TIGER & BUNNY 1

ART BY **MIZUKI SAKAKIBARA**

PLANNING / STORY **SUNRISE** | ORIGINAL SCRIPT **Masafumi Nishida**

ORIGINAL CHARACTER AND HERO DESIGN **Masakazu Katsura**

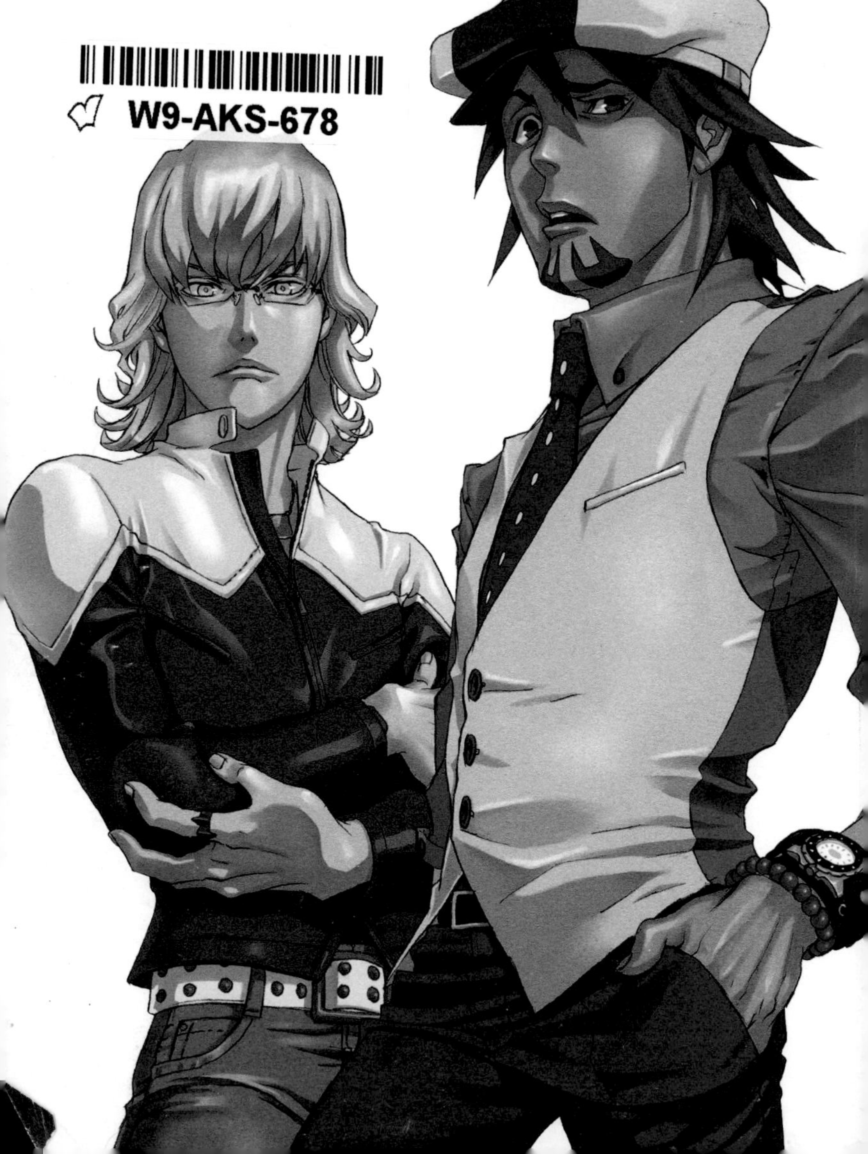

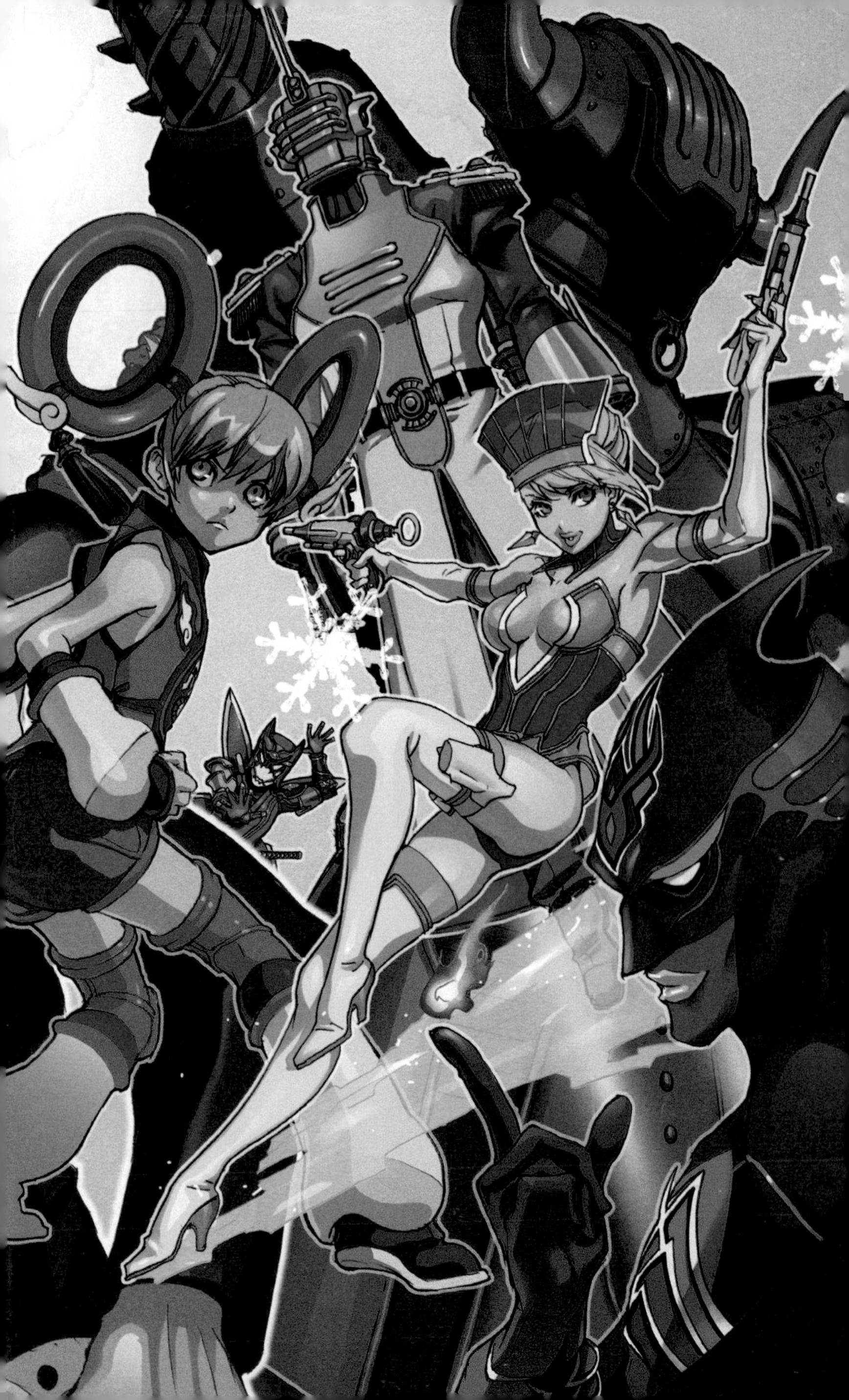

CONTENTS

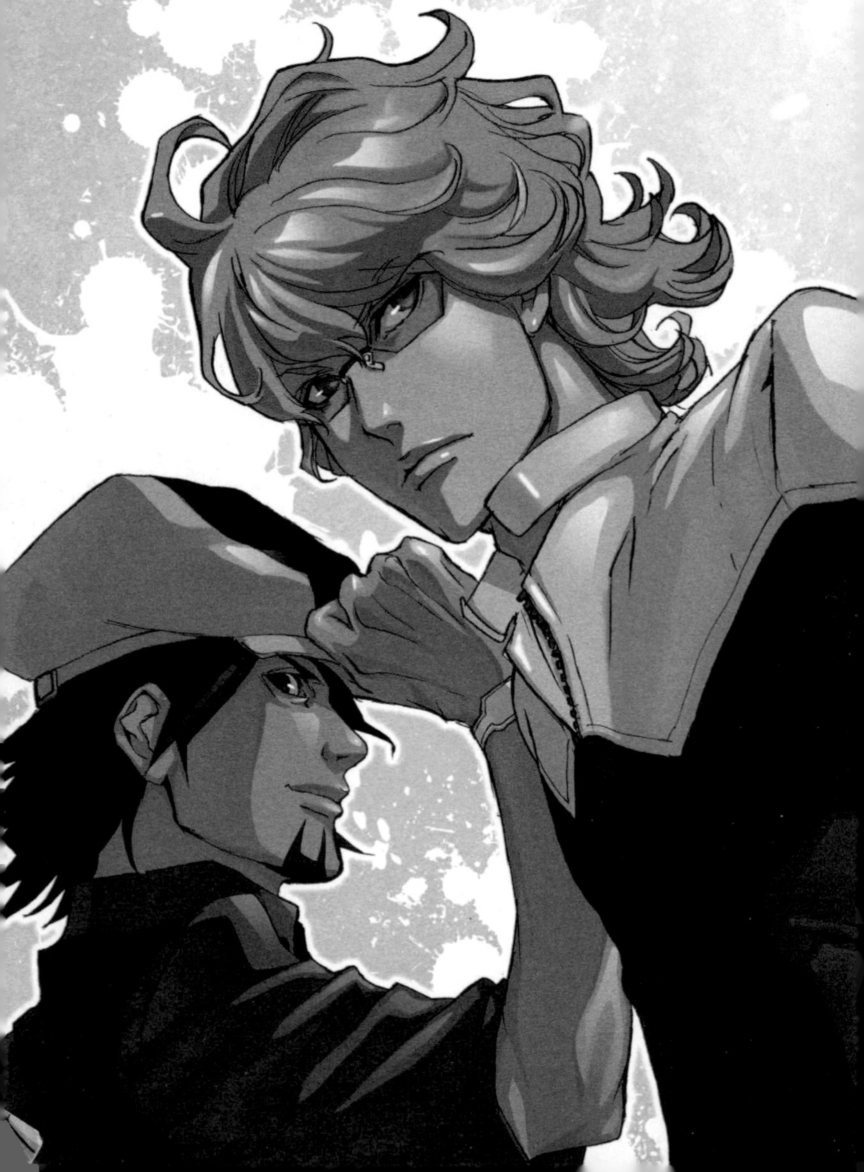

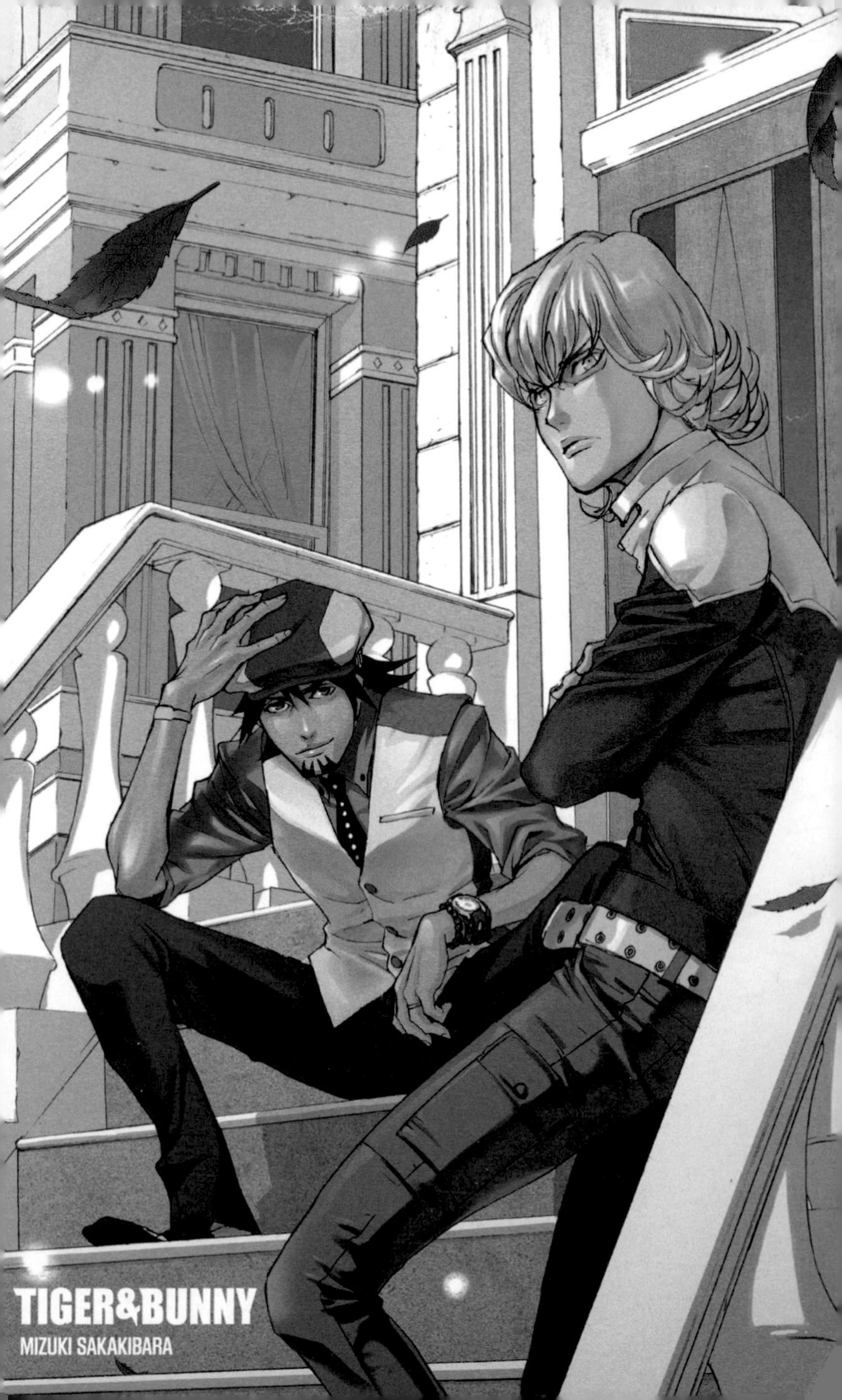
TIGER&BUNNY
MIZUKI SAKAKIBARA

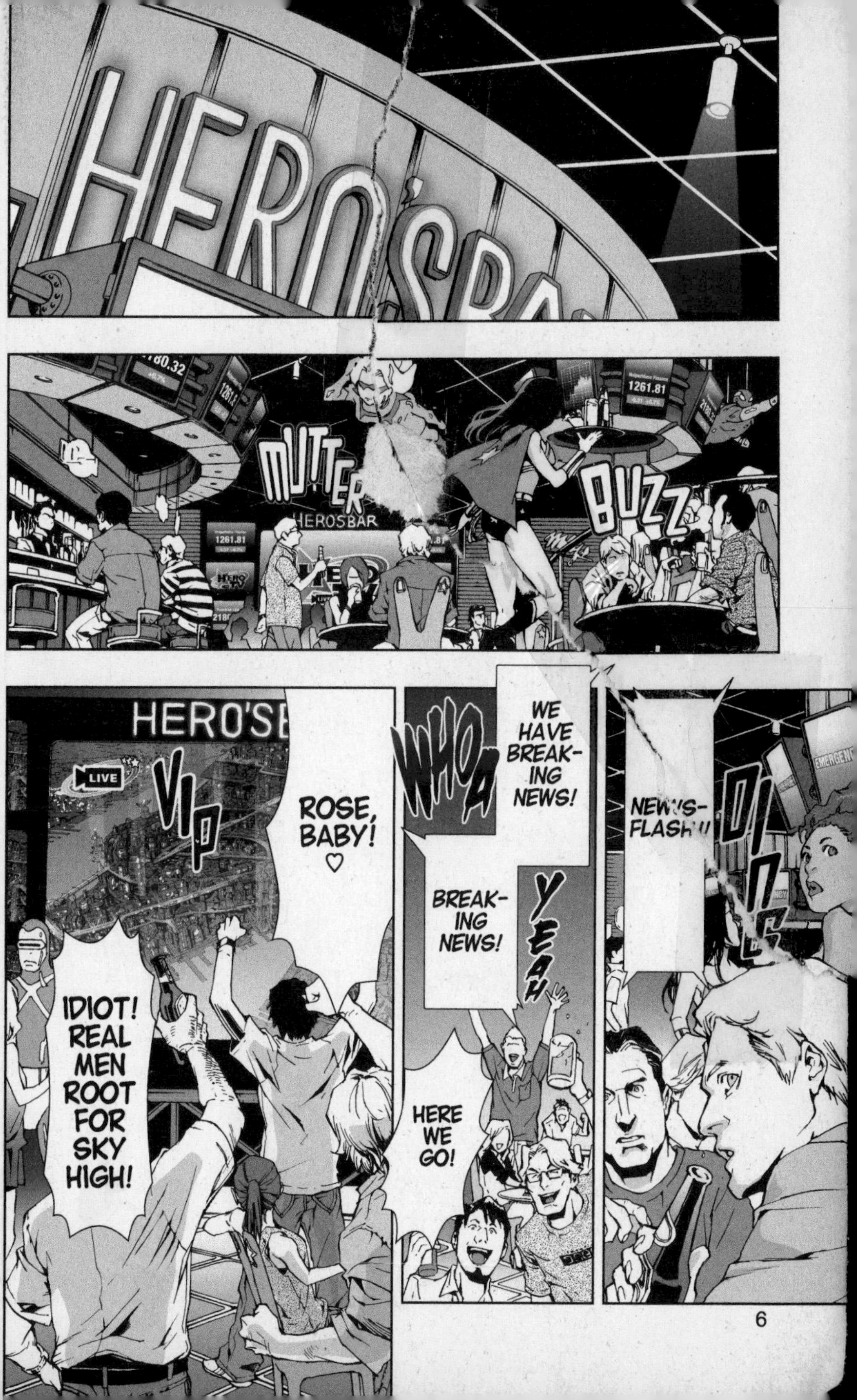
HERO'S BAR
BUZZ
MUTTER
HEROSBAR
1261.81
1261.81
2180.32
NEWS-FLASH!!
DING
WE HAVE BREAKING-ING NEWS!
WHOA
BREAK-ING NEWS!
YEAH
HERE WE GO!
HERO'SB
ROSE, BABY! ♡
VIP
LIVE
IDIOT! REAL MEN ROOT FOR SKY HIGH!

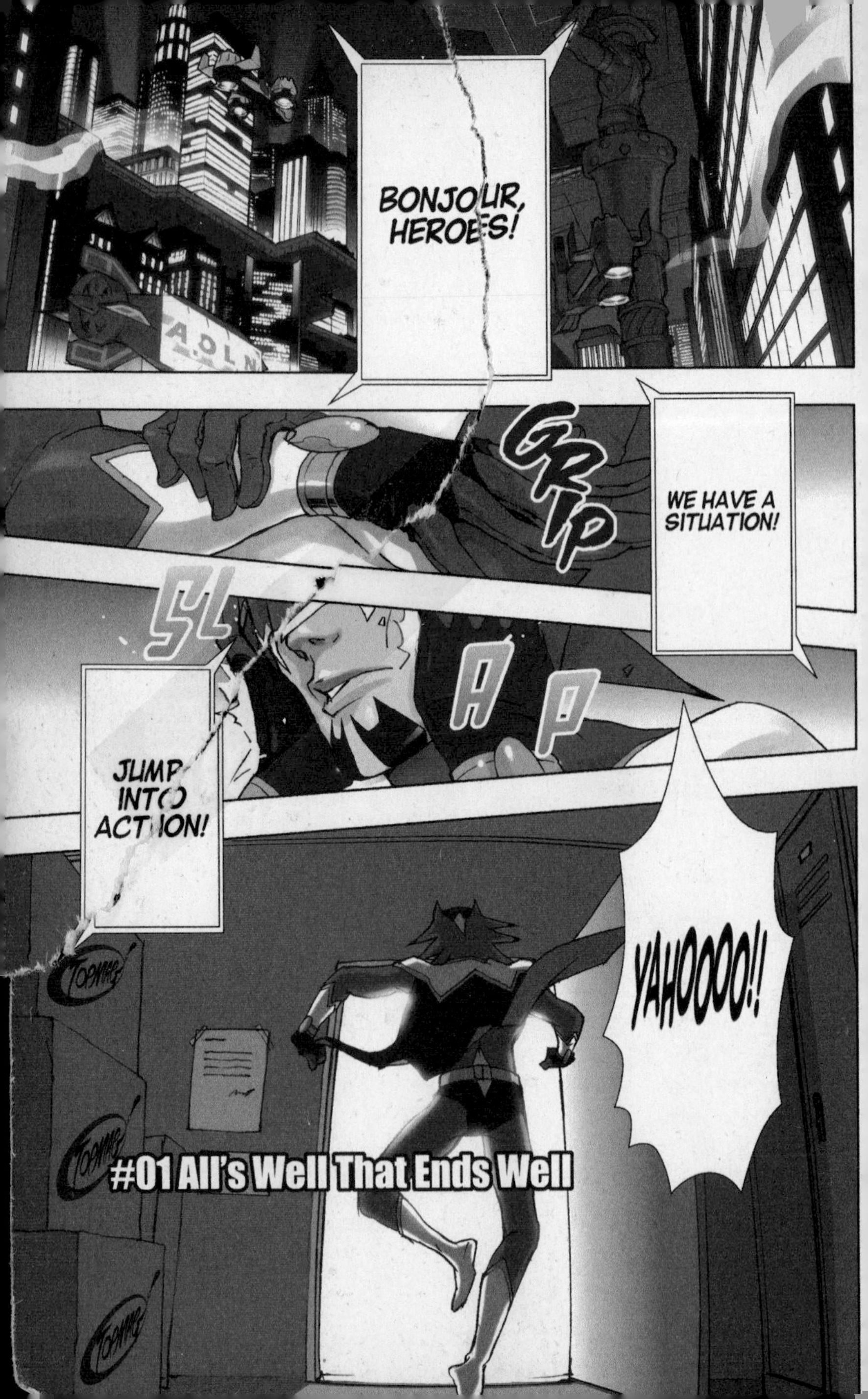
BONJOUR, HEROES!
WE HAVE A SITUATION!
GRIP
SLAP
JUMP INTO ACTION!
YAHOOOO!!
#01 All's Well That Ends Well

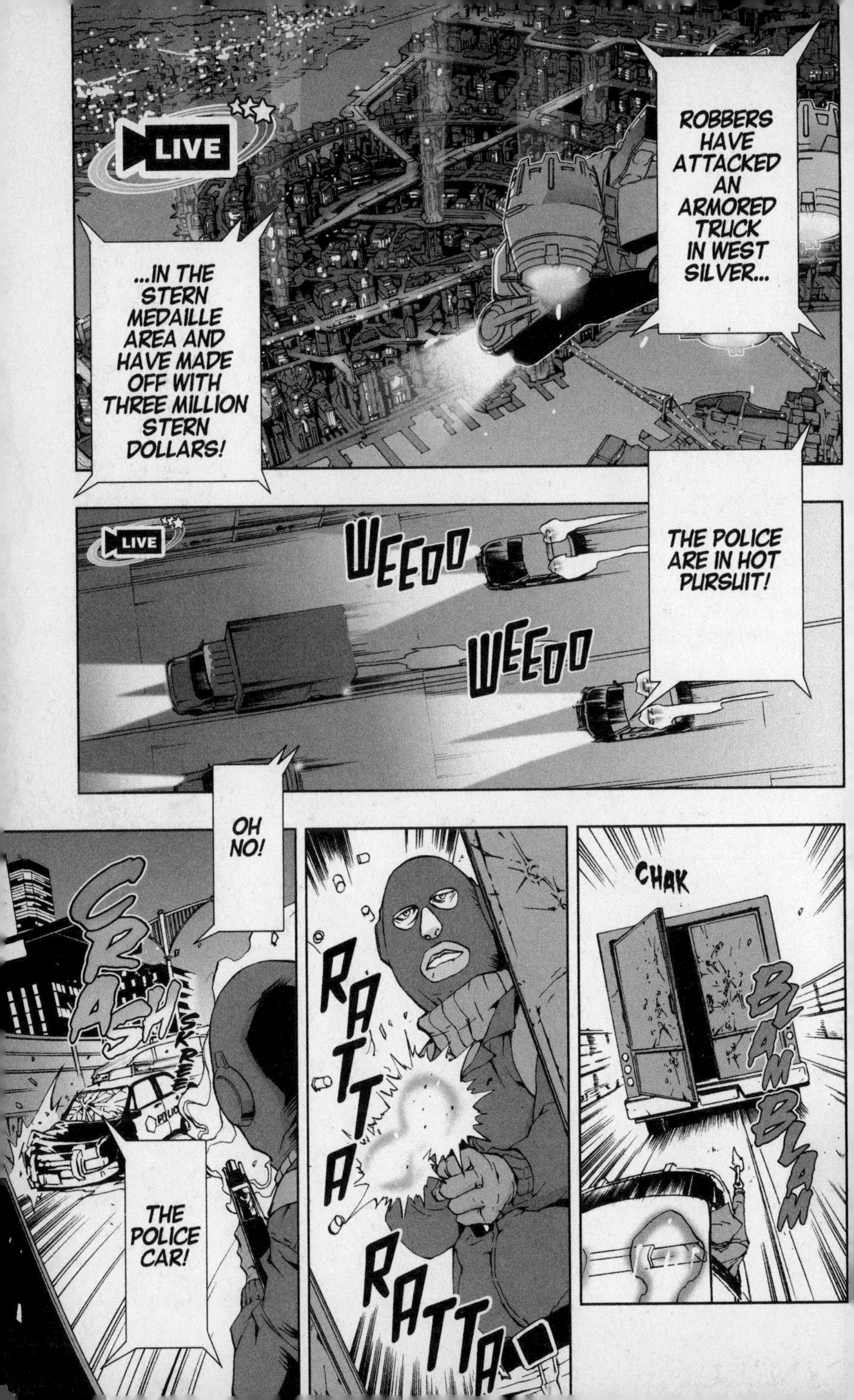
LIVE
ROBBERS HAVE ATTACKED AN ARMORED TRUCK IN WEST SILVER...
...IN THE STERN MEDAILLE AREA AND HAVE MADE OFF WITH THREE MILLION STERN DOLLARS!
LIVE
THE POLICE ARE IN HOT PURSUIT!
WEEOO
WEEOO
CHAK
BLAM BLAM
RATTA RATTA
OH NO!
CRASH
SKREE
POLICE
THE POLICE CAR!

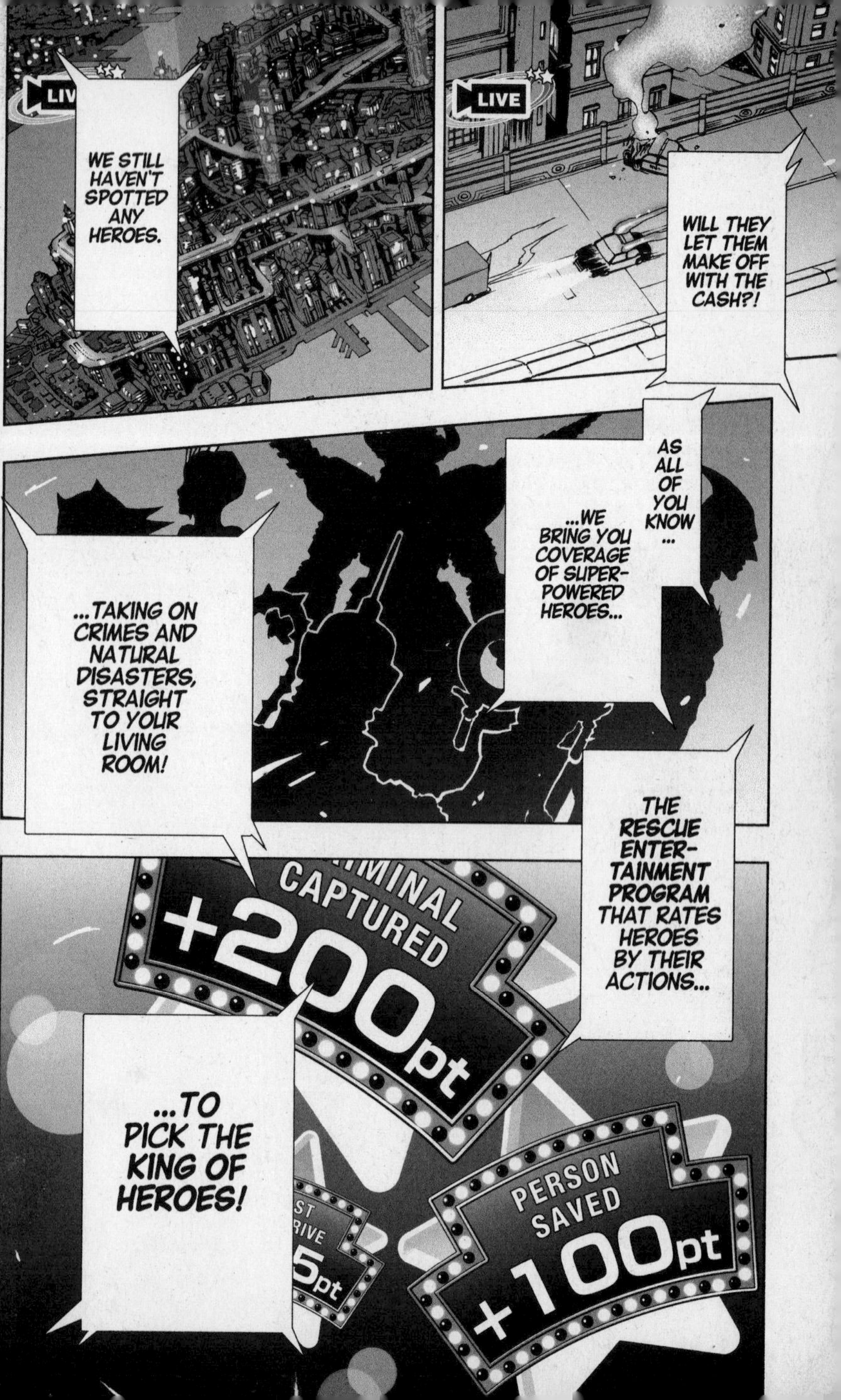
LIVE
WILL THEY LET THEM MAKE OFF WITH THE CASH?!
LIV
WE STILL HAVEN'T SPOTTED ANY HEROES.
AS ALL OF YOU KNOW...
...WE BRING YOU COVERAGE OF SUPER-POWERED HEROES...
...TAKING ON CRIMES AND NATURAL DISASTERS, STRAIGHT TO YOUR LIVING ROOM!
THE RESCUE ENTERTAINMENT PROGRAM THAT RATES HEROES BY THEIR ACTIONS...
IMINAL CAPTURED +200pt
...TO PICK THE KING OF HEROES!
PERSON SAVED +100pt

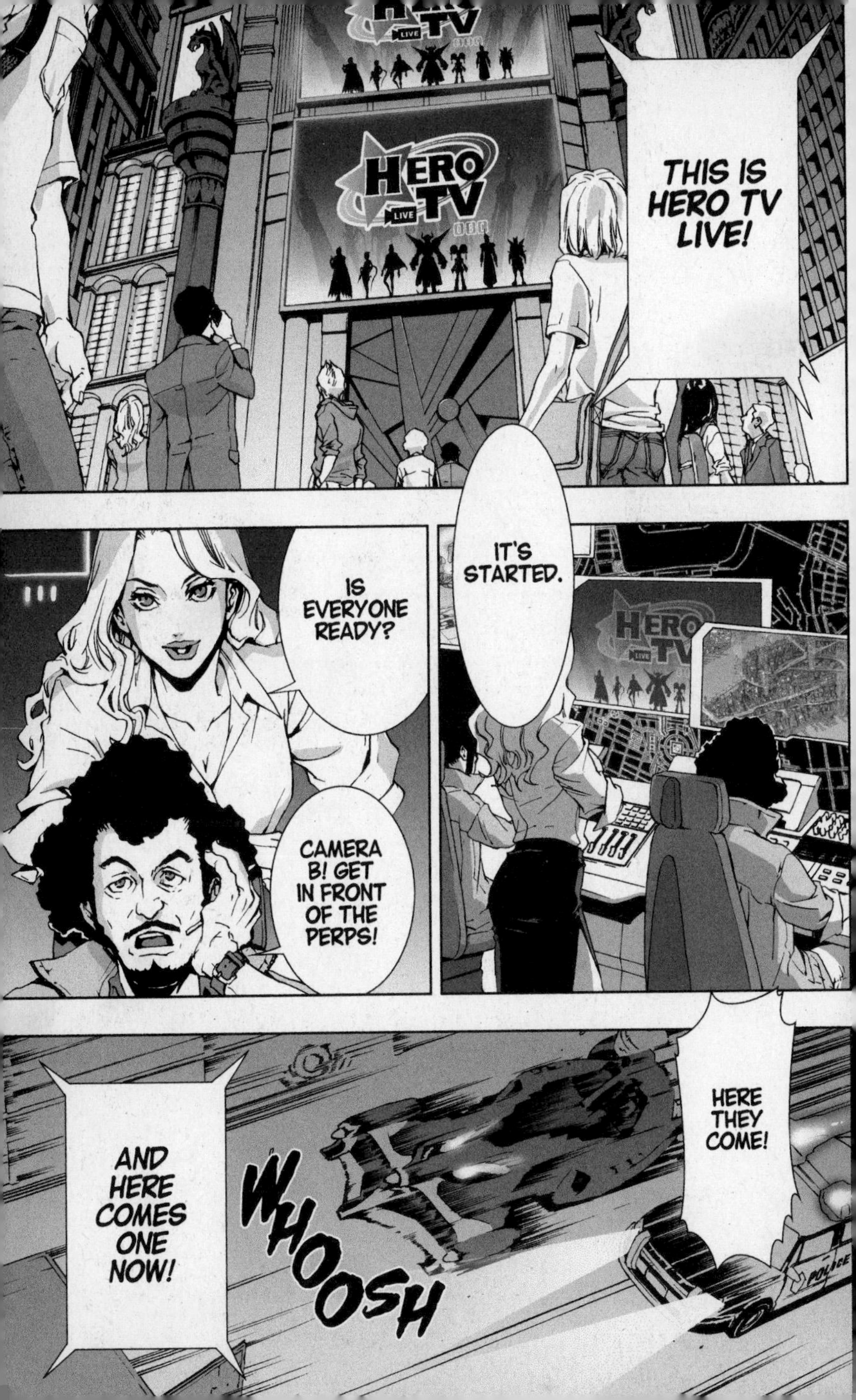
HERO TV LIVE
THIS IS HERO TV LIVE!
IT'S STARTED.
IS EVERYONE READY?
CAMERA B! GET IN FRONT OF THE PERPS!
HERE THEY COME!
POLICE
WHOOSH
AND HERE COMES ONE NOW!

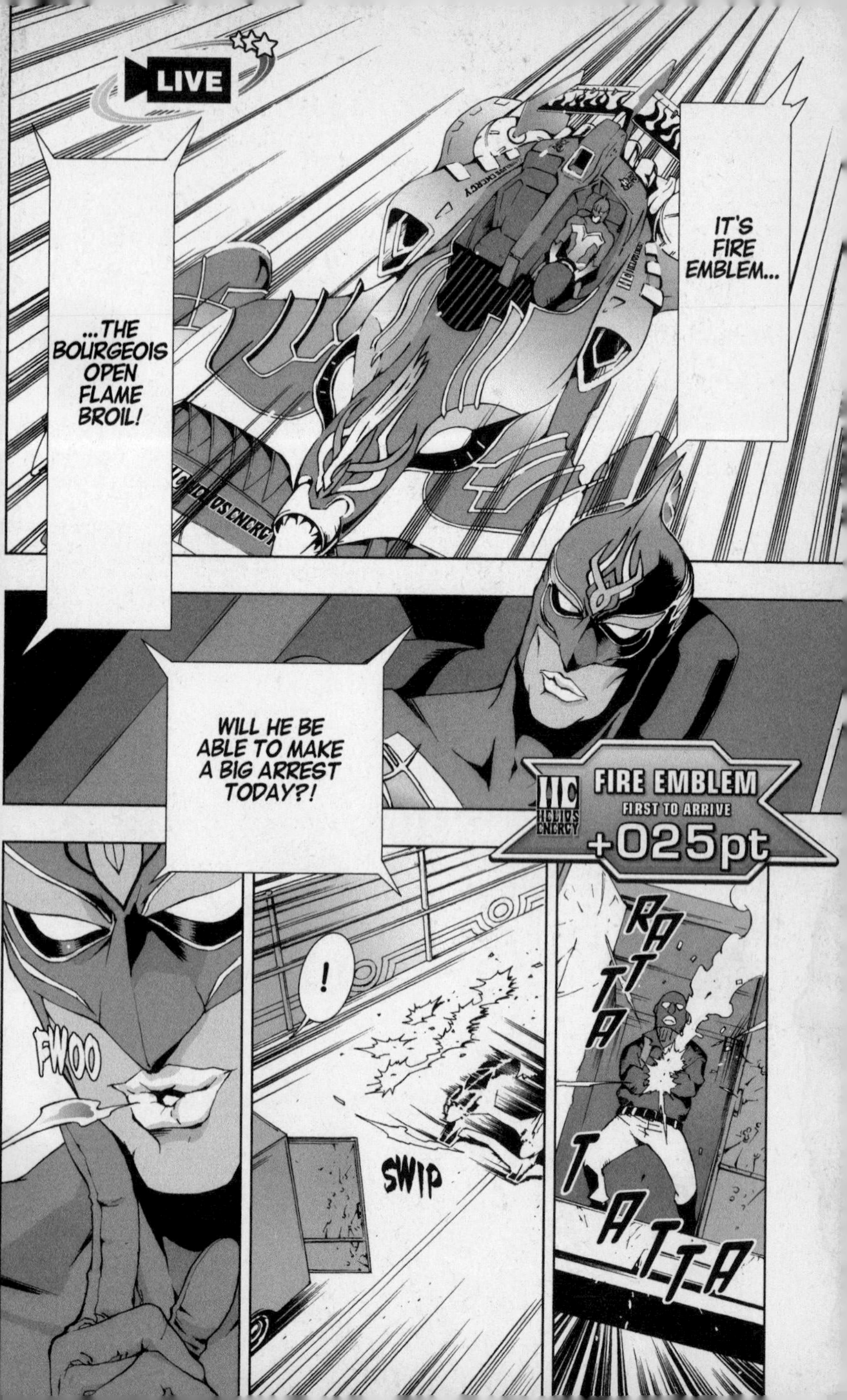
LIVE
IT'S FIRE EMBLEM...
...THE BOURGEOIS OPEN FLAME BROIL!
WILL HE BE ABLE TO MAKE A BIG ARREST TODAY?!
FIRE EMBLEM
FIRST TO ARRIVE
+025pt
HELIOS ENERGY
RATTA
TATTA
!
SWIP
FWOO

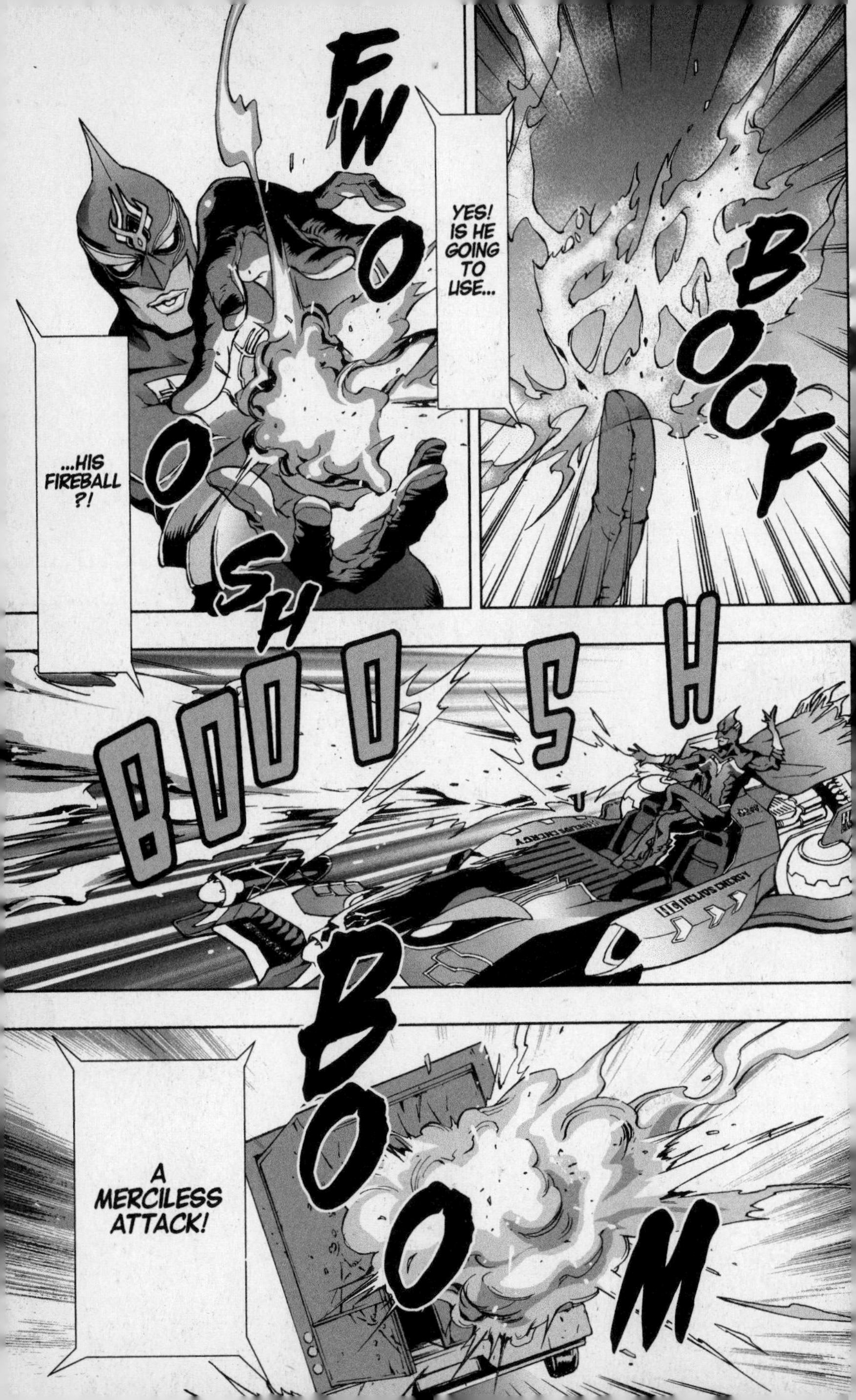
BOOF
YES! IS HE GOING TO USE...
FWOOSH
...HIS FIREBALL ?!
BOOOSH
HELIOS ENERGY
A MERCILESS ATTACK!
BOOM

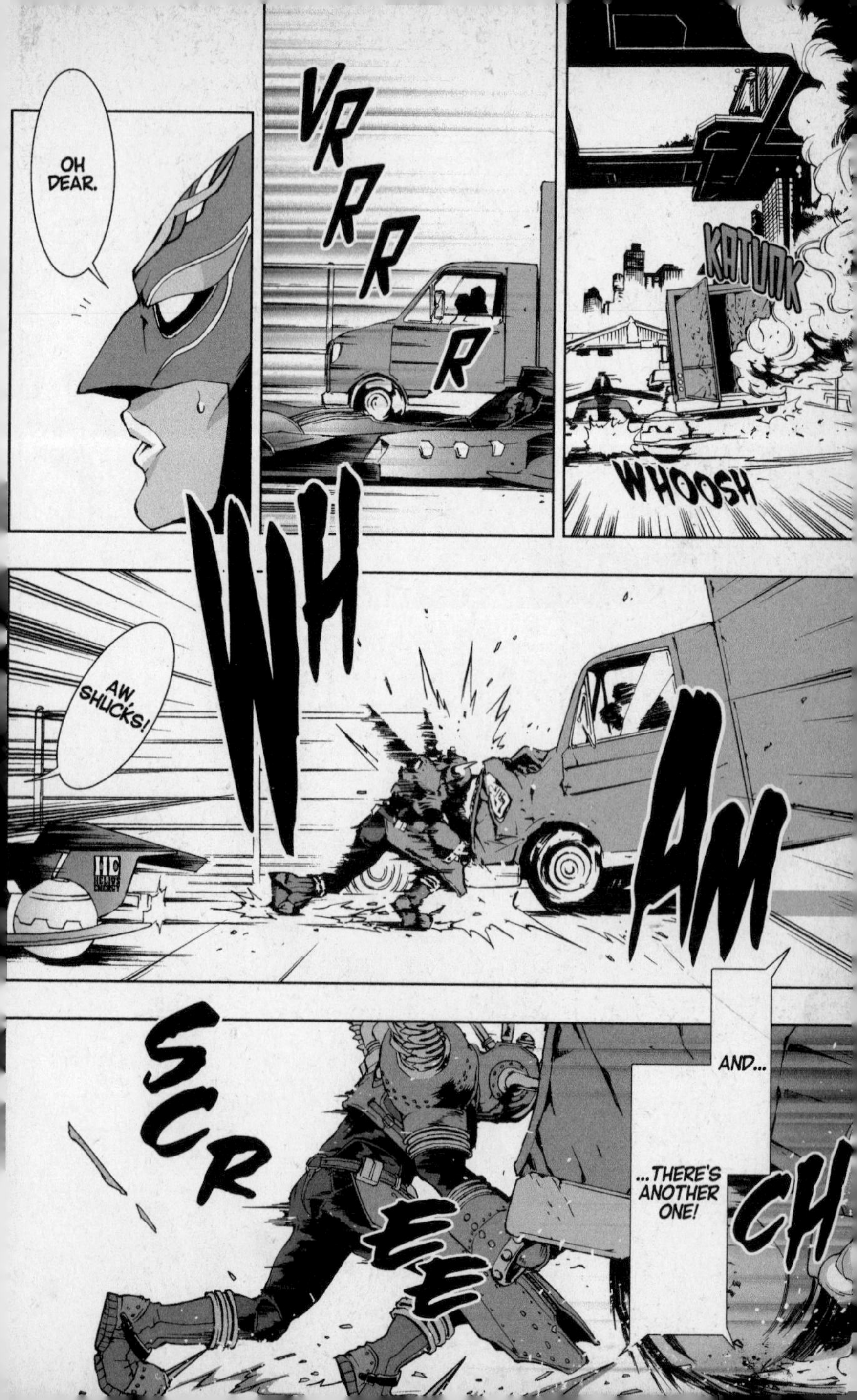
KATUNK
WHOOSH
VRRRRR
OH DEAR.
WHAM
AW, SHUCKS!
AND...
...THERE'S ANOTHER ONE!
CH
SCREE

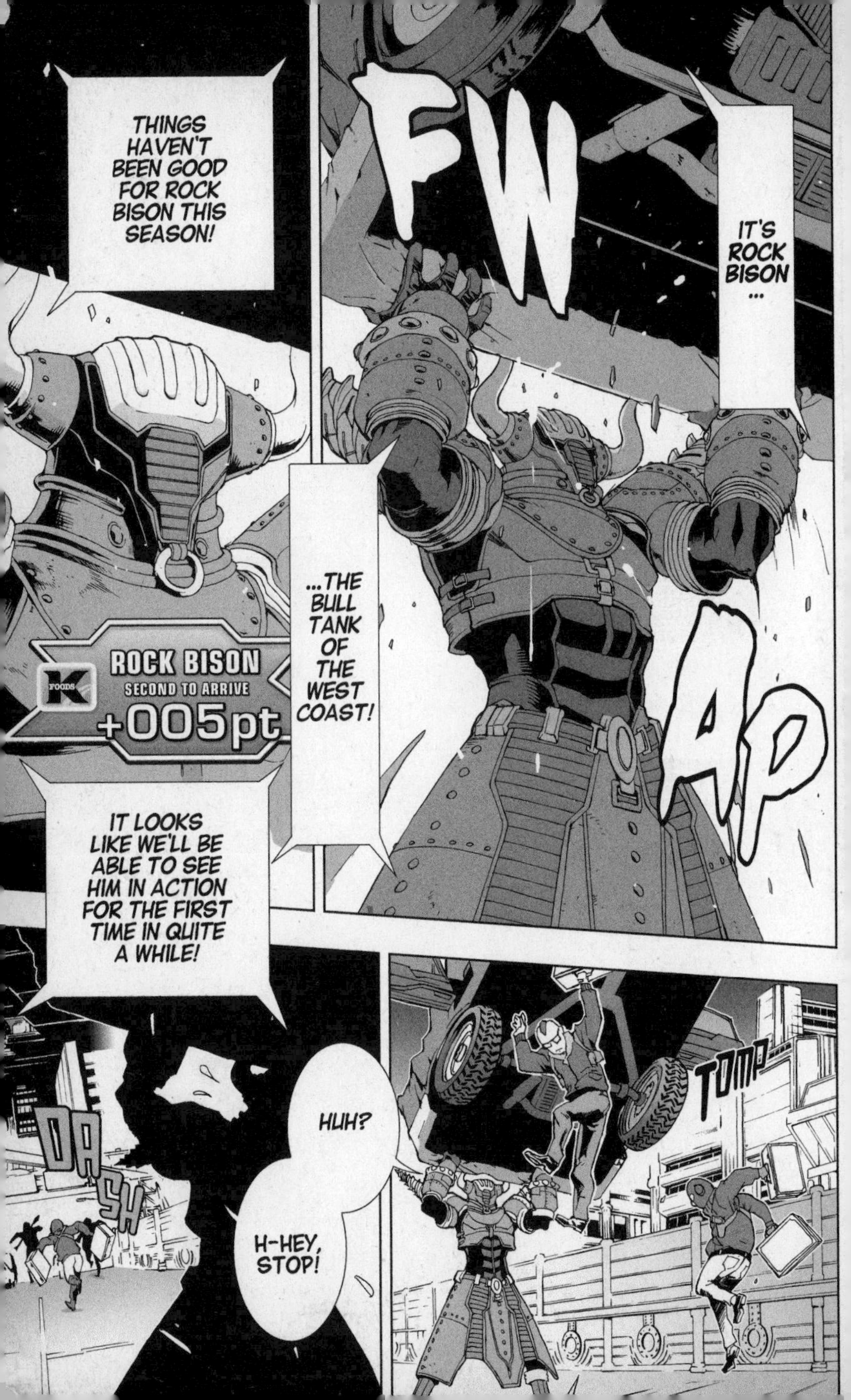
FW
IT'S ROCK BISON...
...THE BULL TANK OF THE WEST COAST!
AP
THINGS HAVEN'T BEEN GOOD FOR ROCK BISON THIS SEASON!
K FOODS
ROCK BISON
SECOND TO ARRIVE
+005pt
IT LOOKS LIKE WE'LL BE ABLE TO SEE HIM IN ACTION FOR THE FIRST TIME IN QUITE A WHILE!
TOMP
HUH?
H-HEY, STOP!
DASH

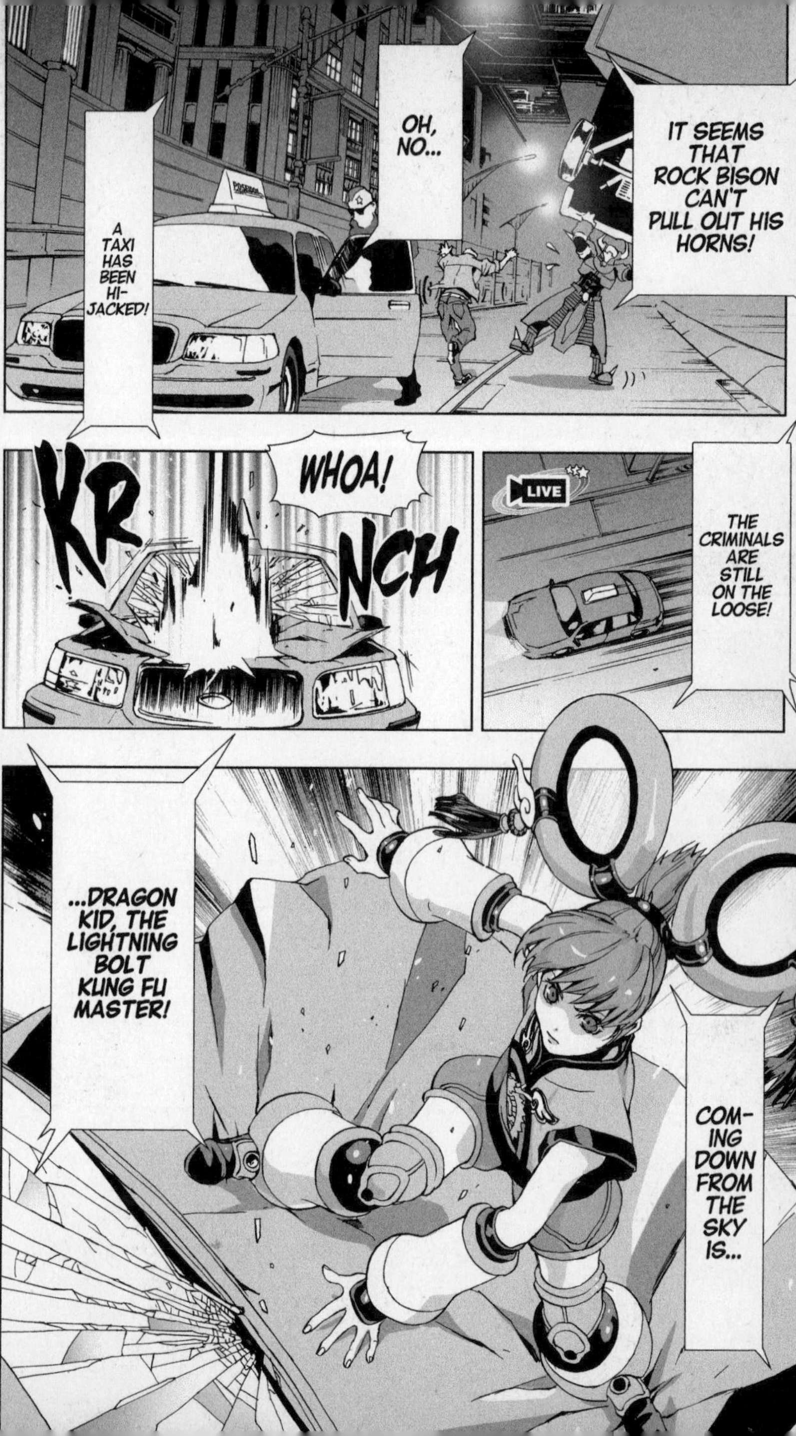
IT SEEMS THAT ROCK BISON CAN'T PULL OUT HIS HORNS!
OH, NO...
A TAXI HAS BEEN HI-JACKED!
LIVE
THE CRIMINALS ARE STILL ON THE LOOSE!
WHOA!
KR
NCH
COM-ING DOWN FROM THE SKY IS...
...DRAGON KID, THE LIGHTNING BOLT KUNG FU MASTER!

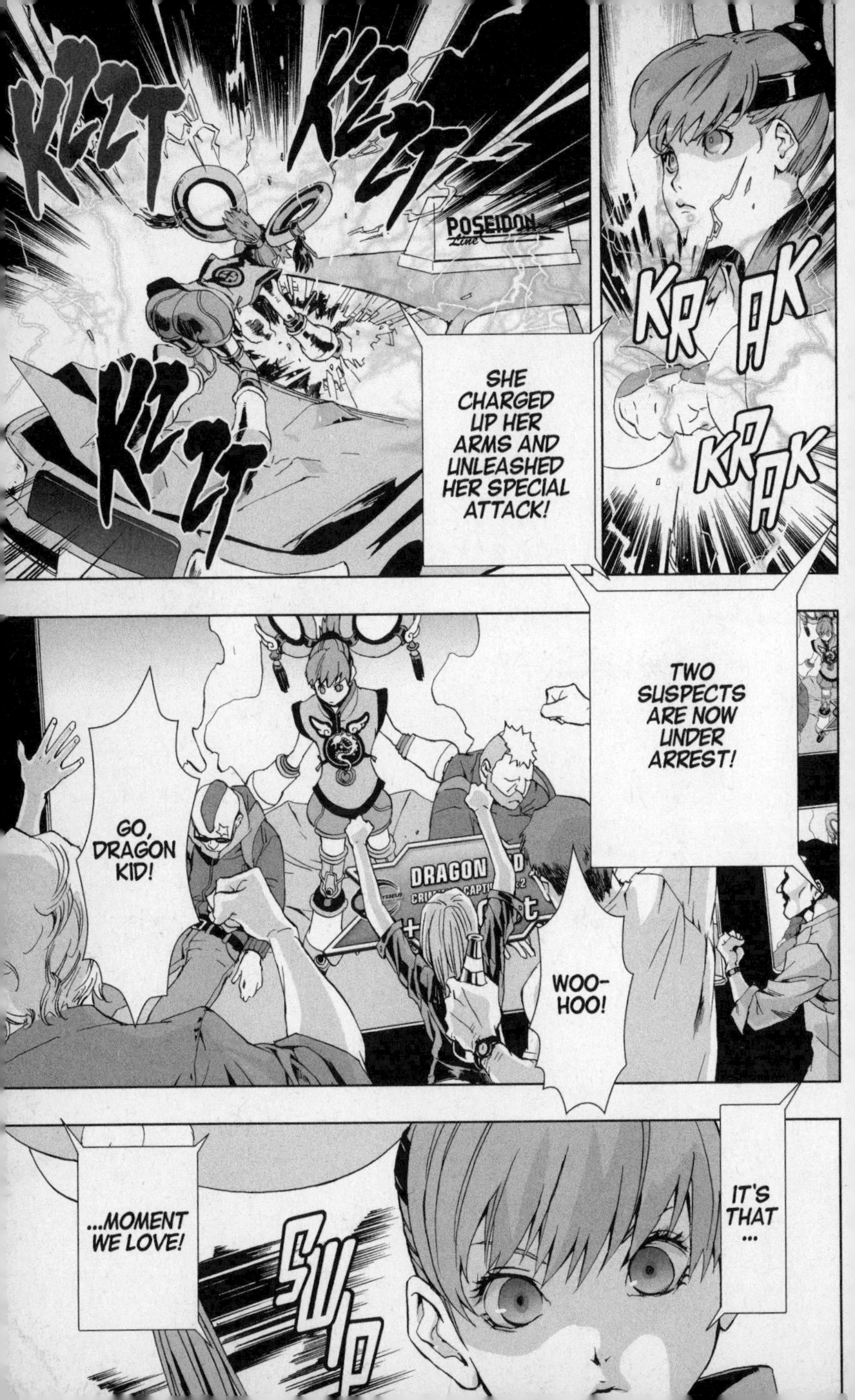
KRAAK
KRAAK
KZZT
KZZT
KZZT
POSEIDON Line
SHE CHARGED UP HER ARMS AND UNLEASHED HER SPECIAL ATTACK!
TWO SUSPECTS ARE NOW UNDER ARREST!
GO, DRAGON KID!
WOO-HOO!
IT'S THAT...
SWIP
...MOMENT WE LOVE!

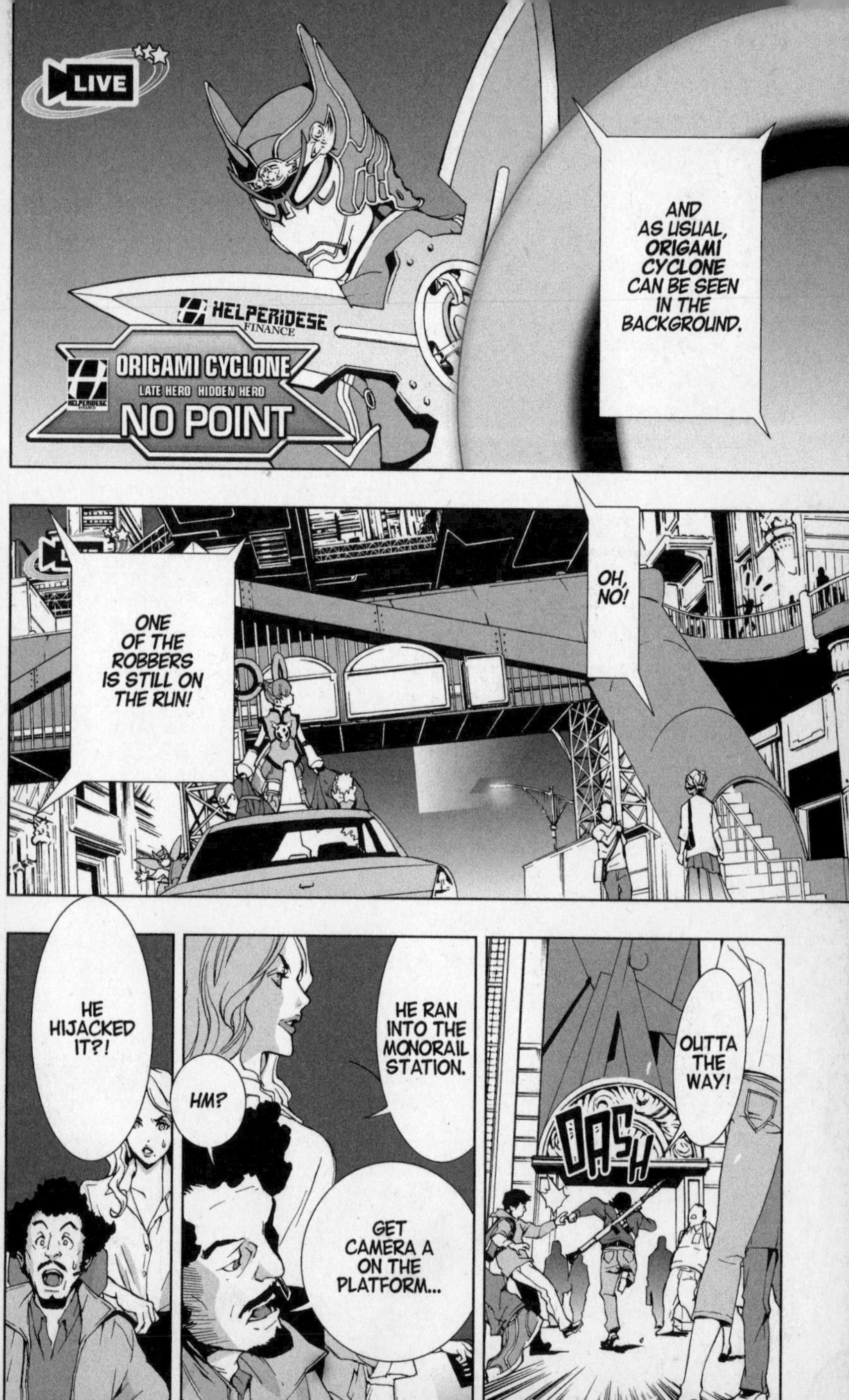
AND AS USUAL, ORIGAMI CYCLONE CAN BE SEEN IN THE BACKGROUND.
LIVE
HELPERIDESE FINANCE
ORIGAMI CYCLONE
LATE HERO HIDDEN HERO
NO POINT
OH, NO!
ONE OF THE ROBBERS IS STILL ON THE RUN!
OUTTA THE WAY!
DASH
HE RAN INTO THE MONORAIL STATION.
HM?
GET CAMERA A ON THE PLATFORM...
HE HIJACKED IT?!

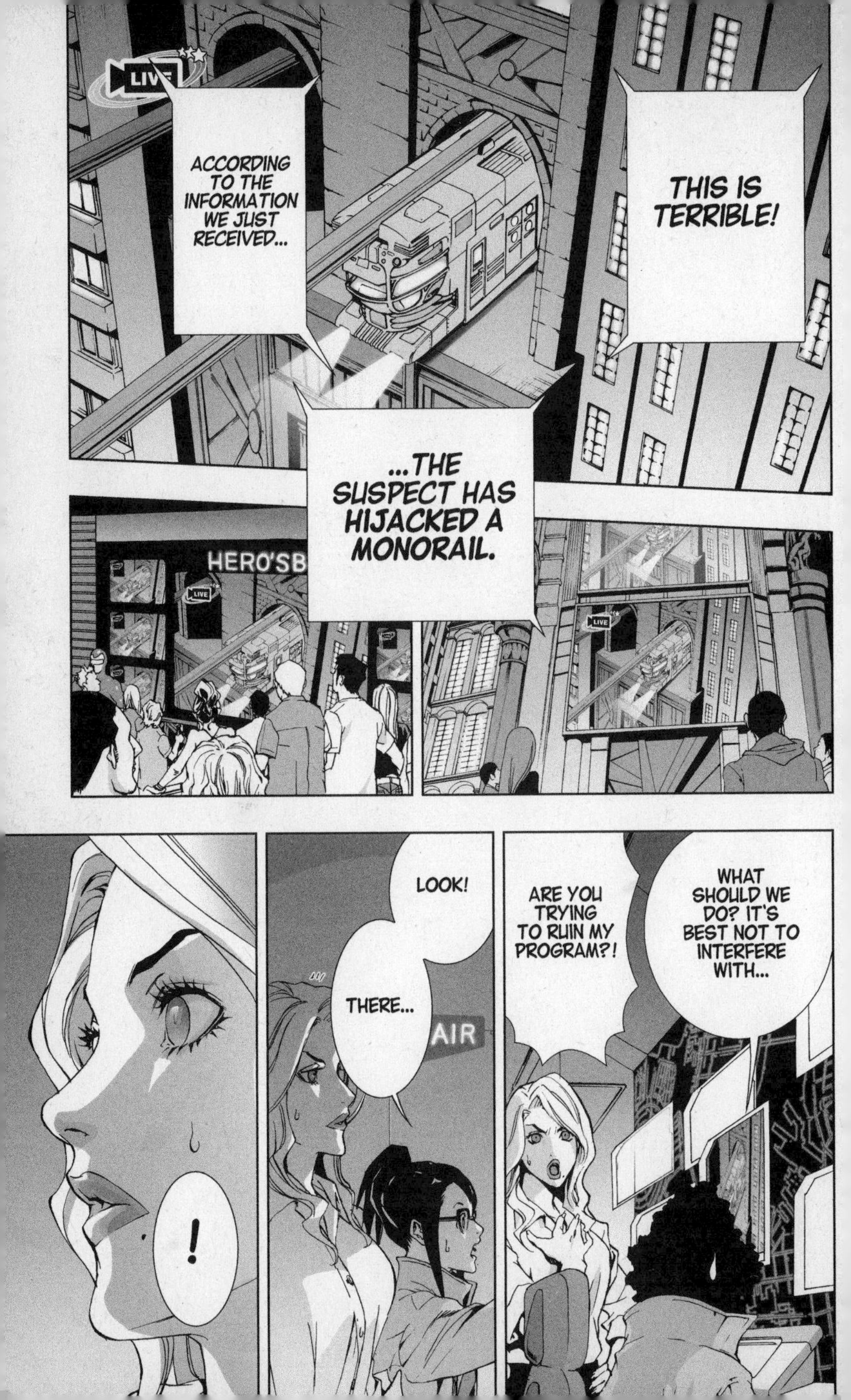
LIVE
THIS IS TERRIBLE!
ACCORDING TO THE INFORMATION WE JUST RECEIVED...
...THE SUSPECT HAS HIJACKED A MONORAIL.
LIVE
HERO'SB
LIVE
WHAT SHOULD WE DO? IT'S BEST NOT TO INTERFERE WITH...
ARE YOU TRYING TO RUIN MY PROGRAM?!
LOOK!
THERE...
AIR
!

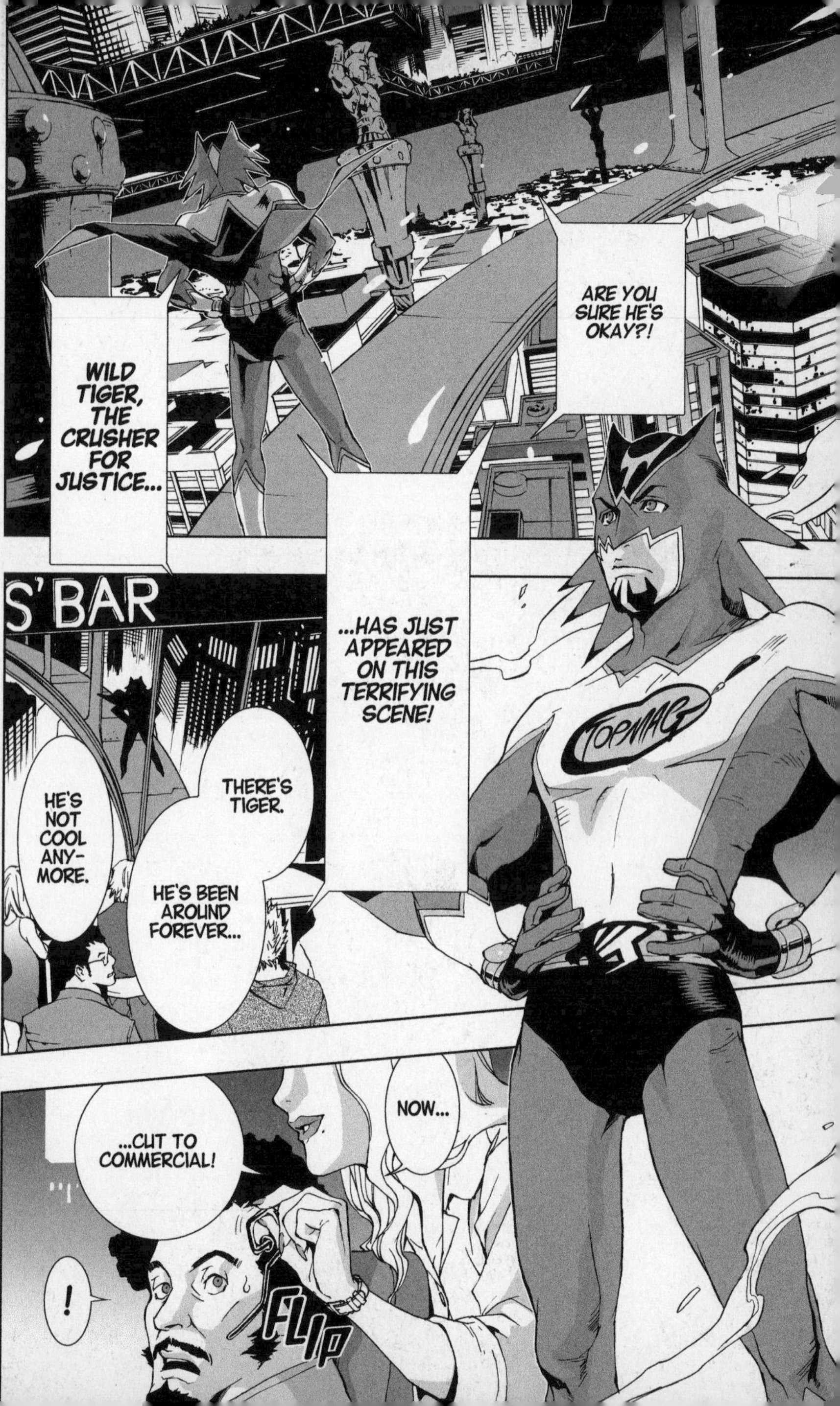

ARE YOU SURE HE'S OKAY?!
WILD TIGER, THE CRUSHER FOR JUSTICE...
...HAS JUST APPEARED ON THIS TERRIFYING SCENE!
TOPMAG
S' BAR
THERE'S TIGER.
HE'S BEEN AROUND FOREVER...
HE'S NOT COOL ANY-MORE.
NOW...
...CUT TO COMMERCIAL!
!
FLIP

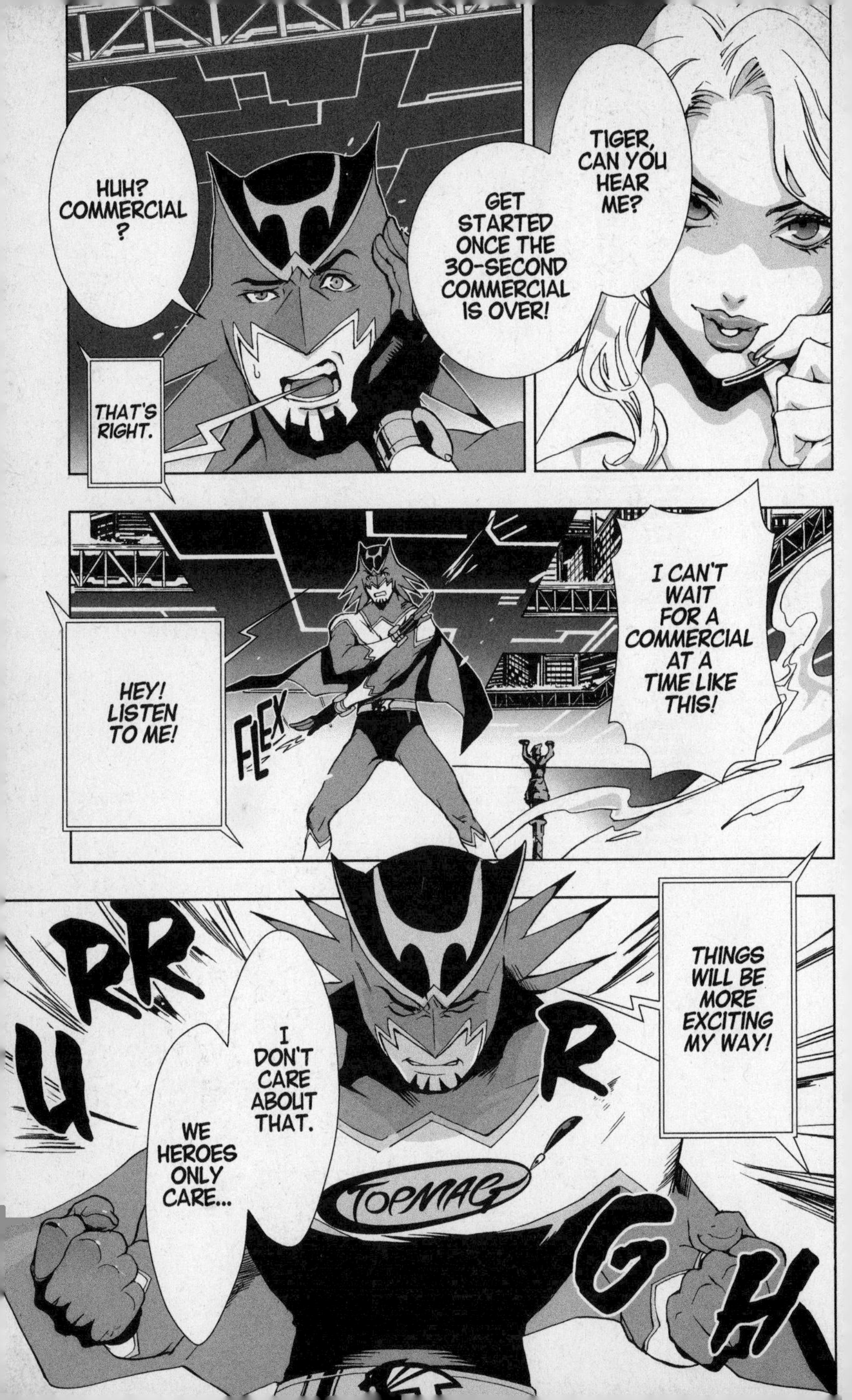
TIGER, CAN YOU HEAR ME?
GET STARTED ONCE THE 30-SECOND COMMERCIAL IS OVER!
HUH? COMMERCIAL?
THAT'S RIGHT.
I CAN'T WAIT FOR A COMMERCIAL AT A TIME LIKE THIS!
HEY! LISTEN TO ME!
FLEX
THINGS WILL BE MORE EXCITING MY WAY!
I DON'T CARE ABOUT THAT.
WE HEROES ONLY CARE...
URRRGH
TOPMAG

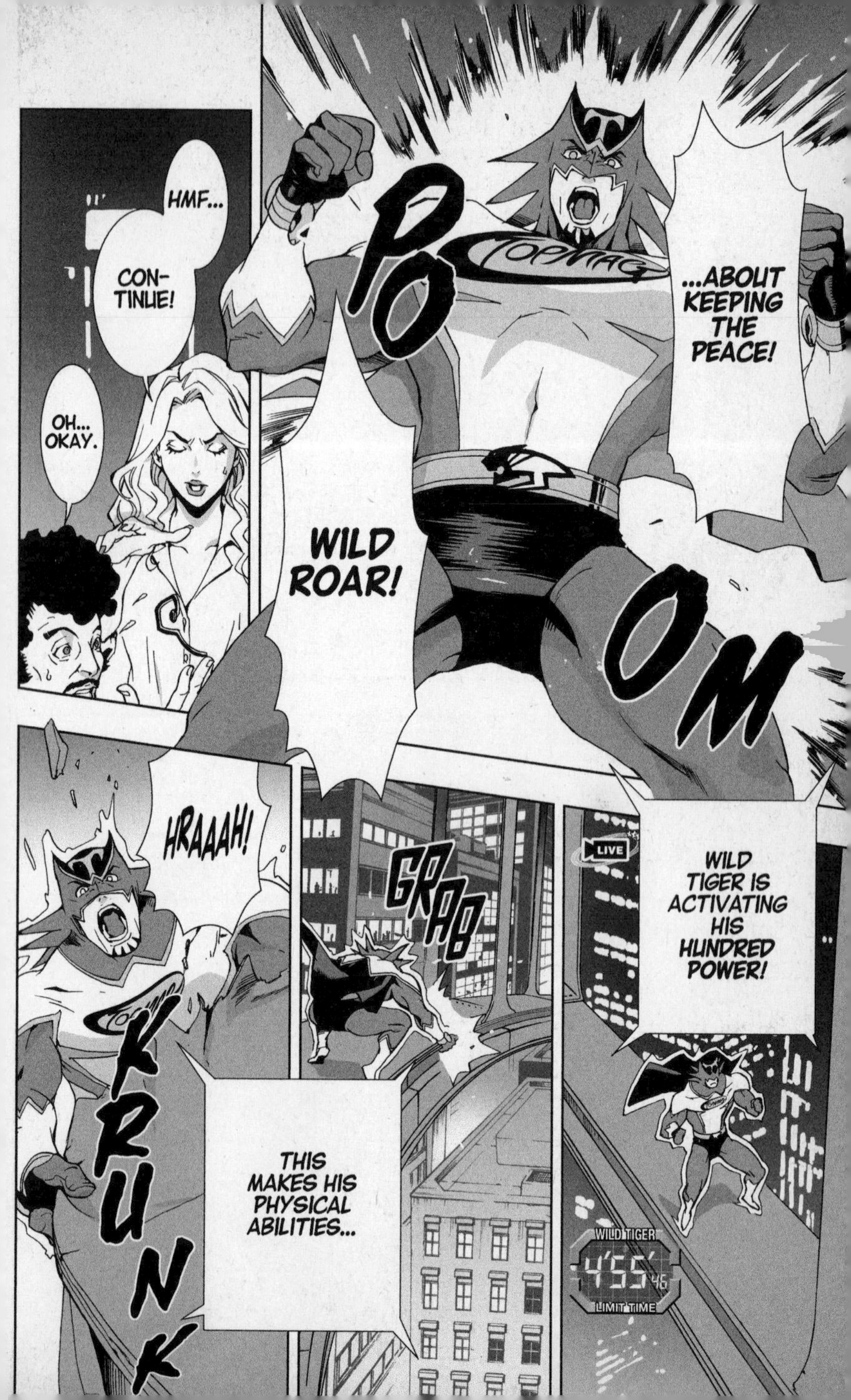
...ABOUT KEEPING THE PEACE!
TOPMAG
POOM
WILD ROAR!
HMF...
CON-TINUE!
OH... OKAY.
LIVE
WILD TIGER IS ACTIVATING HIS HUNDRED POWER!
WILD TIGER
4'55'46
LIMIT TIME
GRAB
THIS MAKES HIS PHYSICAL ABILITIES...
HRAAAH!
KRUNK

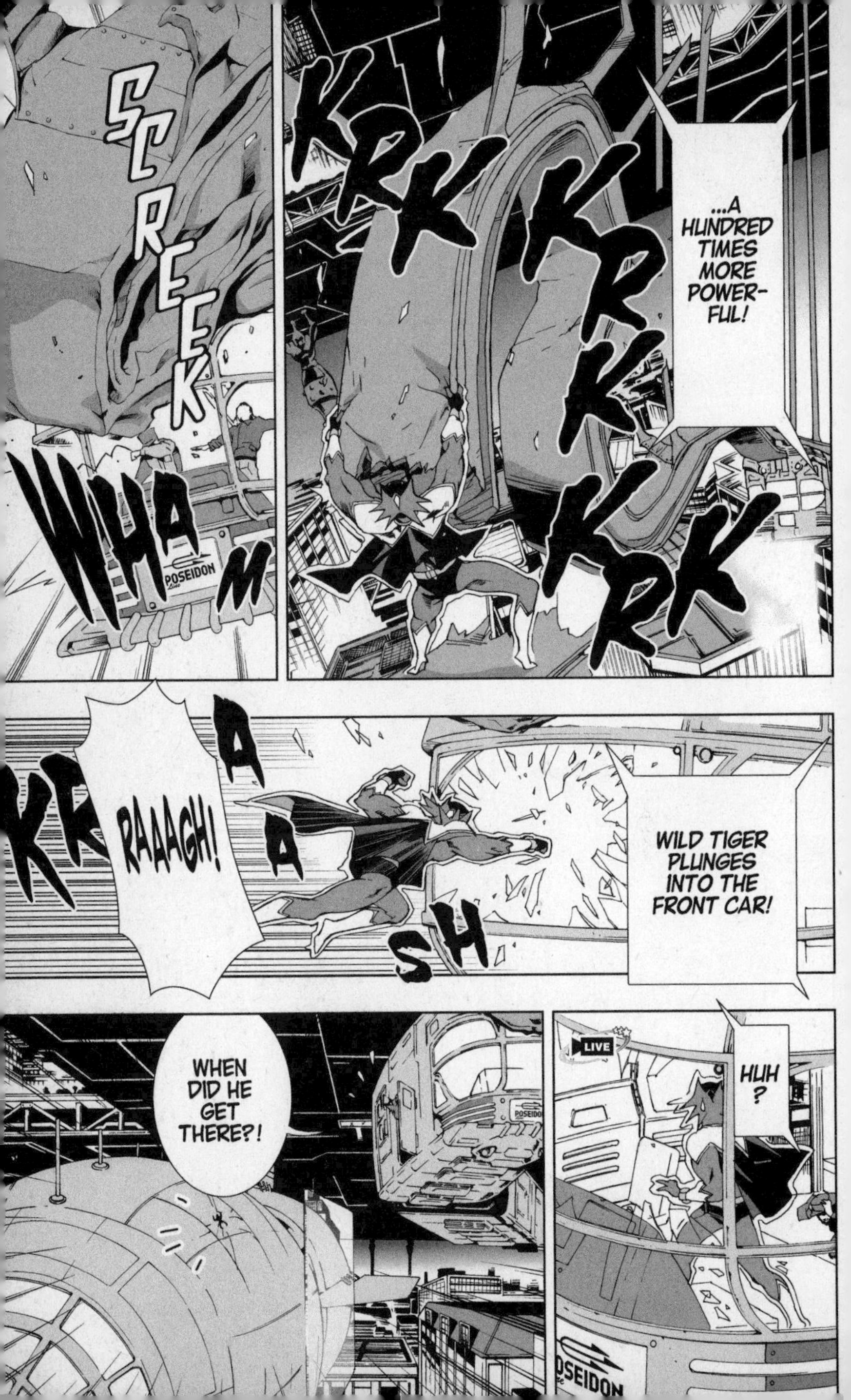
...A HUNDRED TIMES MORE POWER-FUL!
KRKKRKKRK
SCREEK
POSEIDON
WHAM
WILD TIGER PLUNGES INTO THE FRONT CAR!
KRRAASH
RAAAGH!
LIVE
HUH?
POSEIDON
WHEN DID HE GET THERE?!
POSEIDON

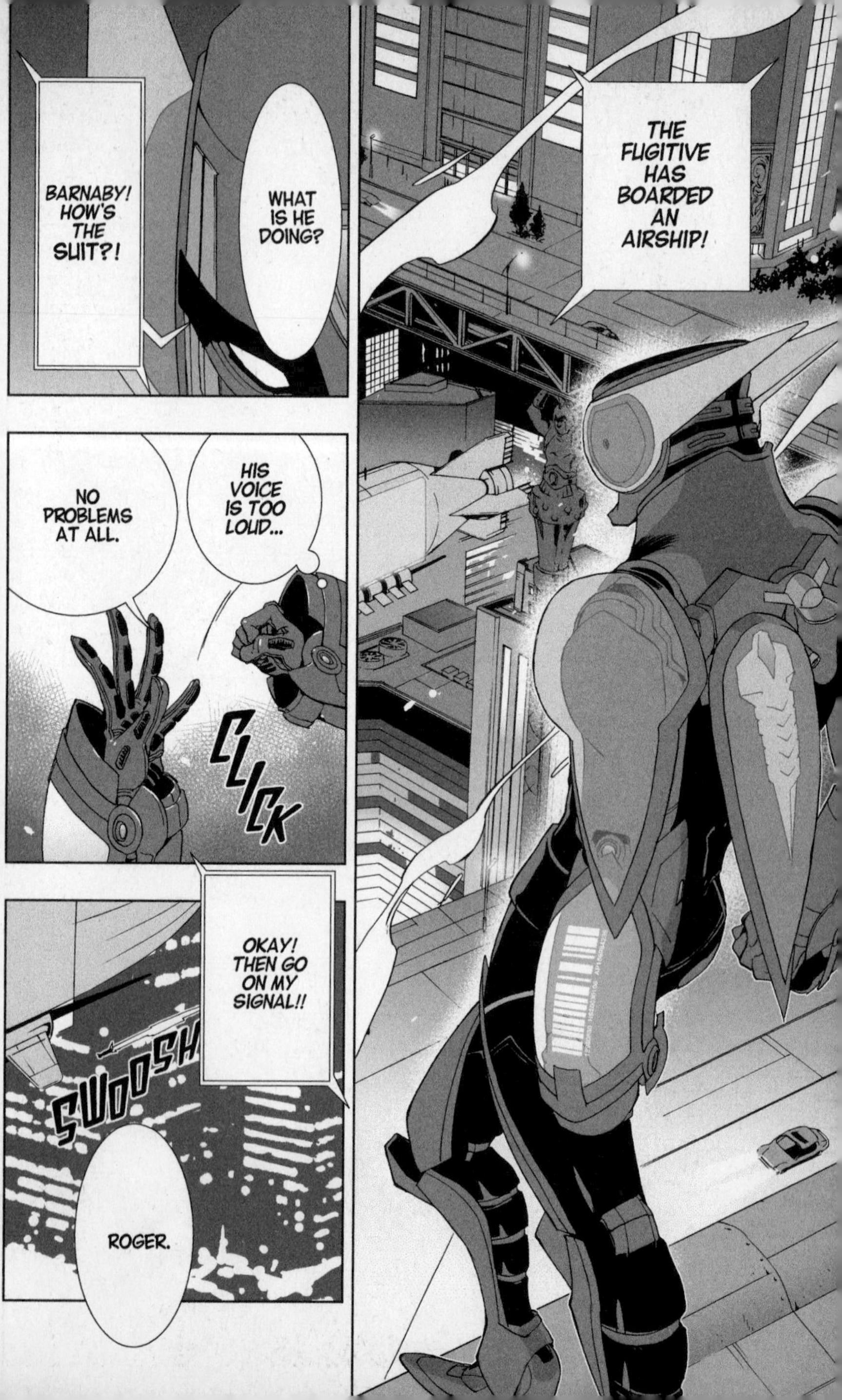
THE FUGITIVE HAS BOARDED AN AIRSHIP!
WHAT IS HE DOING?
BARNABY! HOW'S THE SUIT?!
HIS VOICE IS TOO LOUD...
NO PROBLEMS AT ALL.
CLICK
OKAY! THEN GO ON MY SIGNAL!!
SWOOSH
ROGER.

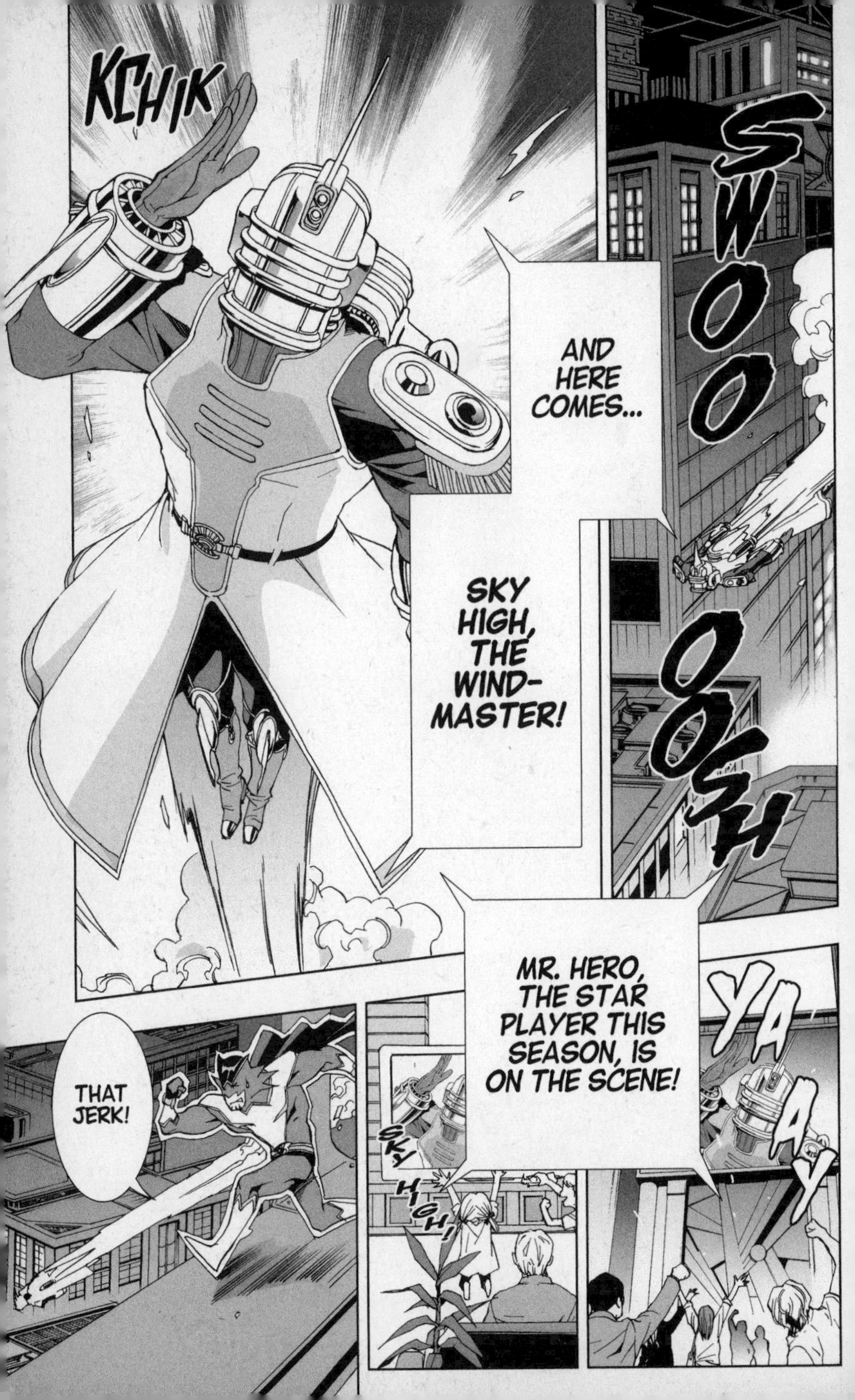
SWOOOOSH
AND HERE COMES...
SKY HIGH, THE WIND-MASTER!
KCHIK
YAAY
MR. HERO, THE STAR PLAYER THIS SEASON, IS ON THE SCENE!
SKY HIGH!
THAT JERK!

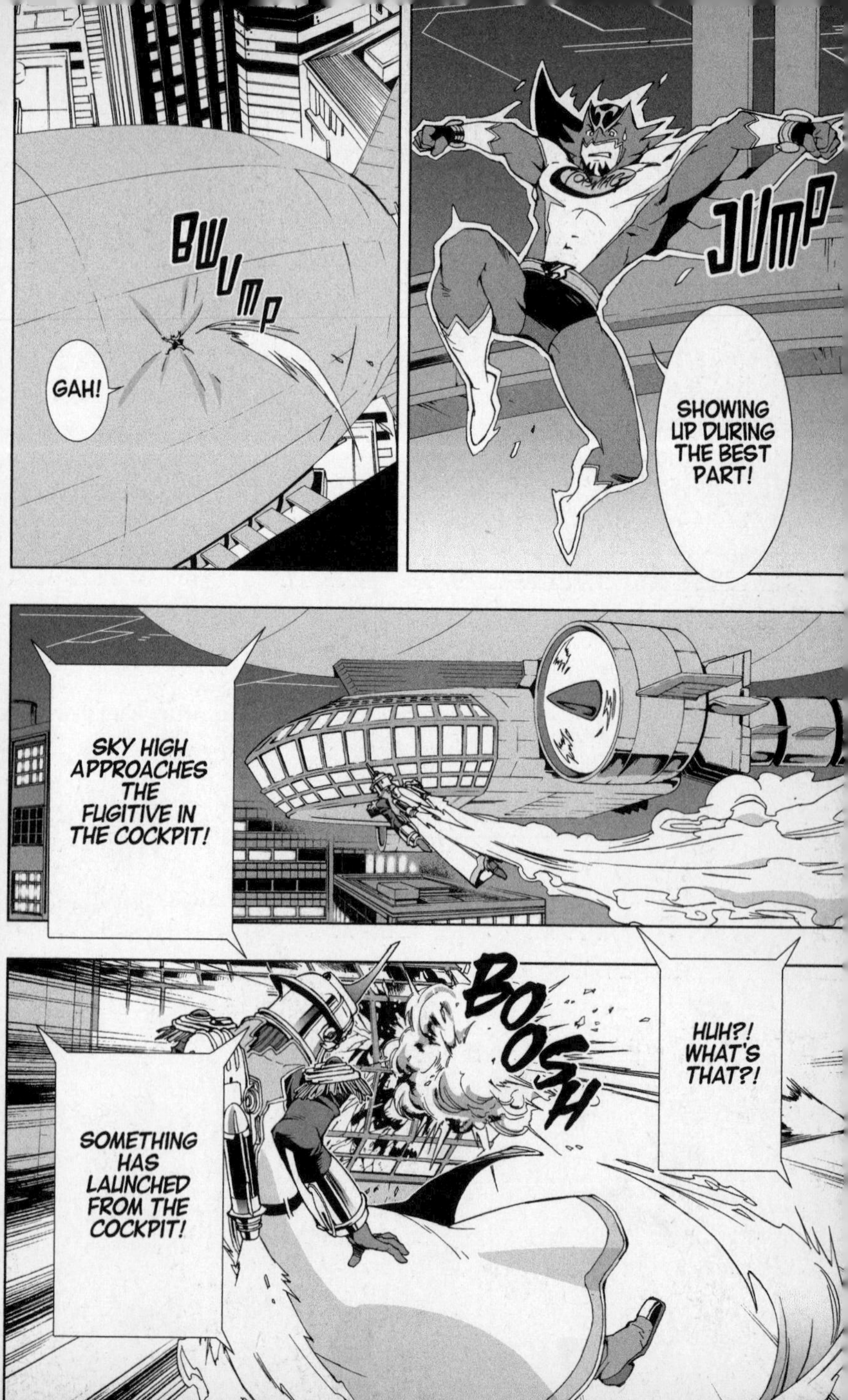
JUMP
SHOWING UP DURING THE BEST PART!
BWUMP
GAH!
SKY HIGH APPROACHES THE FUGITIVE IN THE COCKPIT!
HUH?! WHAT'S THAT?!
BOOSH
SOMETHING HAS LAUNCHED FROM THE COCKPIT!

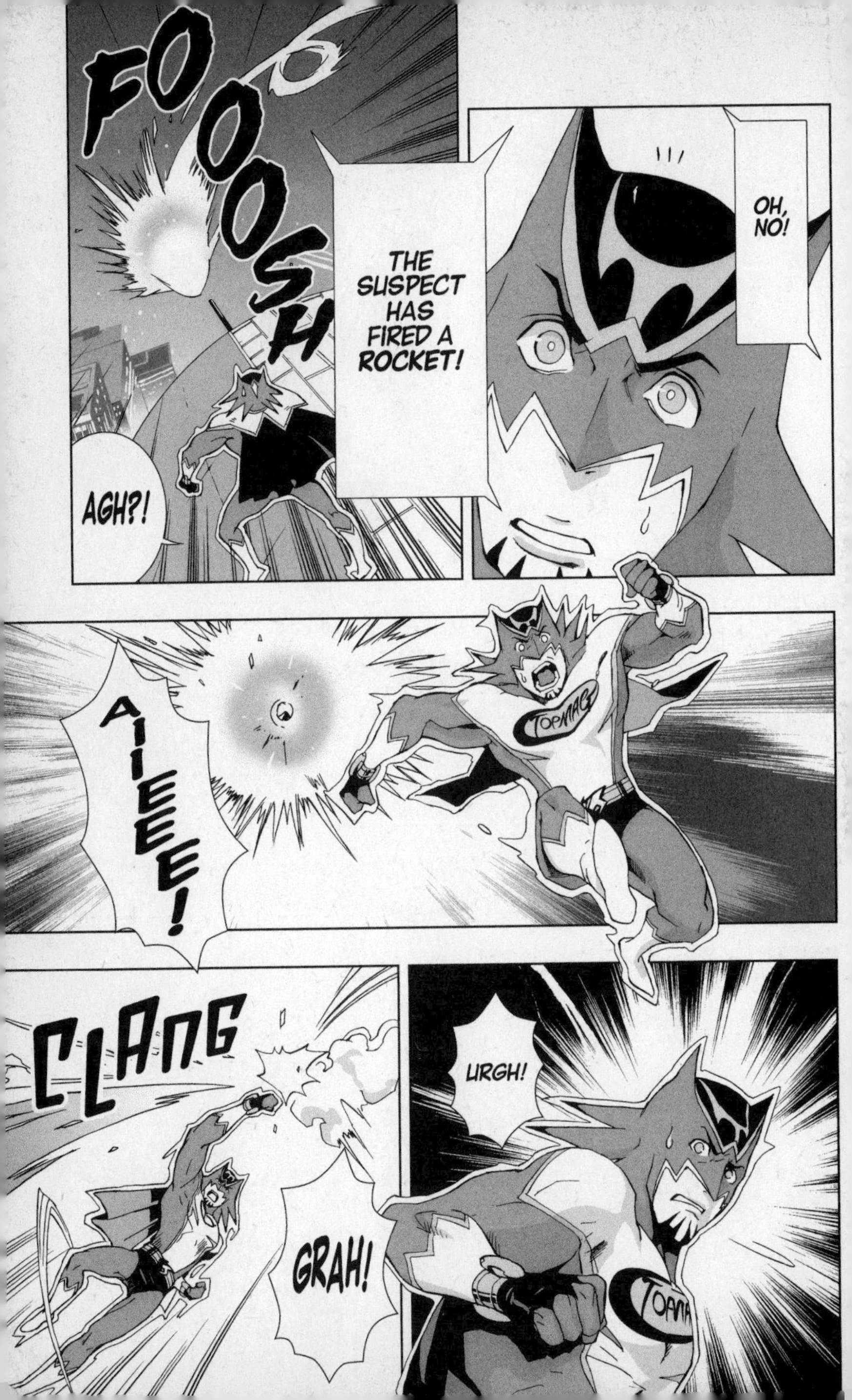

OH, NO!
THE SUSPECT HAS FIRED A ROCKET!
FOOOSH
AGH?!
AIEEE!
URGH!
CLANG
GRAH!

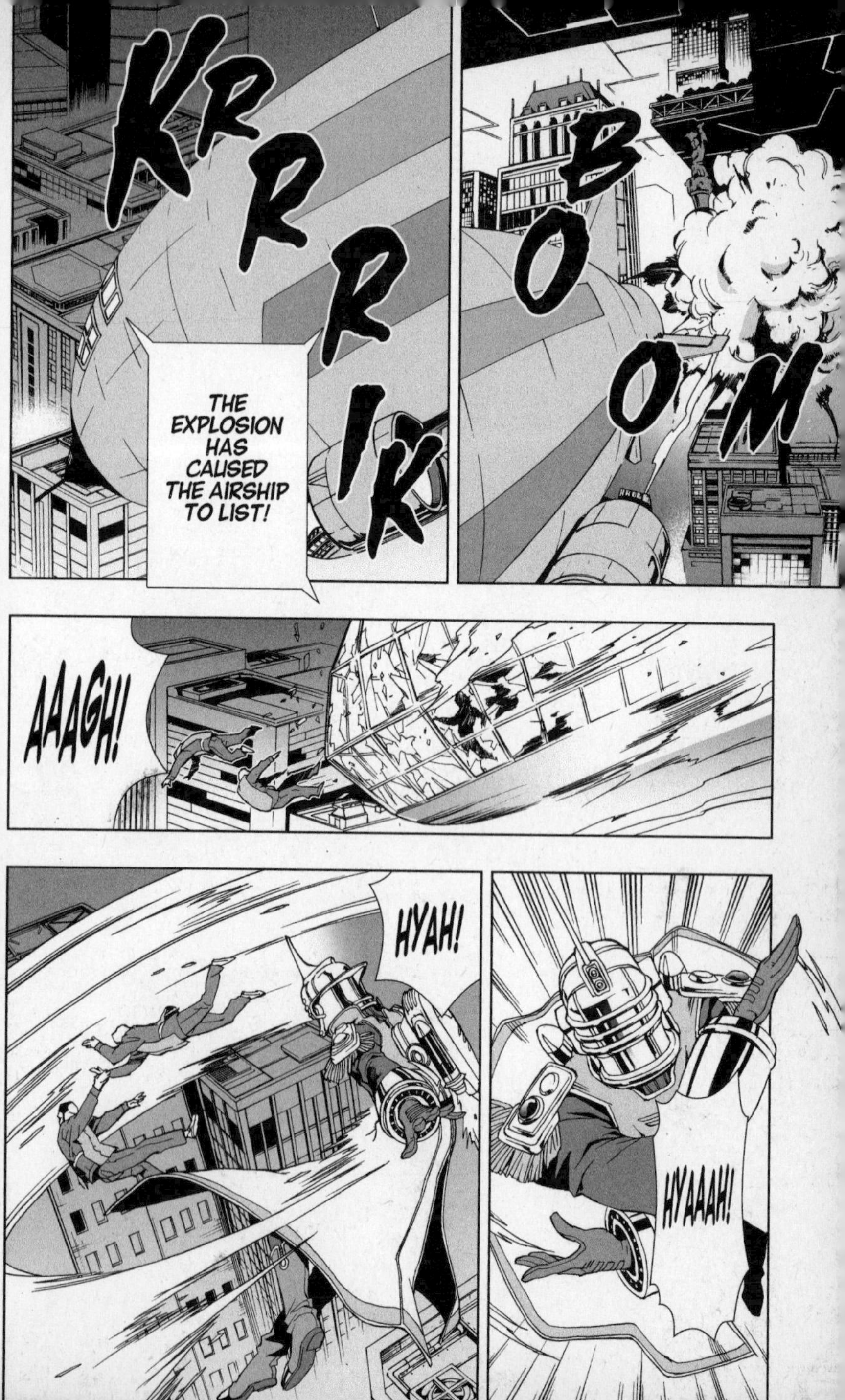
BOOOM
KRRRIK
THE EXPLOSION HAS CAUSED THE AIRSHIP TO LIST!
AAAGH!
HYAAAH!
HYAH!

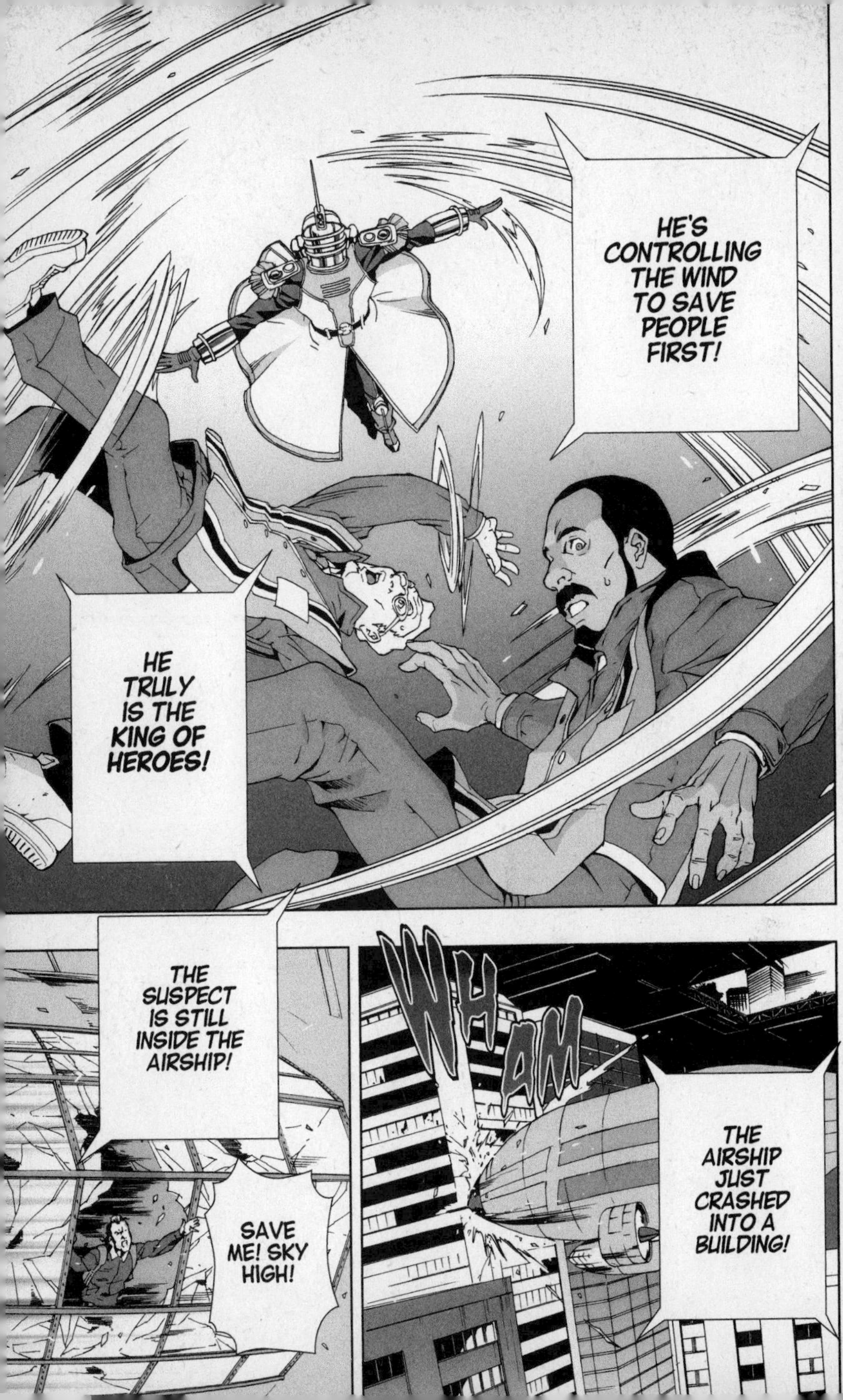
HE'S CONTROLLING THE WIND TO SAVE PEOPLE FIRST!
HE TRULY IS THE KING OF HEROES!
WHAM
THE AIRSHIP JUST CRASHED INTO A BUILDING!
THE SUSPECT IS STILL INSIDE THE AIRSHIP!
SAVE ME! SKY HIGH!

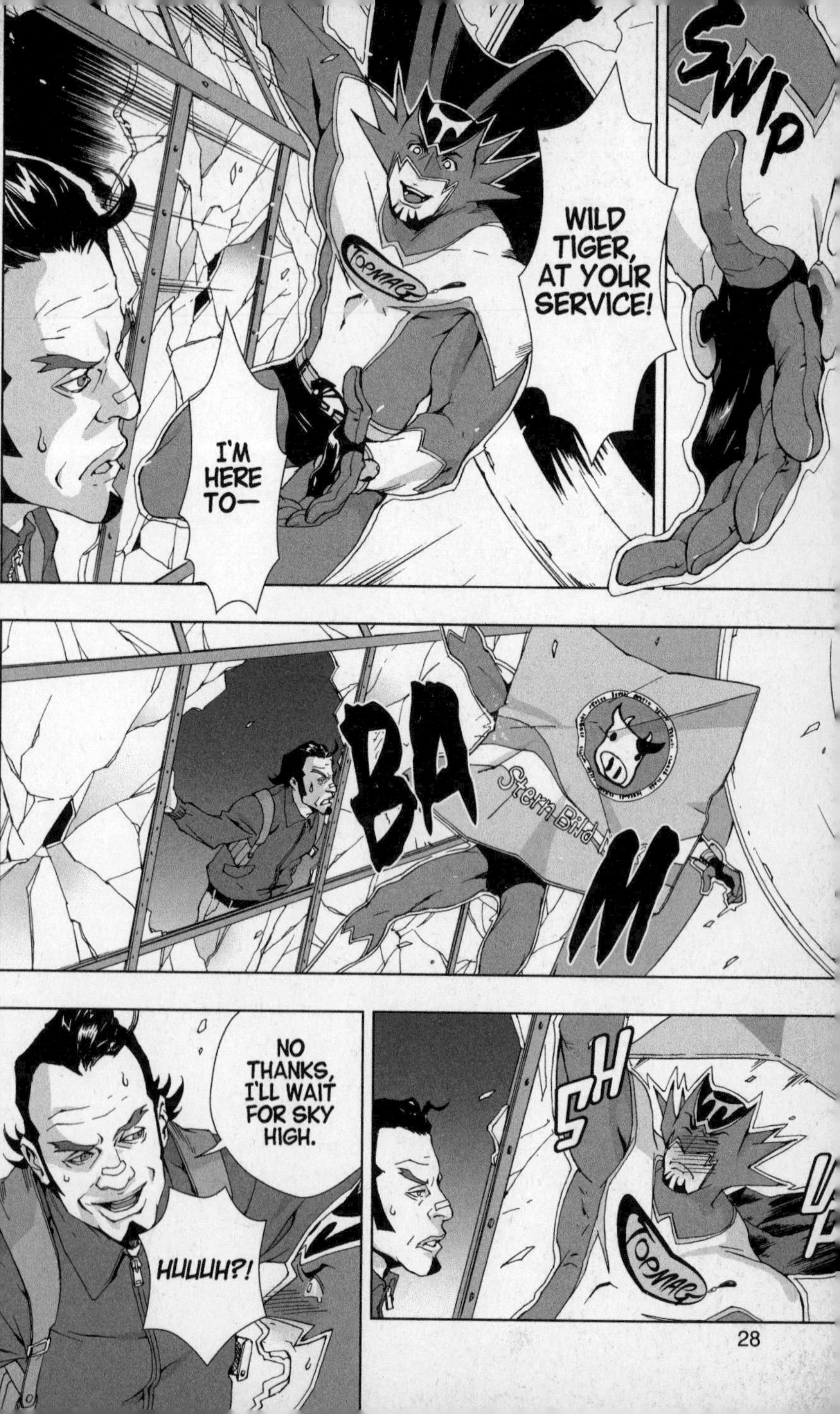
SWIP
WILD TIGER, AT YOUR SERVICE!
TOPMAG
I'M HERE TO—
BAM
Stern Bild
SH
TOPMAG
NO THANKS, I'LL WAIT FOR SKY HIGH.
HUUUH?!

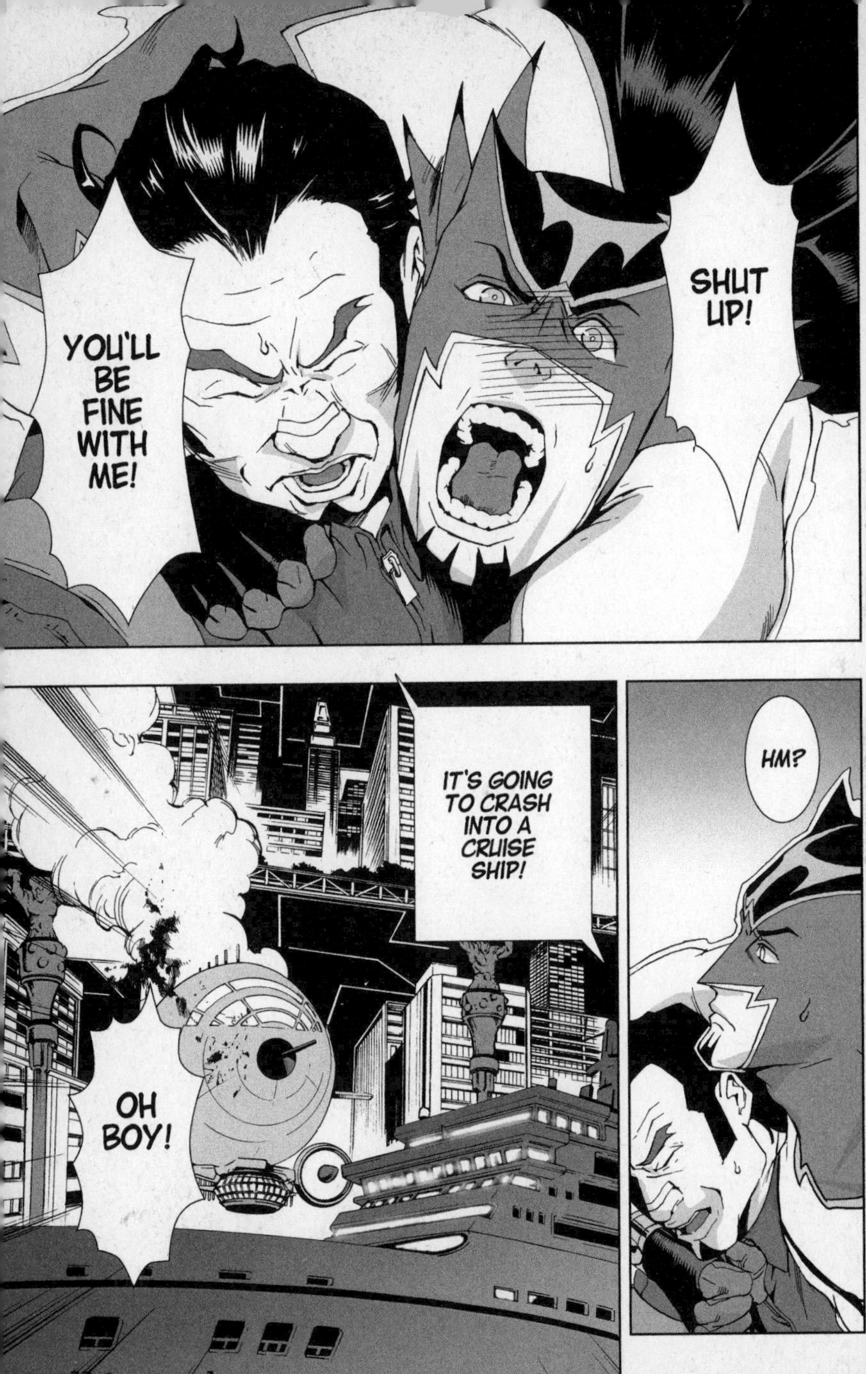
SHUT UP!
YOU'LL BE FINE WITH ME!
HM?
IT'S GOING TO CRASH INTO A CRUISE SHIP!
OH BOY!

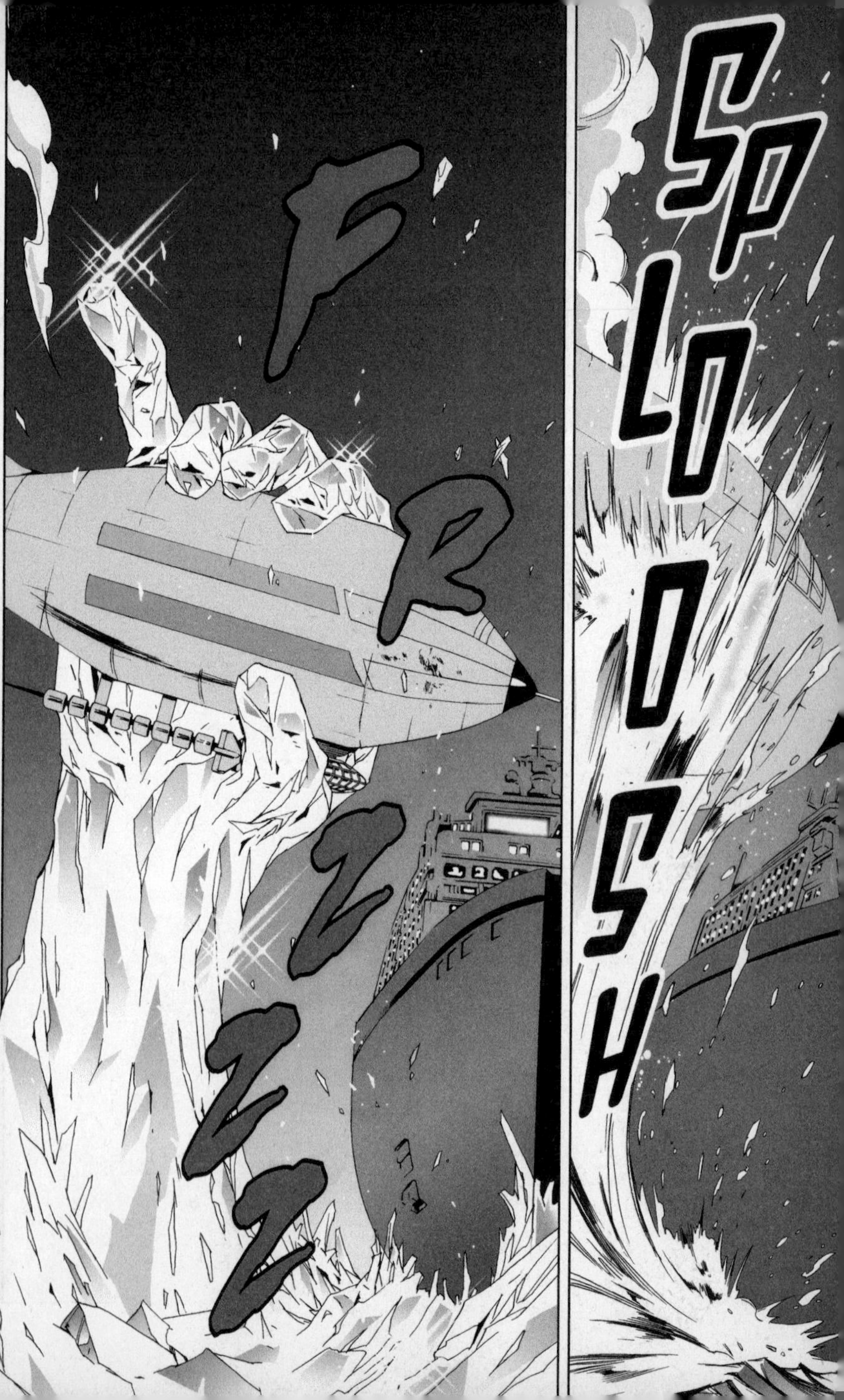
SPLOOSH
FRZZZZ

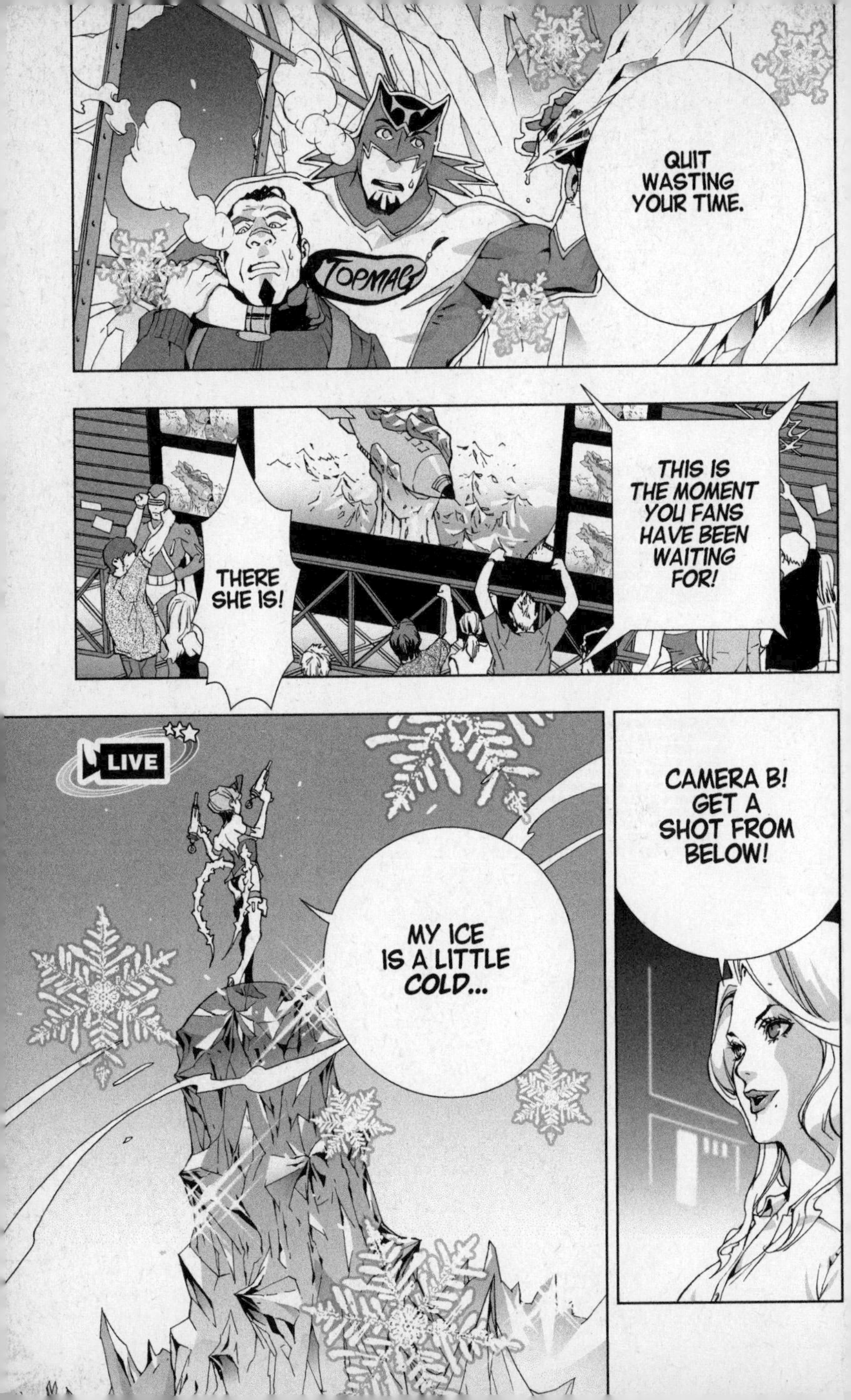
QUIT WASTING YOUR TIME.
TOPMAG
THIS IS THE MOMENT YOU FANS HAVE BEEN WAITING FOR!
THERE SHE IS!
CAMERA B! GET A SHOT FROM BELOW!
LIVE
MY ICE IS A LITTLE COLD...

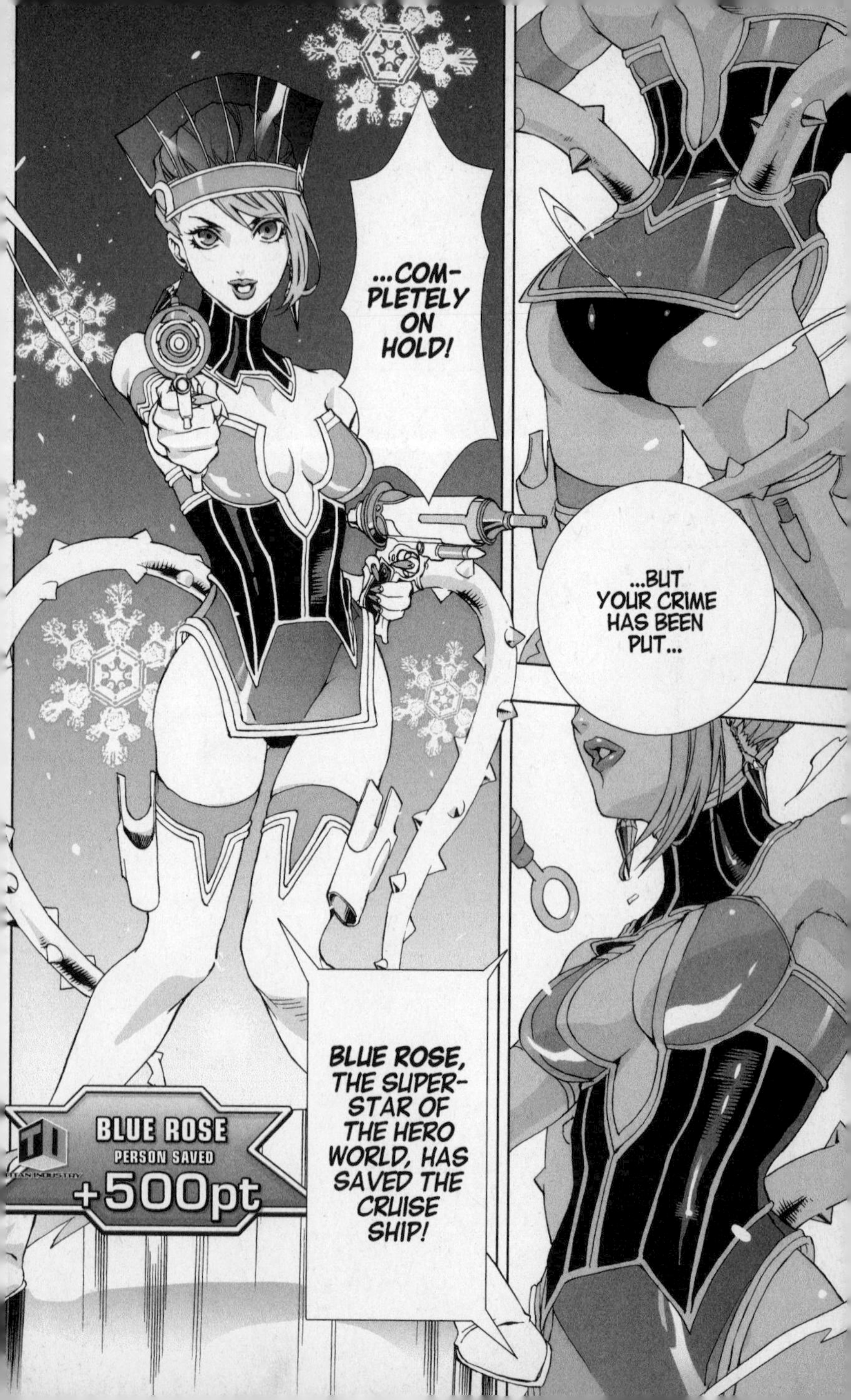

...BUT YOUR CRIME HAS BEEN PUT...
...COM-PLETELY ON HOLD!
BLUE ROSE, THE SUPER-STAR OF THE HERO WORLD, HAS SAVED THE CRUISE SHIP!
TI
TITAN INDUSTRY
BLUE ROSE
PERSON SAVED
+500pt

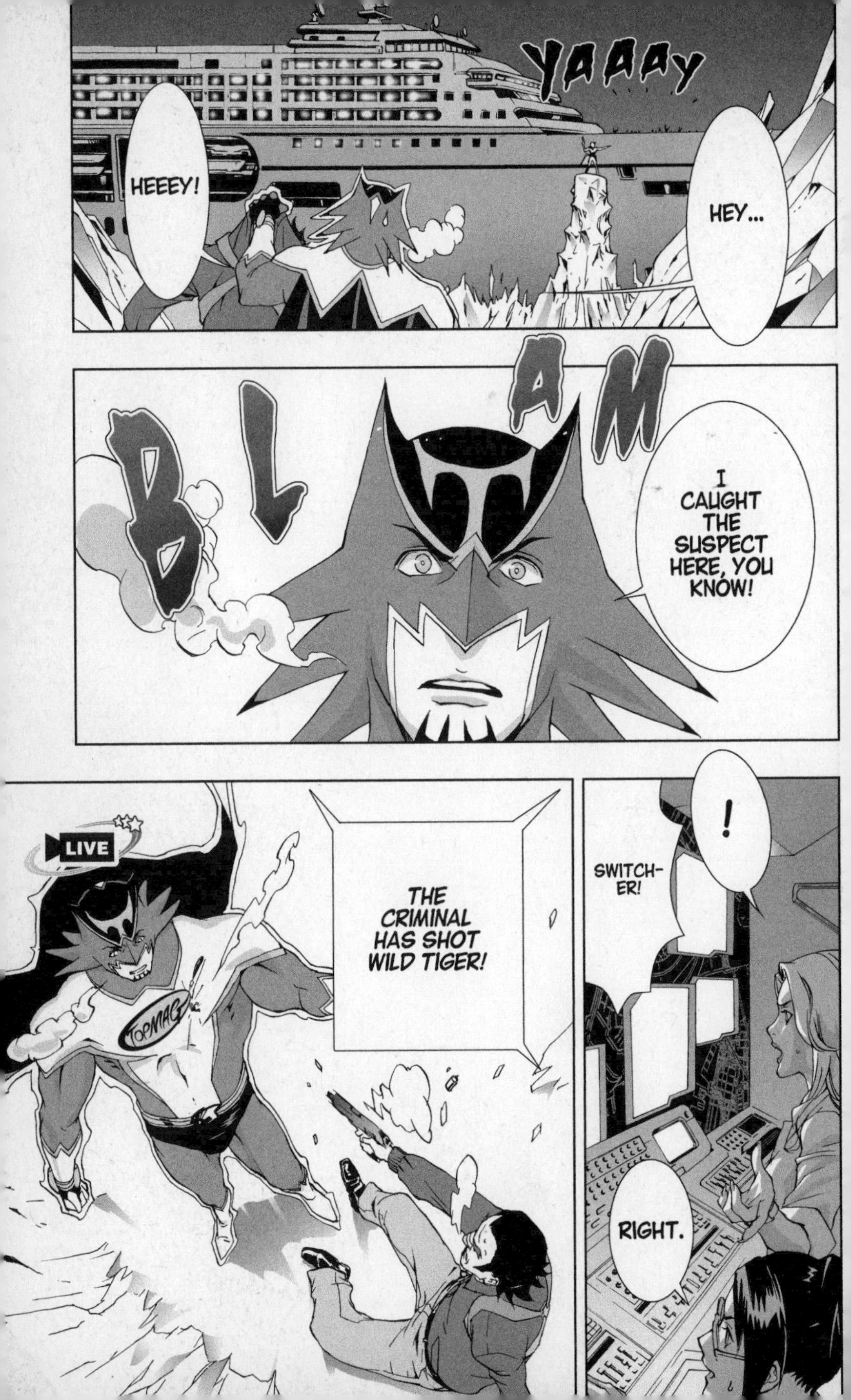
YAAAY
HEY...
HEEEY!
BLAM
I CAUGHT THE SUSPECT HERE, YOU KNOW!
!
SWITCHER!
RIGHT.
LIVE
THE CRIMINAL HAS SHOT WILD TIGER!
TOPMAG

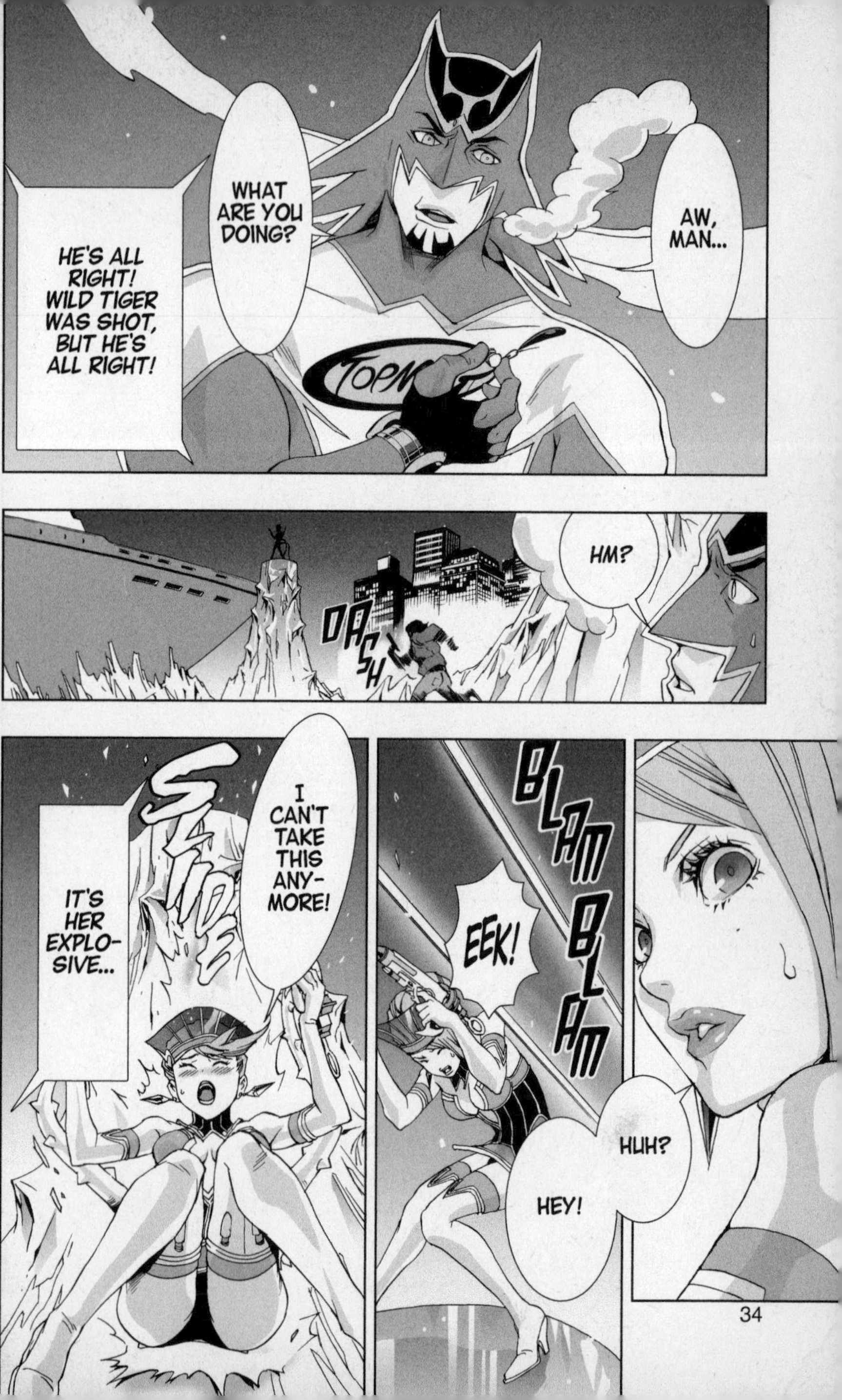
AW, MAN...
WHAT ARE YOU DOING?
HE'S ALL RIGHT! WILD TIGER WAS SHOT, BUT HE'S ALL RIGHT!
HM?
DASH
HUH?
HEY!
BLAM BLAM BLAM
EEK!
I CAN'T TAKE THIS ANYMORE!
IT'S HER EXPLOSIVE...
SLIDE

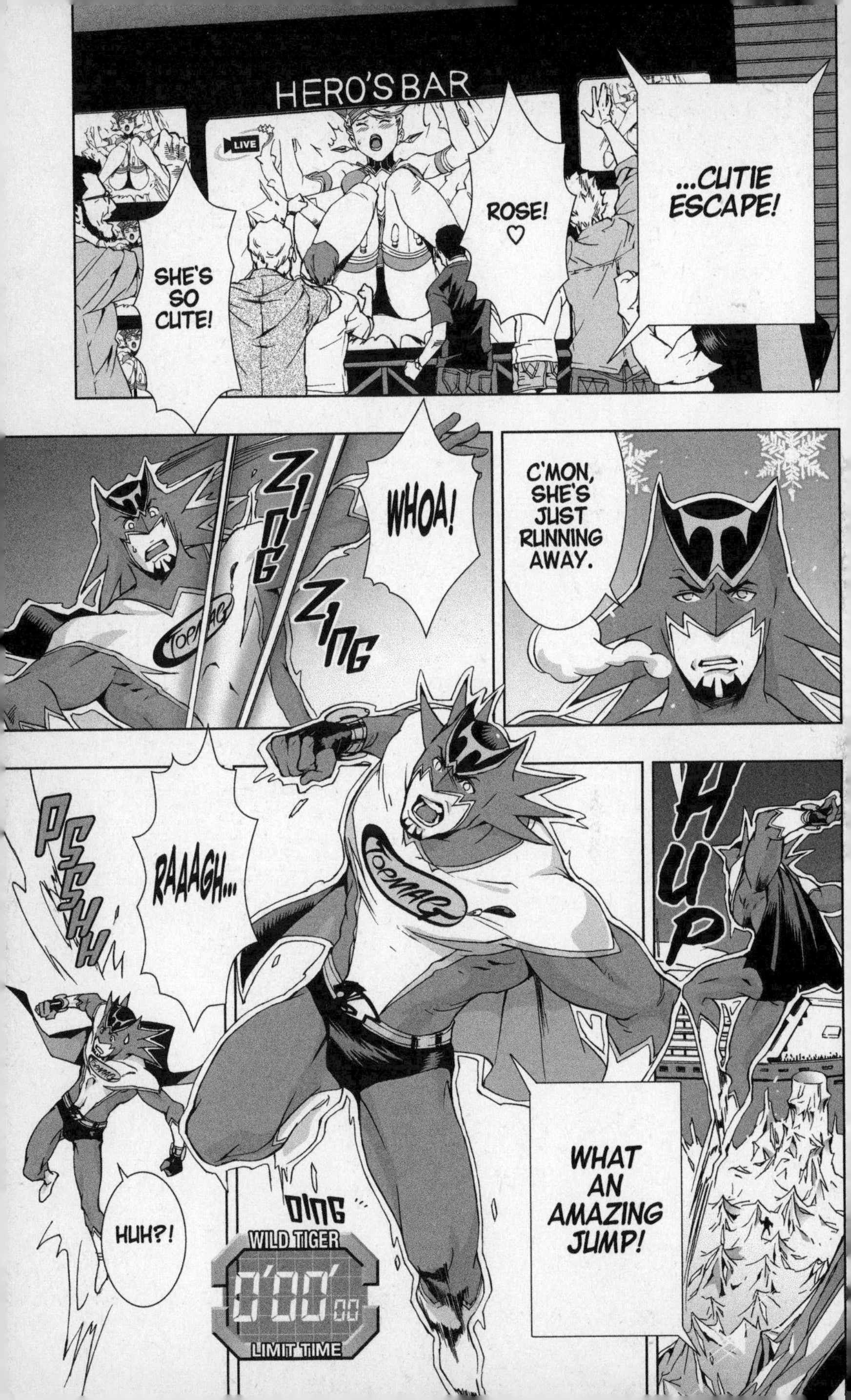
...CUTIE ESCAPE!
HERO'S BAR
ROSE! ♡
LIVE
SHE'S SO CUTE!
C'MON, SHE'S JUST RUNNING AWAY.
WHOA!
ZING
ZING
HUP
RAAAGH...
PSSHH
WHAT AN AMAZING JUMP!
DING
WILD TIGER
0'00"00
LIMIT TIME
HUH?!

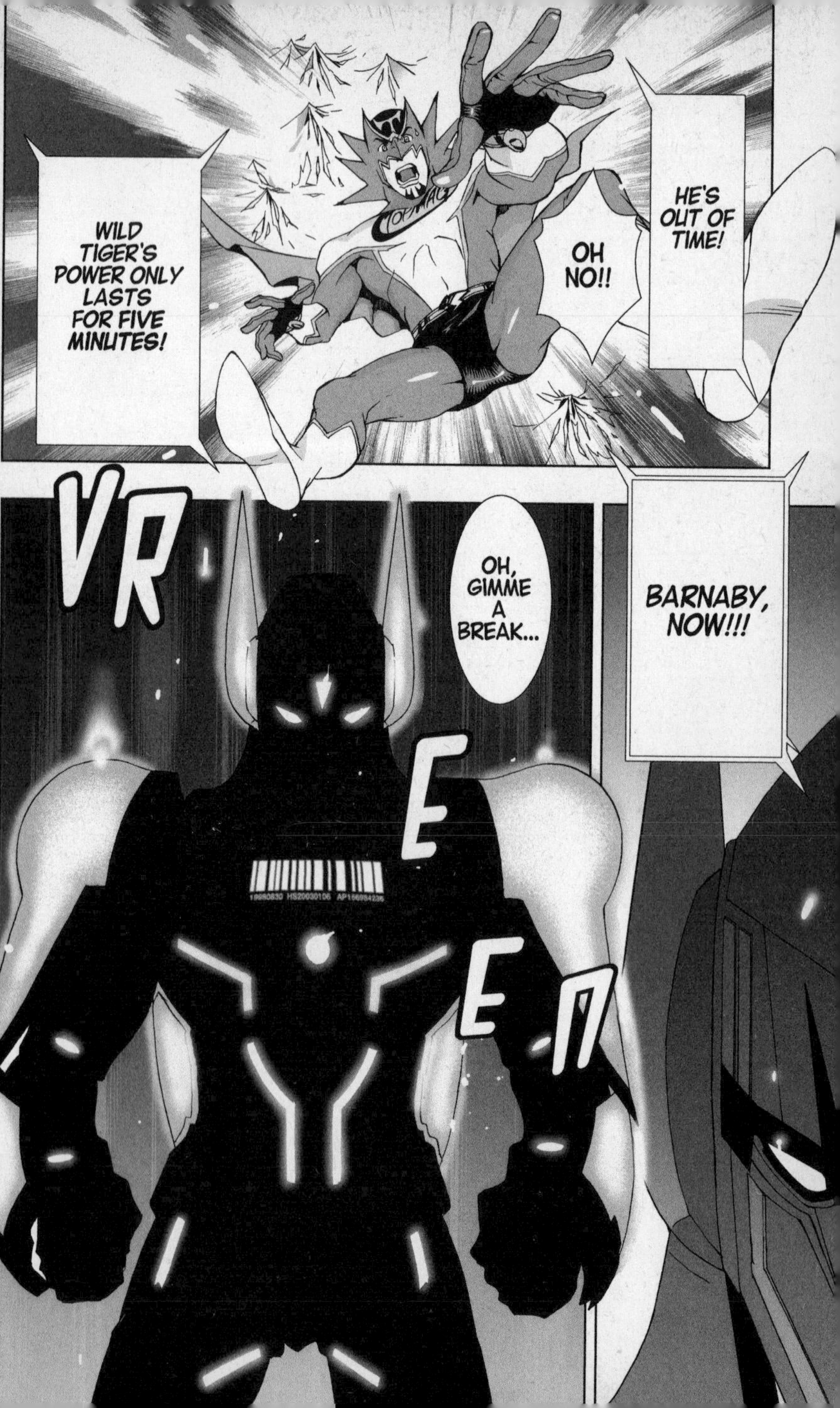
HE'S OUT OF TIME!
OH NO!!
WILD TIGER'S POWER ONLY LASTS FOR FIVE MINUTES!
BARNABY, NOW!!!
OH, GIMME A BREAK...
VREEM

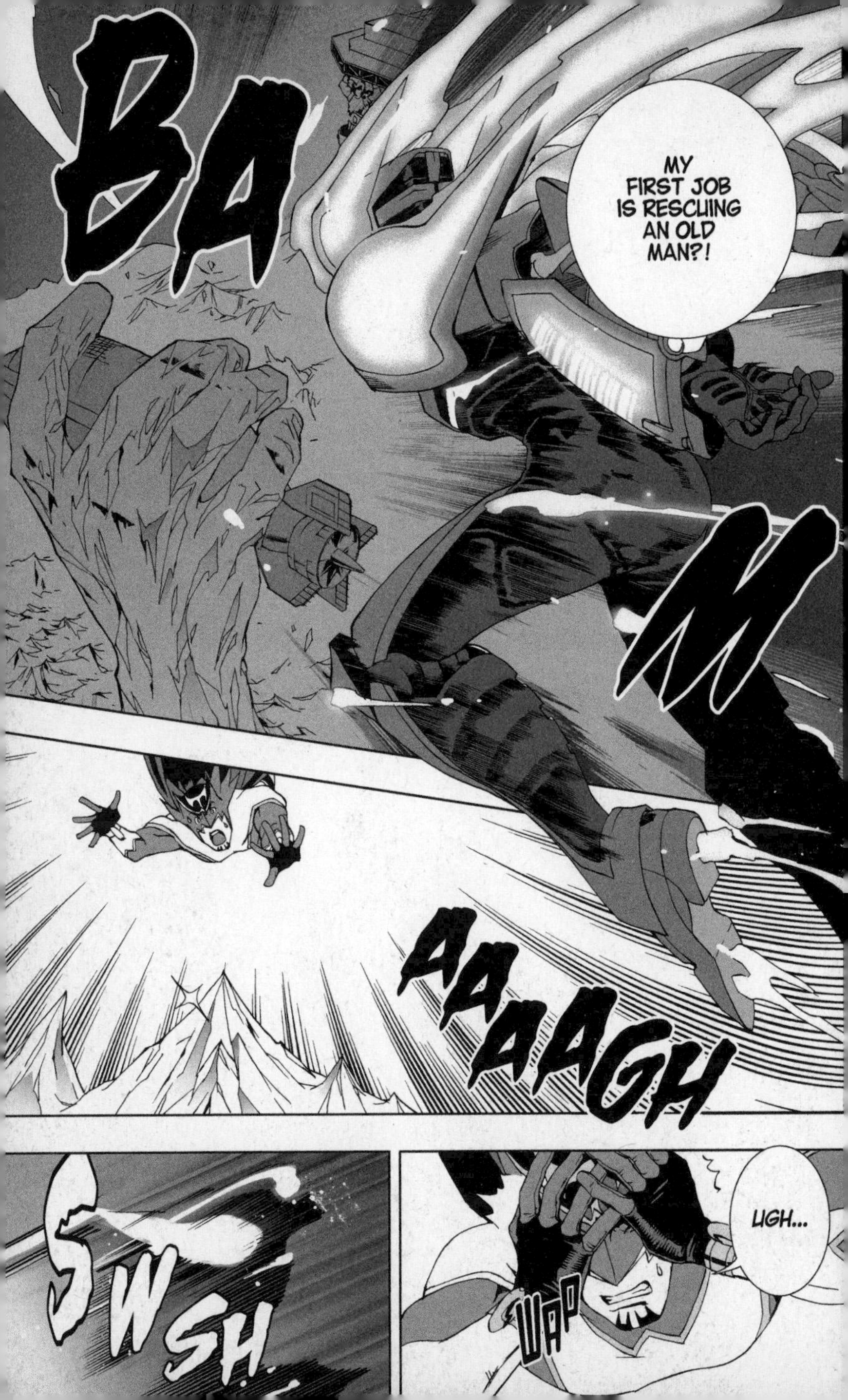
MY FIRST JOB IS RESCUING AN OLD MAN?!
BAM
AAAAAGH
UGH...
WAP
SWSH

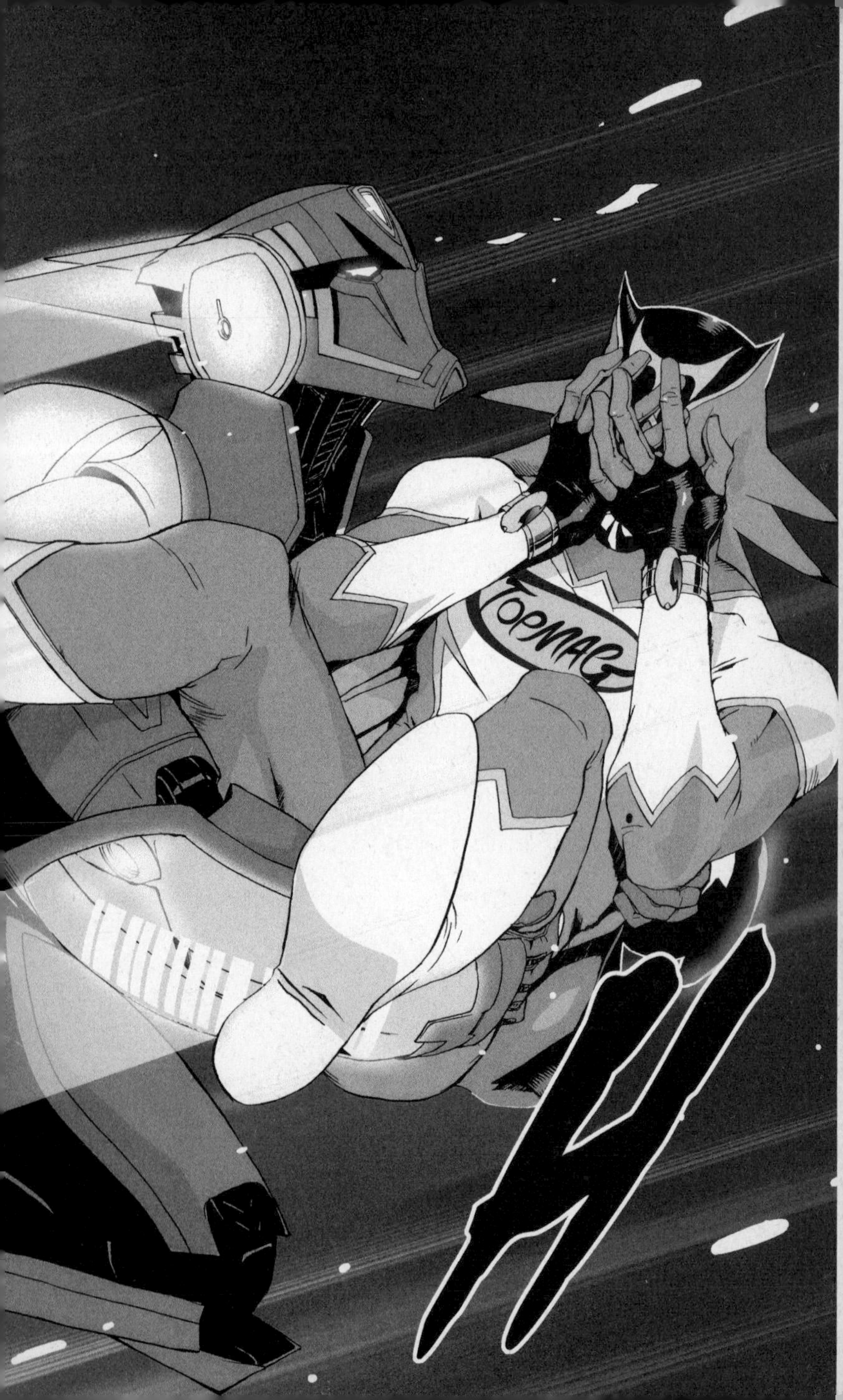
TOPMAG

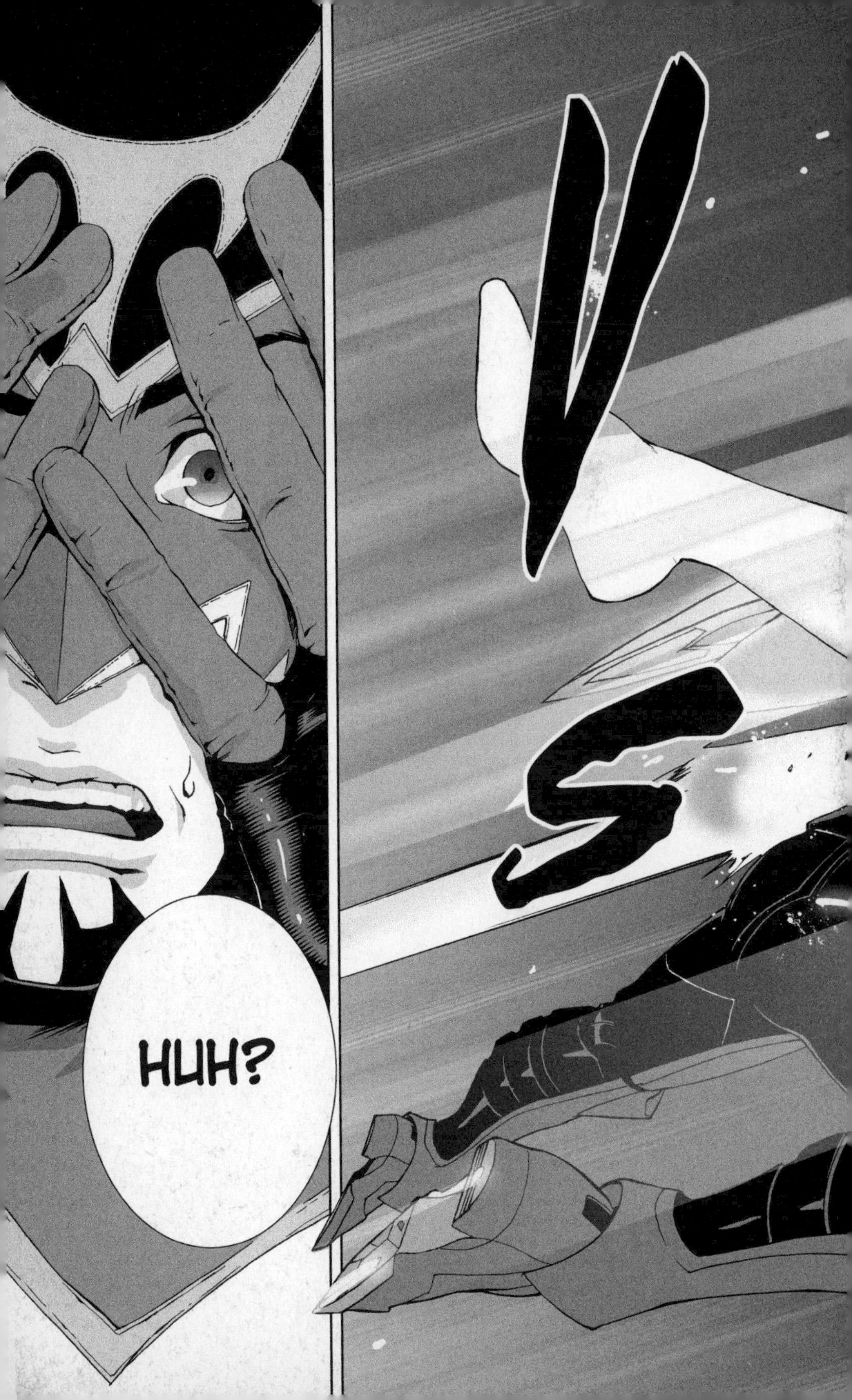
HUH?

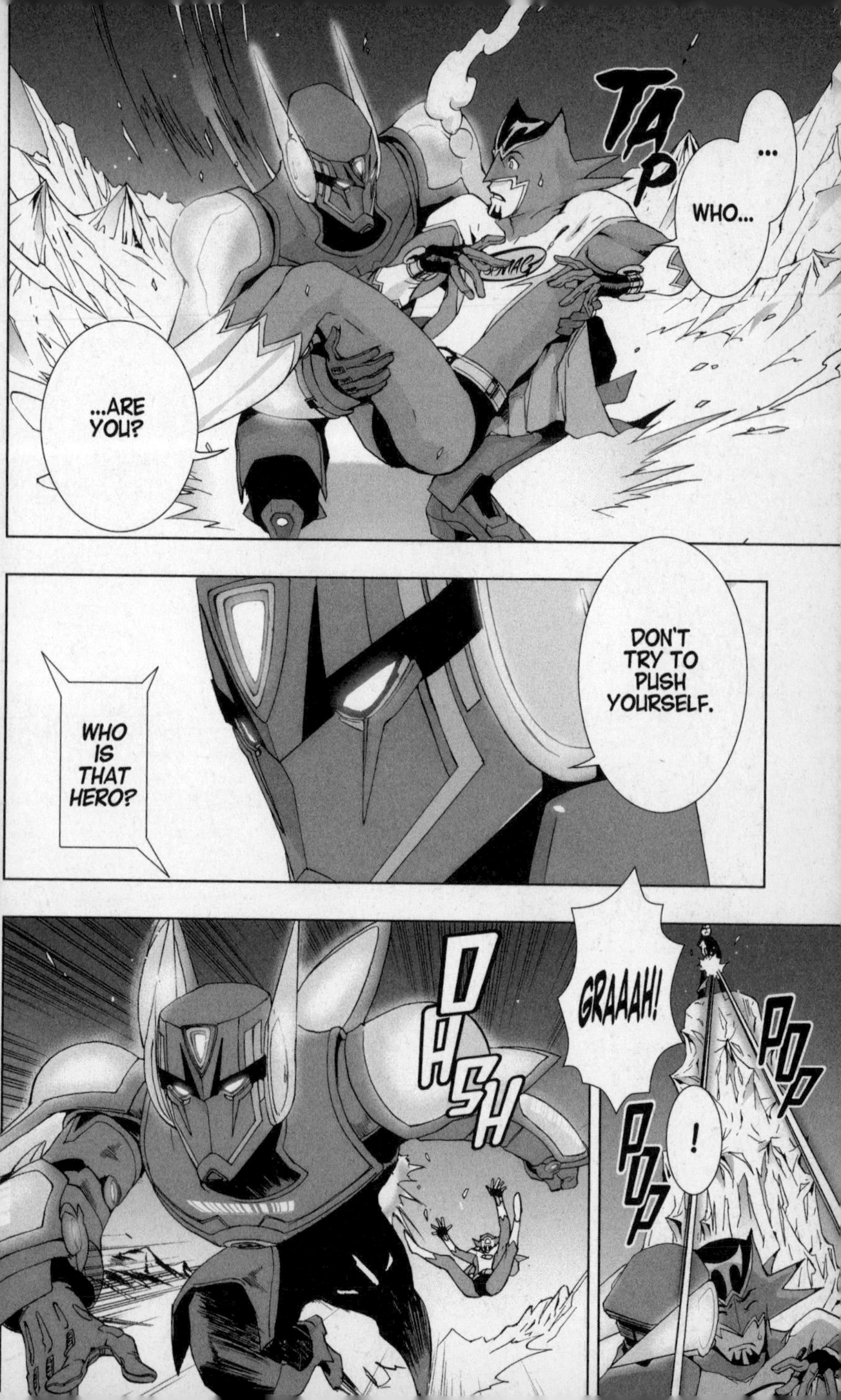
TAP
...
WHO...
...ARE YOU?
DON'T TRY TO PUSH YOURSELF.
WHO IS THAT HERO?
GRAAAH!
POP
POP
POP
POP
!
DASH

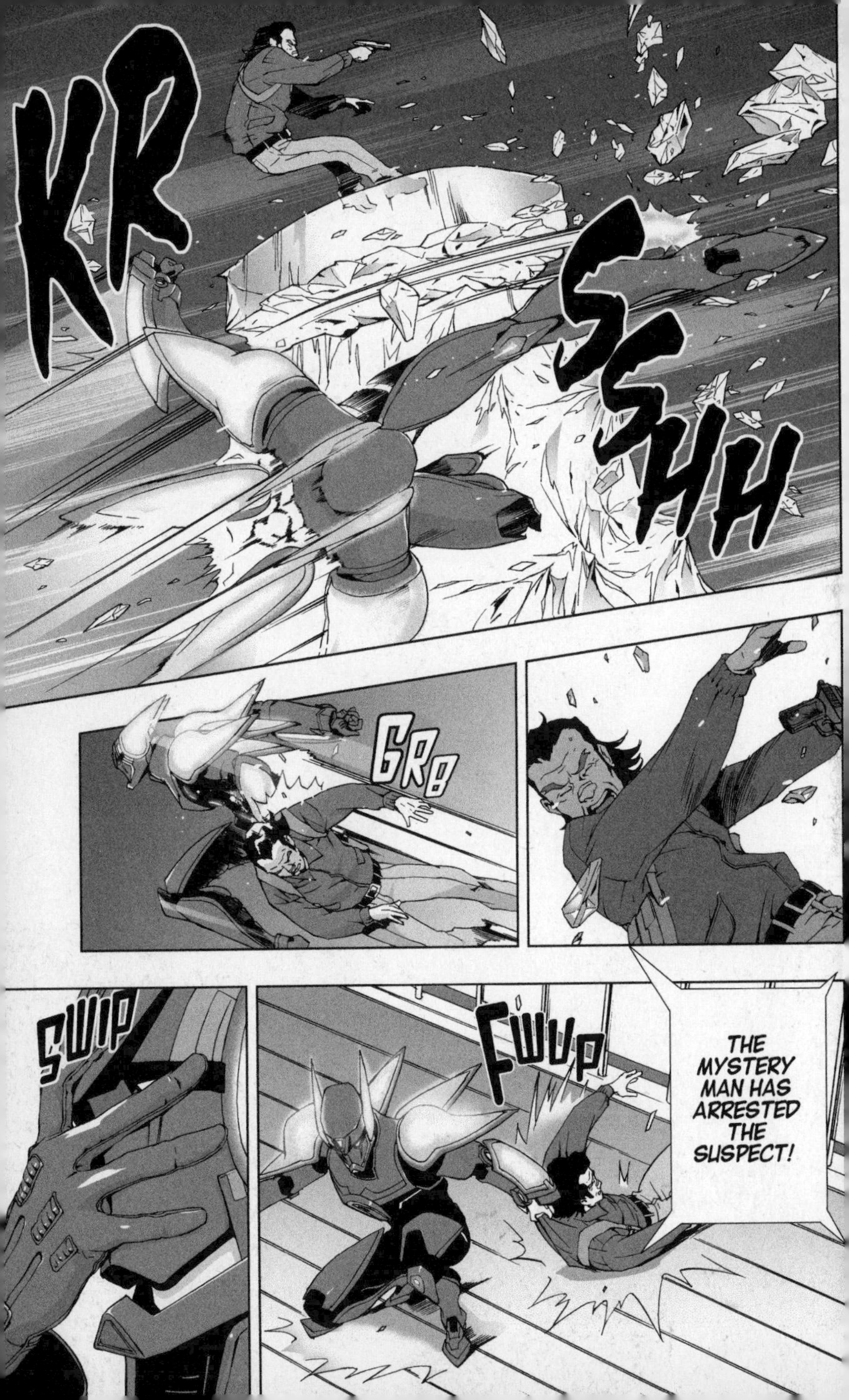
KR
SSHH
GRB
THE MYSTERY MAN HAS ARRESTED THE SUSPECT!
FWUP
SWIP

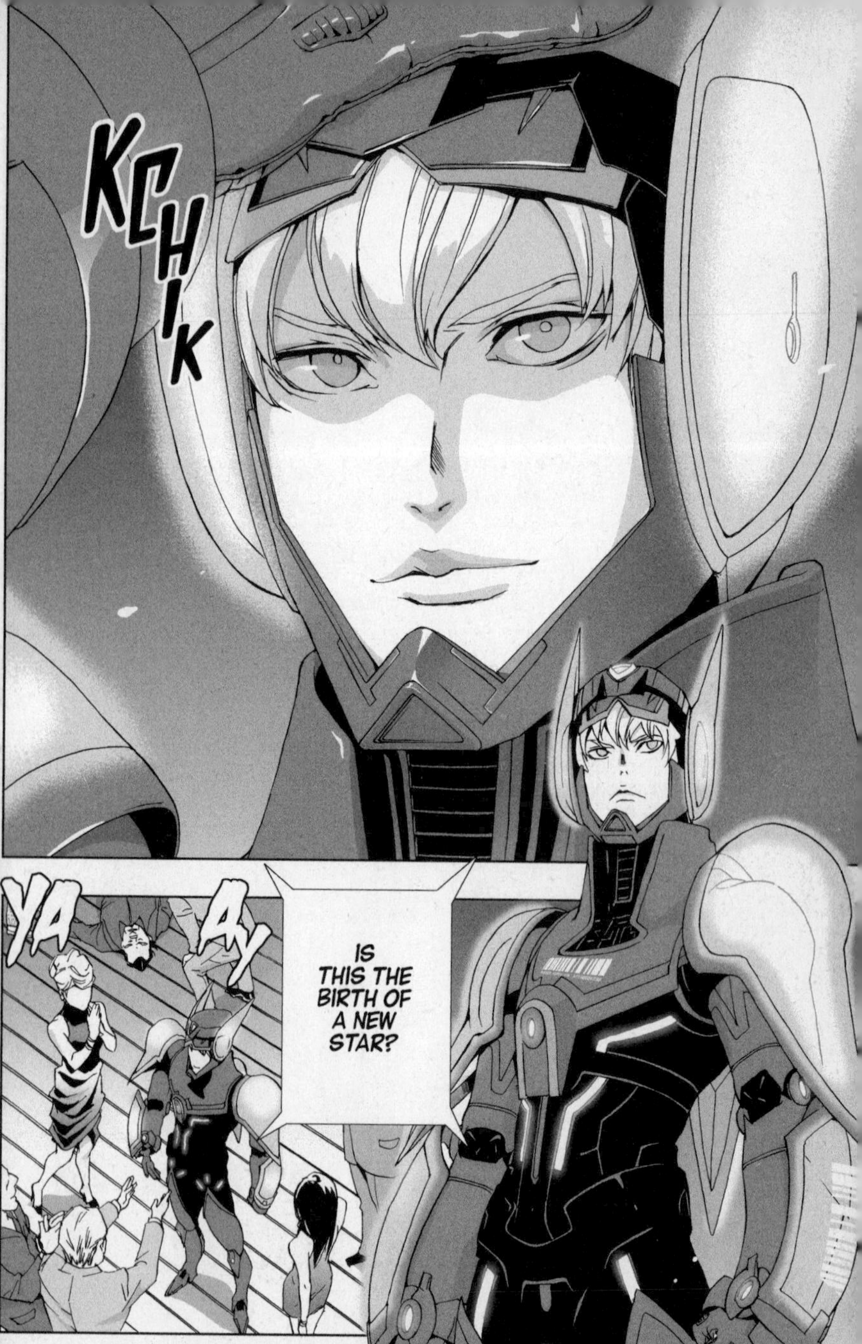
KCHIK
YAAY
IS THIS THE BIRTH OF A NEW STAR?

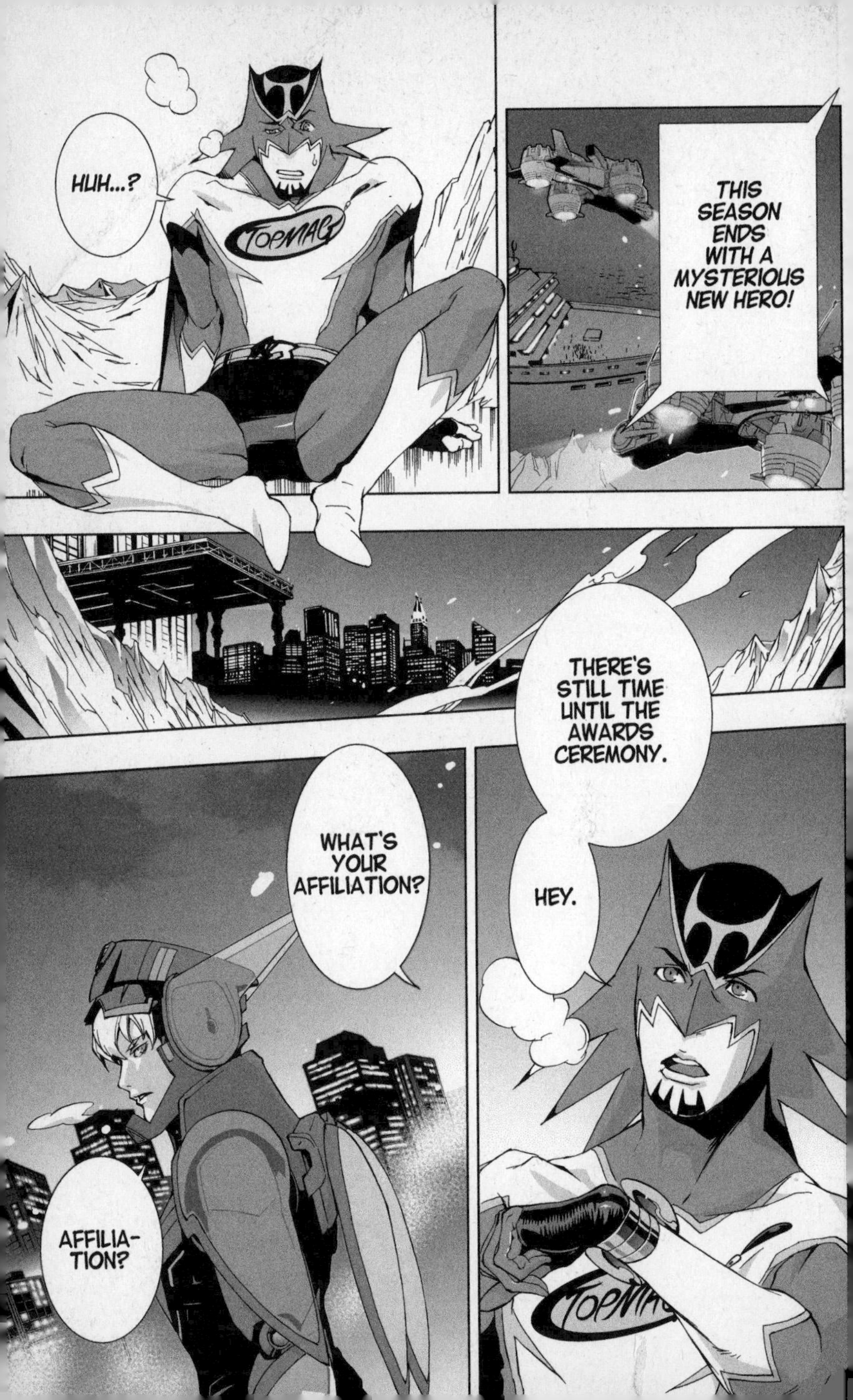
THIS SEASON ENDS WITH A MYSTERIOUS NEW HERO!
HUH...?
THERE'S STILL TIME UNTIL THE AWARDS CEREMONY.
HEY.
WHAT'S YOUR AFFILIATION?
AFFILIA- TION?

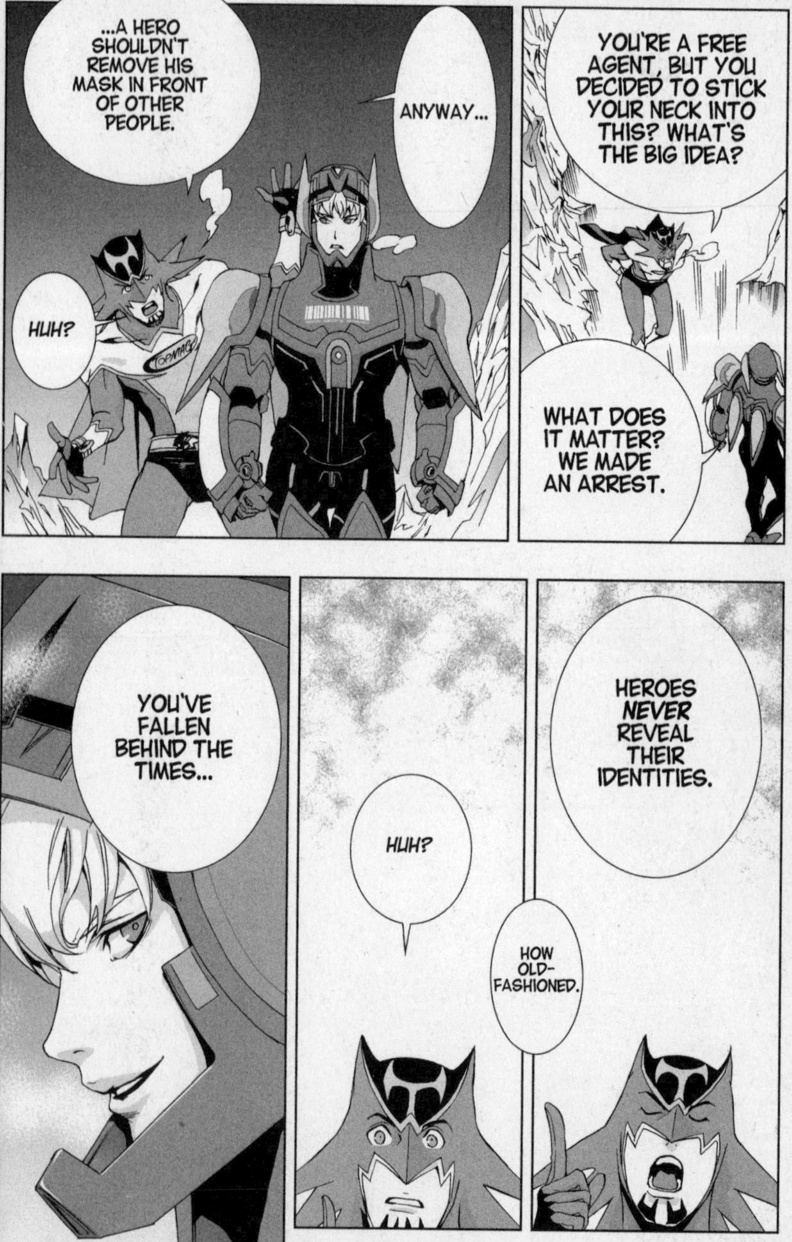
YOU'RE A FREE AGENT, BUT YOU DECIDED TO STICK YOUR NECK INTO THIS? WHAT'S THE BIG IDEA?
WHAT DOES IT MATTER? WE MADE AN ARREST.
ANYWAY...
...A HERO SHOULDN'T REMOVE HIS MASK IN FRONT OF OTHER PEOPLE.
HUH?
HEROES *NEVER* REVEAL THEIR IDENTITIES.
HOW OLD-FASHIONED.
HUH?
YOU'VE FALLEN BEHIND THE TIMES...

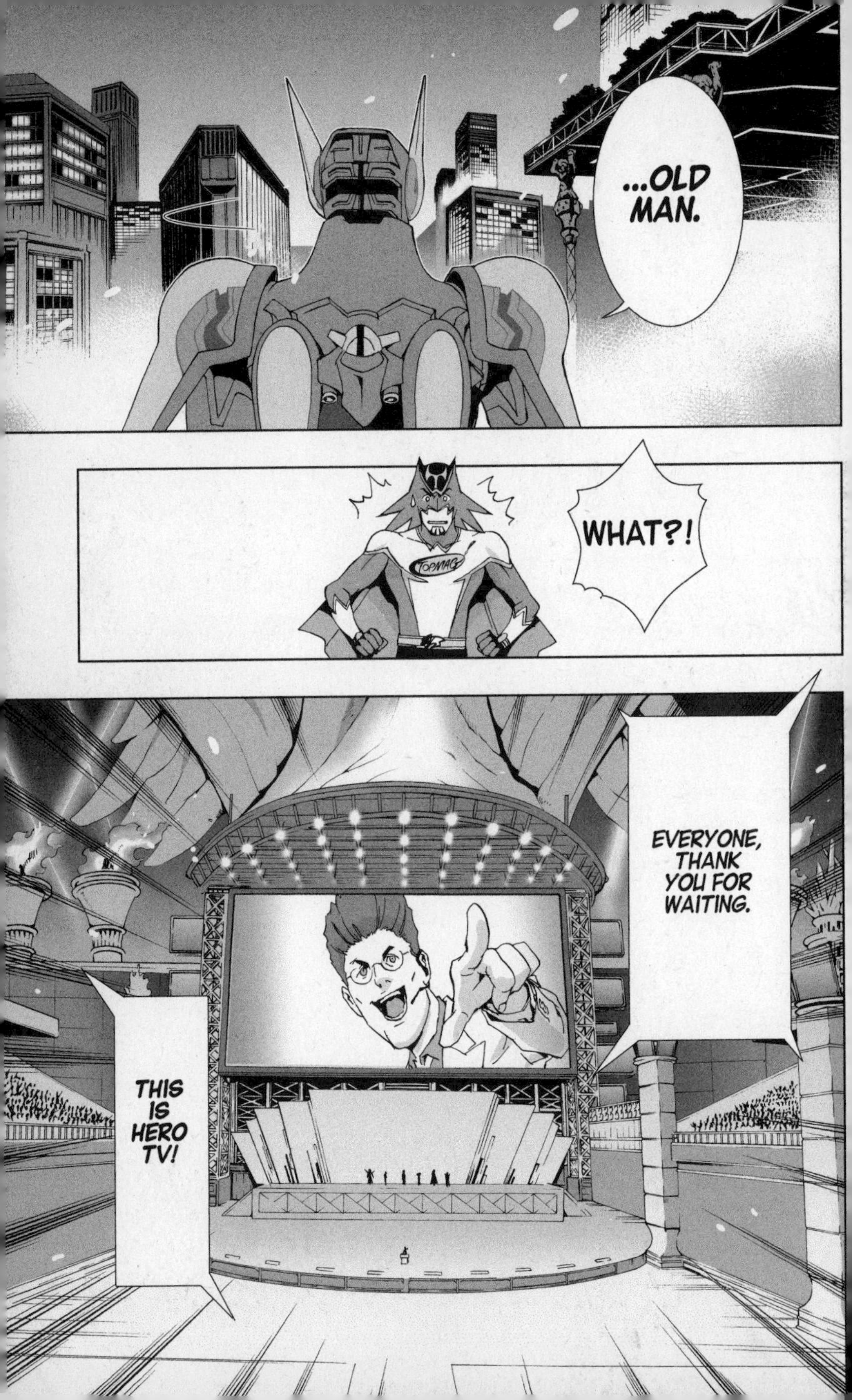
...OLD MAN.
WHAT?!
EVERYONE, THANK YOU FOR WAITING.
THIS IS HERO TV!

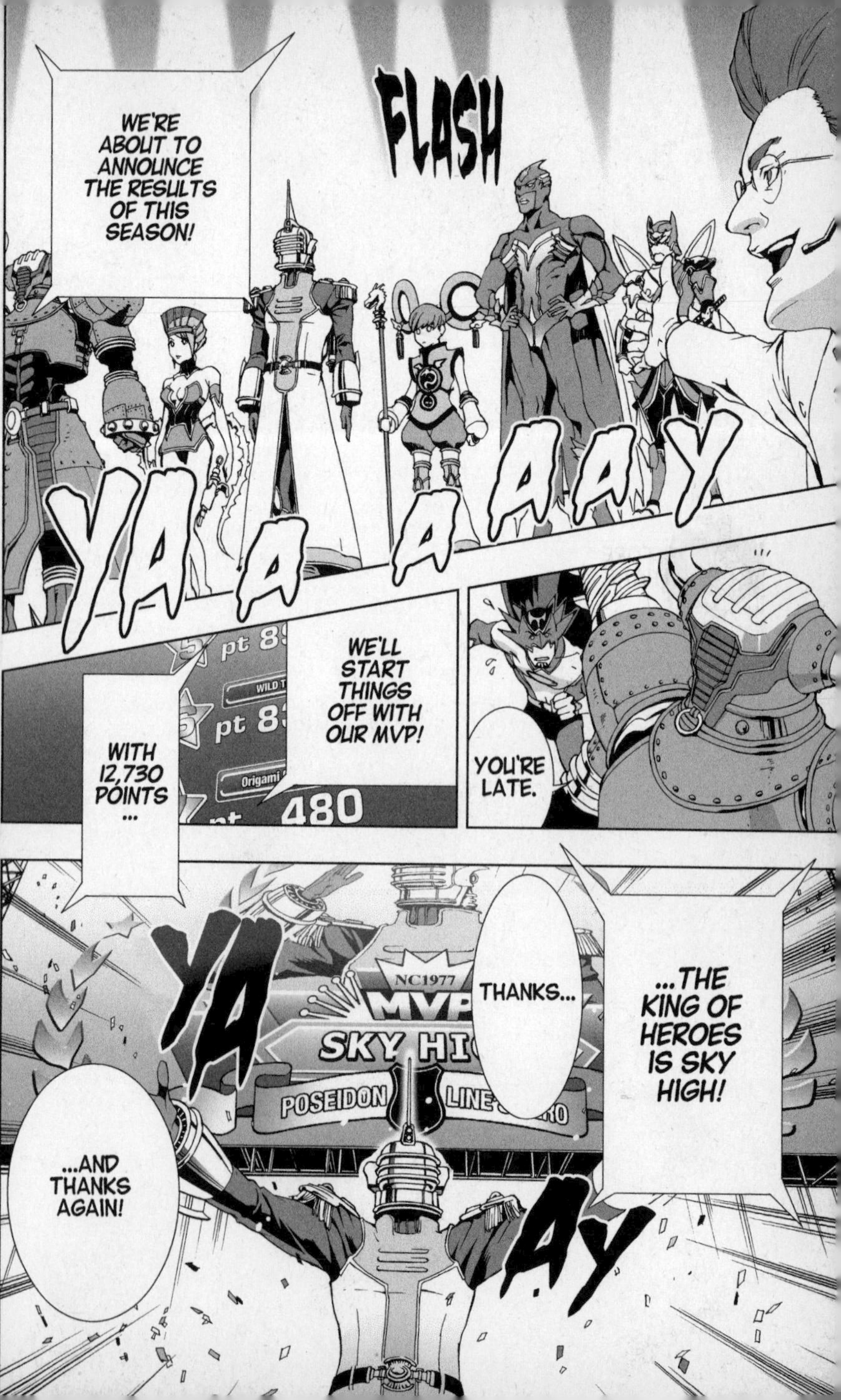
FLASH
WE'RE ABOUT TO ANNOUNCE THE RESULTS OF THIS SEASON!
YAAAAAY
YOU'RE LATE.
WE'LL START THINGS OFF WITH OUR MVP!
480
WITH 12,730 POINTS ...
...THE KING OF HEROES IS SKY HIGH!
THANKS...
NC1977
POSEIDON
YAAY
...AND THANKS AGAIN!

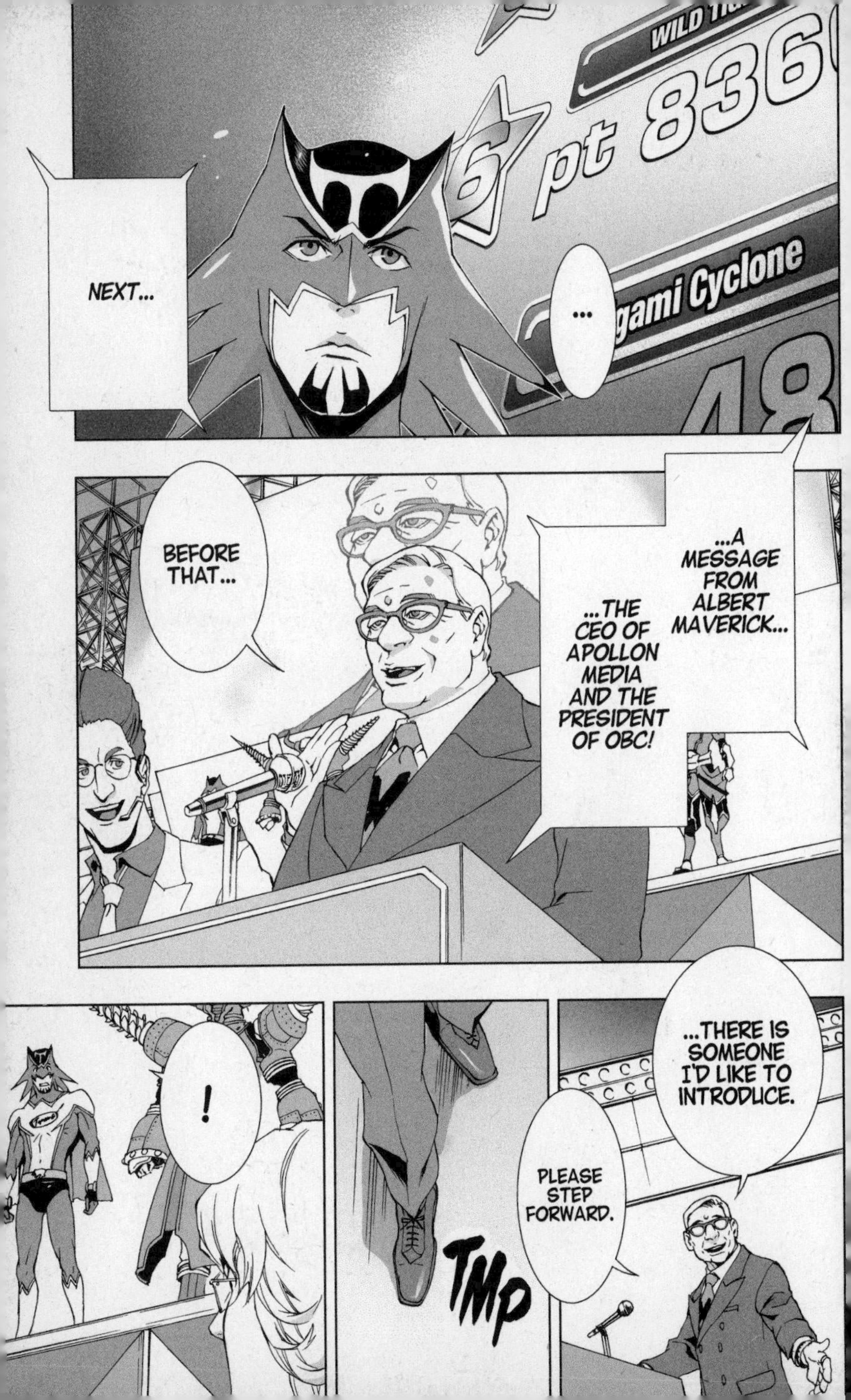
...
NEXT...
...A MESSAGE FROM ALBERT MAVERICK...
...THE CEO OF APOLLON MEDIA AND THE PRESIDENT OF OBC!
BEFORE THAT...
...THERE IS SOMEONE I'D LIKE TO INTRODUCE.
PLEASE STEP FORWARD.
TMP
!

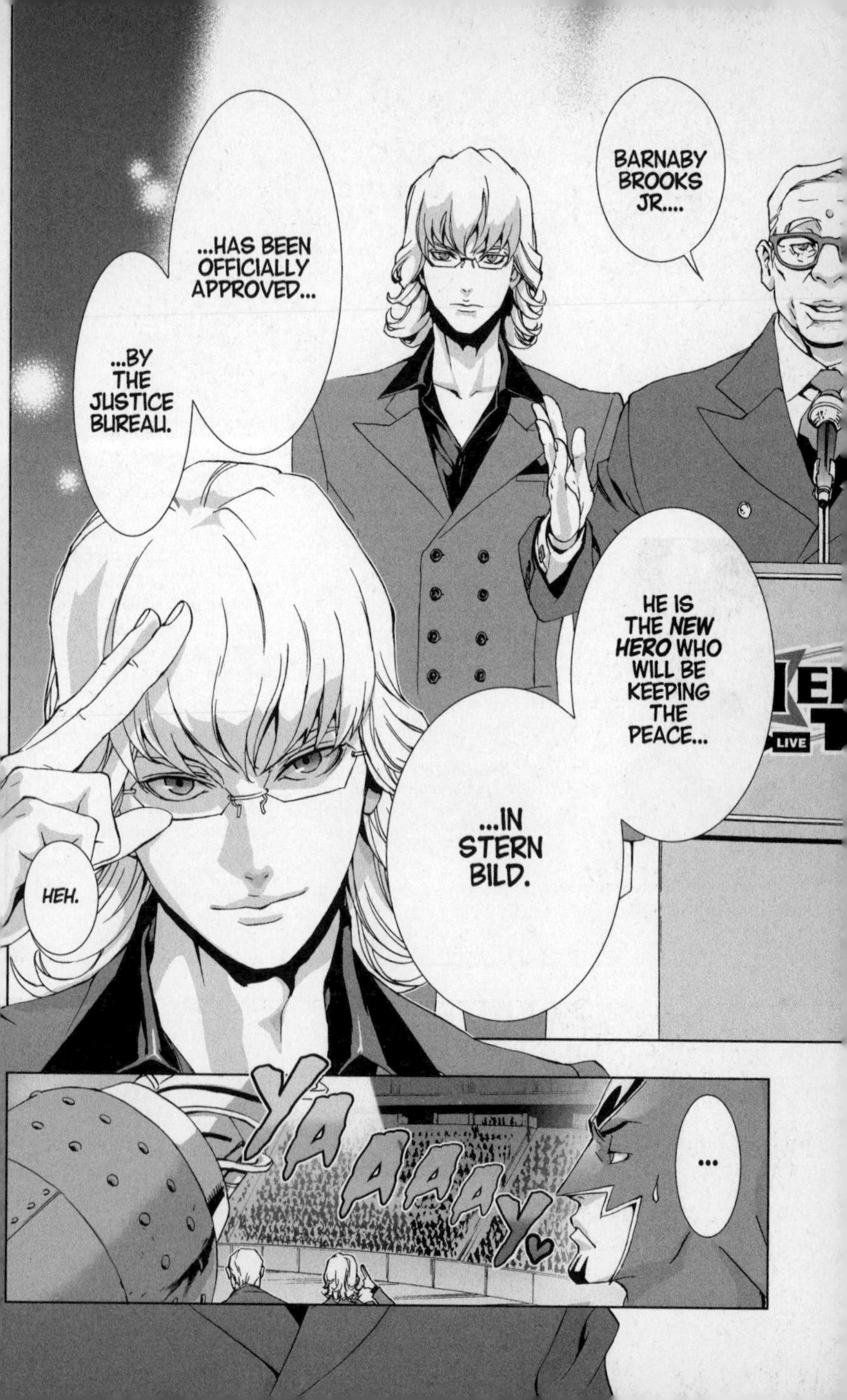
BARNABY BROOKS JR....
...HAS BEEN OFFICIALLY APPROVED...
...BY THE JUSTICE BUREAU.
HE IS THE *NEW HERO* WHO WILL BE KEEPING THE PEACE...
...IN STERN BILD.
LIVE
HEH.
...
YAAAAAY♥

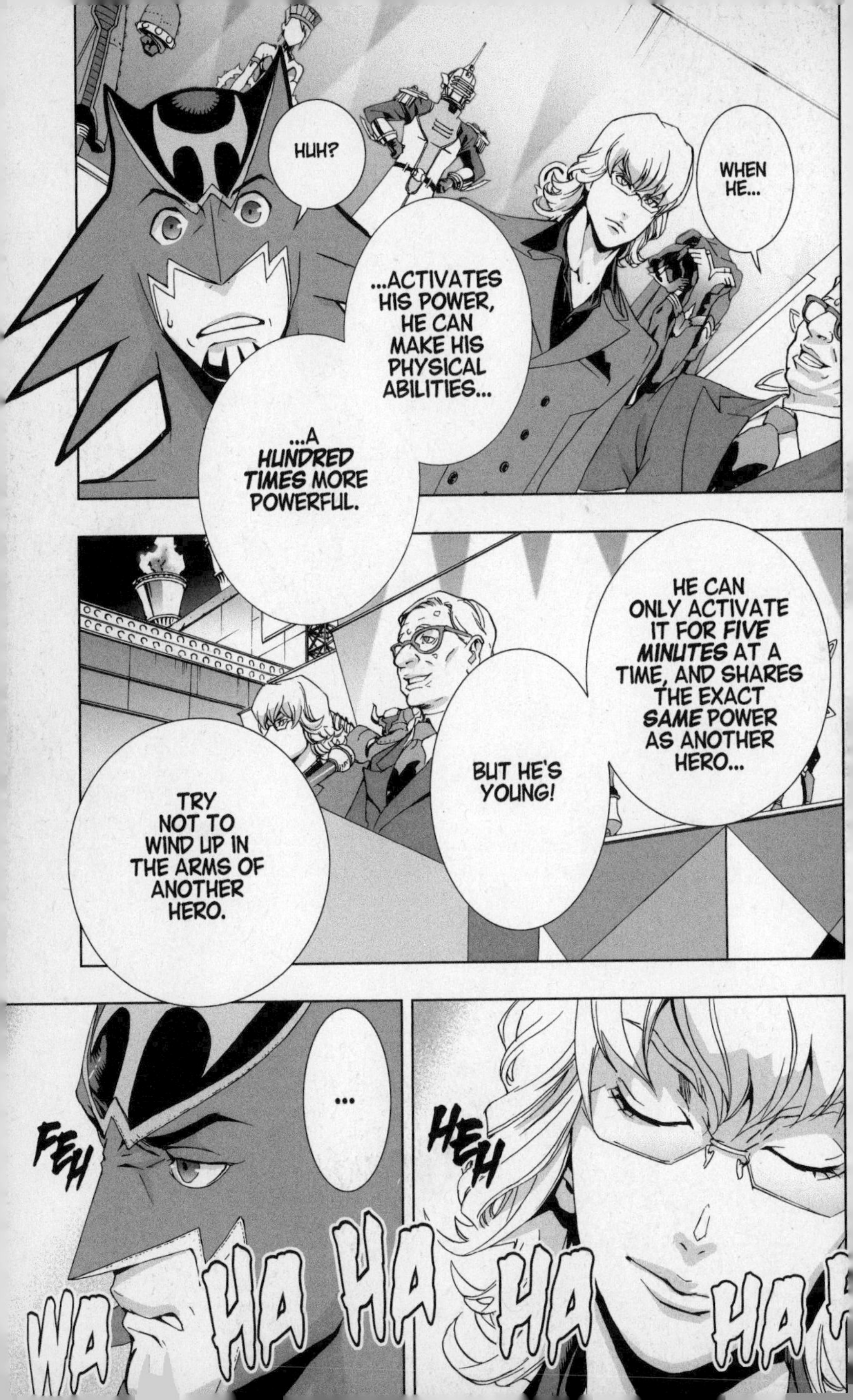
WHEN HE...
HUH?
...ACTIVATES HIS POWER, HE CAN MAKE HIS PHYSICAL ABILITIES...
...A HUNDRED TIMES MORE POWERFUL.
HE CAN ONLY ACTIVATE IT FOR FIVE MINUTES AT A TIME, AND SHARES THE EXACT SAME POWER AS ANOTHER HERO...
BUT HE'S YOUNG!
TRY NOT TO WIND UP IN THE ARMS OF ANOTHER HERO.
HEH
...
FEH
WA HA HA HA HA

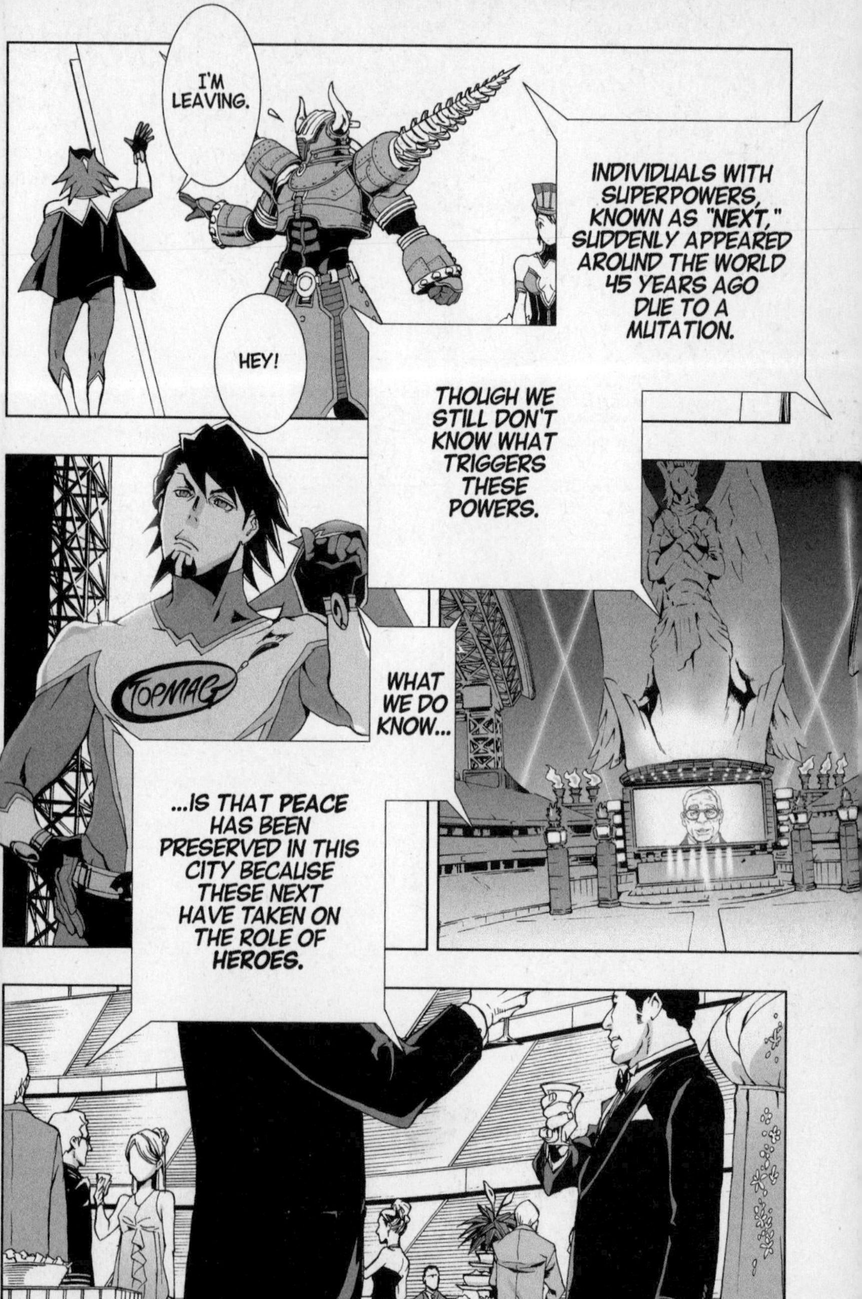
INDIVIDUALS WITH SUPERPOWERS, KNOWN AS "NEXT," SUDDENLY APPEARED AROUND THE WORLD 45 YEARS AGO DUE TO A MUTATION.
I'M LEAVING.
HEY!
THOUGH WE STILL DON'T KNOW WHAT TRIGGERS THESE POWERS.
WHAT WE DO KNOW...
...IS THAT PEACE HAS BEEN PRESERVED IN THIS CITY BECAUSE THESE NEXT HAVE TAKEN ON THE ROLE OF HEROES.
TOPMAG

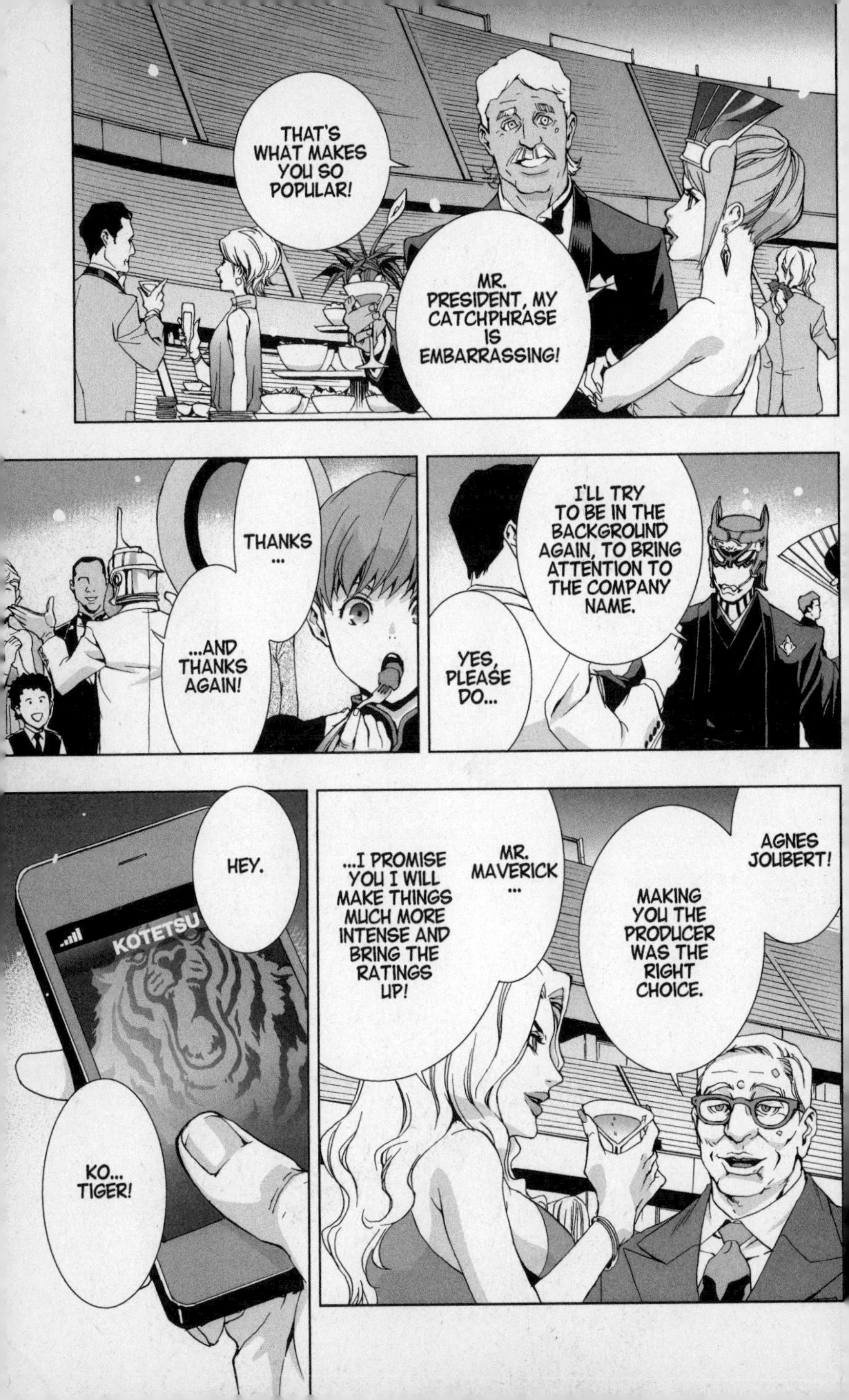
THAT'S WHAT MAKES YOU SO POPULAR!
MR. PRESIDENT, MY CATCHPHRASE IS EMBARRASSING!
I'LL TRY TO BE IN THE BACKGROUND AGAIN, TO BRING ATTENTION TO THE COMPANY NAME.
YES, PLEASE DO...
THANKS...
...AND THANKS AGAIN!
AGNES JOUBERT!
MAKING YOU THE PRODUCER WAS THE RIGHT CHOICE.
MR. MAVERICK...
...I PROMISE YOU I WILL MAKE THINGS MUCH MORE INTENSE AND BRING THE RATINGS UP!
HEY.
KOTETSU
KO... TIGER!

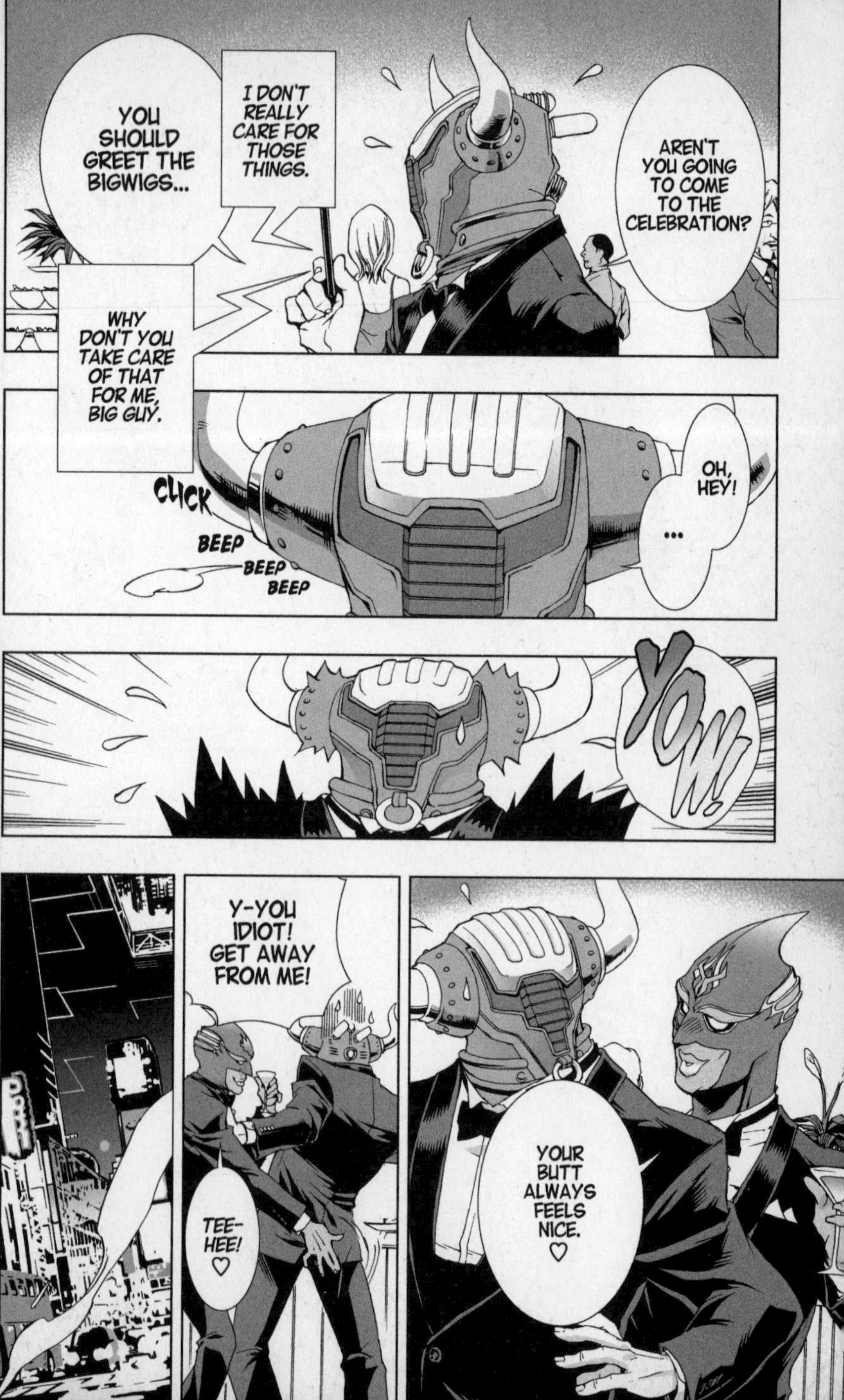
AREN'T YOU GOING TO COME TO THE CELEBRATION?
I DON'T REALLY CARE FOR THOSE THINGS.
YOU SHOULD GREET THE BIGWIGS...
WHY DON'T YOU TAKE CARE OF THAT FOR ME, BIG GUY.
OH, HEY!
...
CLICK
BEEP
BEEP
BEEP
YOW!
YOUR BUTT ALWAYS FEELS NICE. ♡
Y-YOU IDIOT! GET AWAY FROM ME!
TEE-HEE! ♡

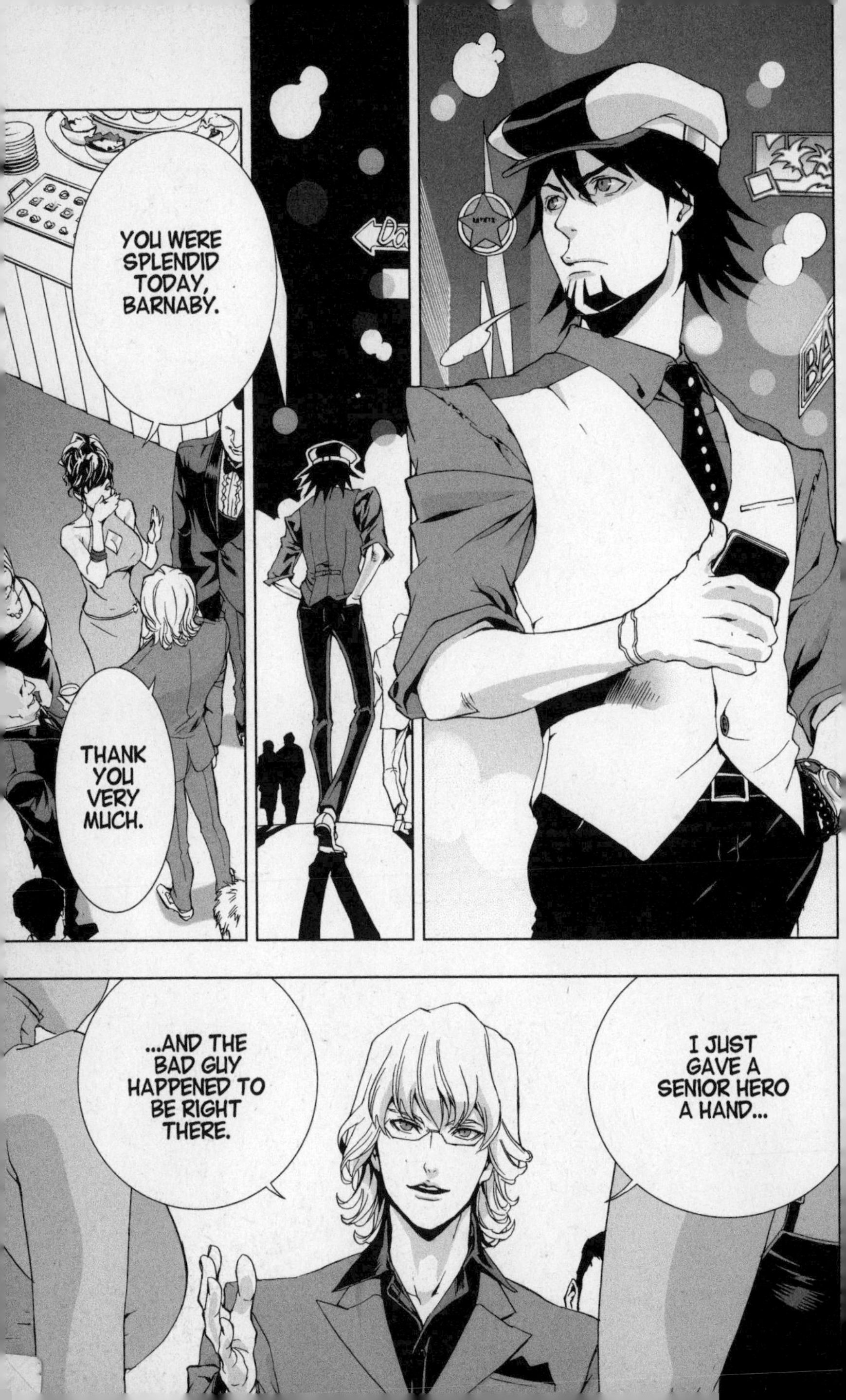
YOU WERE SPLENDID TODAY, BARNABY.
THANK YOU VERY MUCH.
I JUST GAVE A SENIOR HERO A HAND...
...AND THE BAD GUY HAPPENED TO BE RIGHT THERE.

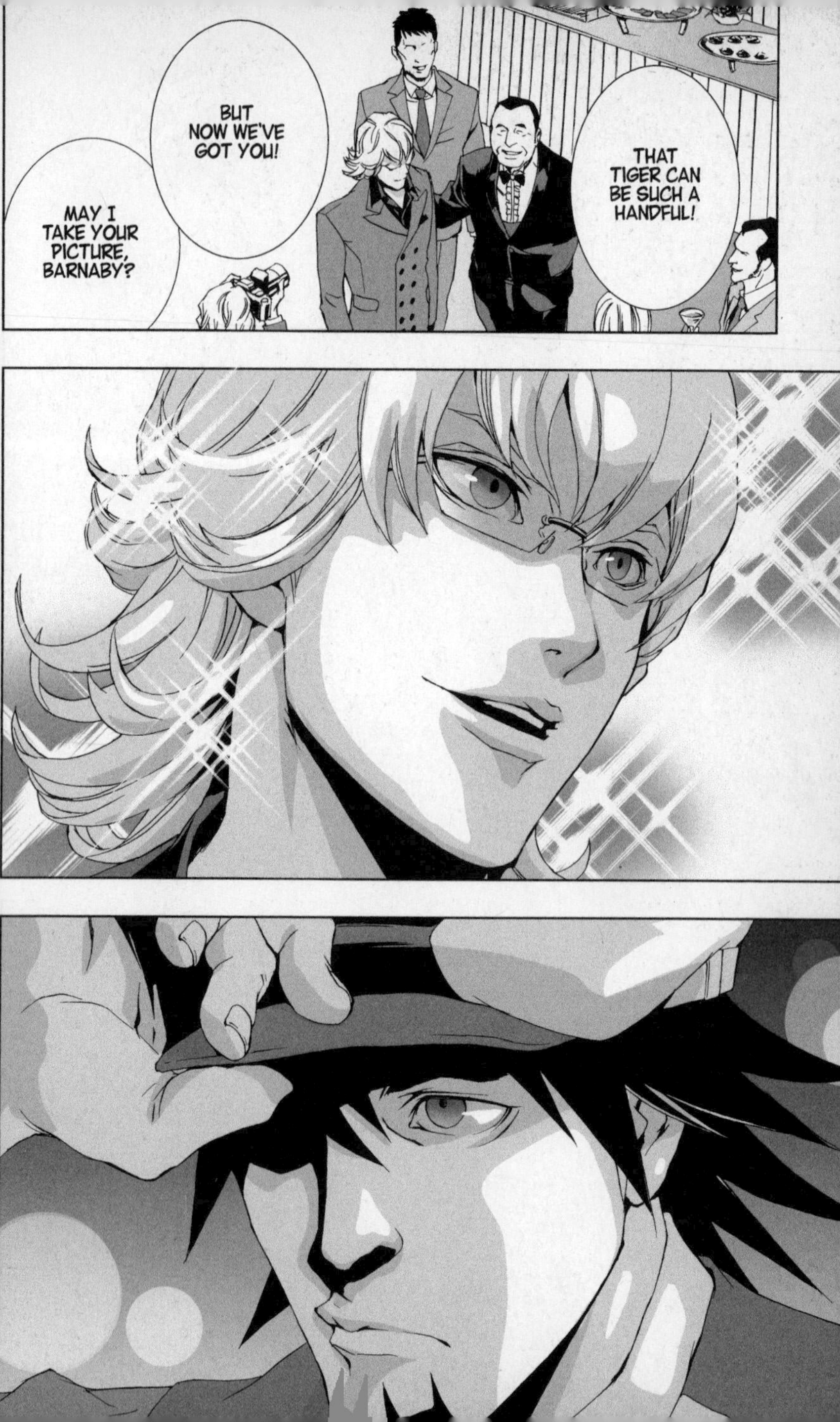
THAT TIGER CAN BE SUCH A HANDFUL!
BUT NOW WE'VE GOT YOU!
MAY I TAKE YOUR PICTURE, BARNABY?

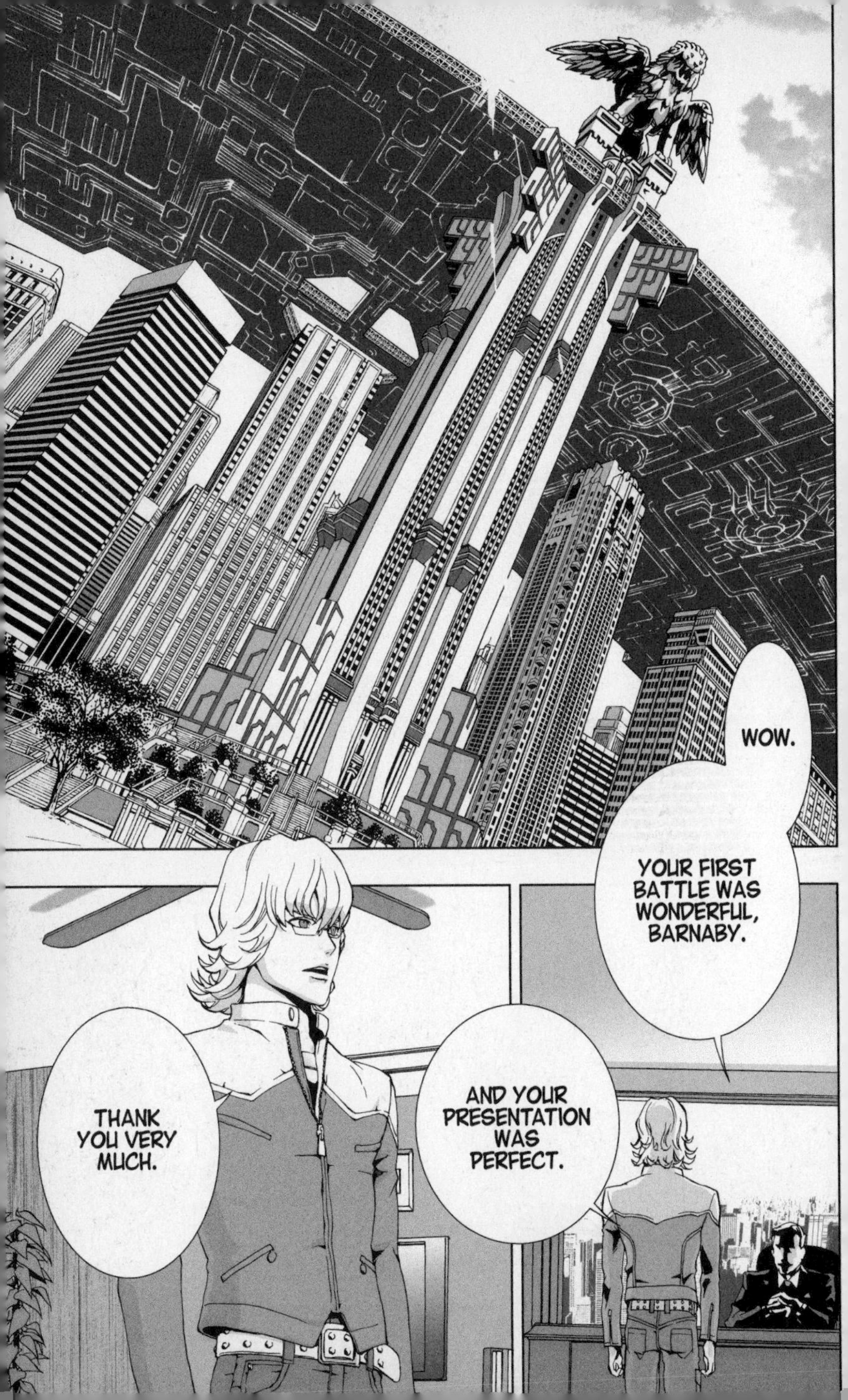
WOW.
YOUR FIRST BATTLE WAS WONDERFUL, BARNABY.
AND YOUR PRESENTATION WAS PERFECT.
THANK YOU VERY MUCH.

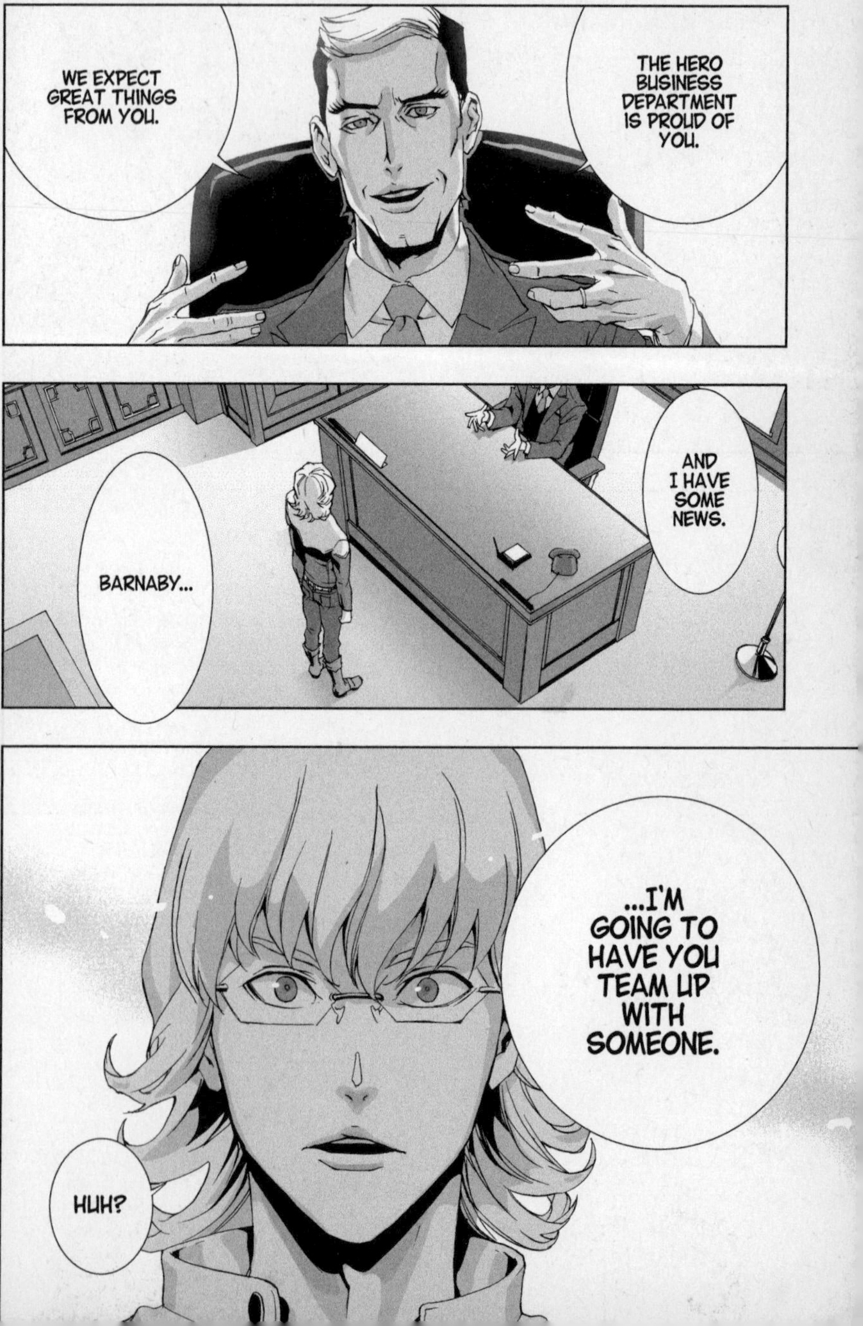
THE HERO BUSINESS DEPARTMENT IS PROUD OF YOU.
WE EXPECT GREAT THINGS FROM YOU.
AND I HAVE SOME NEWS.
BARNABY...
...I'M GOING TO HAVE YOU TEAM UP WITH SOMEONE.
HUH?

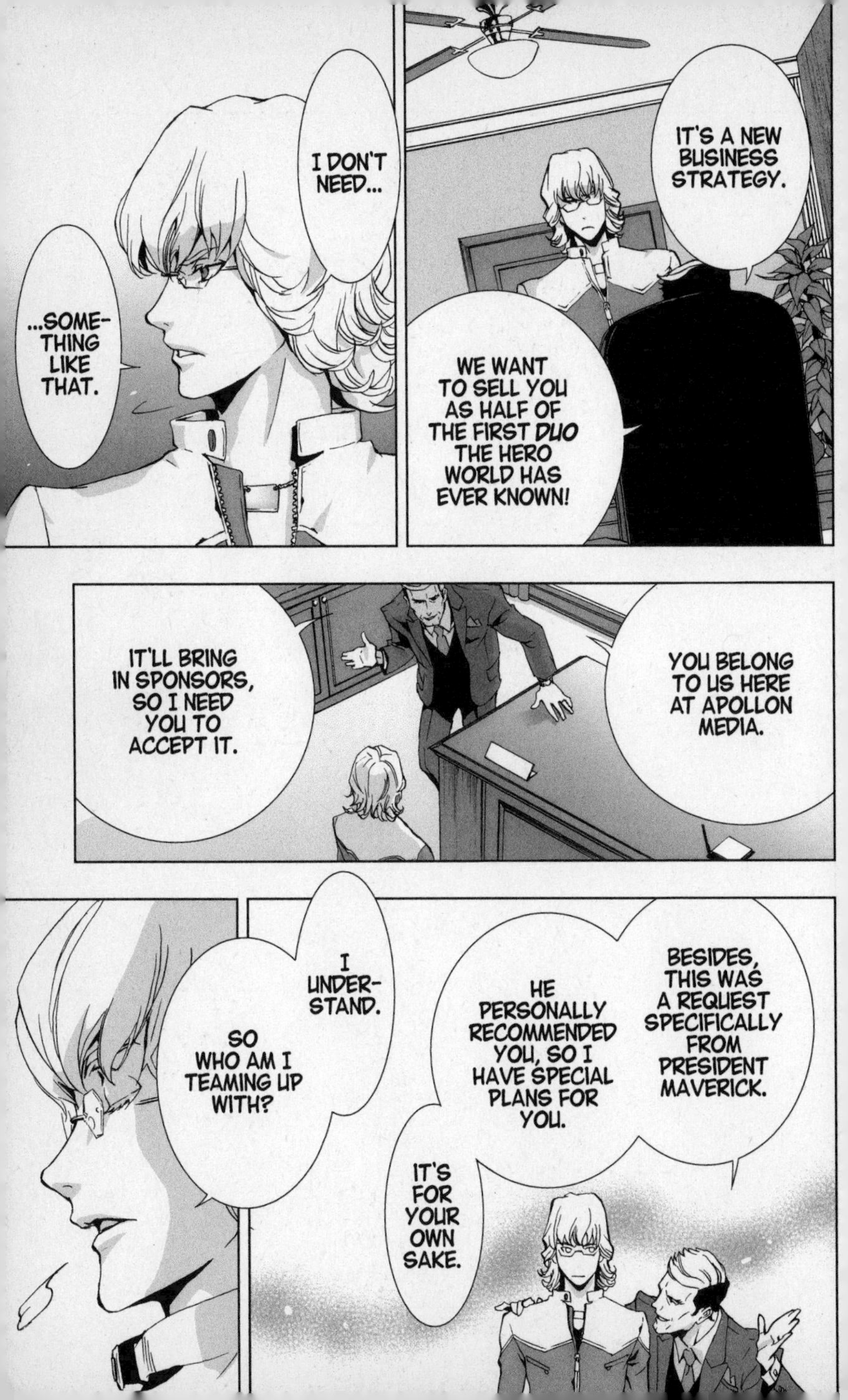
IT'S A NEW BUSINESS STRATEGY.
WE WANT TO SELL YOU AS HALF OF THE FIRST DUO THE HERO WORLD HAS EVER KNOWN!
I DON'T NEED...
...SOMETHING LIKE THAT.
YOU BELONG TO US HERE AT APOLLON MEDIA.
IT'LL BRING IN SPONSORS, SO I NEED YOU TO ACCEPT IT.
BESIDES, THIS WAS A REQUEST SPECIFICALLY FROM PRESIDENT MAVERICK.
HE PERSONALLY RECOMMENDED YOU, SO I HAVE SPECIAL PLANS FOR YOU.
IT'S FOR YOUR OWN SAKE.
I UNDERSTAND.
SO WHO AM I TEAMING UP WITH?

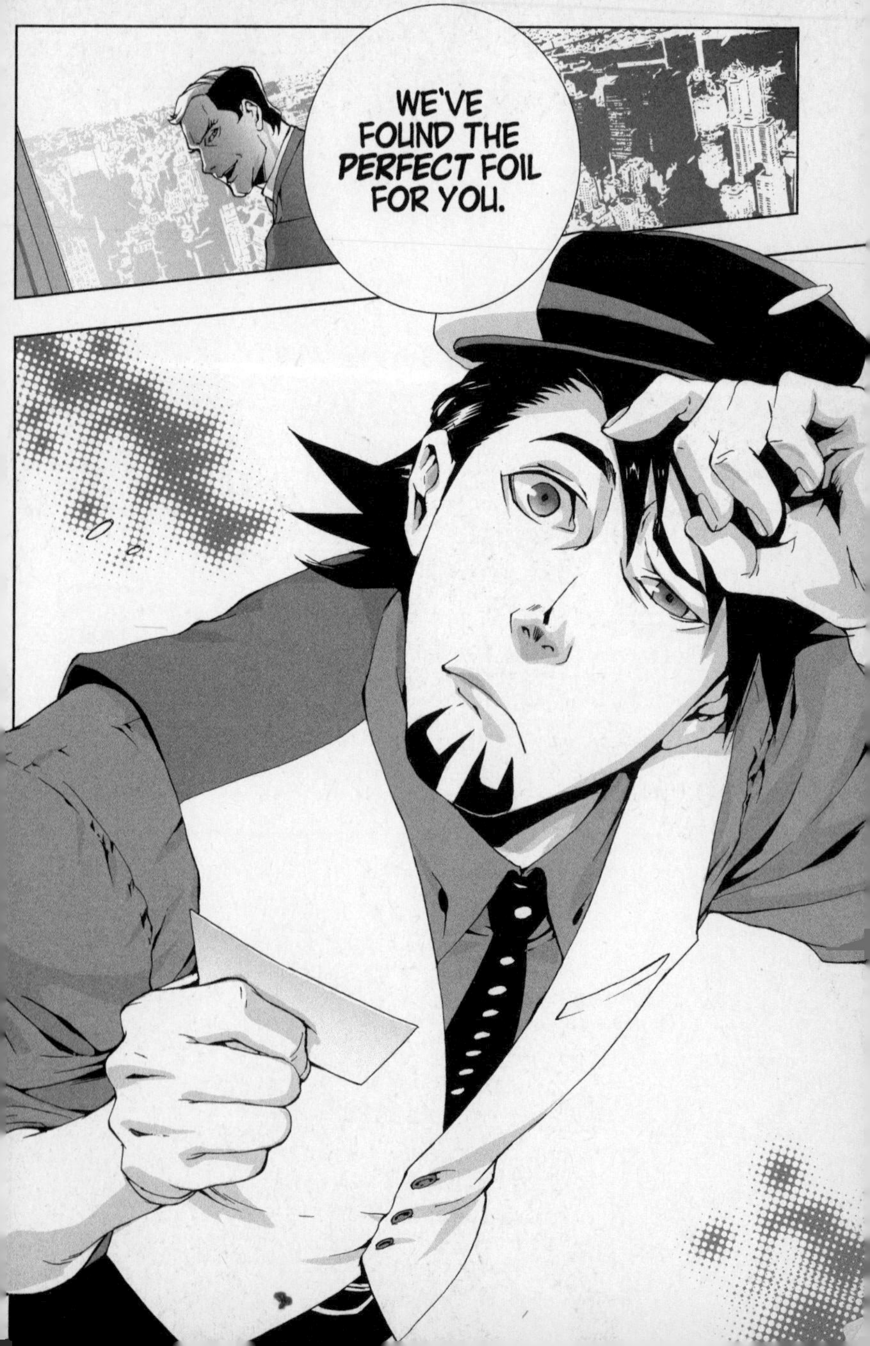
WE'VE FOUND THE *PERFECT* FOIL FOR YOU.

#02 A Good Beginning Makes a Good Ending, Part 1

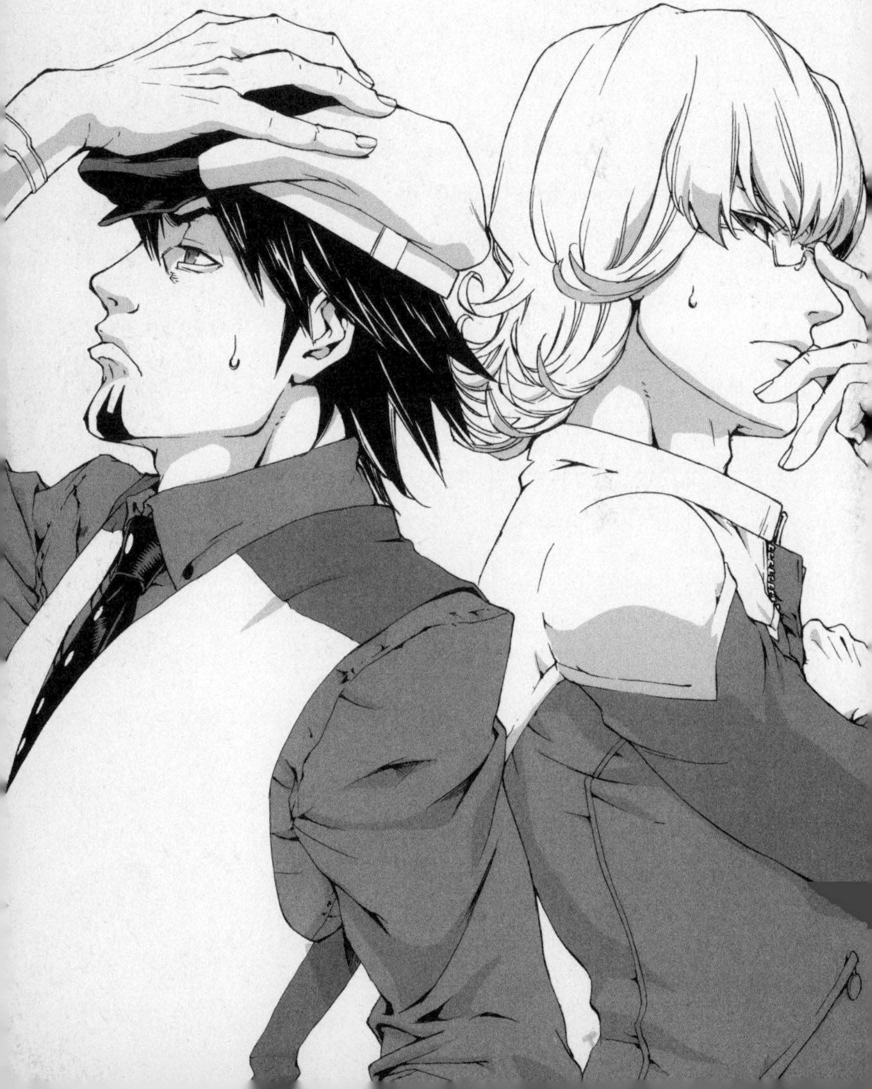

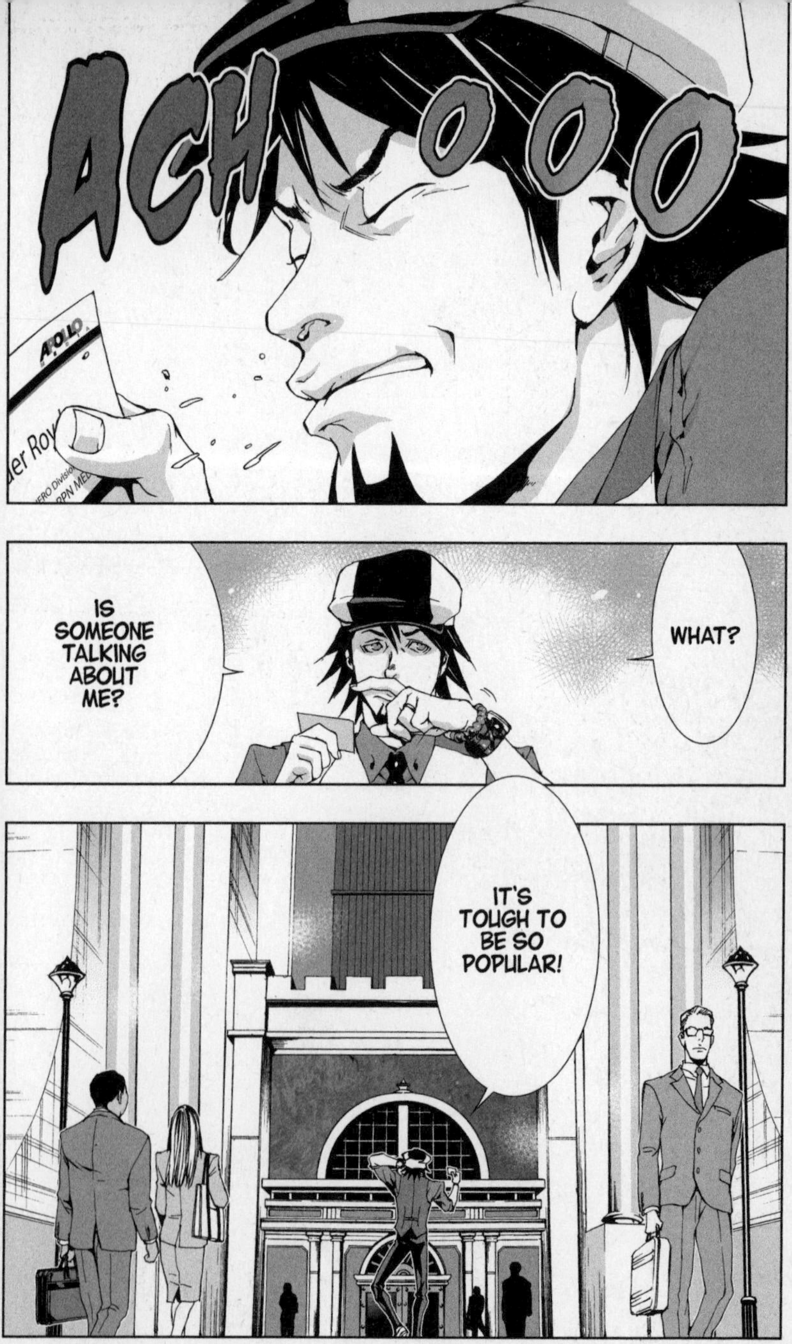
ACHOOOO
APOLLO
WHAT?
IS SOMEONE TALKING ABOUT ME?
IT'S TOUGH TO BE SO POPULAR!

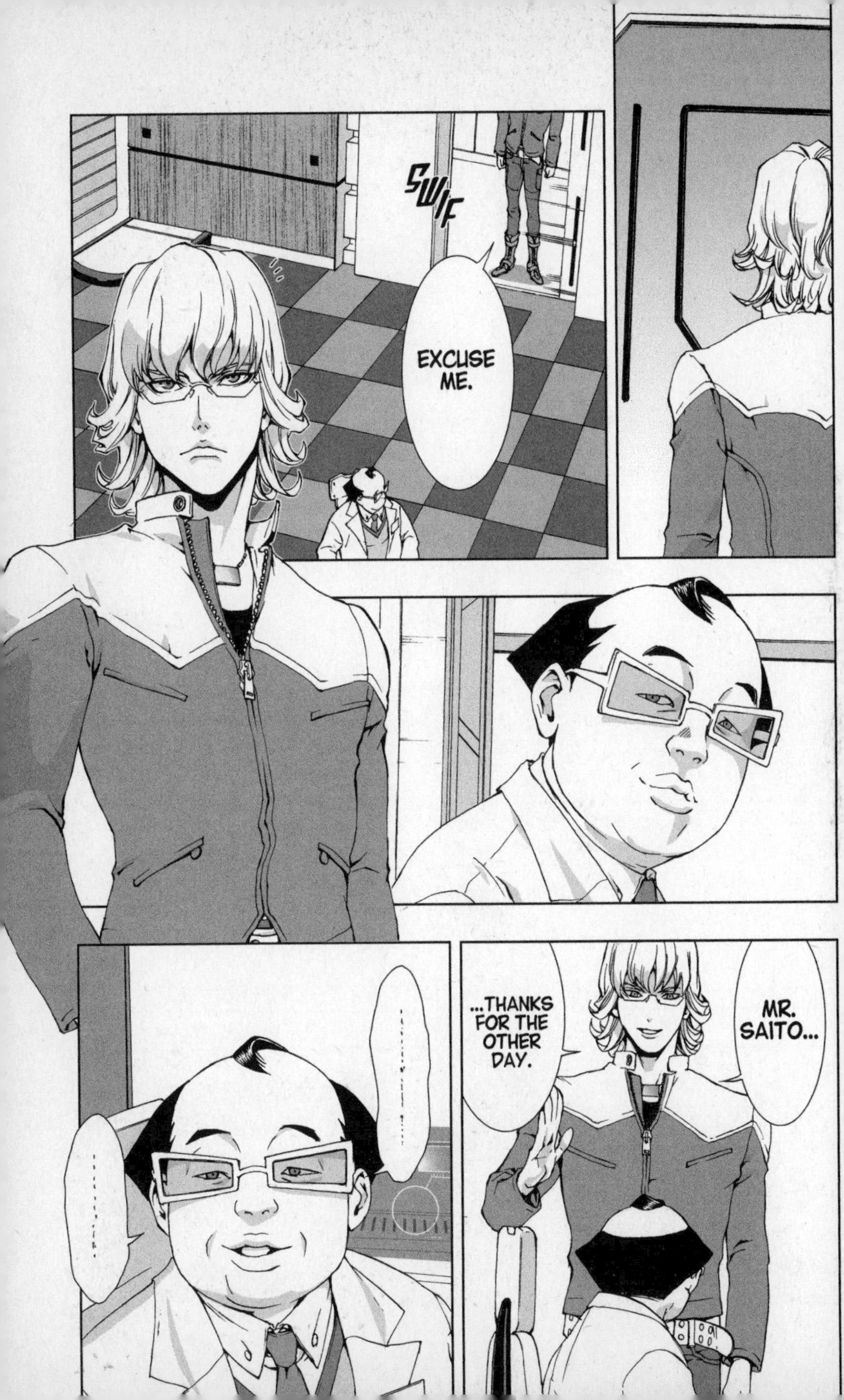
SWIF
EXCUSE ME.
MR. SAITO...
...THANKS FOR THE OTHER DAY.
......
......

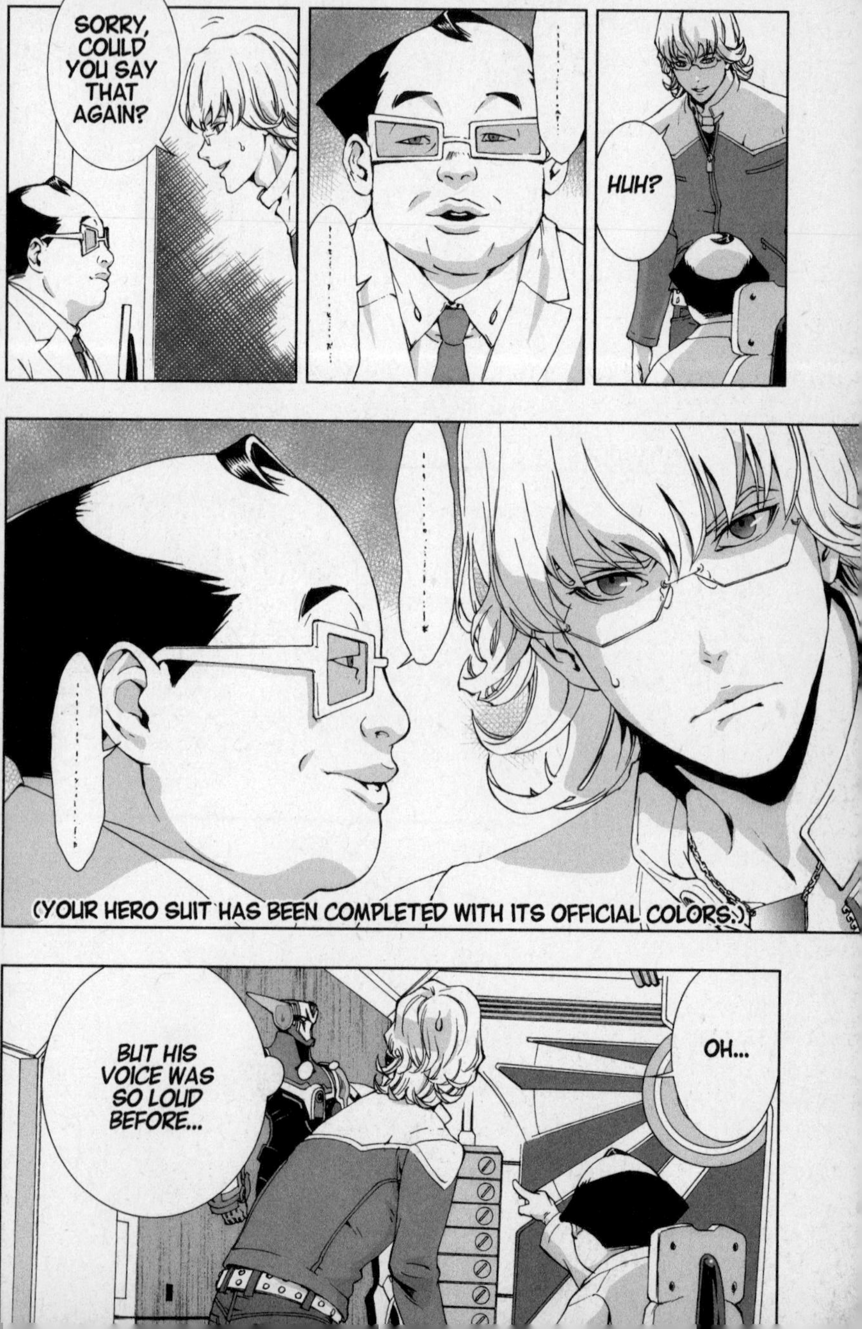
HUH?
SORRY, COULD YOU SAY THAT AGAIN?
(YOUR HERO SUIT HAS BEEN COMPLETED WITH ITS OFFICIAL COLORS.)
OH...
BUT HIS VOICE WAS SO LOUD BEFORE...

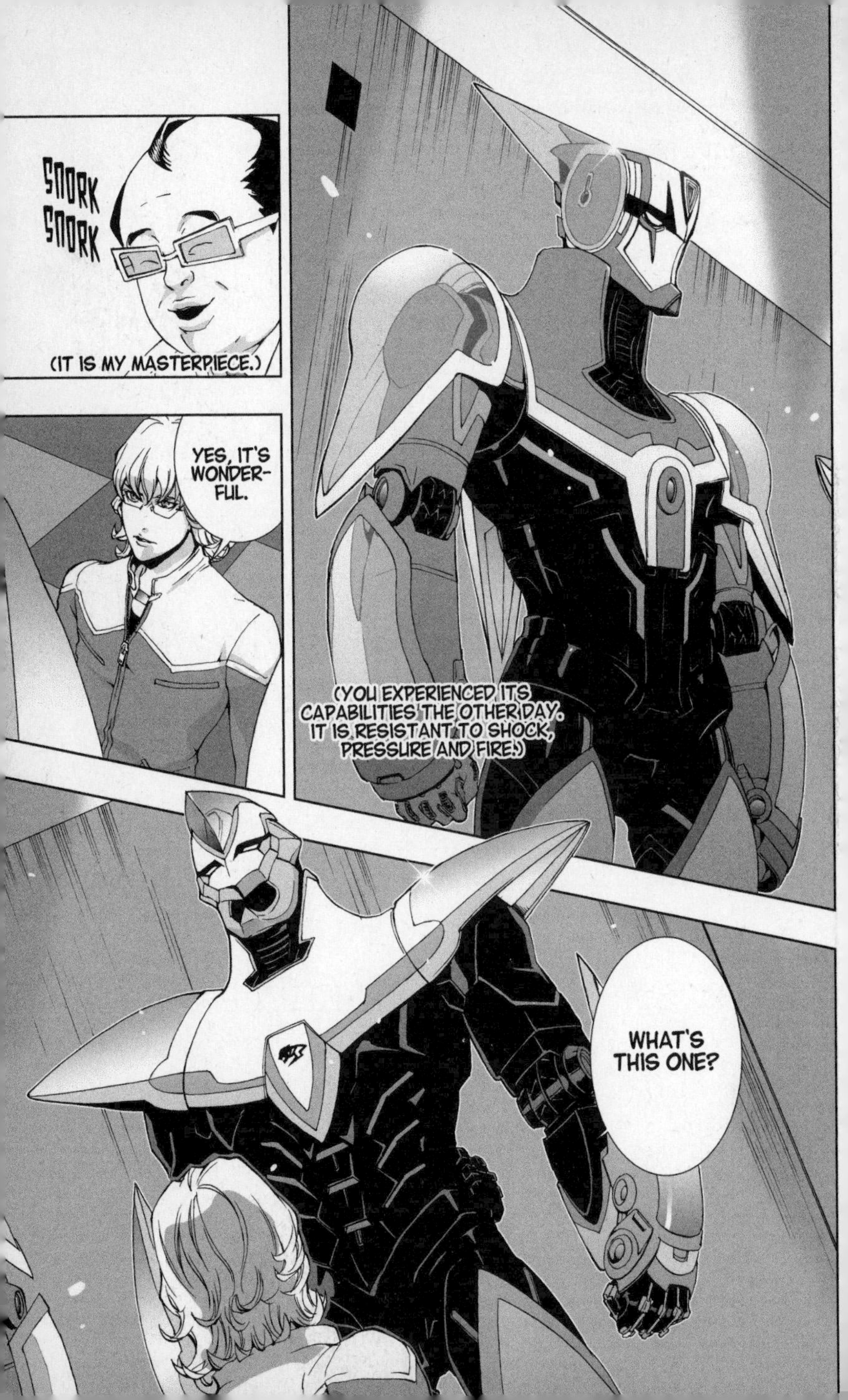
(YOU EXPERIENCED ITS CAPABILITIES THE OTHER DAY. IT IS RESISTANT TO SHOCK, PRESSURE AND FIRE.)
SNORK SNORK
(IT IS MY MASTERPIECE.)
YES, IT'S WONDERFUL.
WHAT'S THIS ONE?

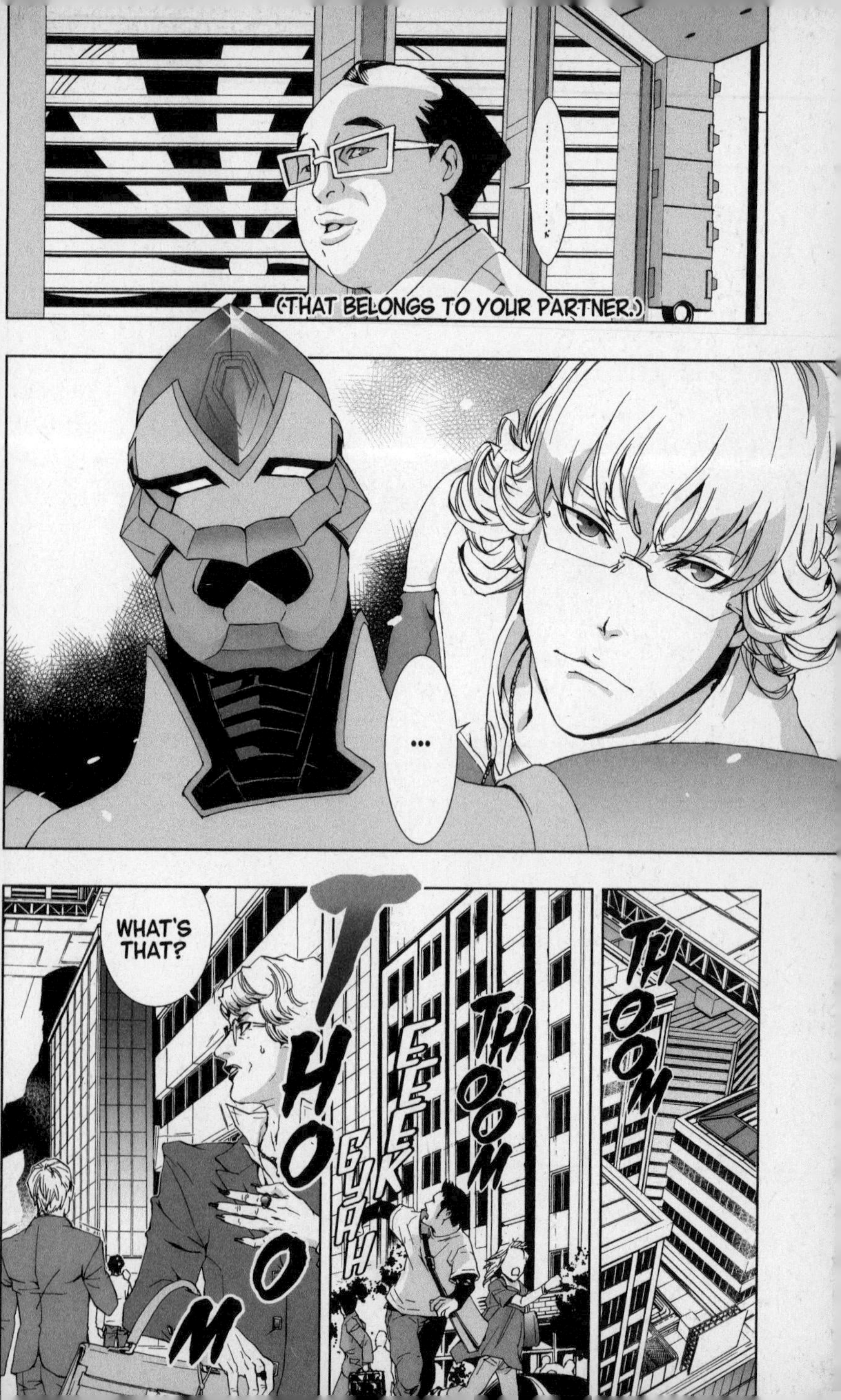
(THAT BELONGS TO YOUR PARTNER.)
...
THOOM
THOOOM
EEEEK
GUAHH
WHAT'S THAT?
THOOOM

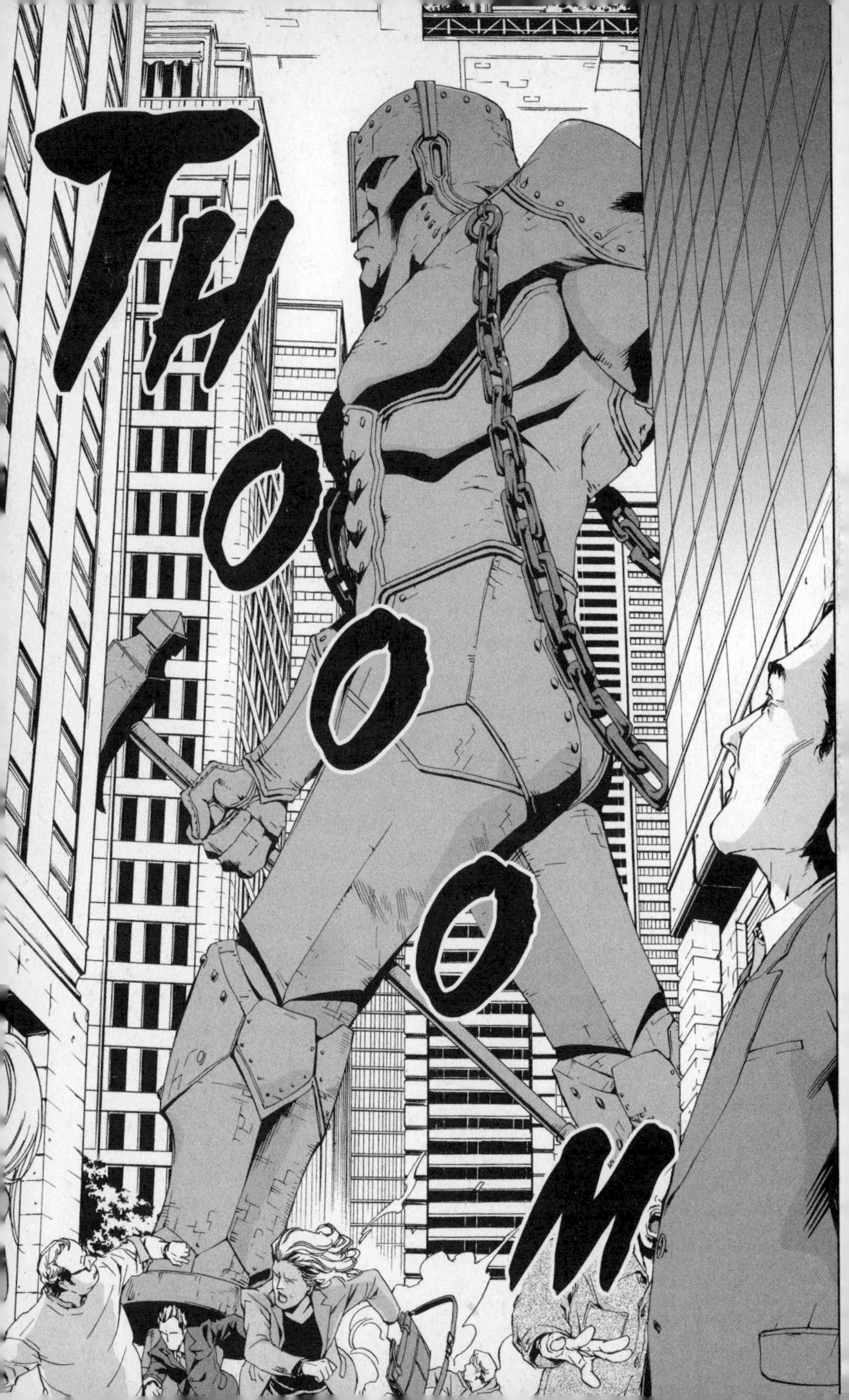
THOOOM

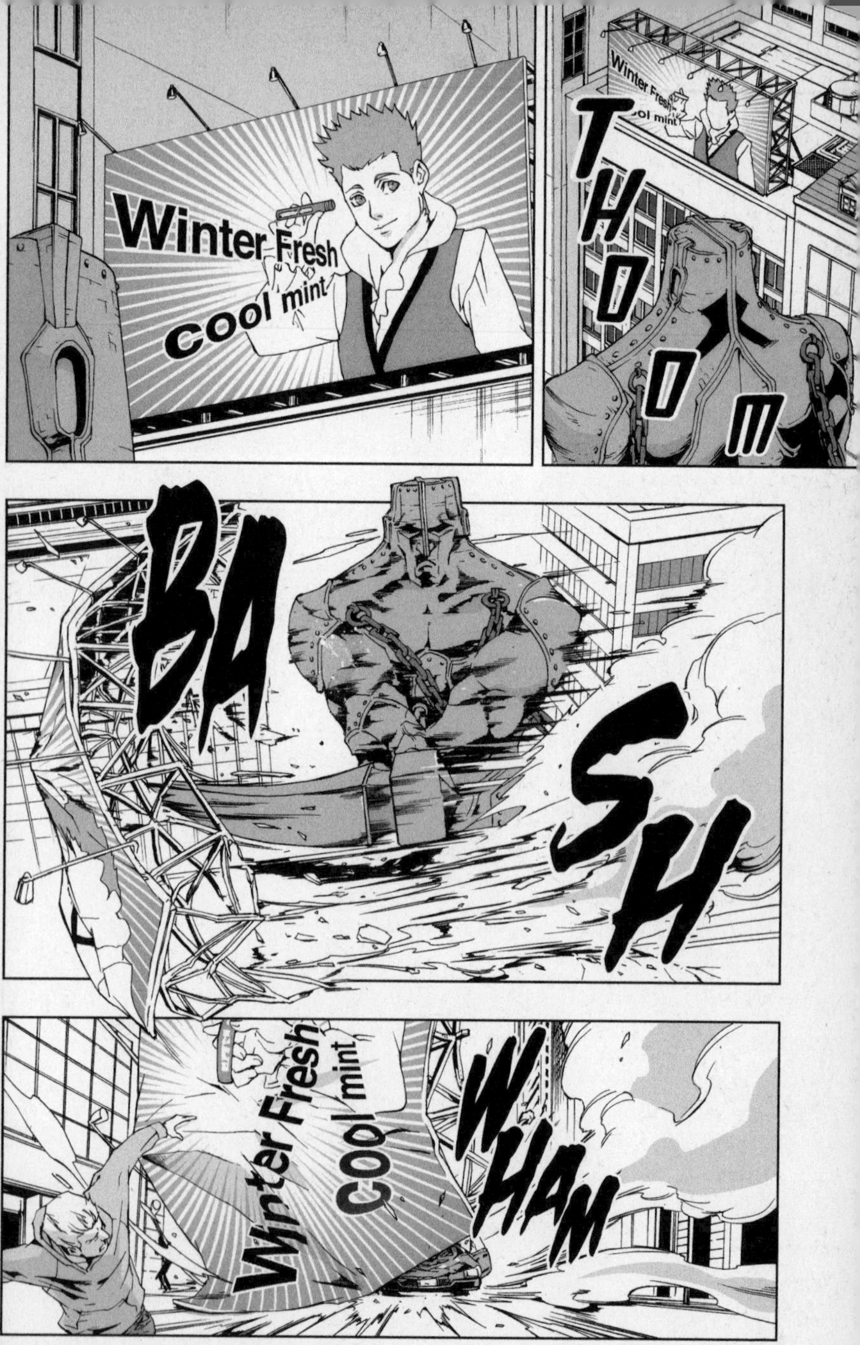
Winter Fresh cool mint
THOOM
Winter Fresh
cool mint
BASH
Winter Fresh
cool mint
WHAM

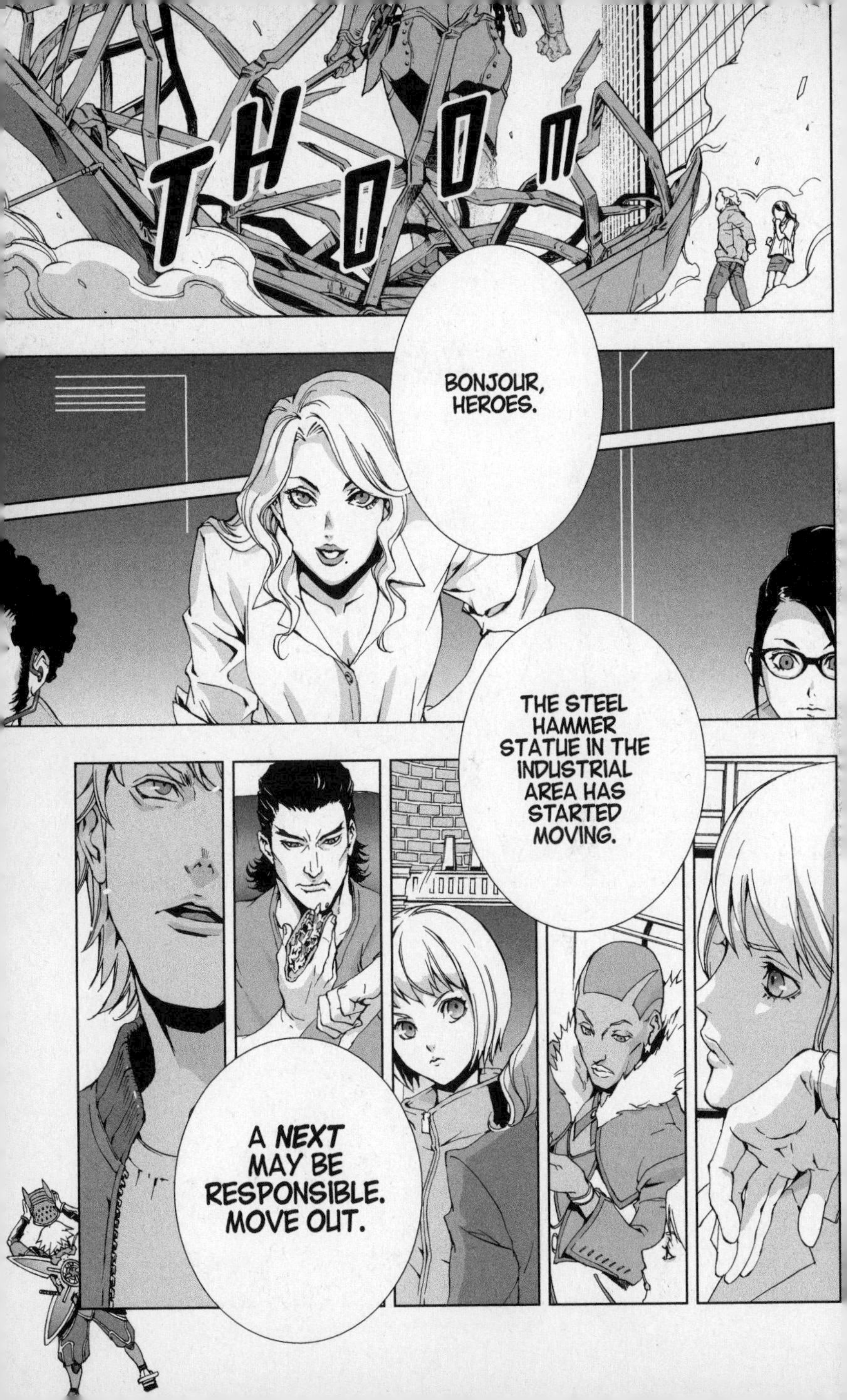
THOOM
BONJOUR, HEROES.
THE STEEL HAMMER STATUE IN THE INDUSTRIAL AREA HAS STARTED MOVING.
A NEXT MAY BE RESPONSIBLE. MOVE OUT.

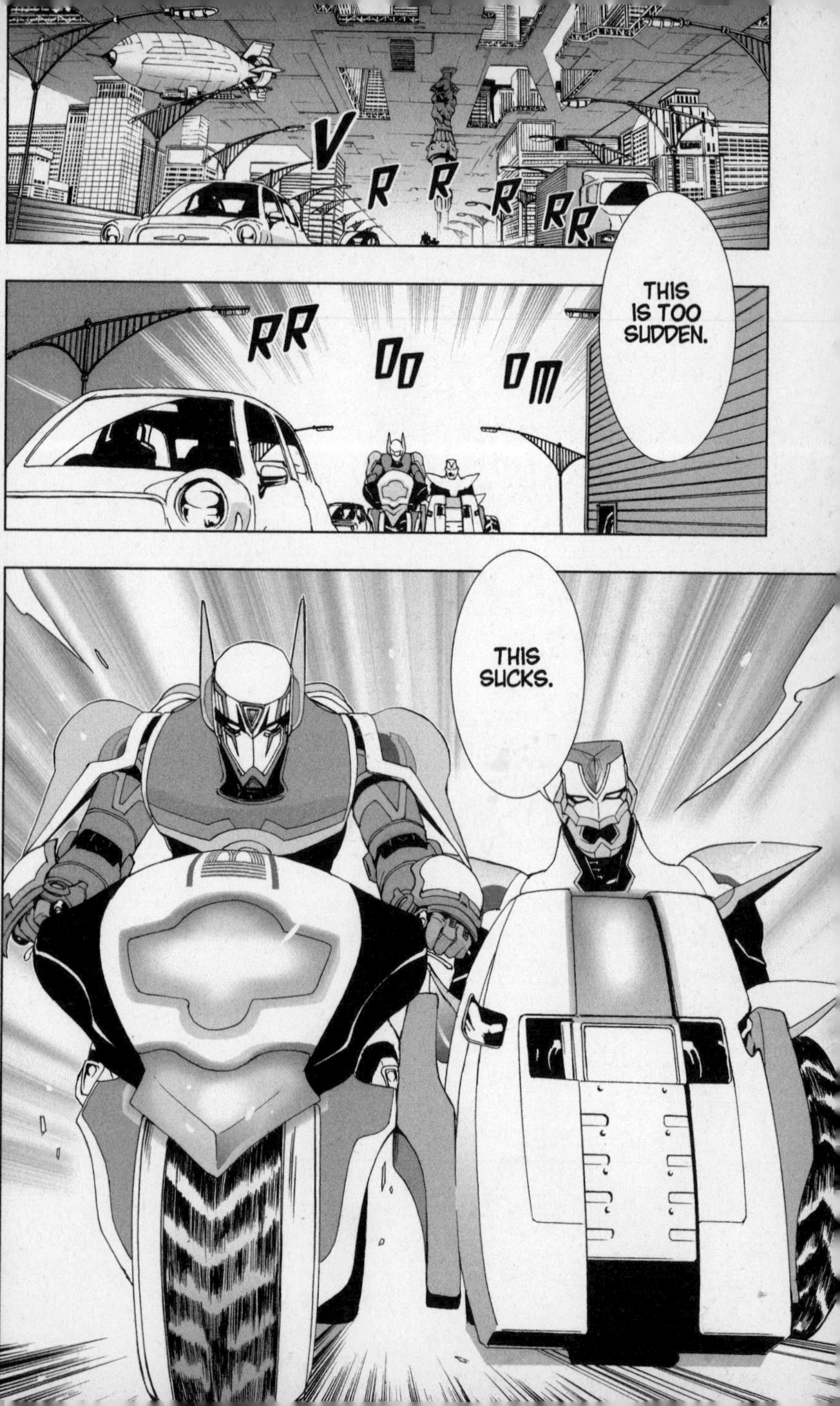
VRRRRRR
THIS IS TOO SUDDEN.
RROOOM
THIS SUCKS.

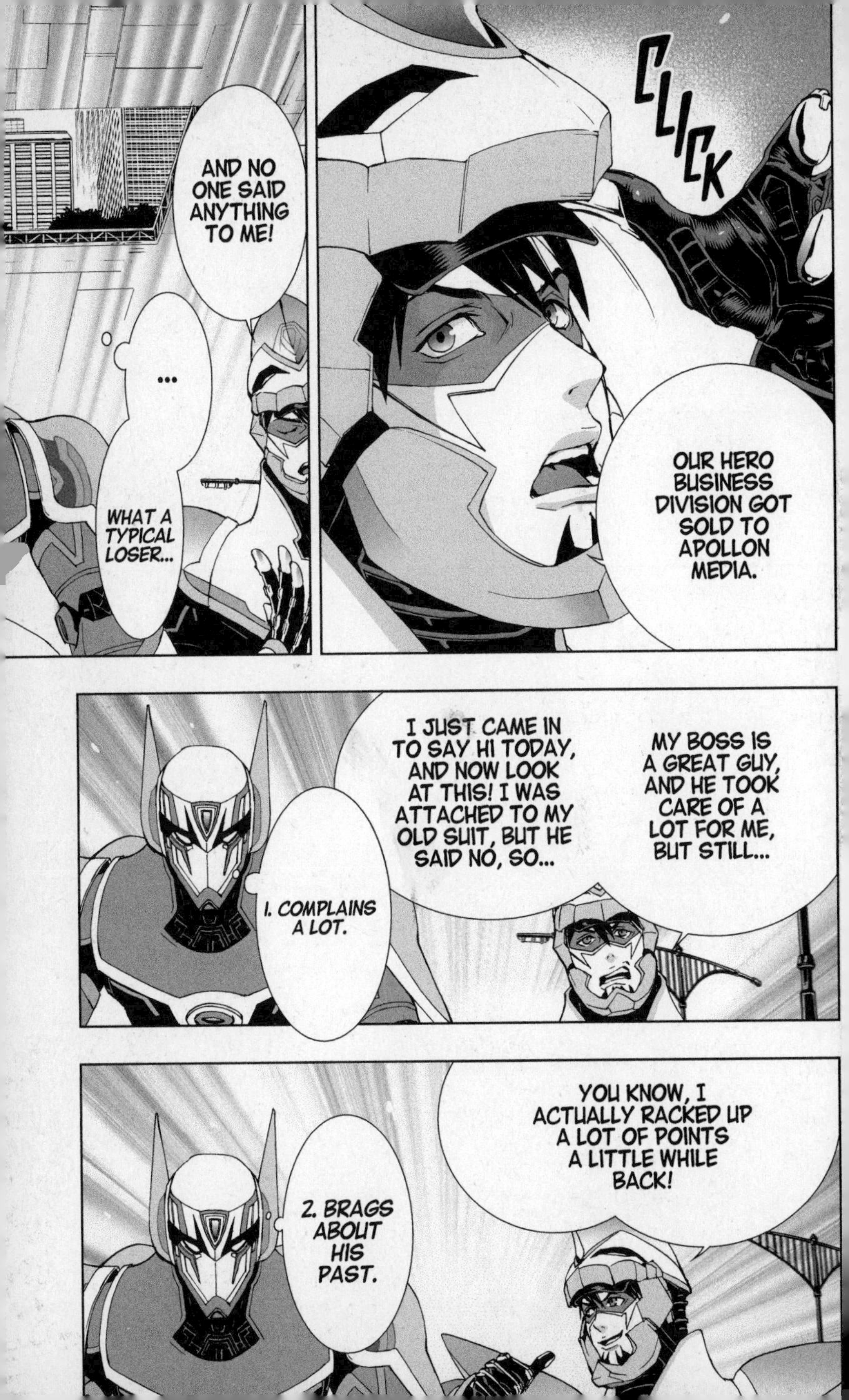
CLICK
OUR HERO BUSINESS DIVISION GOT SOLD TO APOLLON MEDIA.
AND NO ONE SAID ANYTHING TO ME!
...
WHAT A TYPICAL LOSER...
MY BOSS IS A GREAT GUY, AND HE TOOK CARE OF A LOT FOR ME, BUT STILL...
I JUST CAME IN TO SAY HI TODAY, AND NOW LOOK AT THIS! I WAS ATTACHED TO MY OLD SUIT, BUT HE SAID NO, SO...
1. COMPLAINS A LOT.
YOU KNOW, I ACTUALLY RACKED UP A LOT OF POINTS A LITTLE WHILE BACK!
2. BRAGS ABOUT HIS PAST.

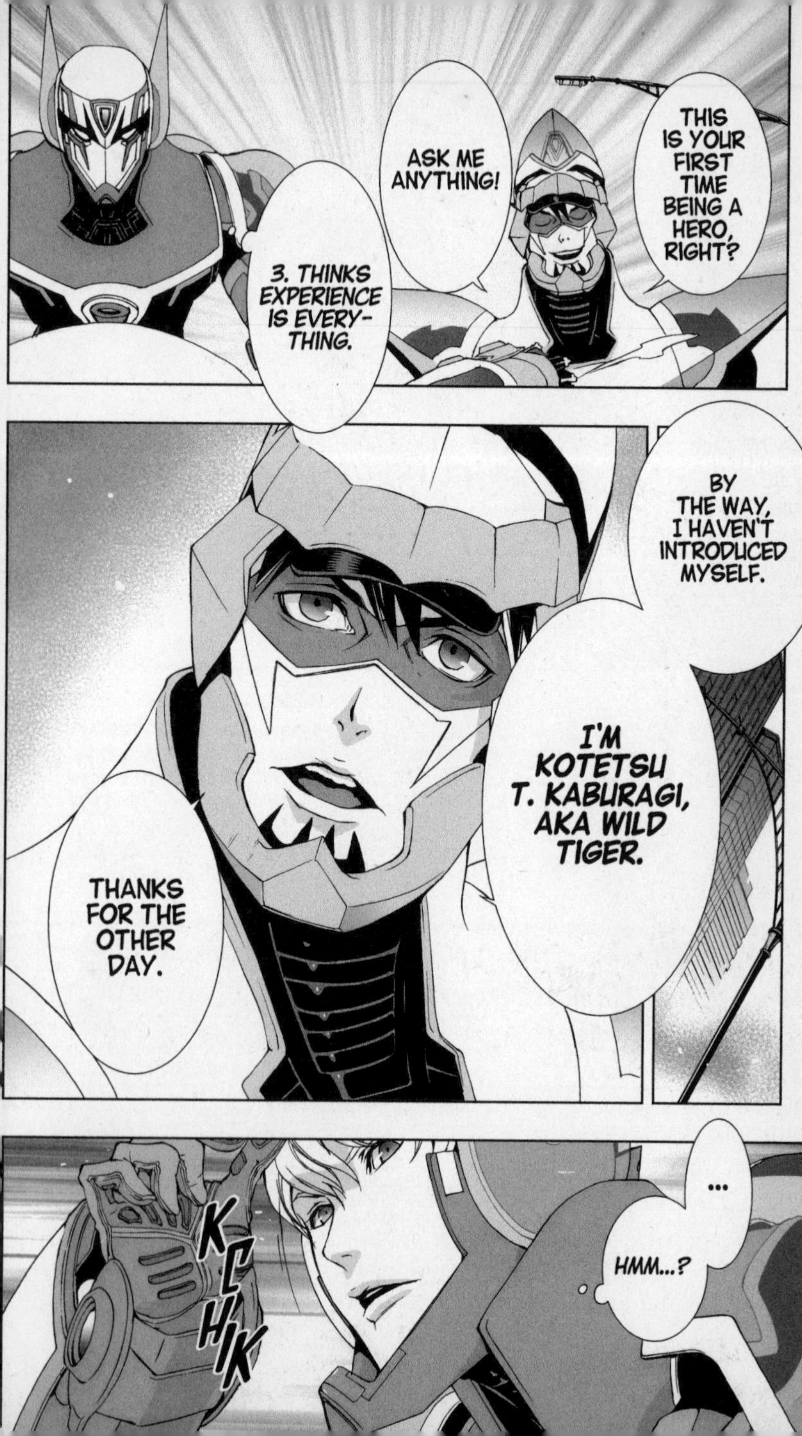
THIS IS YOUR FIRST TIME BEING A HERO, RIGHT?
ASK ME ANYTHING!
3. THINKS EXPERIENCE IS EVERY-THING.
BY THE WAY, I HAVEN'T INTRODUCED MYSELF.
I'M KOTETSU T. KABURAGI, AKA WILD TIGER.
THANKS FOR THE OTHER DAY.
...
HMM...?
KCHIK

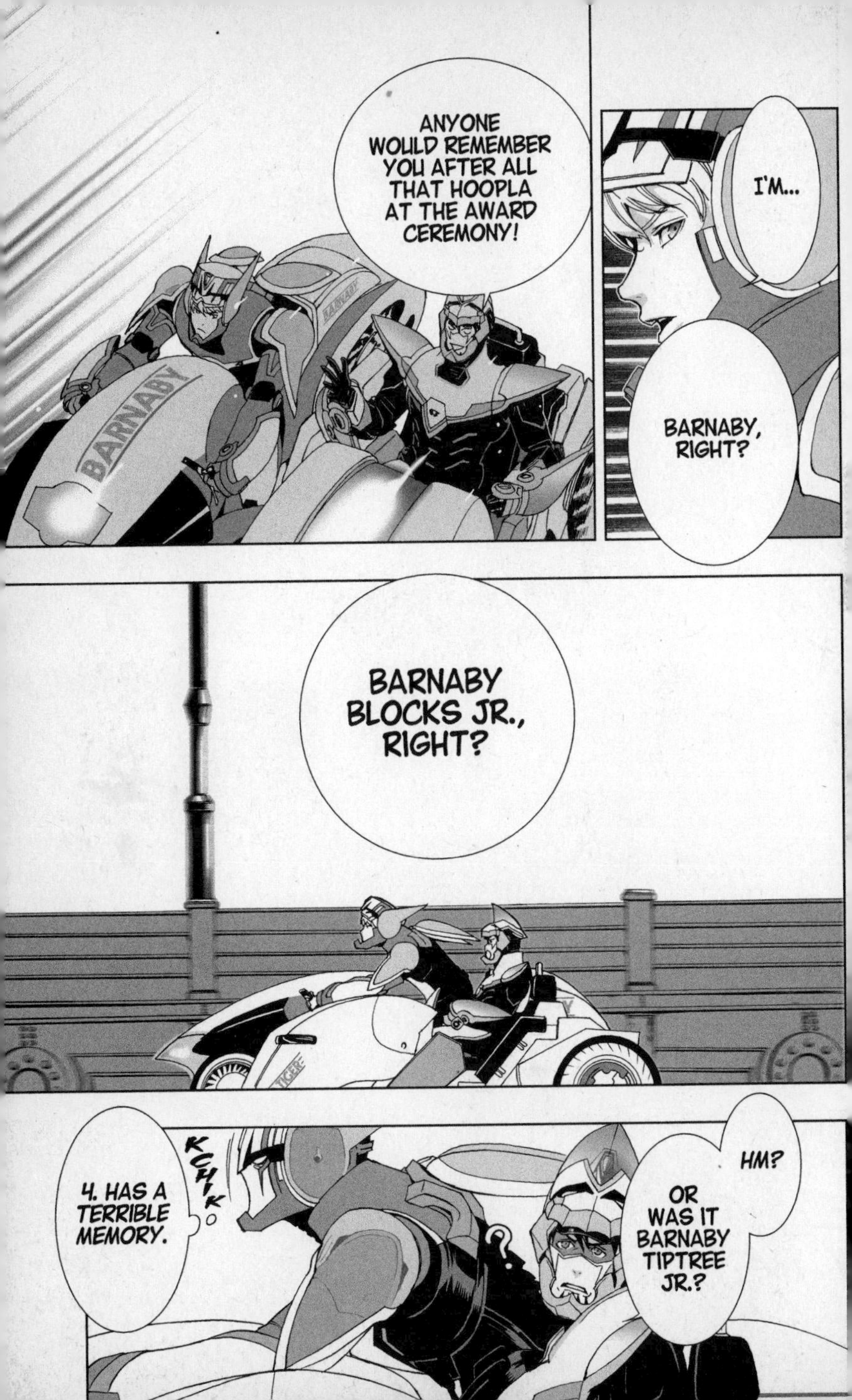
I'M...
BARNABY, RIGHT?
ANYONE WOULD REMEMBER YOU AFTER ALL THAT HOOPLA AT THE AWARD CEREMONY!
BARNABY BLOCKS JR., RIGHT?
HM?
OR WAS IT BARNABY TIPTREE JR.?
KCHIK
4. HAS A TERRIBLE MEMORY.

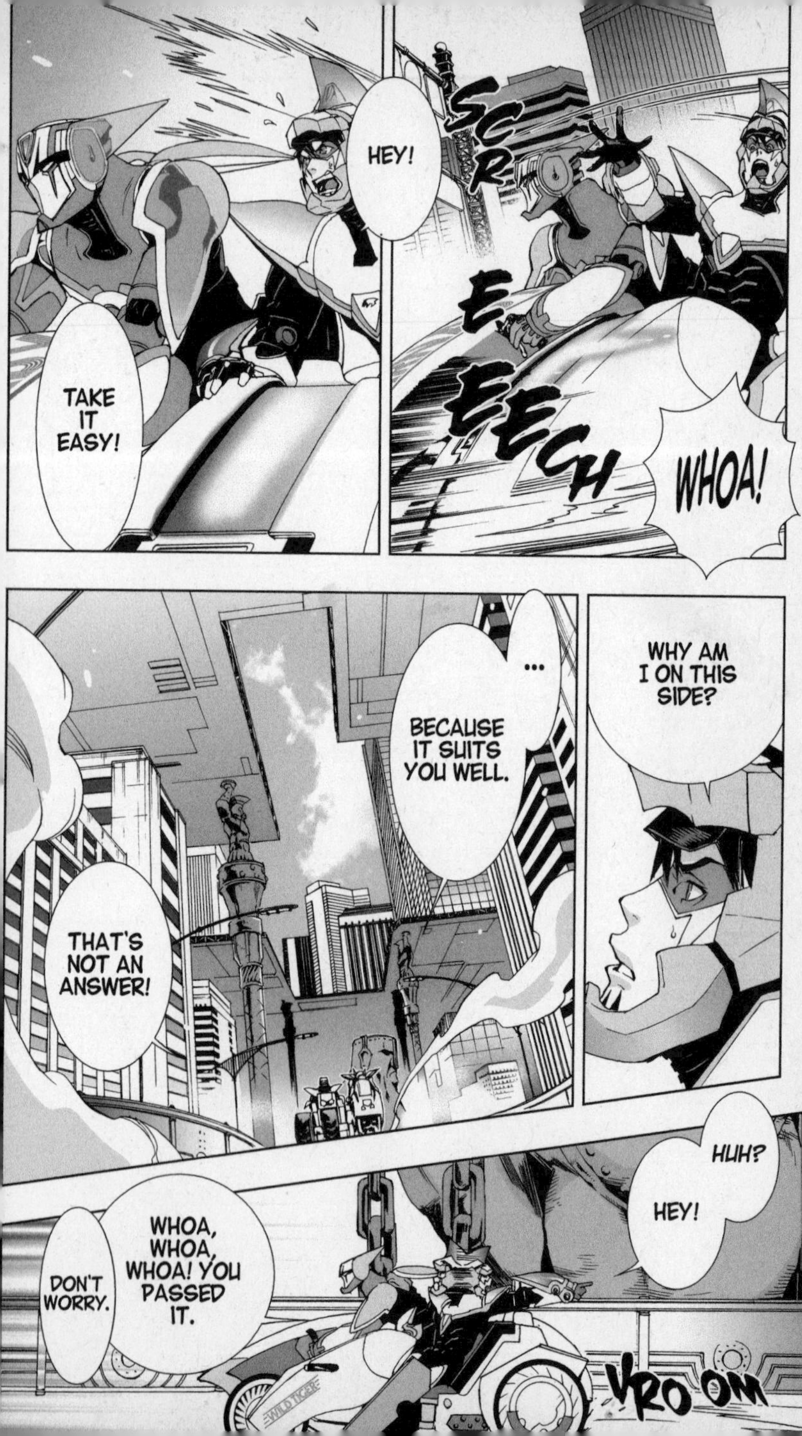
SCREEEECH
WHOA!
HEY!
TAKE IT EASY!
WHY AM I ON THIS SIDE?
...
BECAUSE IT SUITS YOU WELL.
THAT'S NOT AN ANSWER!
HUH?
HEY!
WHOA, WHOA, WHOA! YOU PASSED IT.
DON'T WORRY.
VROOM
WILD TIGER

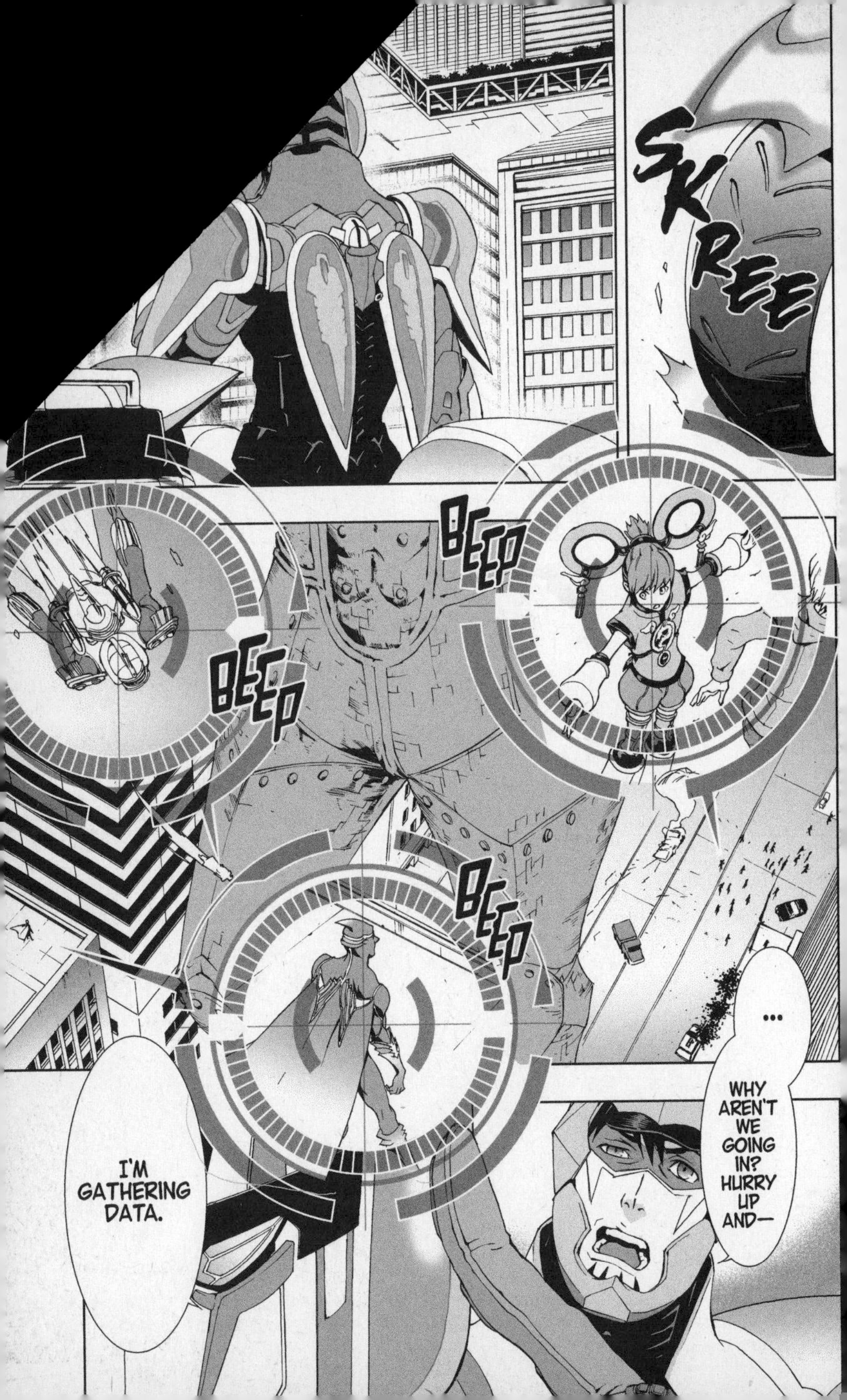
SKREE
BEEP
BEEP
BEEP
...
WHY AREN'T WE GOING IN? HURRY UP AND—
I'M GATHERING DATA.

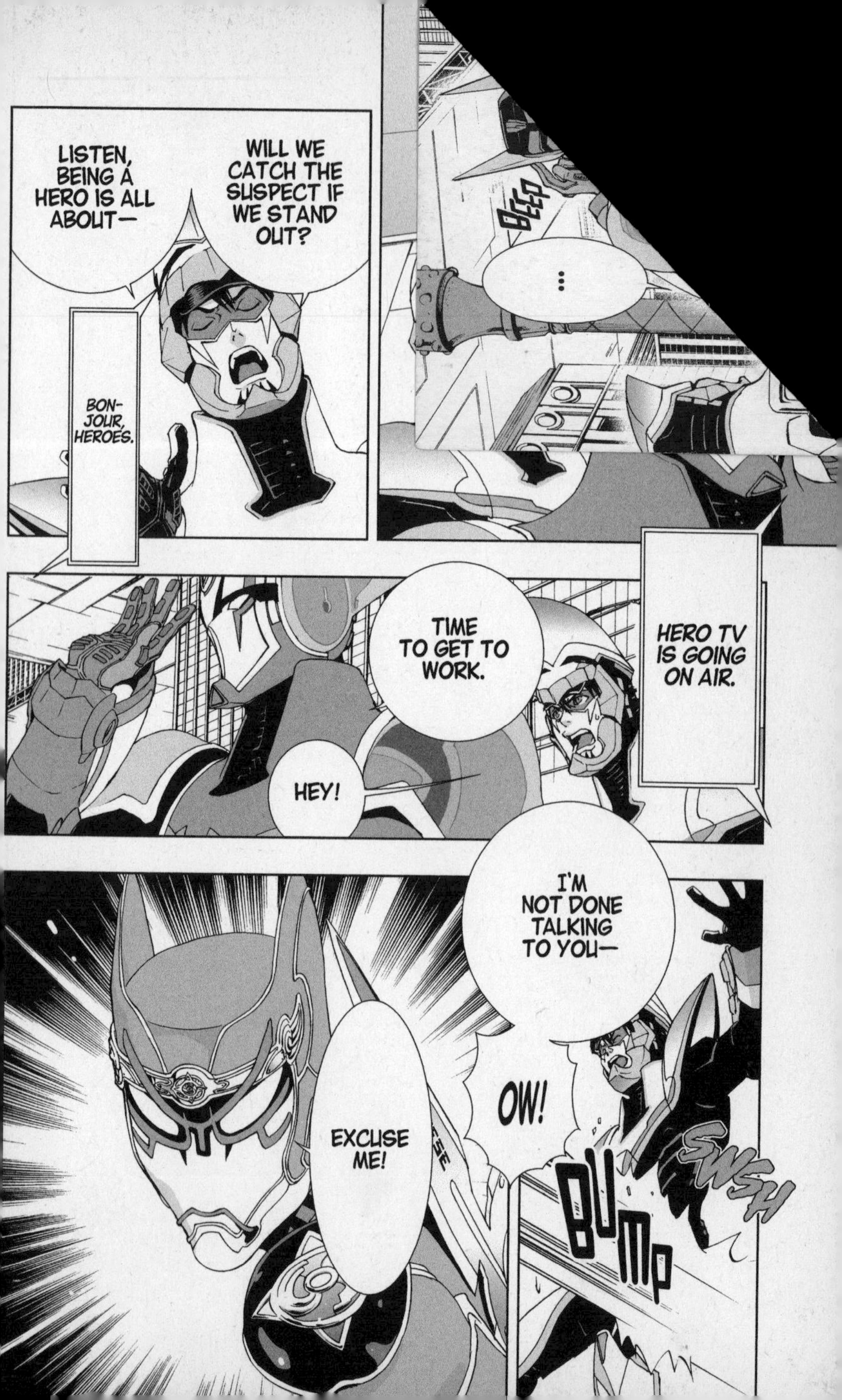
BEEP
...
WILL WE CATCH THE SUSPECT IF WE STAND OUT?
LISTEN, BEING A HERO IS ALL ABOUT—
BON-JOUR, HEROES.
HERO TV IS GOING ON AIR.
TIME TO GET TO WORK.
HEY!
I'M NOT DONE TALKING TO YOU—
SWSH
BUMP
OW!
EXCUSE ME!

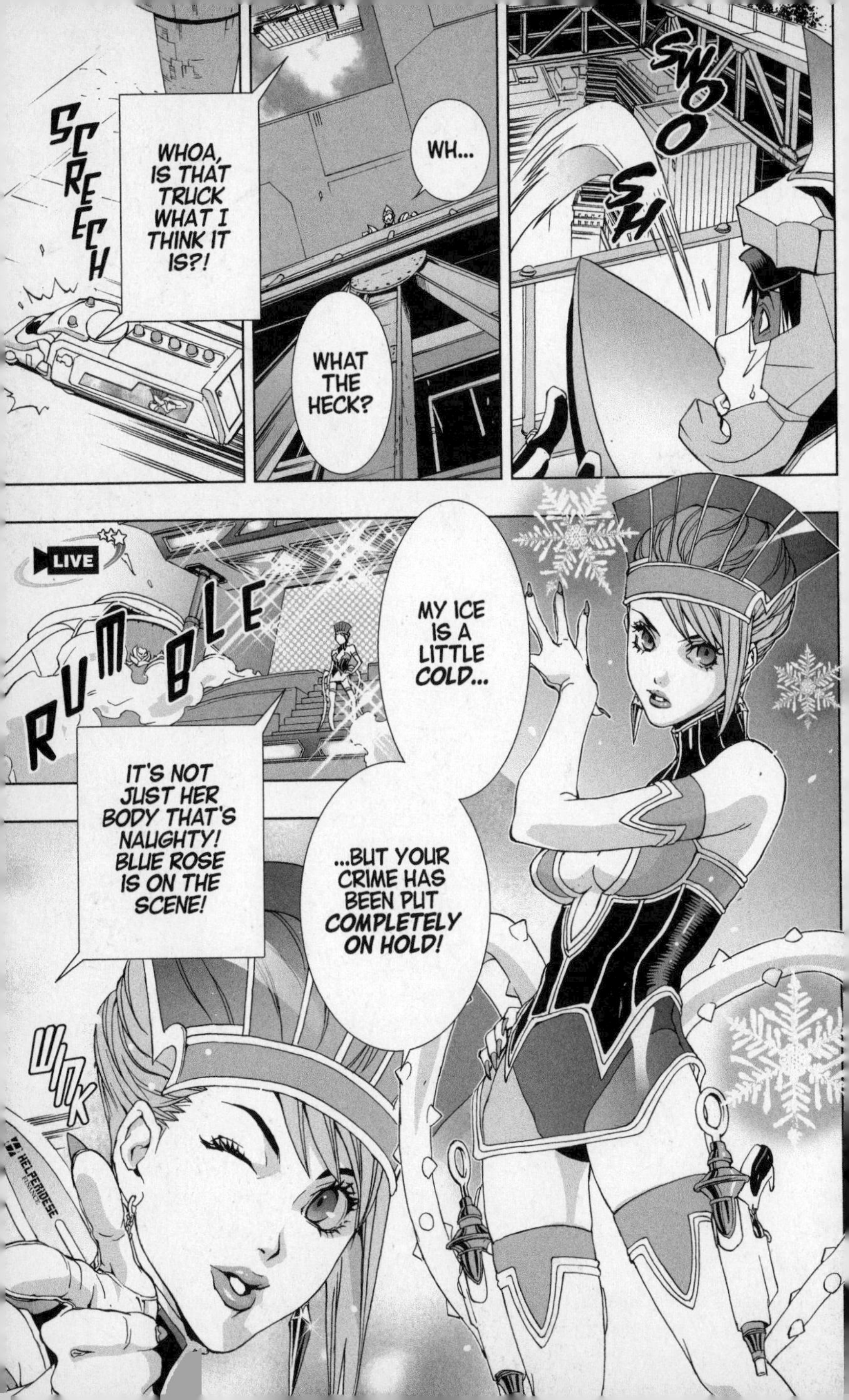
SWOOSH
WH...
WHAT THE HECK?
SCREECH
WHOA, IS THAT TRUCK WHAT I THINK IT IS?!
MY ICE IS A LITTLE COLD...
...BUT YOUR CRIME HAS BEEN PUT COMPLETELY ON HOLD!
LIVE
RUMBLE
IT'S NOT JUST HER BODY THAT'S NAUGHTY! BLUE ROSE IS ON THE SCENE!
WINK

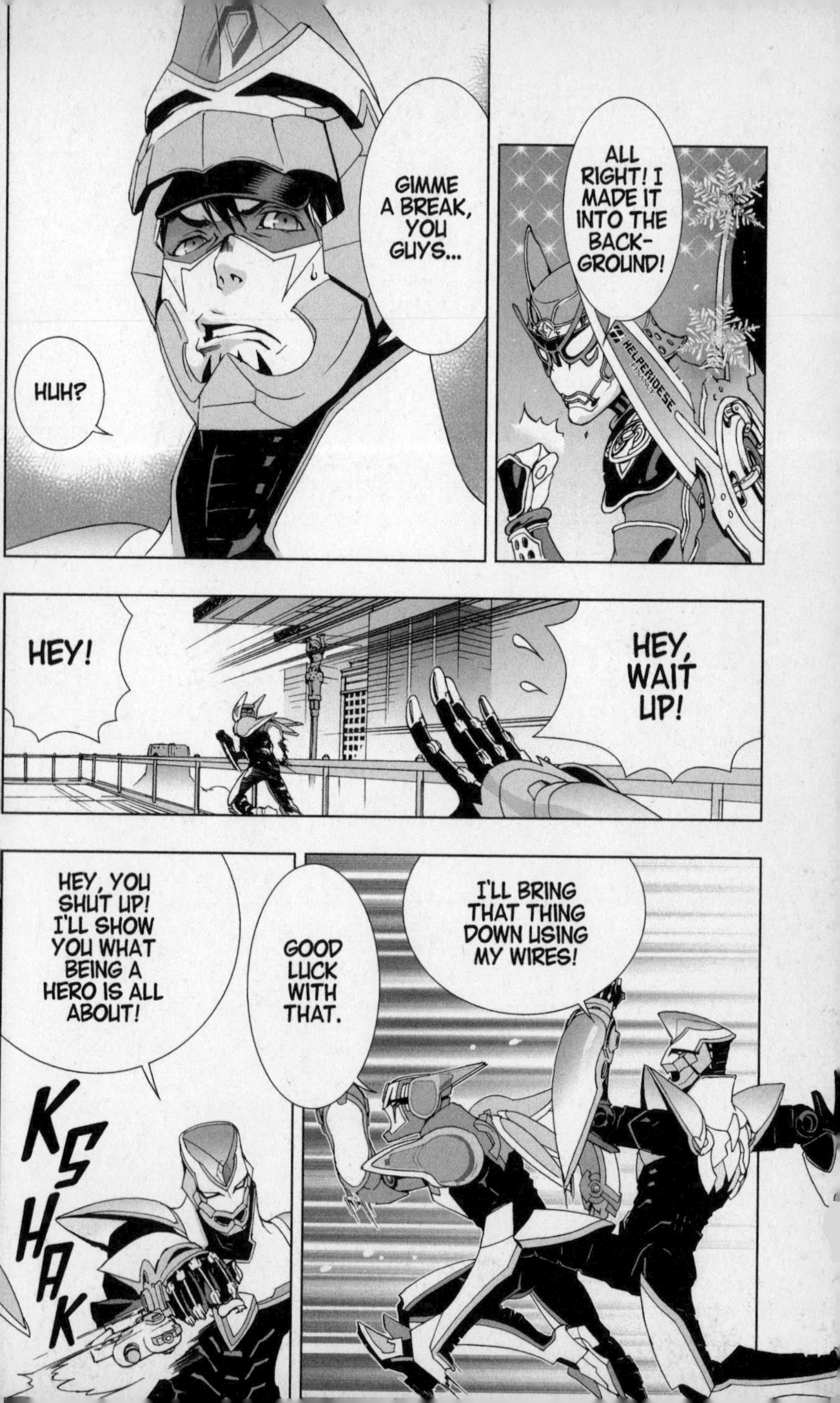
ALL RIGHT! I MADE IT INTO THE BACK-GROUND!
GIMME A BREAK, YOU GUYS...
HUH?
HEY, WAIT UP!
HEY!
I'LL BRING THAT THING DOWN USING MY WIRES!
GOOD LUCK WITH THAT.
HEY, YOU SHUT UP! I'LL SHOW YOU WHAT BEING A HERO IS ALL ABOUT!
KSHAK

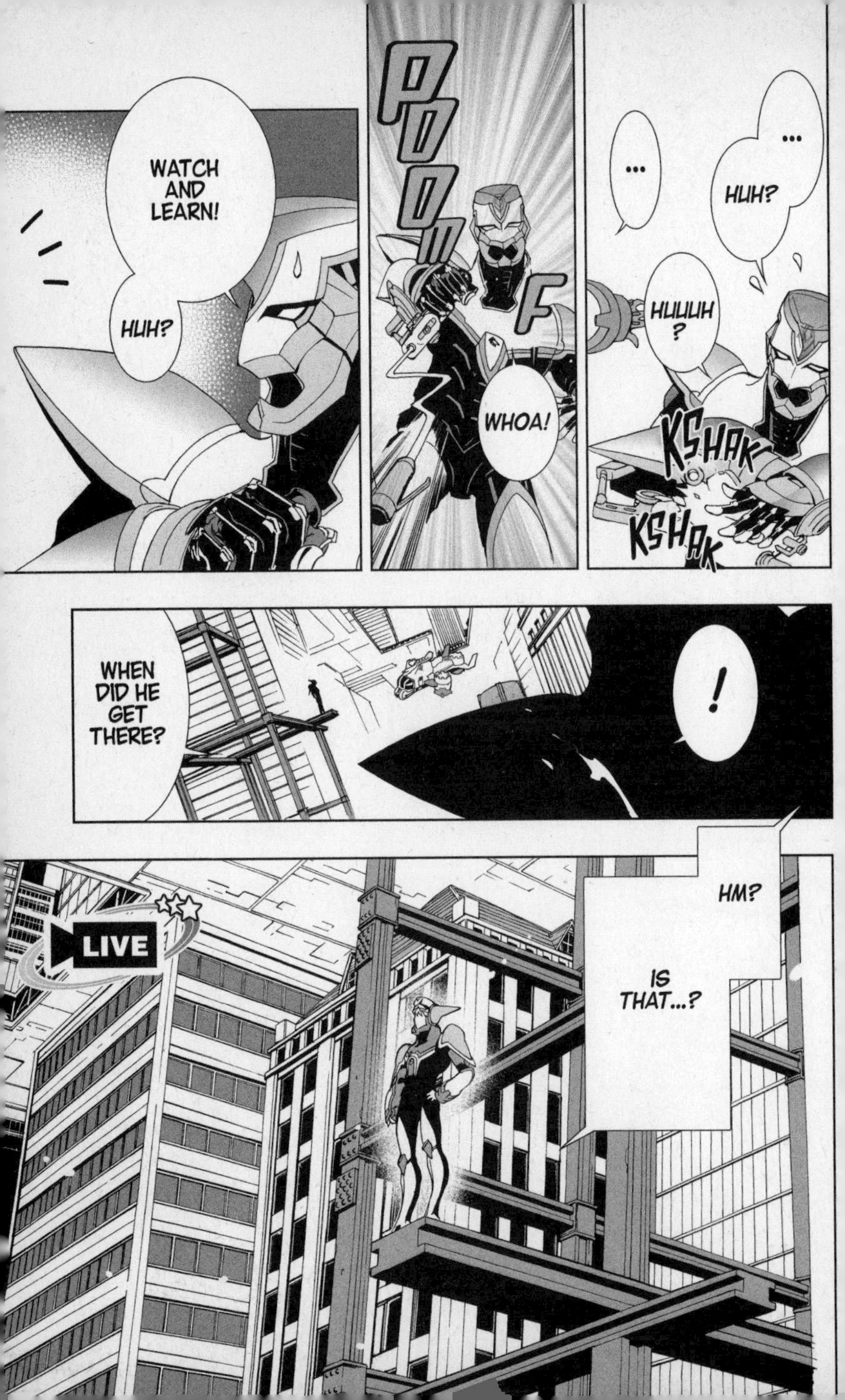
... HUH?
...
HUUUH ?
KSHAK
KSHAK
POOMF
WHOA!
WATCH AND LEARN!
HUH?
!
WHEN DID HE GET THERE?
HM? IS THAT...?
LIVE

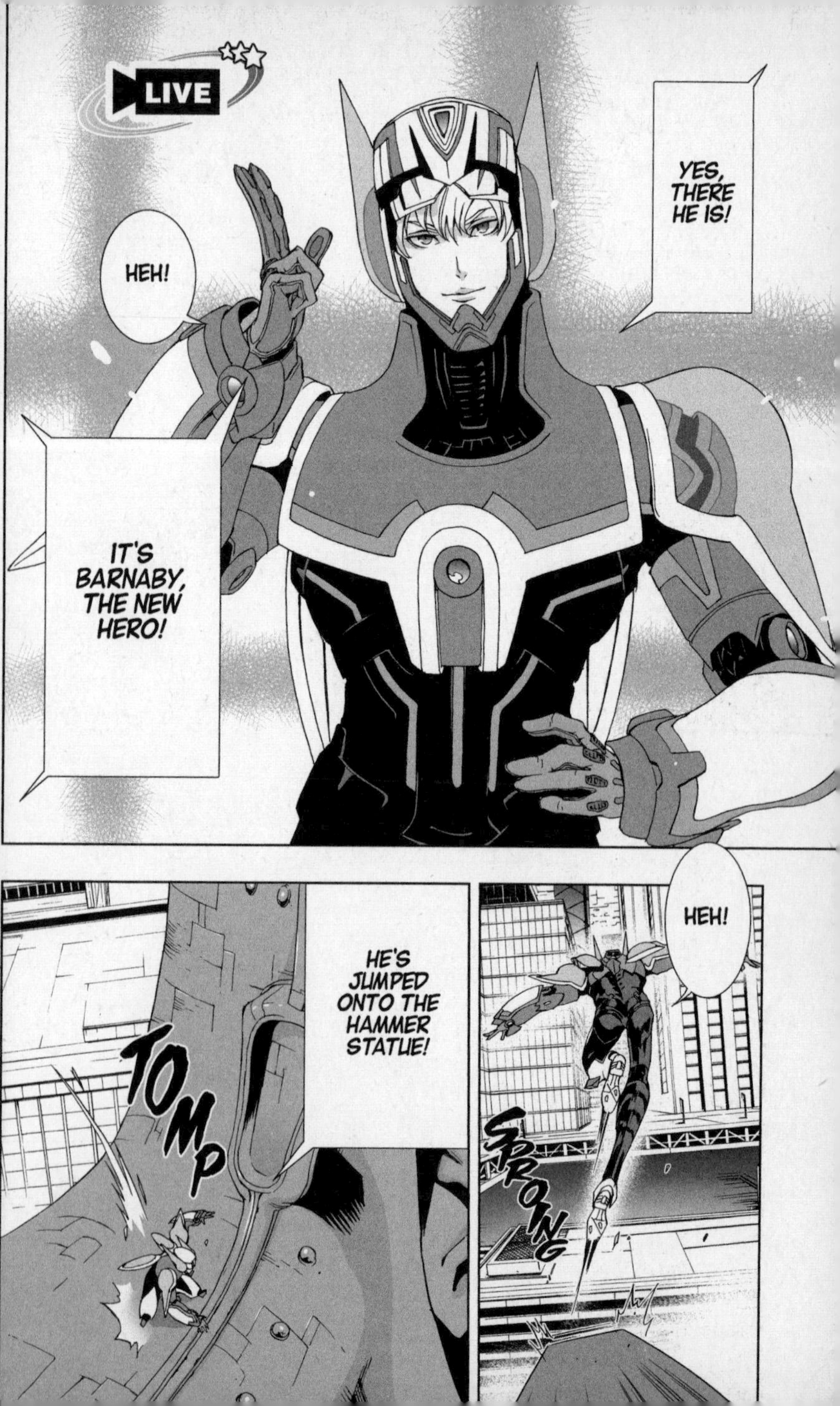
LIVE
YES, THERE HE IS!
HEH!
IT'S BARNABY, THE NEW HERO!
HEH!
SPRONG
HE'S JUMPED ONTO THE HAMMER STATUE!
TOMP

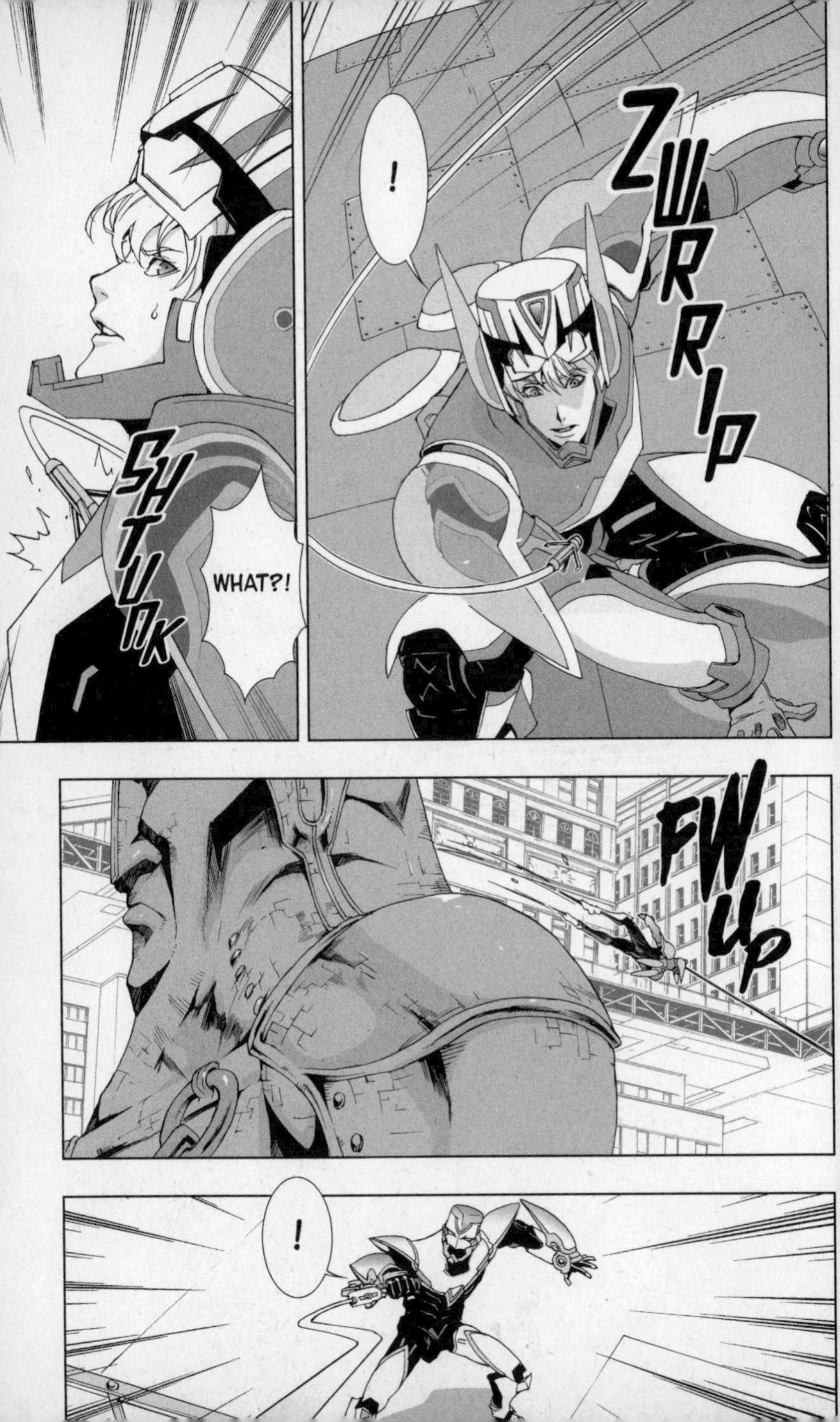
!
ZURRIP
SHTUNK
WHAT?!
FWUP
!

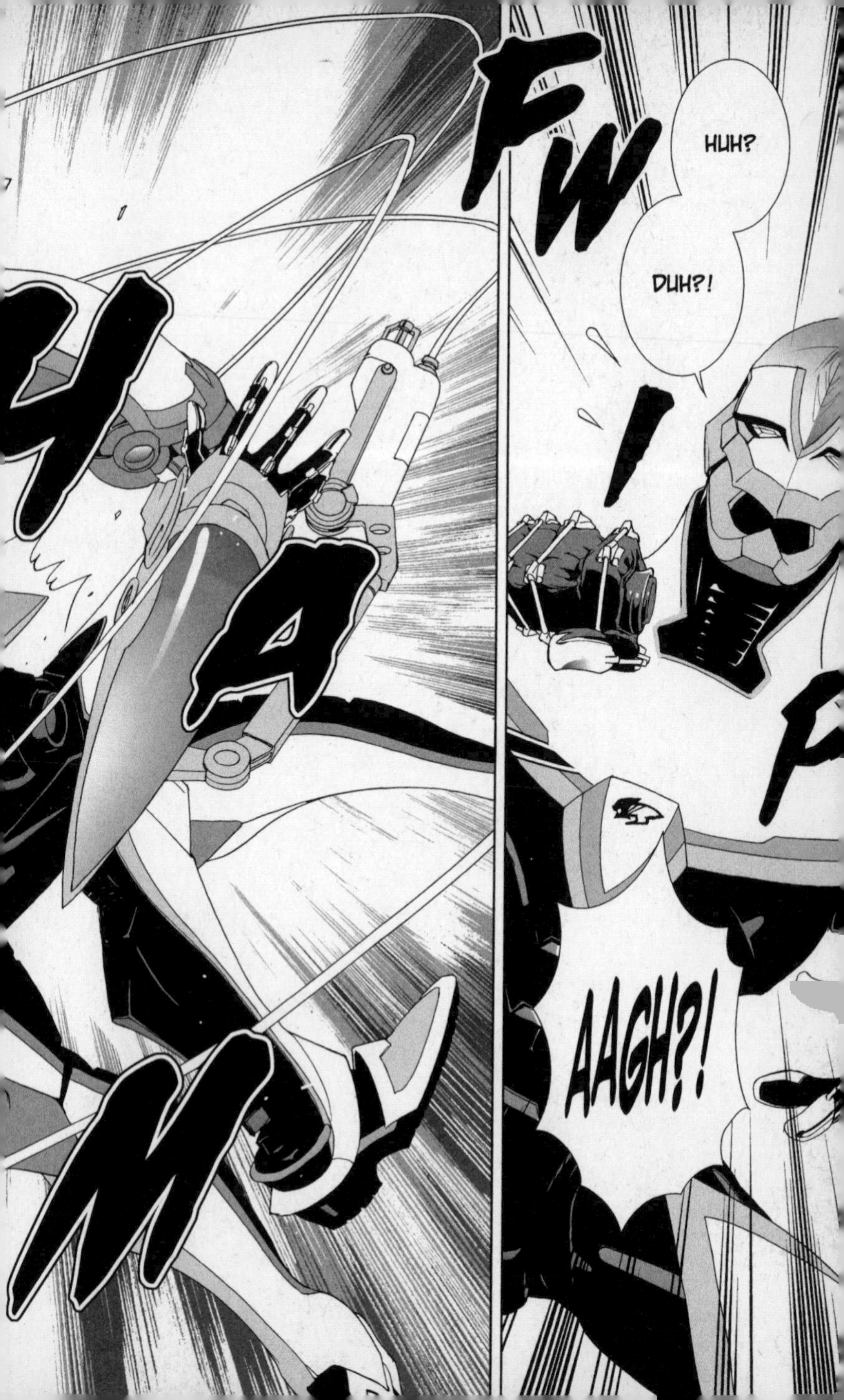
FWIP
HUH?
DUH?!
AAGH?!

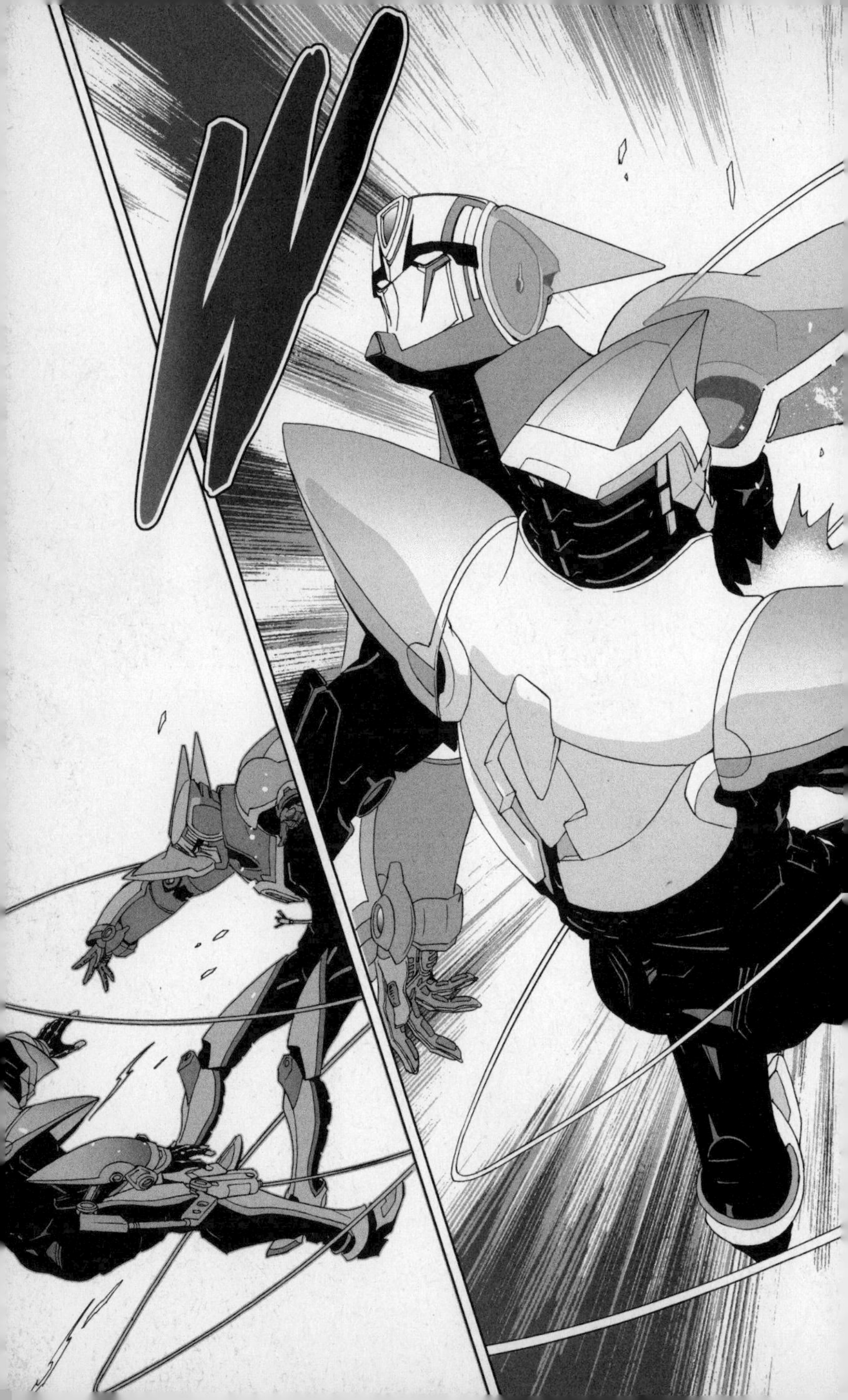

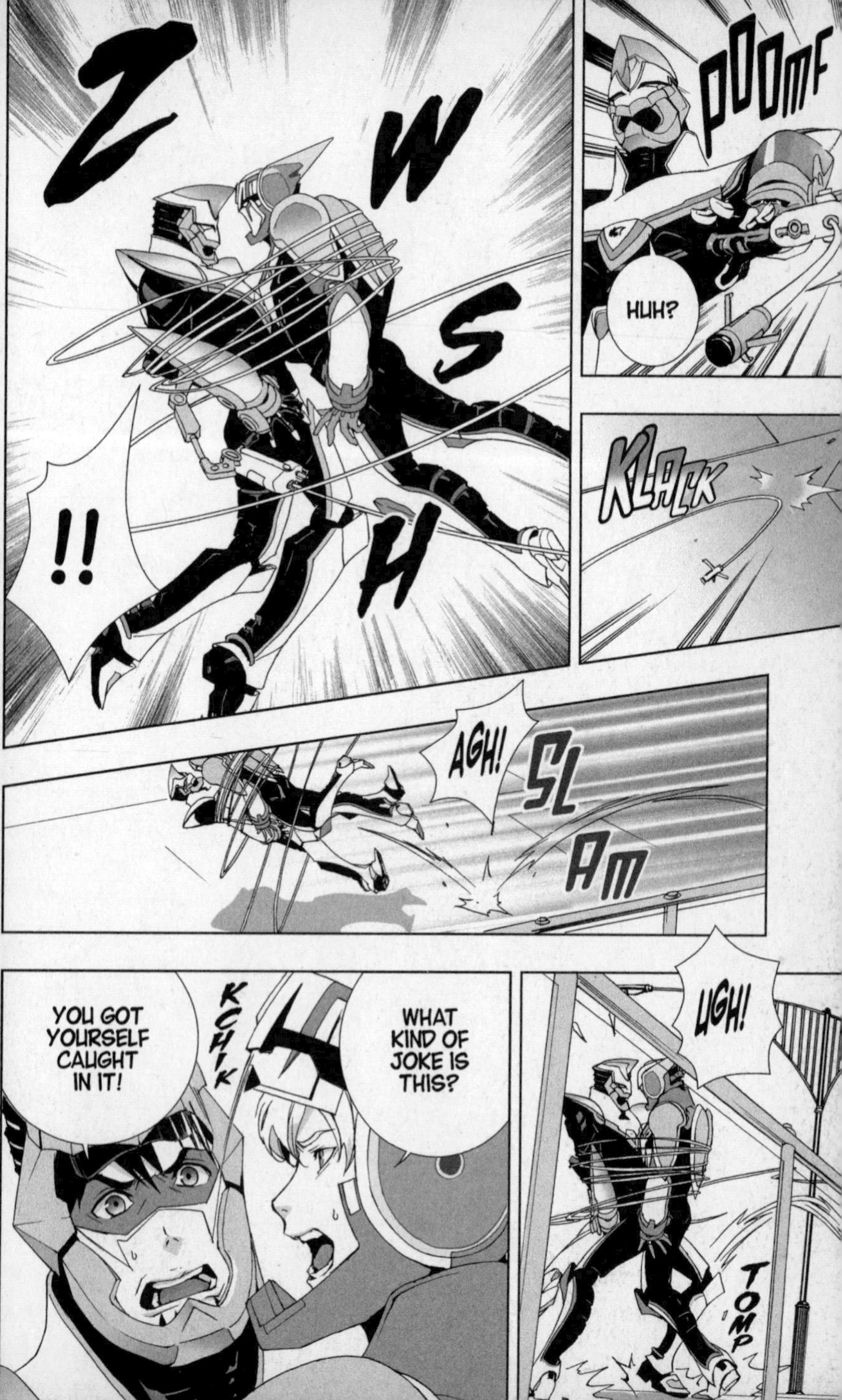
POOMF
HUH?
KLACK
ZWSH
!!
AGH!
SLAM
UGH!
TOMP
WHAT KIND OF JOKE IS THIS?
KCHIK
YOU GOT YOURSELF CAUGHT IN IT!

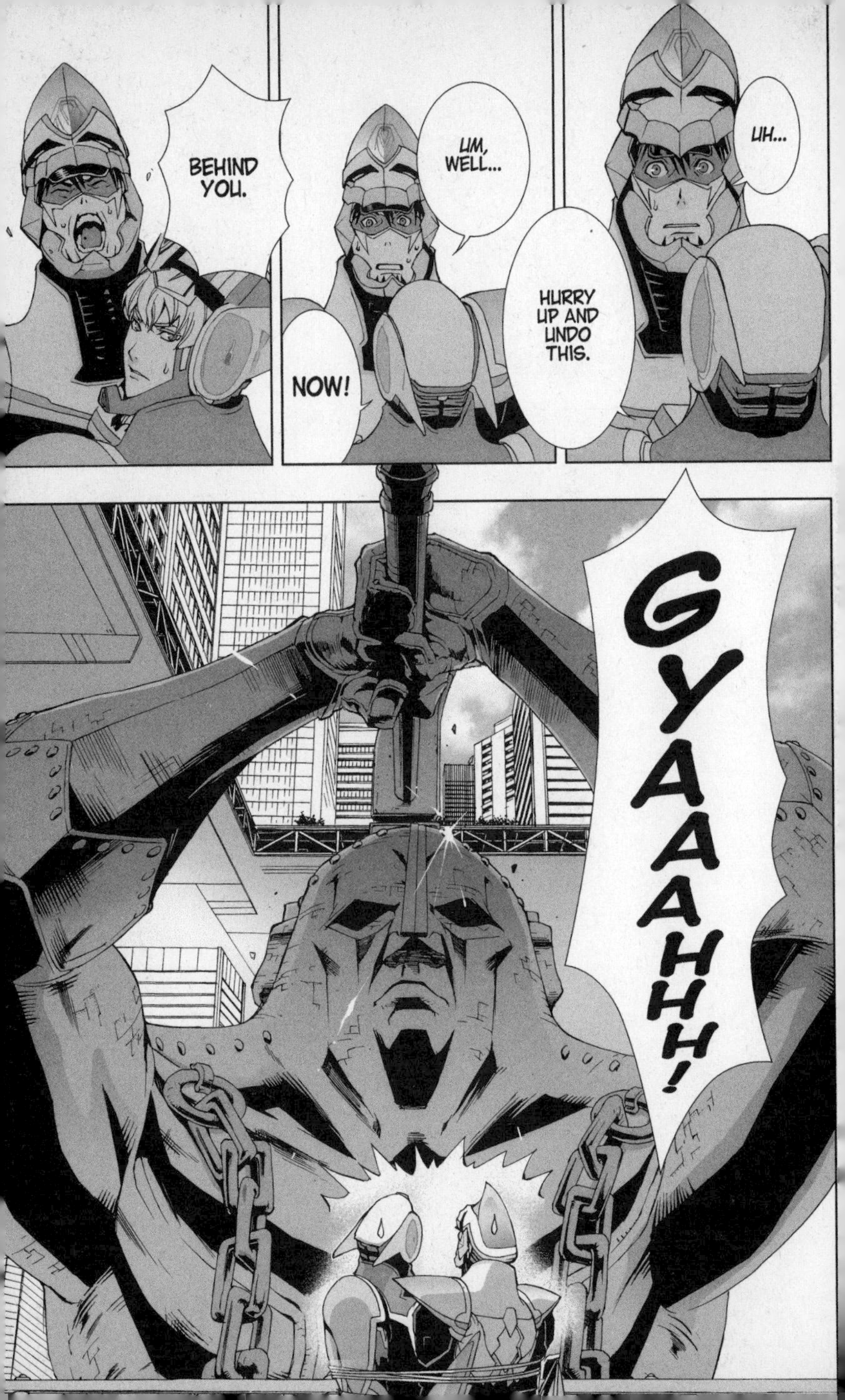
UH...
UM, WELL...
HURRY UP AND UNDO THIS.
NOW!
BEHIND YOU.
GYAAAHHH!

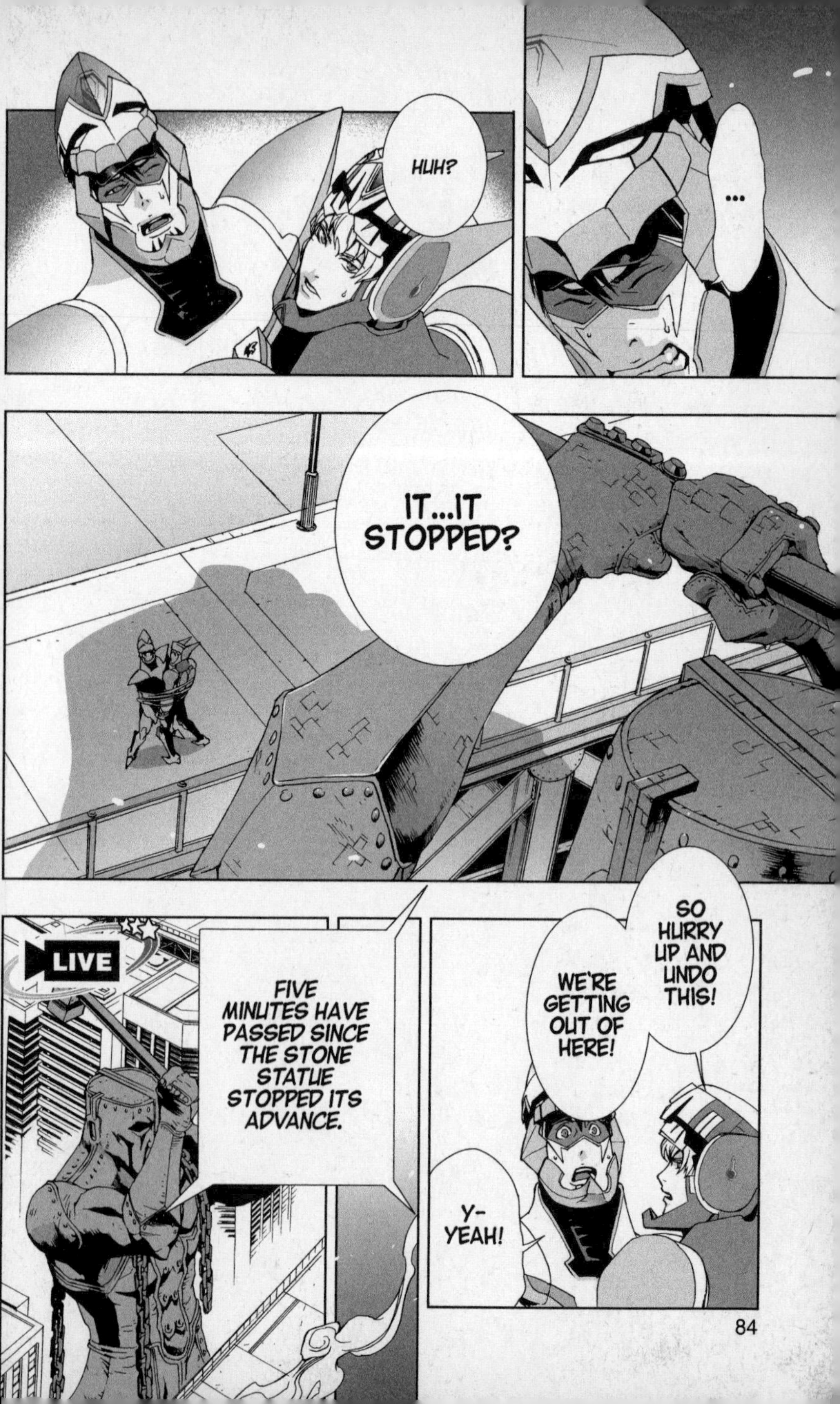
...
HUH?
IT...IT STOPPED?
SO HURRY UP AND UNDO THIS!
WE'RE GETTING OUT OF HERE!
Y-YEAH!
LIVE
FIVE MINUTES HAVE PASSED SINCE THE STONE STATUE STOPPED ITS ADVANCE.

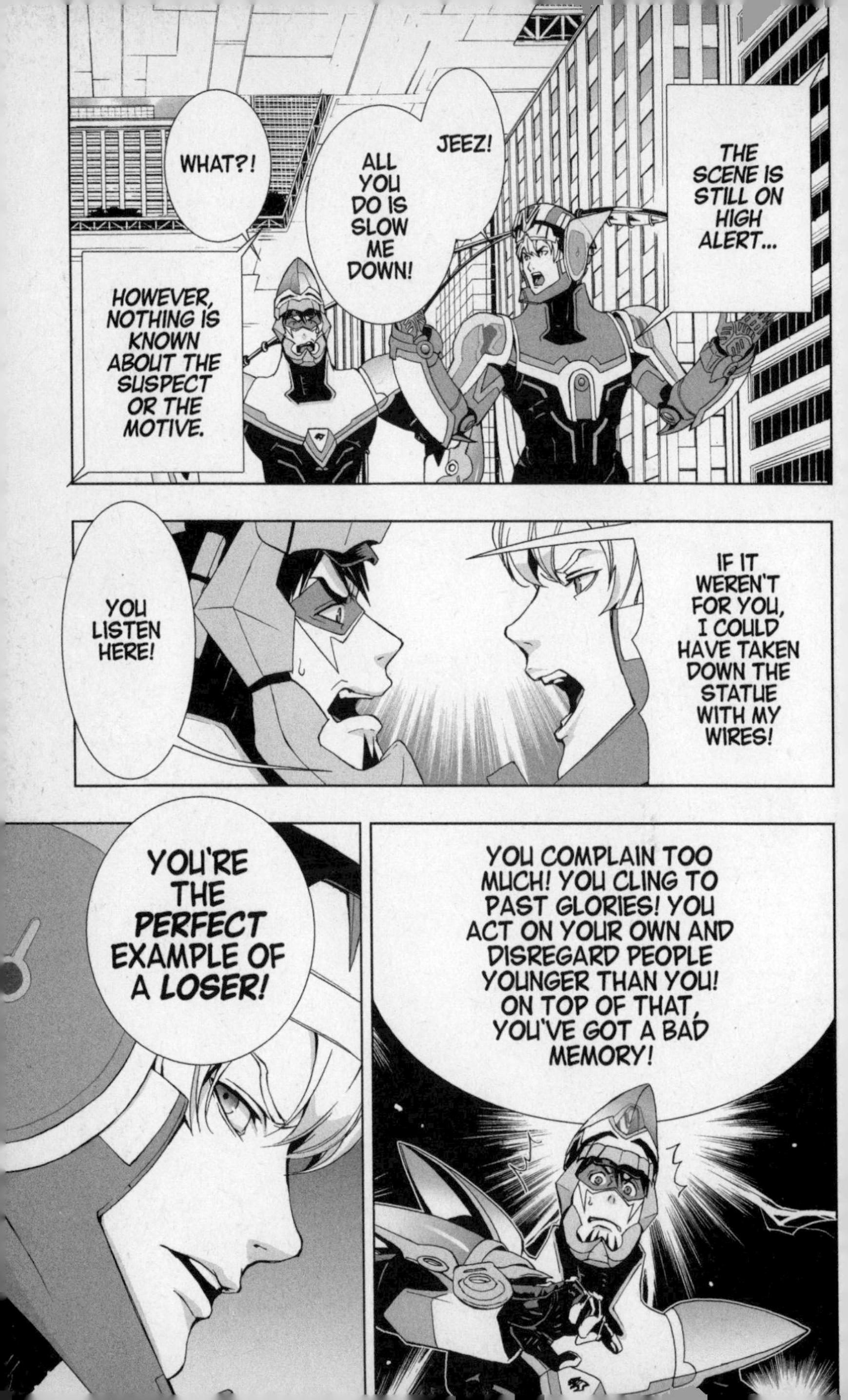
THE SCENE IS STILL ON HIGH ALERT...
JEEZ! ALL YOU DO IS SLOW ME DOWN!
WHAT?!
HOWEVER, NOTHING IS KNOWN ABOUT THE SUSPECT OR THE MOTIVE.
IF IT WEREN'T FOR YOU, I COULD HAVE TAKEN DOWN THE STATUE WITH MY WIRES!
YOU LISTEN HERE!
YOU COMPLAIN TOO MUCH! YOU CLING TO PAST GLORIES! YOU ACT ON YOUR OWN AND DISREGARD PEOPLE YOUNGER THAN YOU! ON TOP OF THAT, YOU'VE GOT A BAD MEMORY!
YOU'RE THE PERFECT EXAMPLE OF A LOSER!

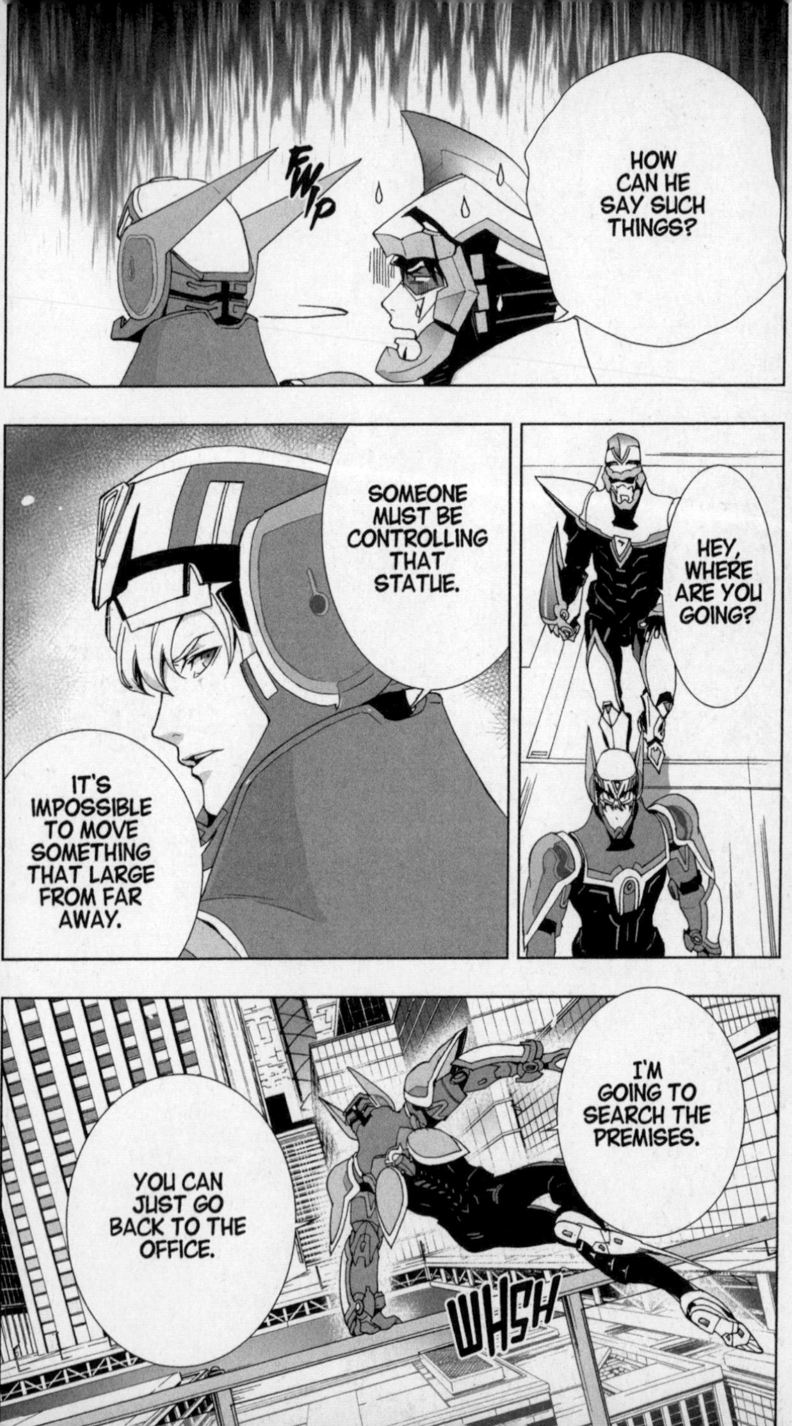
HOW CAN HE SAY SUCH THINGS?
FWIP
HEY, WHERE ARE YOU GOING?
SOMEONE MUST BE CONTROLLING THAT STATUE.
IT'S IMPOSSIBLE TO MOVE SOMETHING THAT LARGE FROM FAR AWAY.
I'M GOING TO SEARCH THE PREMISES.
YOU CAN JUST GO BACK TO THE OFFICE.
WHSH

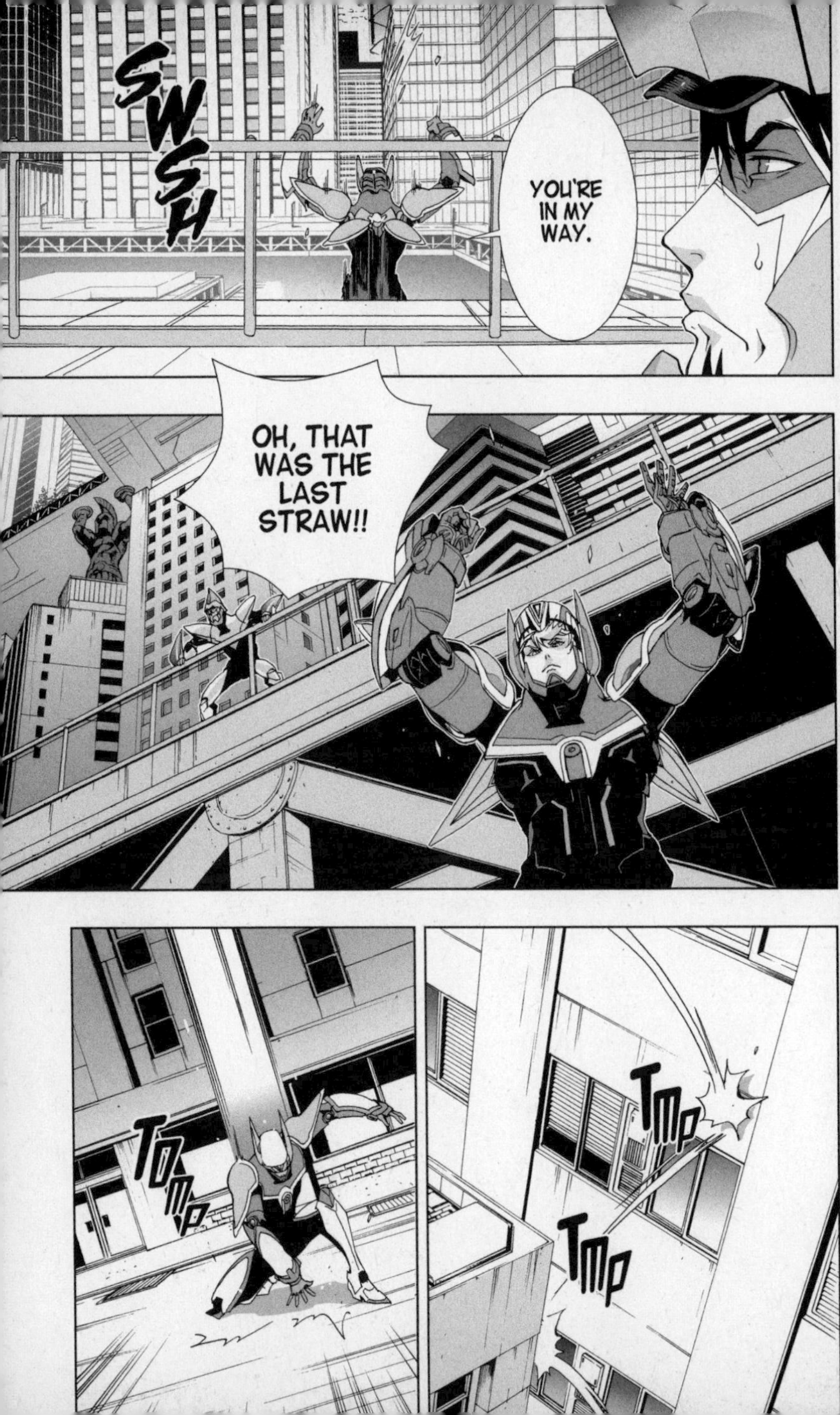
YOU'RE IN MY WAY.
SWSH
OH, THAT WAS THE LAST STRAW!!
TMP
TMP
TOMP

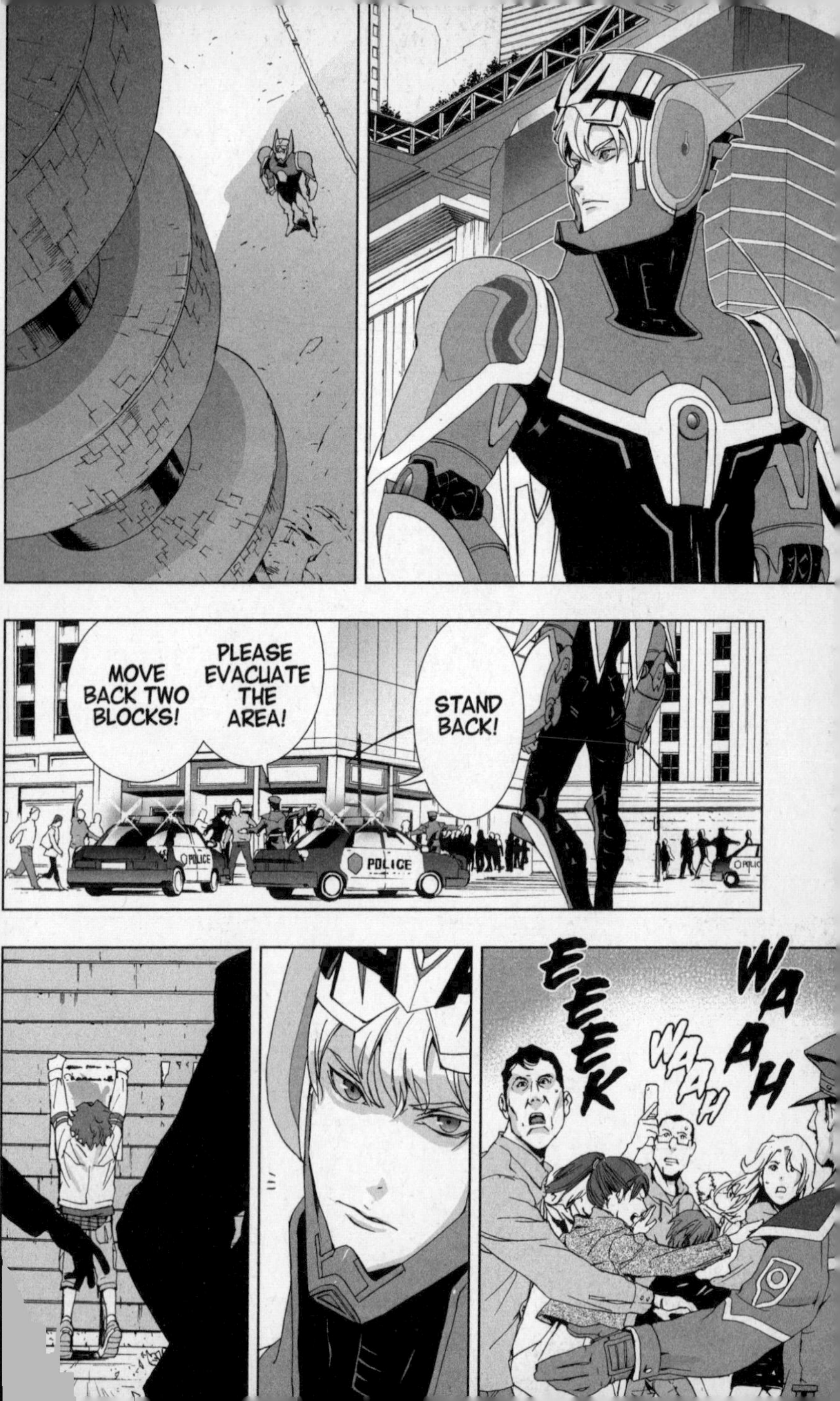
STAND BACK!
PLEASE EVACUATE THE AREA!
MOVE BACK TWO BLOCKS!
POLICE
POLICE
WAAH
WAAH
EEEK

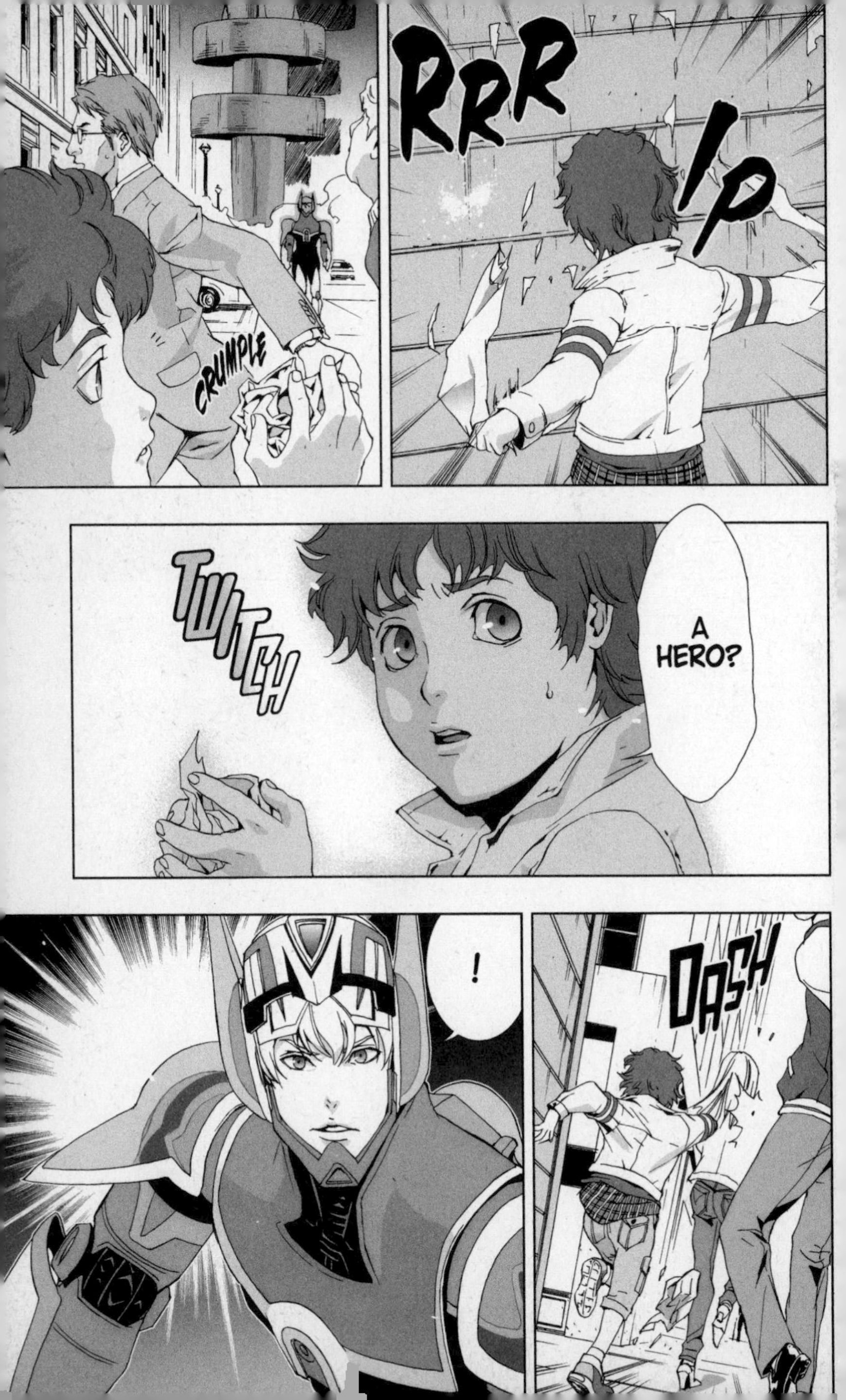
RRRIP
CRUMPLE
A HERO?
TWITCH
DASH
!

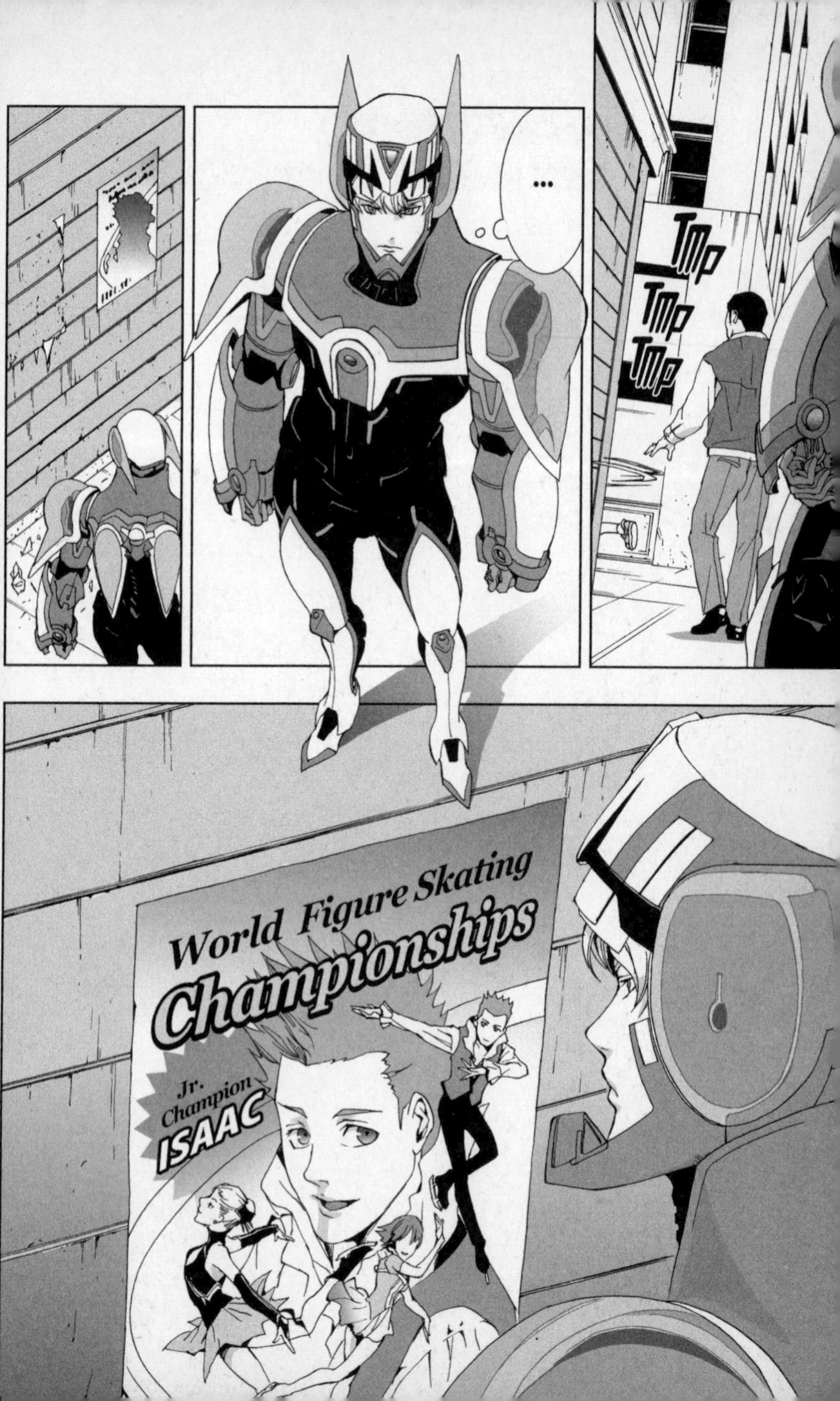
TMP
TMP
TMP
...
World Figure Skating
Championships
Jr. Champion
ISAAC

#03 A Good Beginning Makes a Good Ending, Part 2

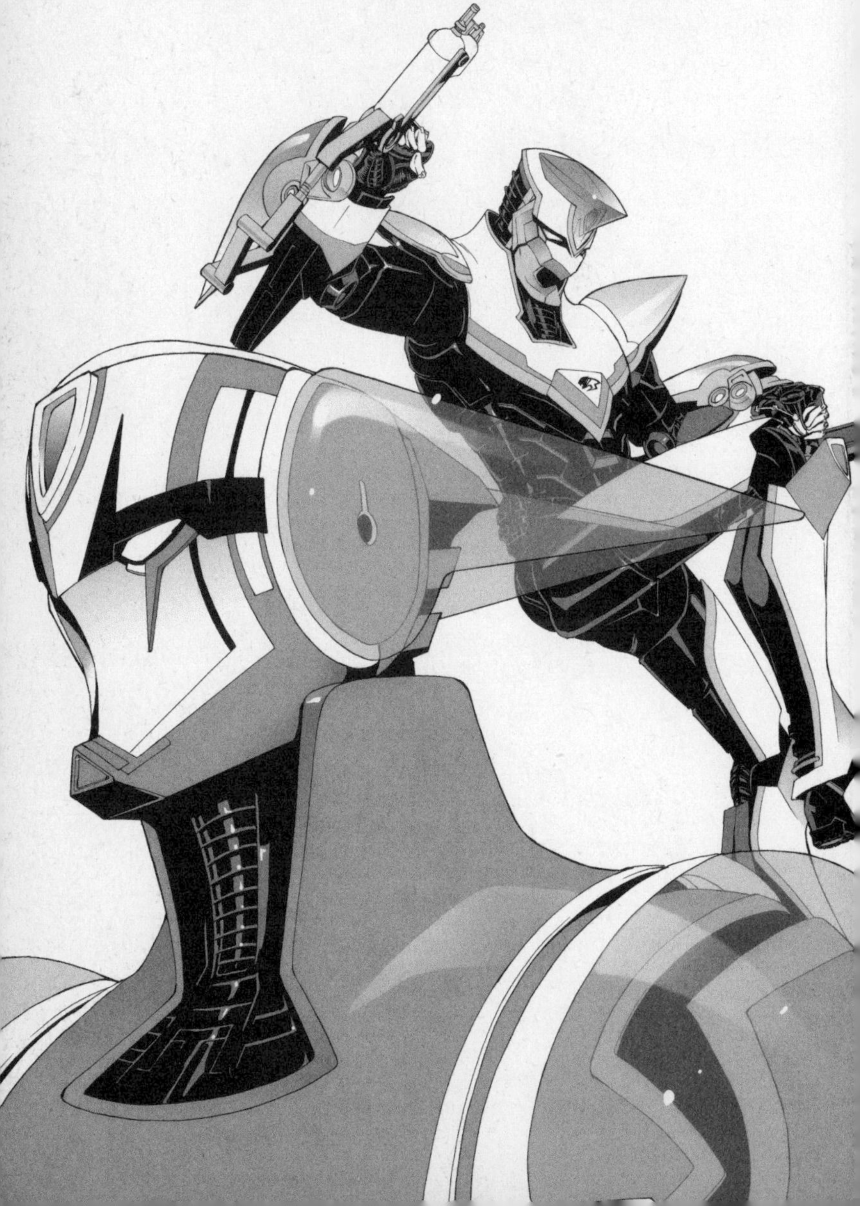

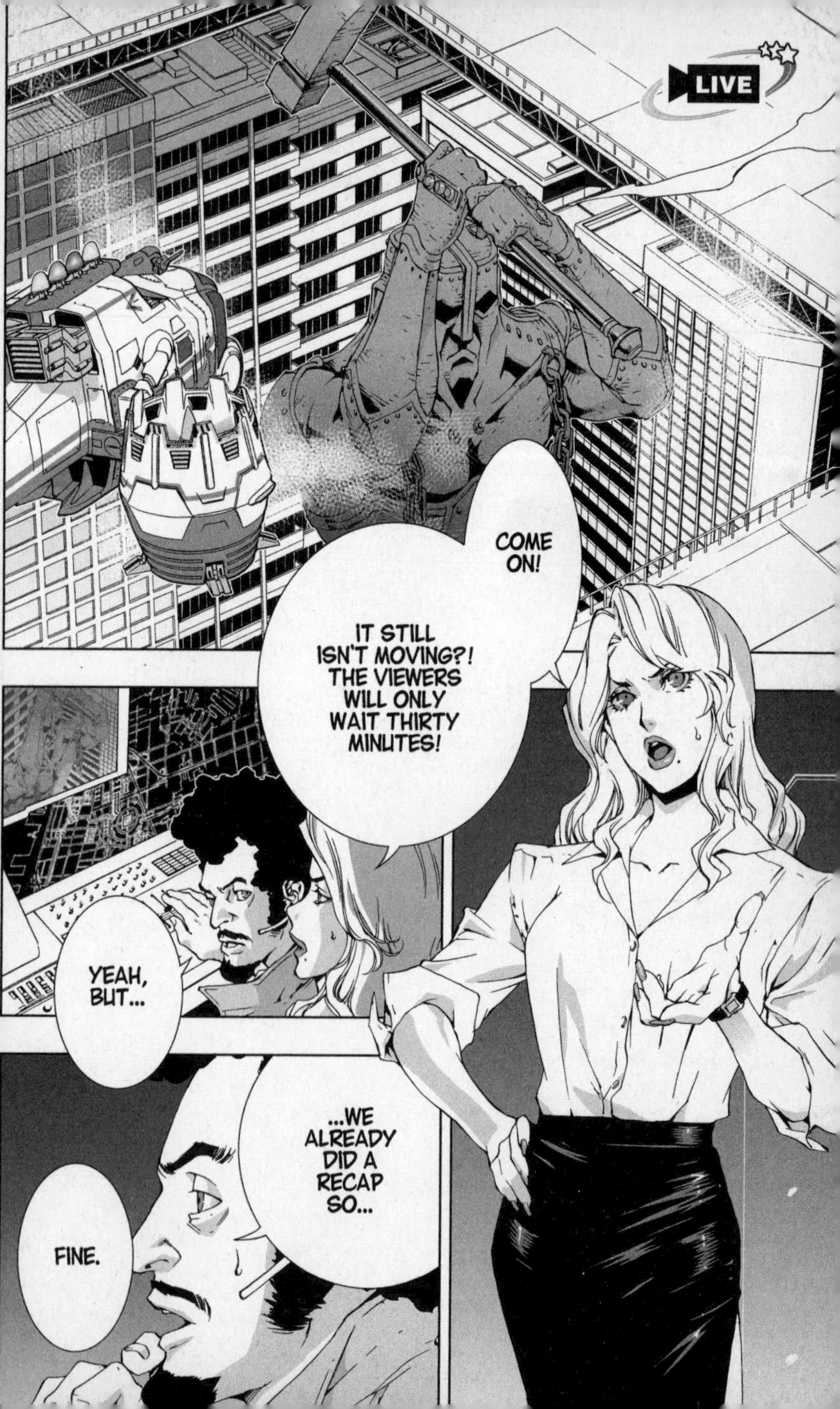
LIVE
COME ON!
IT STILL ISN'T MOVING?! THE VIEWERS WILL ONLY WAIT THIRTY MINUTES!
YEAH, BUT...
...WE ALREADY DID A RECAP SO...
FINE.

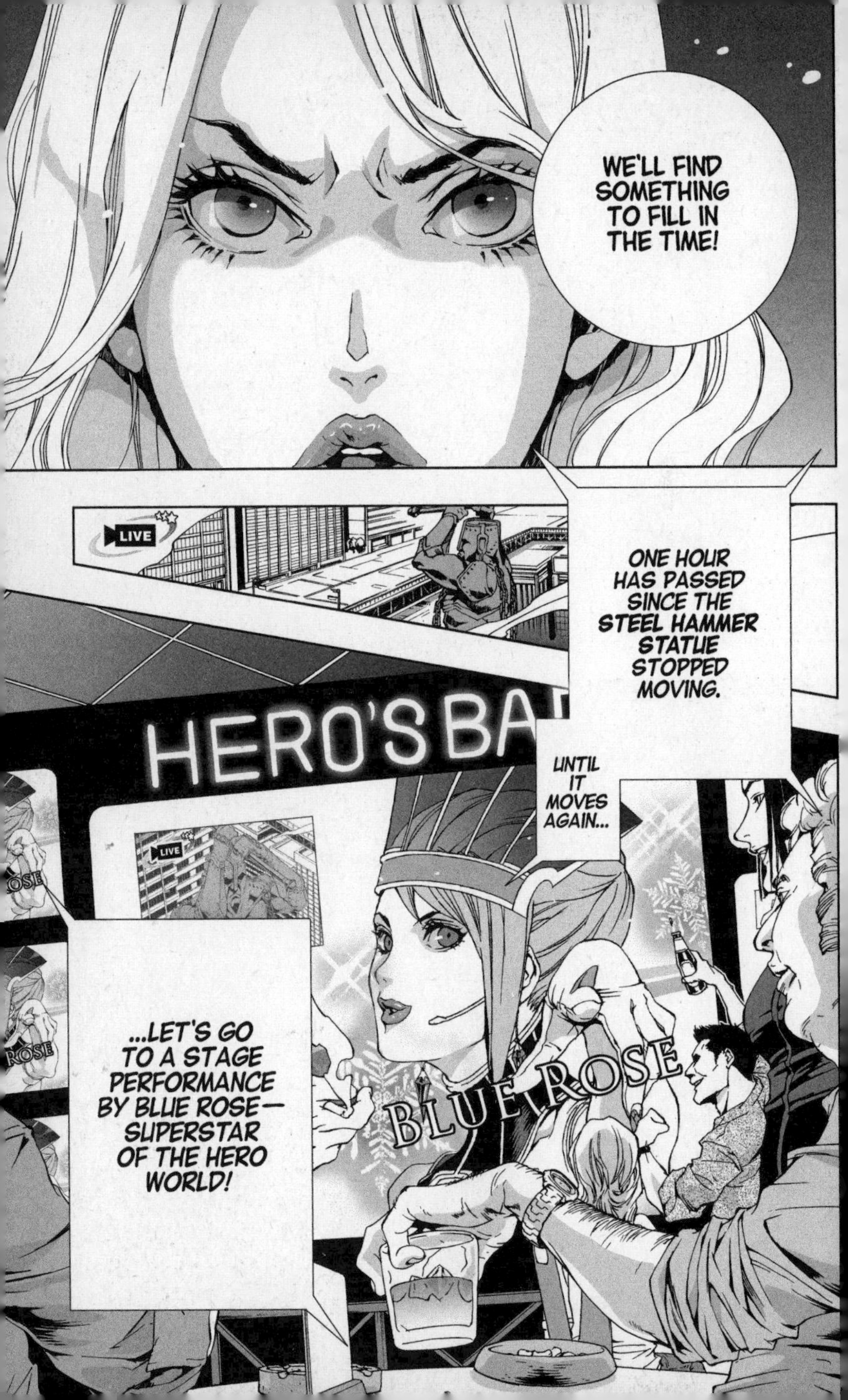
WE'LL FIND SOMETHING TO FILL IN THE TIME!
LIVE
ONE HOUR HAS PASSED SINCE THE STEEL HAMMER STATUE STOPPED MOVING.
HERO'S BA
UNTIL IT MOVES AGAIN...
LIVE
...LET'S GO TO A STAGE PERFORMANCE BY BLUE ROSE—SUPERSTAR OF THE HERO WORLD!
BLUE ROSE

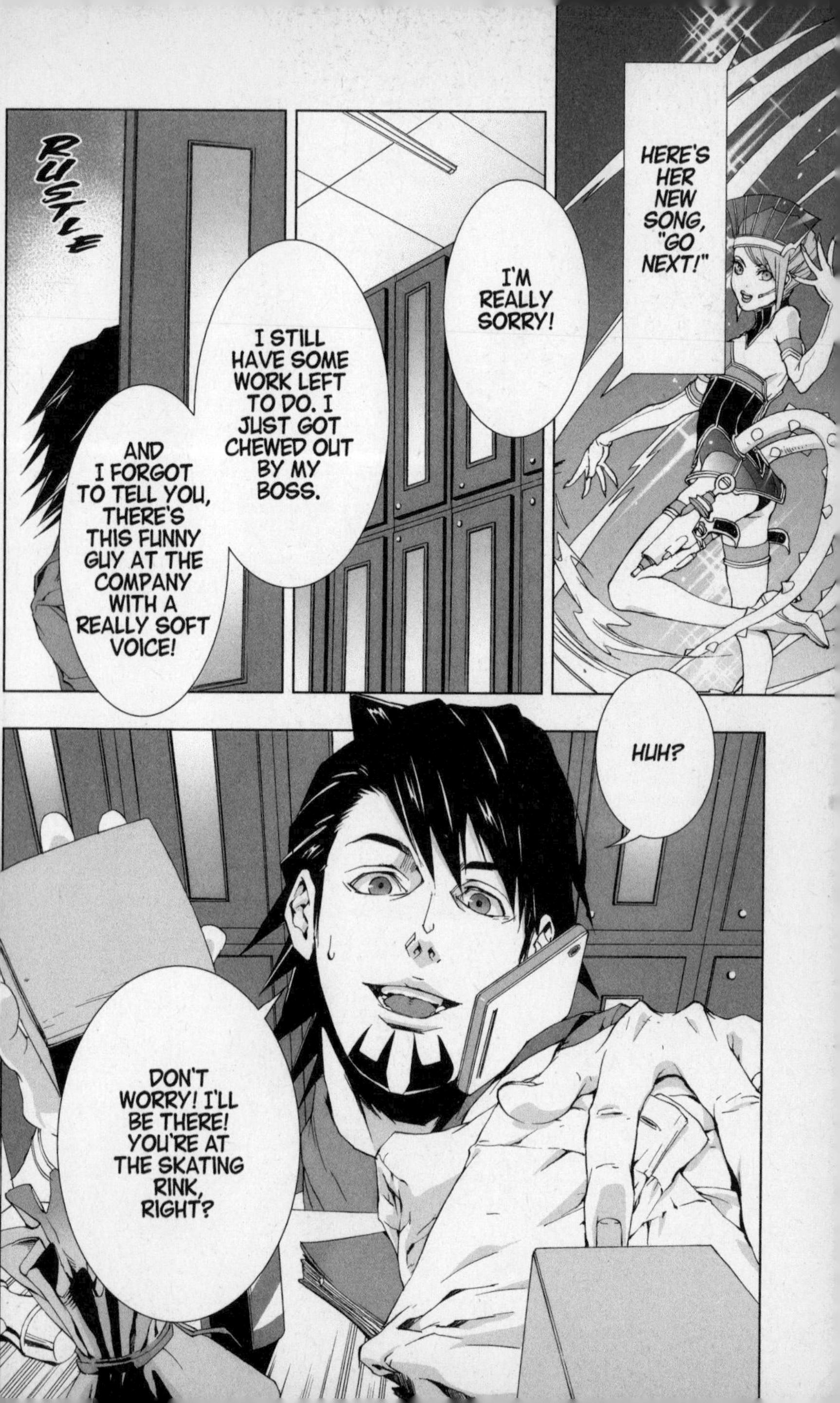
HERE'S HER NEW SONG, "GO NEXT!"
I'M REALLY SORRY!
I STILL HAVE SOME WORK LEFT TO DO. I JUST GOT CHEWED OUT BY MY BOSS.
RUSTLE
AND I FORGOT TO TELL YOU, THERE'S THIS FUNNY GUY AT THE COMPANY WITH A REALLY SOFT VOICE!
HUH?
DON'T WORRY! I'LL BE THERE! YOU'RE AT THE SKATING RINK, RIGHT?

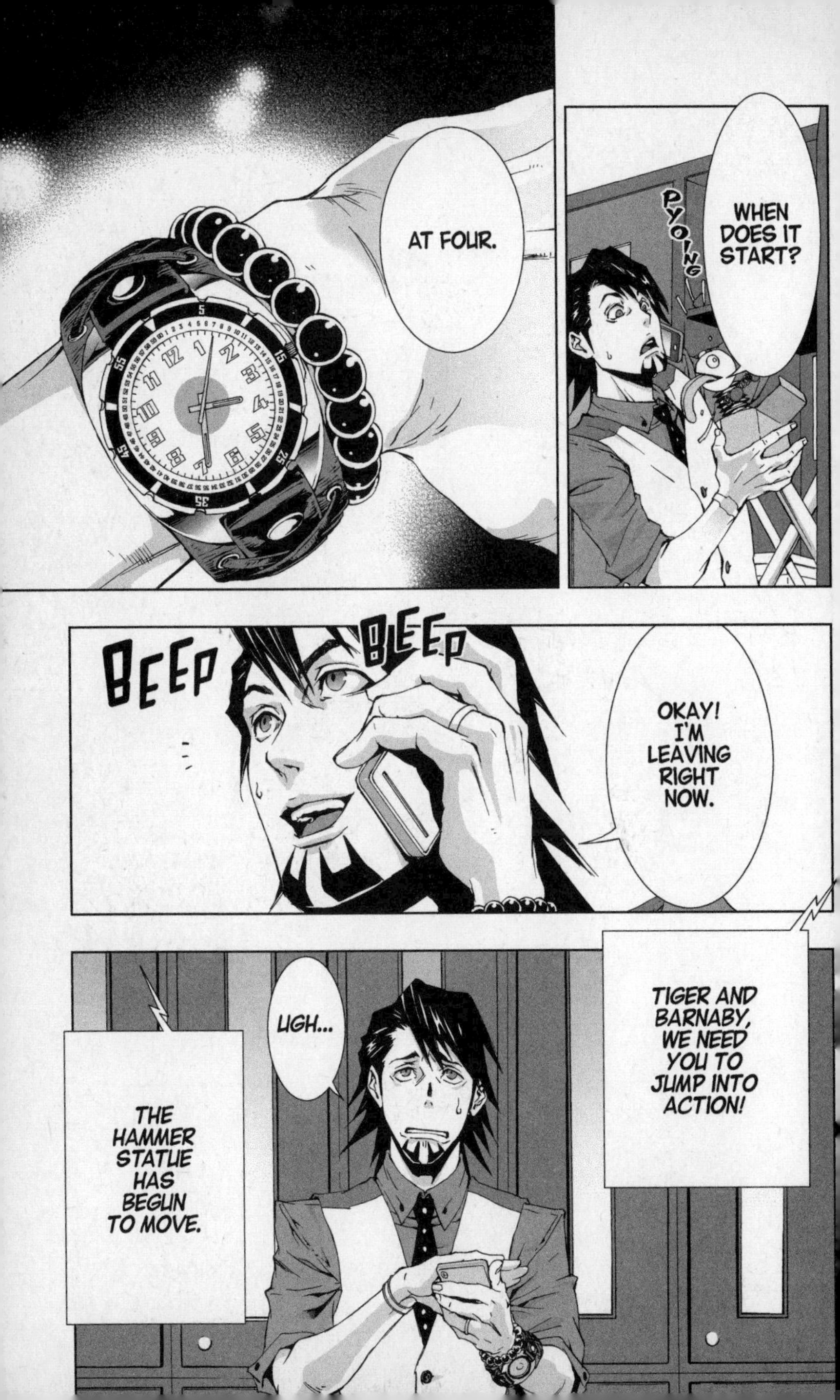
WHEN DOES IT START?
PYOING
AT FOUR.
OKAY! I'M LEAVING RIGHT NOW.
BEEP
BEEP
TIGER AND BARNABY, WE NEED YOU TO JUMP INTO ACTION!
UGH...
THE HAMMER STATUE HAS BEGUN TO MOVE.

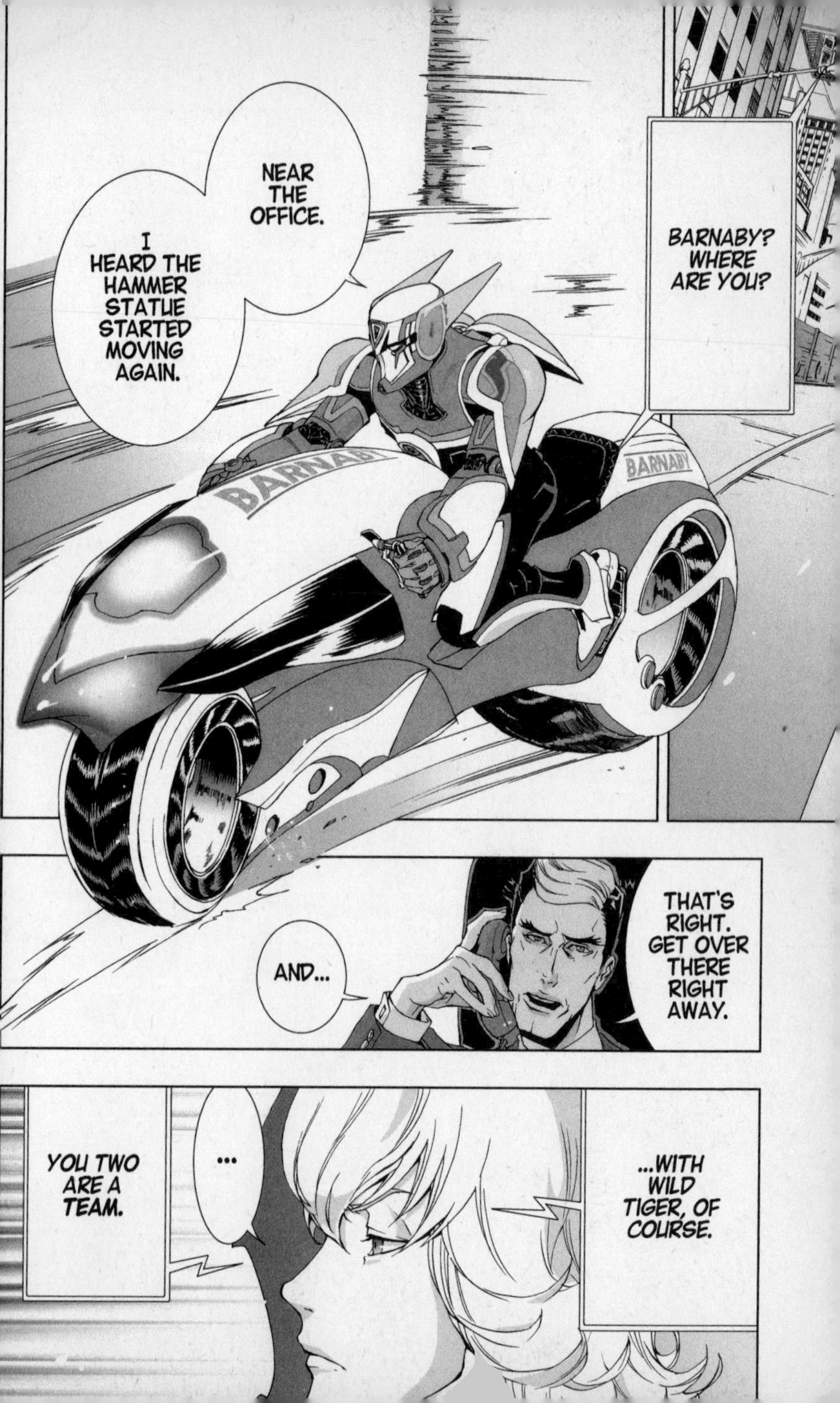
BARNABY? WHERE ARE YOU?
NEAR THE OFFICE.
I HEARD THE HAMMER STATUE STARTED MOVING AGAIN.
THAT'S RIGHT. GET OVER THERE RIGHT AWAY.
AND...
...WITH WILD TIGER, OF COURSE.
...
YOU TWO ARE A TEAM.

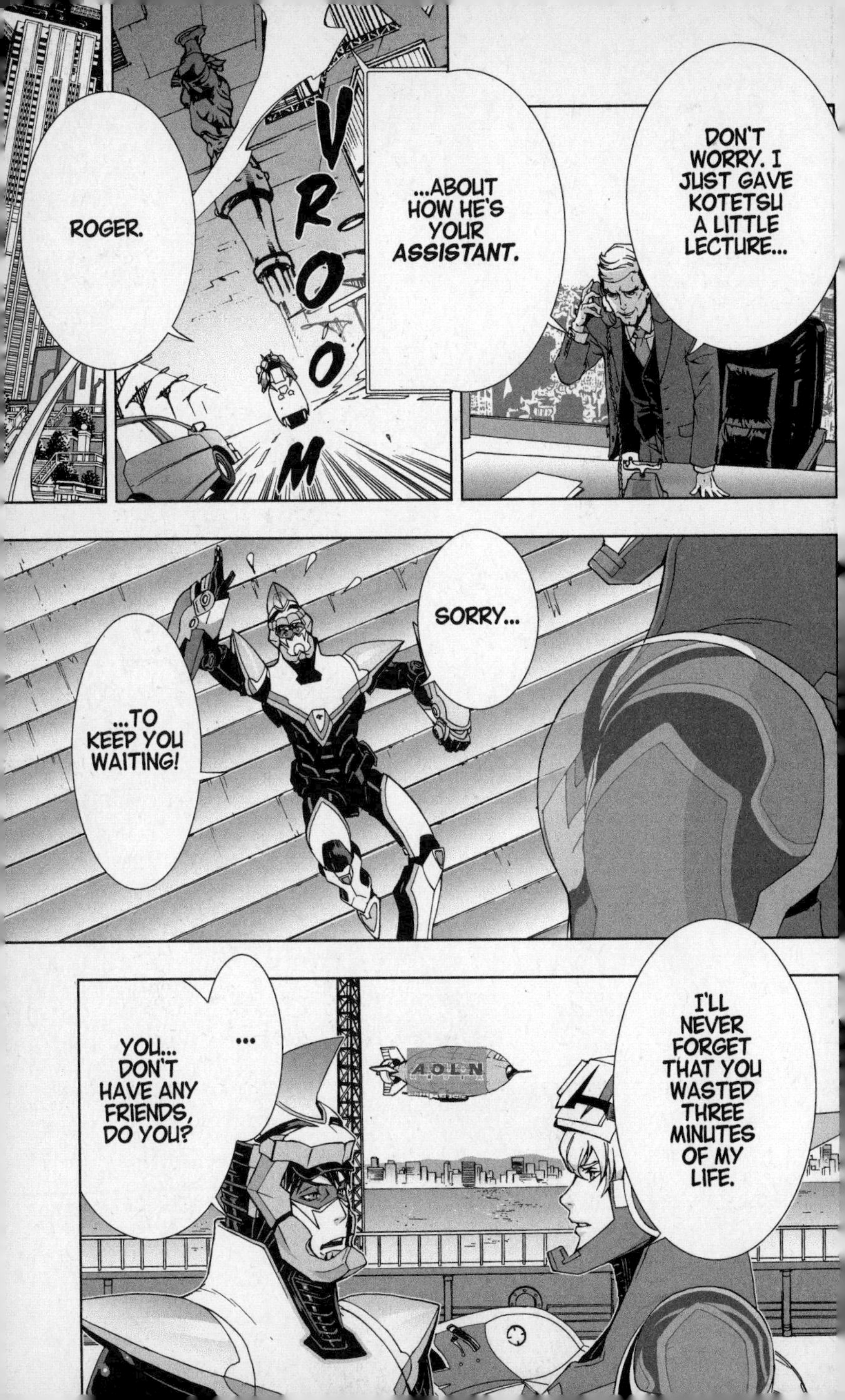
DON'T WORRY. I JUST GAVE KOTETSU A LITTLE LECTURE...
...ABOUT HOW HE'S YOUR ASSISTANT.
VROOM
ROGER.
SORRY...
...TO KEEP YOU WAITING!
I'LL NEVER FORGET THAT YOU WASTED THREE MINUTES OF MY LIFE.
...
YOU... DON'T HAVE ANY FRIENDS, DO YOU?

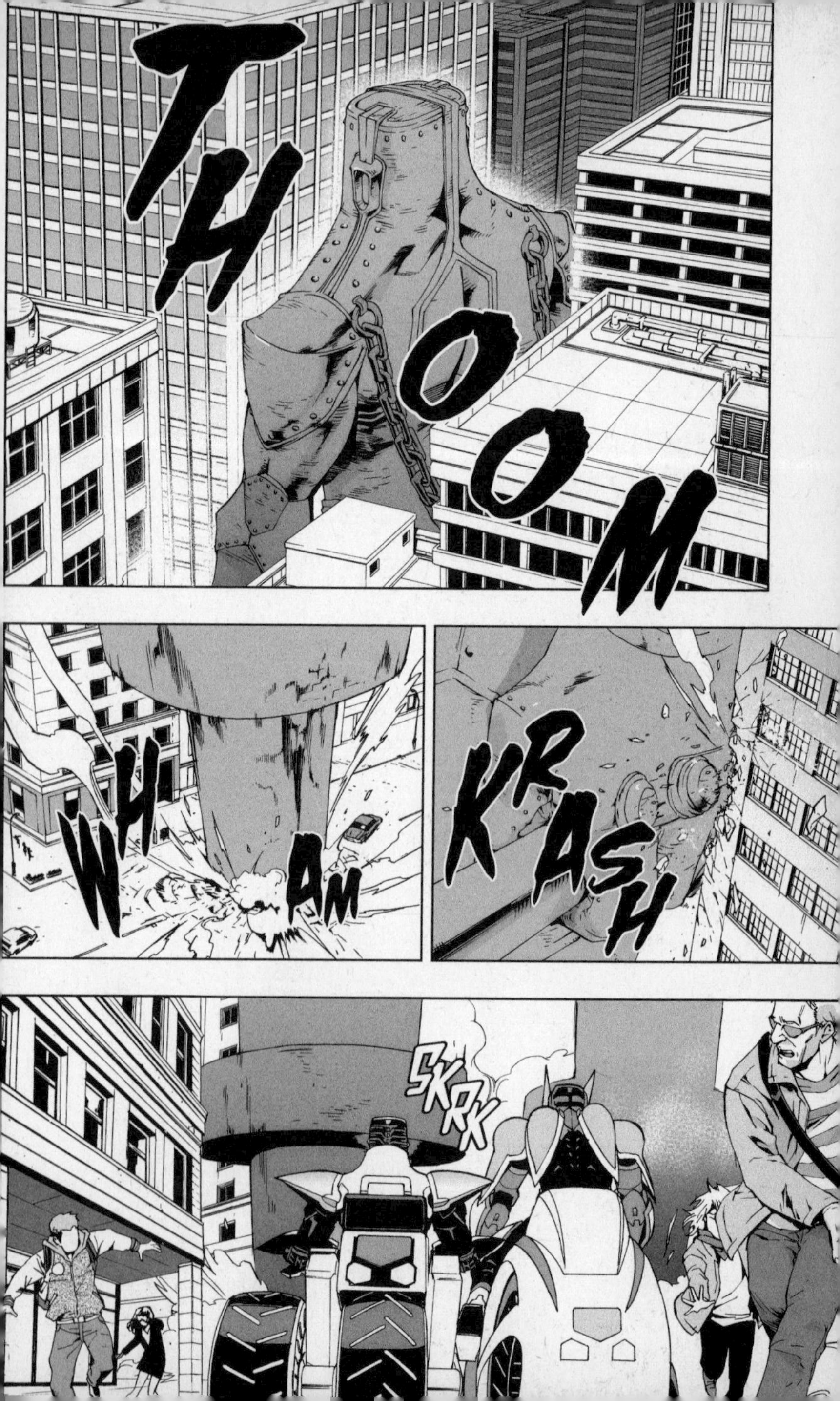
THOOM
KRASH
WHAM
SKRK

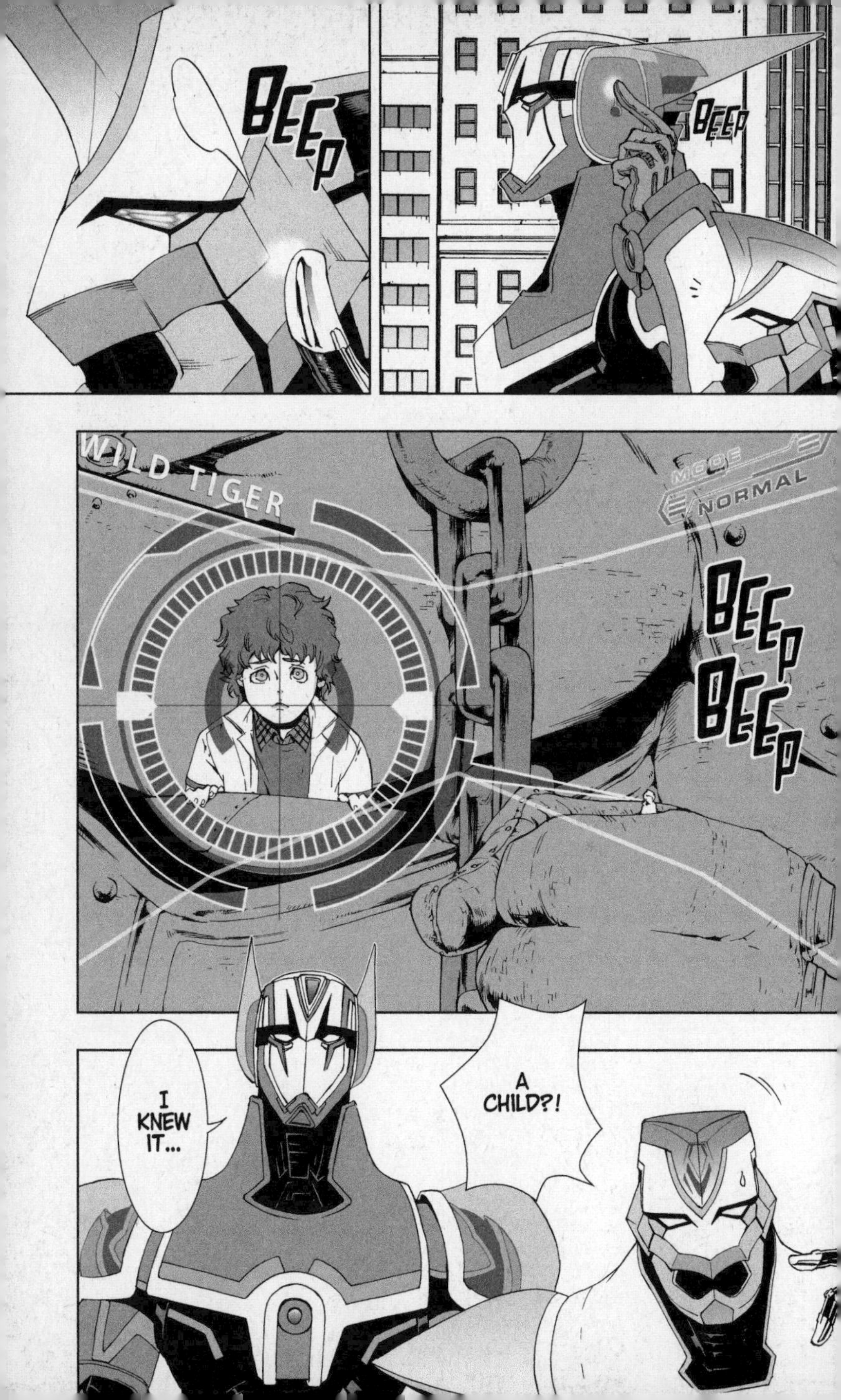
BEEP
BEEP
WILD TIGER
MODE
NORMAL
BEEP BEEP
A CHILD?!
I KNEW IT...

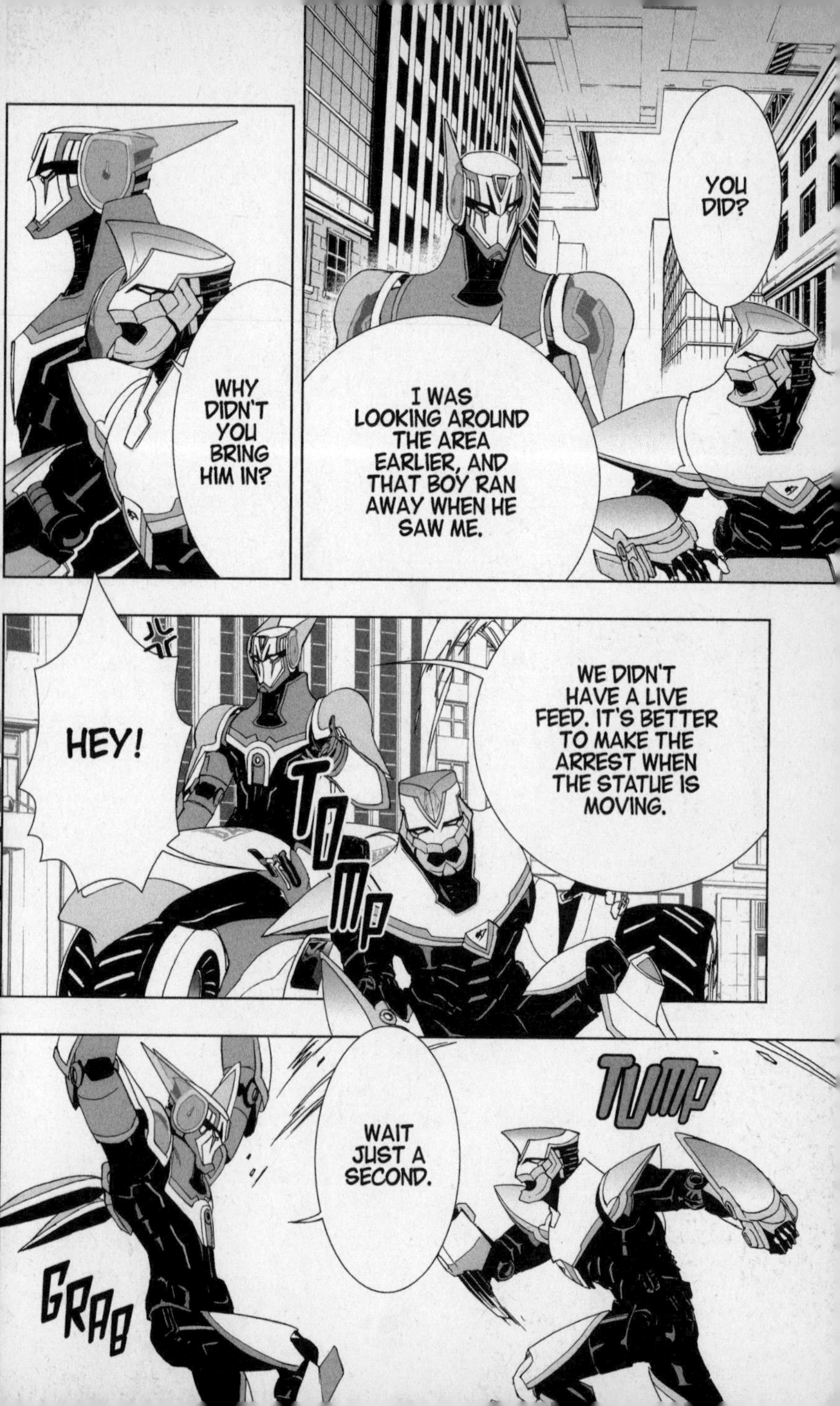
YOU DID?
I WAS LOOKING AROUND THE AREA EARLIER, AND THAT BOY RAN AWAY WHEN HE SAW ME.
WHY DIDN'T YOU BRING HIM IN?
WE DIDN'T HAVE A LIVE FEED. IT'S BETTER TO MAKE THE ARREST WHEN THE STATUE IS MOVING.
TOMP
HEY!
TUMP
WAIT JUST A SECOND.
GRAB

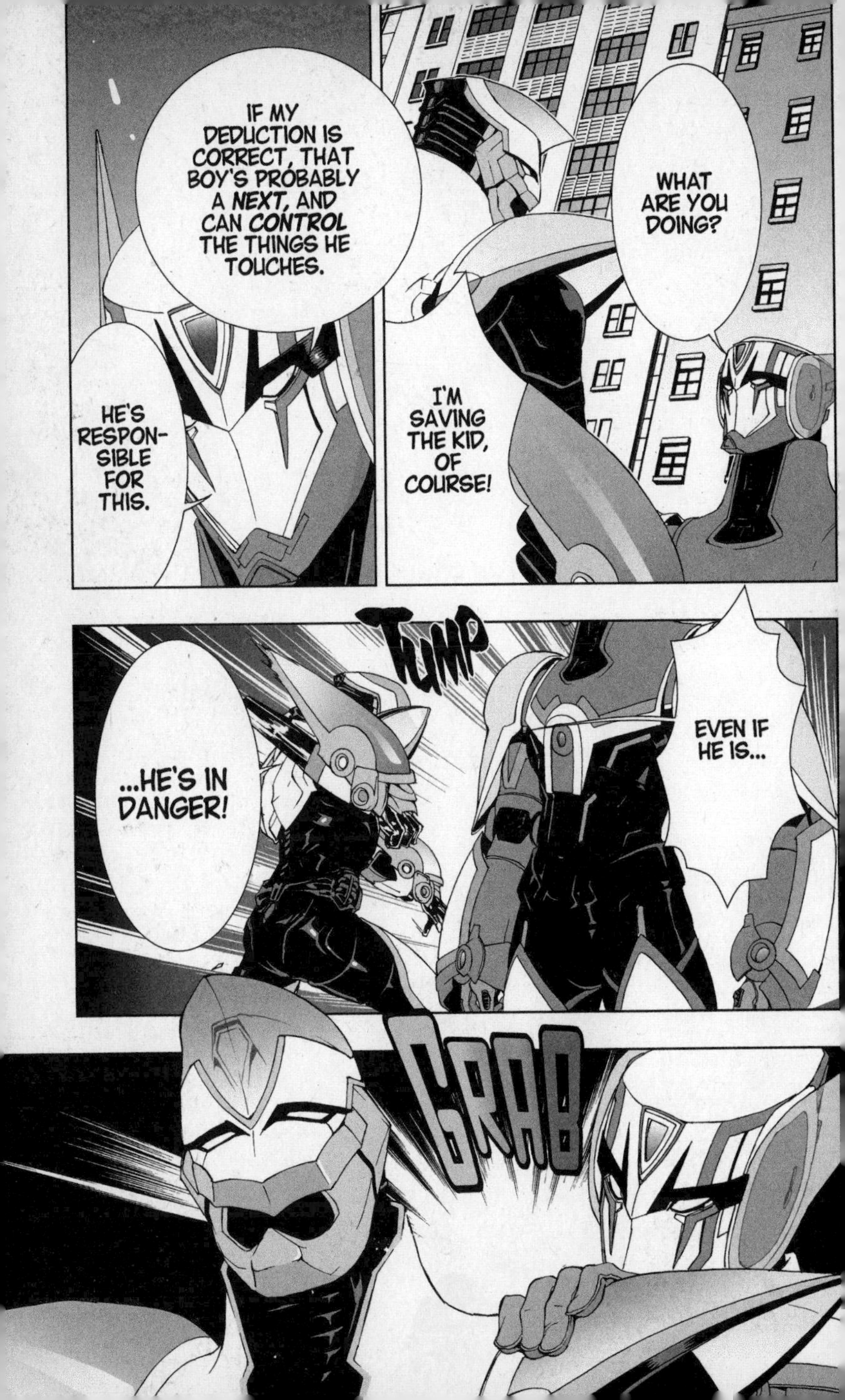
WHAT ARE YOU DOING?
I'M SAVING THE KID, OF COURSE!
IF MY DEDUCTION IS CORRECT, THAT BOY'S PROBABLY A *NEXT*, AND CAN **CONTROL** THE THINGS HE TOUCHES.
HE'S RESPON-SIBLE FOR THIS.
TUMP
EVEN IF HE IS...
...HE'S IN DANGER!
GRAB

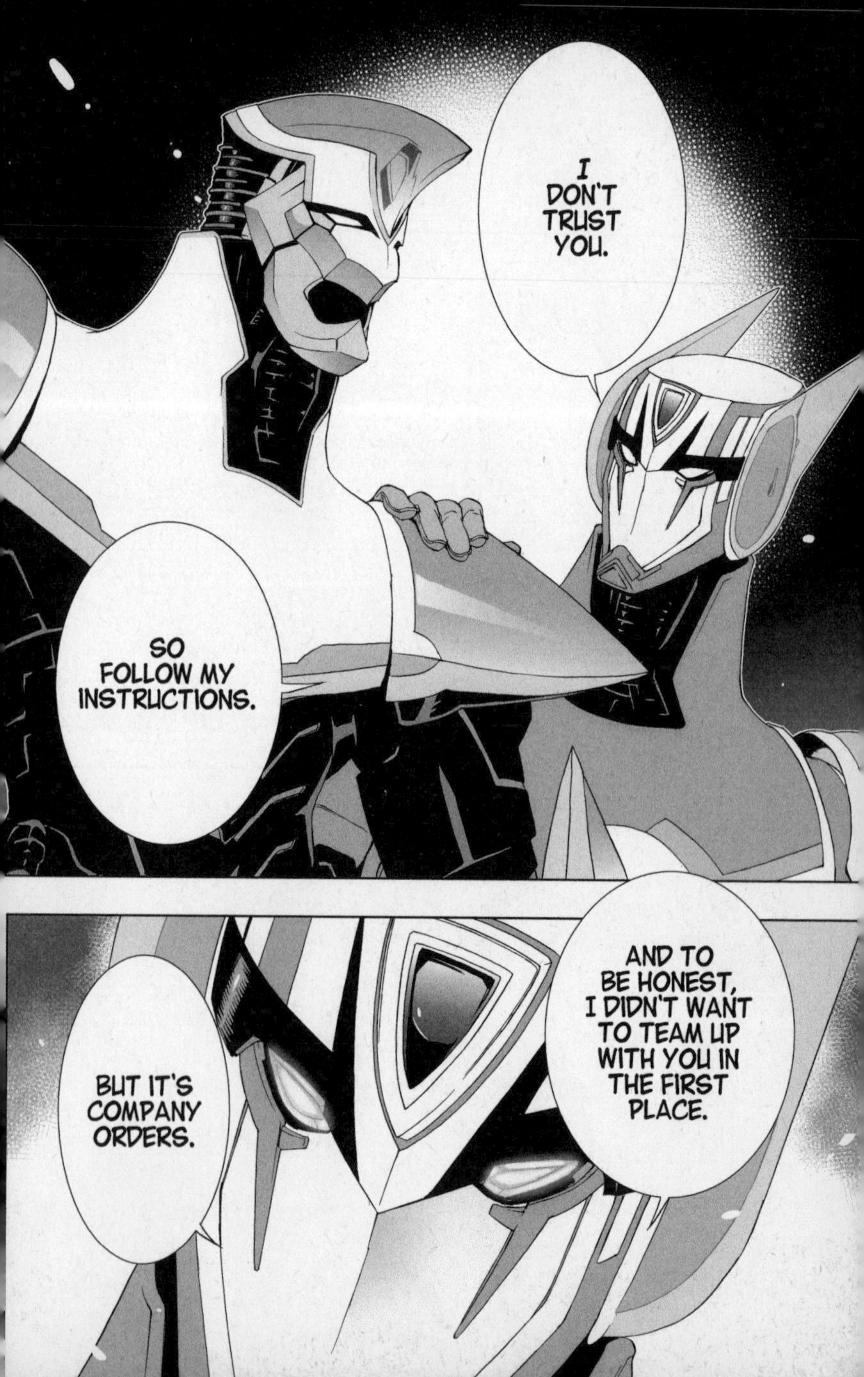
I DON'T TRUST YOU.
SO FOLLOW MY INSTRUCTIONS.
AND TO BE HONEST, I DIDN'T WANT TO TEAM UP WITH YOU IN THE FIRST PLACE.
BUT IT'S COMPANY ORDERS.

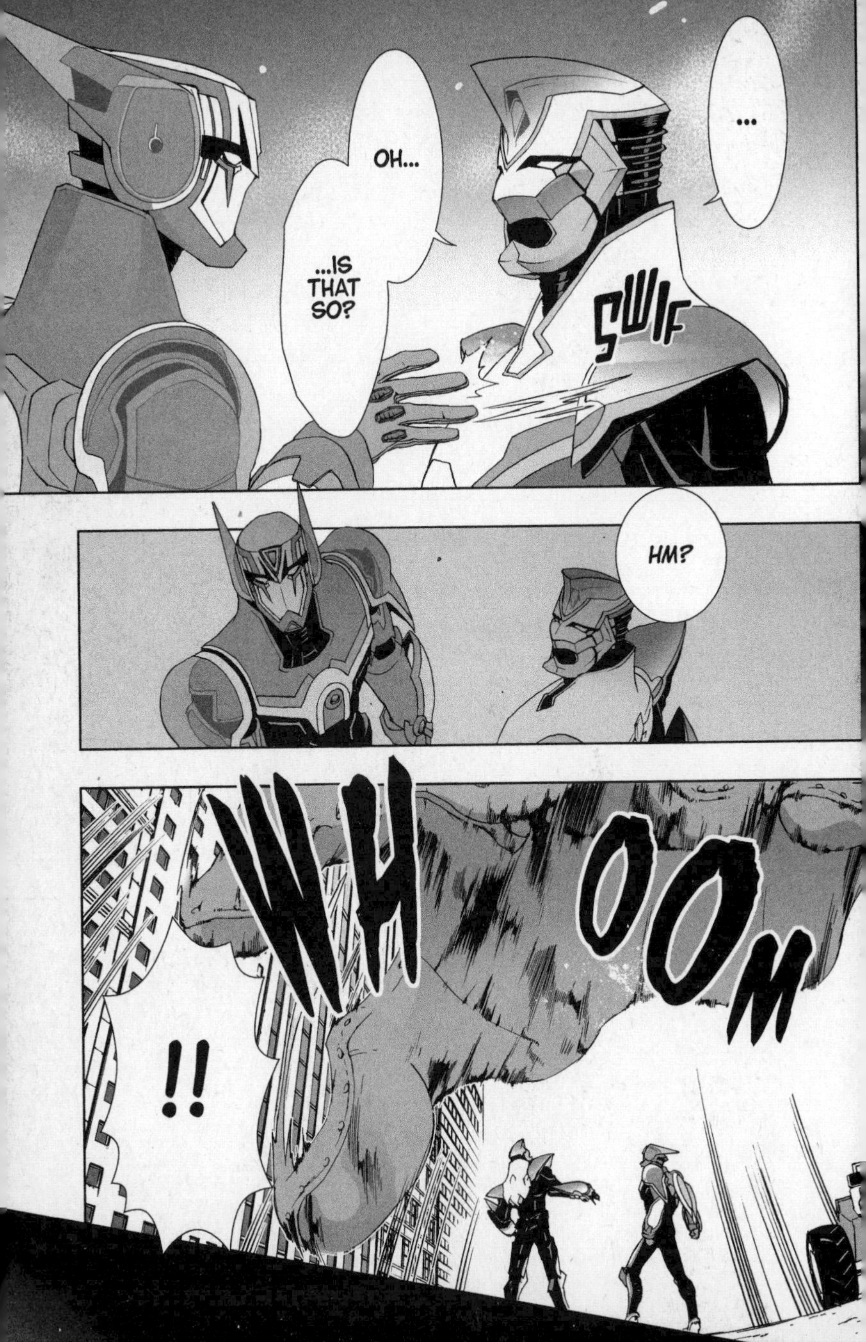
...
OH...
...IS THAT SO?
SWIF
HM?
WHOOOM
!!

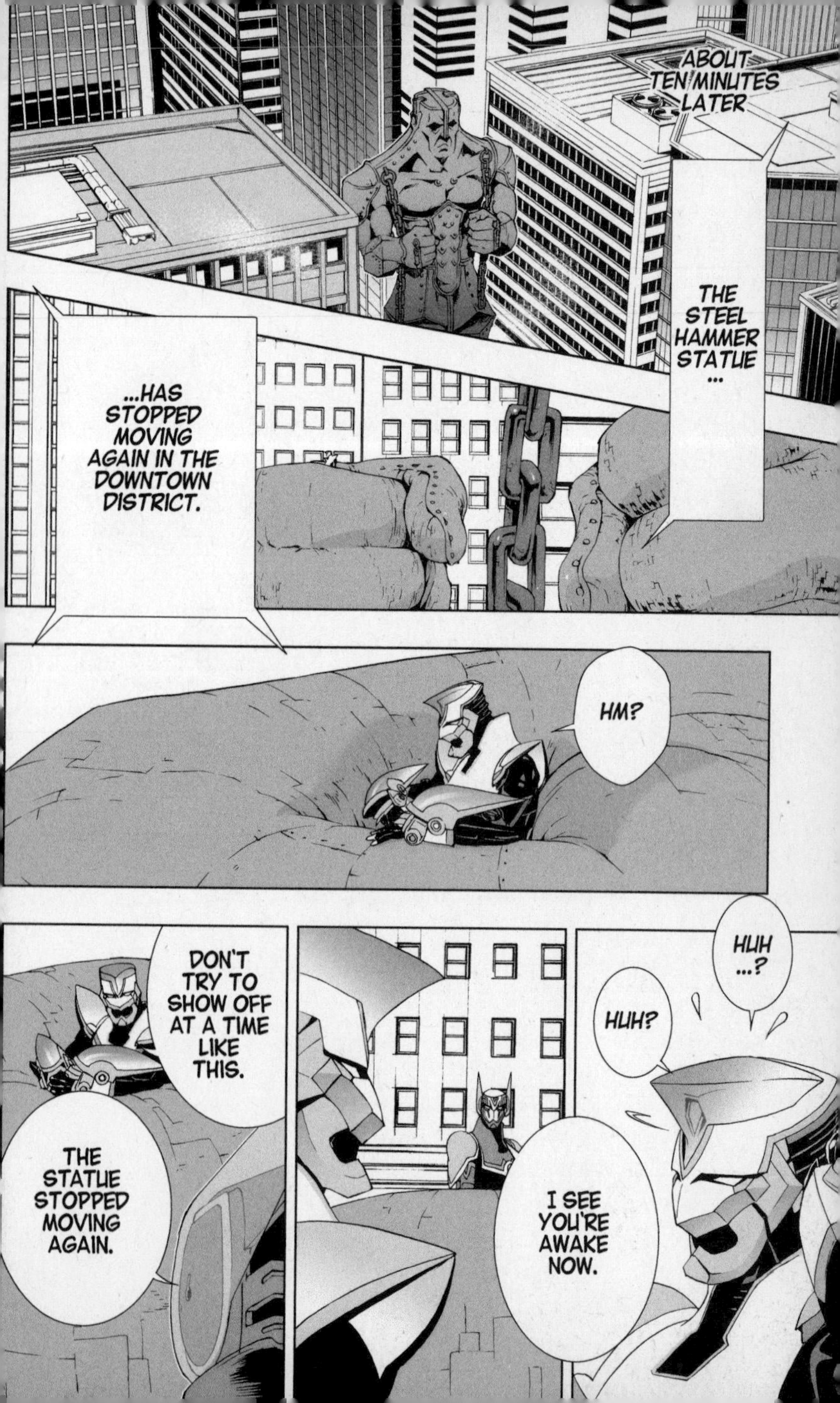
ABOUT TEN MINUTES LATER
THE STEEL HAMMER STATUE ...
...HAS STOPPED MOVING AGAIN IN THE DOWNTOWN DISTRICT.
HM?
HUH ...?
HUH?
I SEE YOU'RE AWAKE NOW.
DON'T TRY TO SHOW OFF AT A TIME LIKE THIS.
THE STATUE STOPPED MOVING AGAIN.

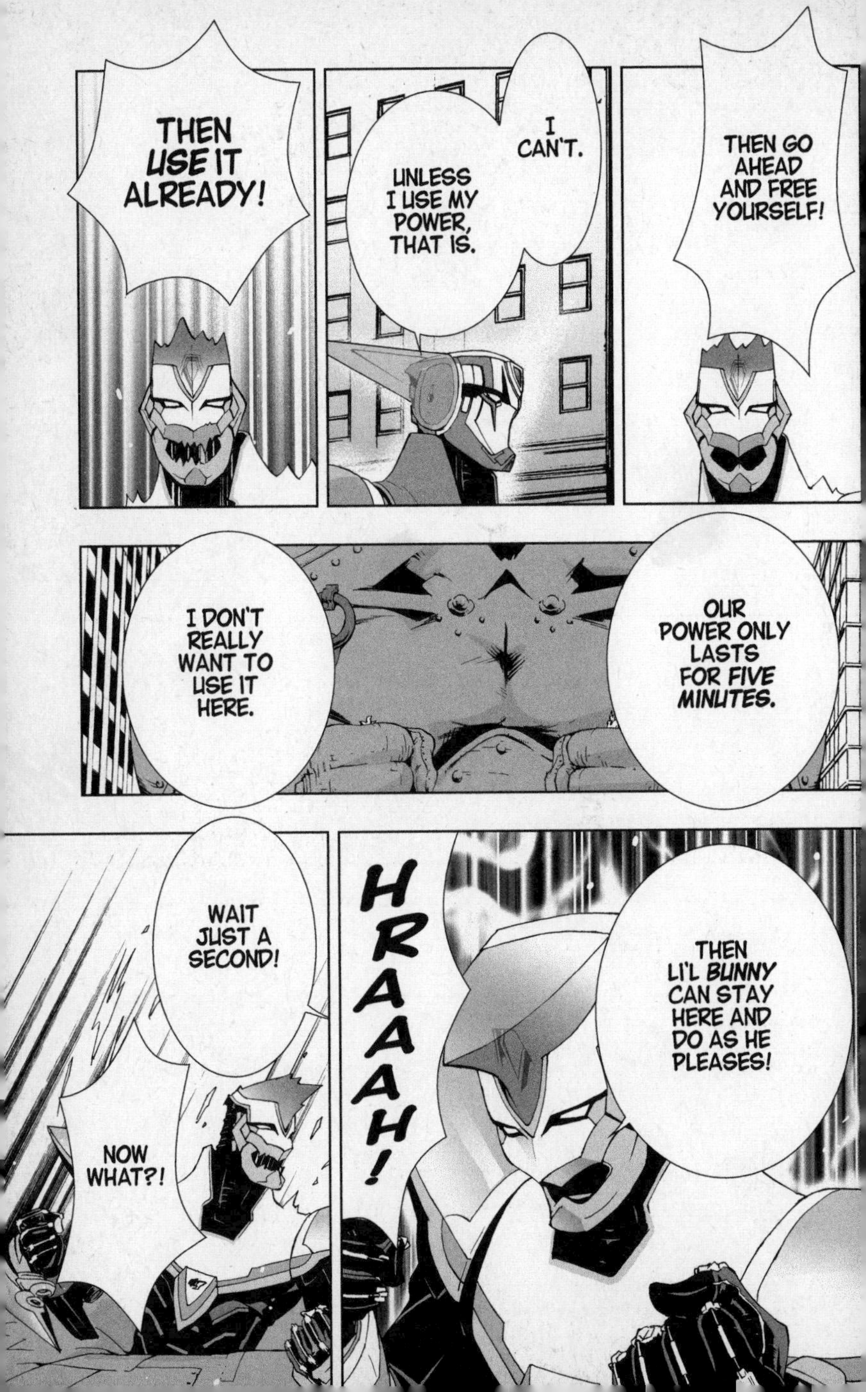
THEN GO AHEAD AND FREE YOURSELF!
I CAN'T.
UNLESS I USE MY POWER, THAT IS.
THEN *USE* IT ALREADY!
OUR POWER ONLY LASTS FOR FIVE MINUTES.
I DON'T REALLY WANT TO USE IT HERE.
THEN LI'L *BUNNY* CAN STAY HERE AND DO AS HE PLEASES!
HRAAAH!
WAIT JUST A SECOND!
NOW WHAT?!

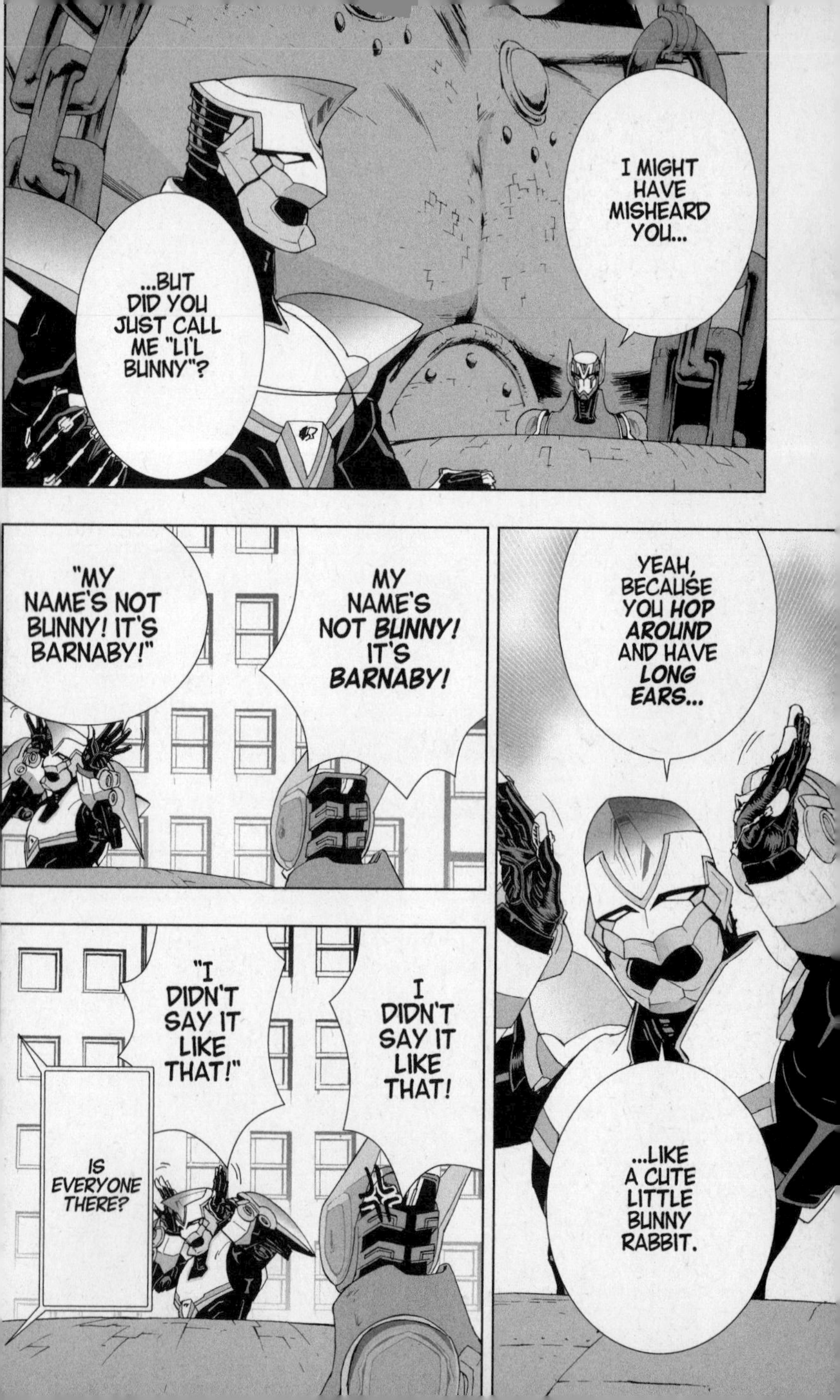
I MIGHT HAVE MISHEARD YOU...
...BUT DID YOU JUST CALL ME "LI'L BUNNY"?
YEAH, BECAUSE YOU HOP AROUND AND HAVE LONG EARS...
...LIKE A CUTE LITTLE BUNNY RABBIT.
MY NAME'S NOT BUNNY! IT'S BARNABY!
"MY NAME'S NOT BUNNY! IT'S BARNABY!"
I DIDN'T SAY IT LIKE THAT!
"I DIDN'T SAY IT LIKE THAT!"
IS EVERYONE THERE?

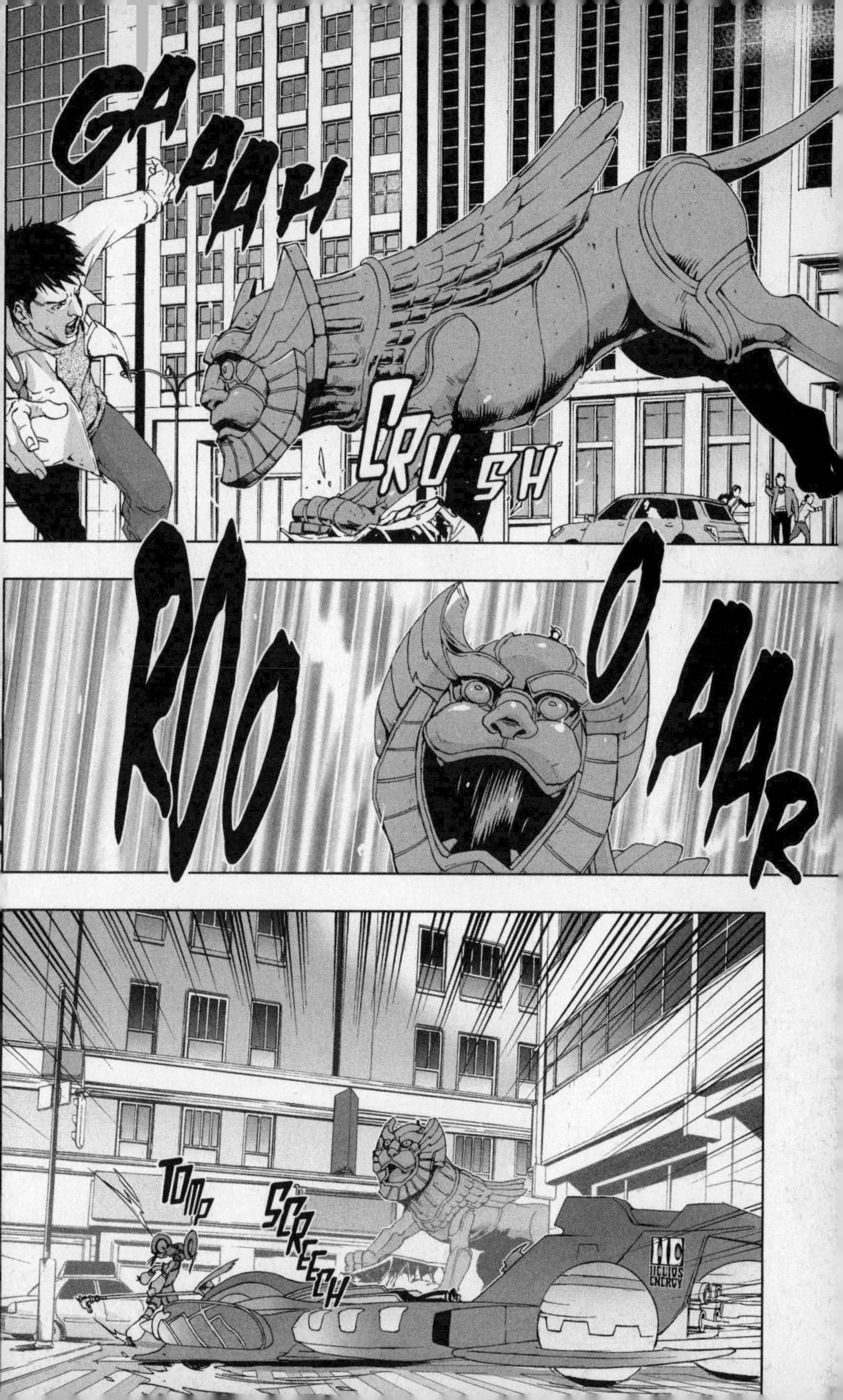
GAAAH
CRUSH
ROOOAAR
HELIOS ENERGY
SCREECH
TOMP

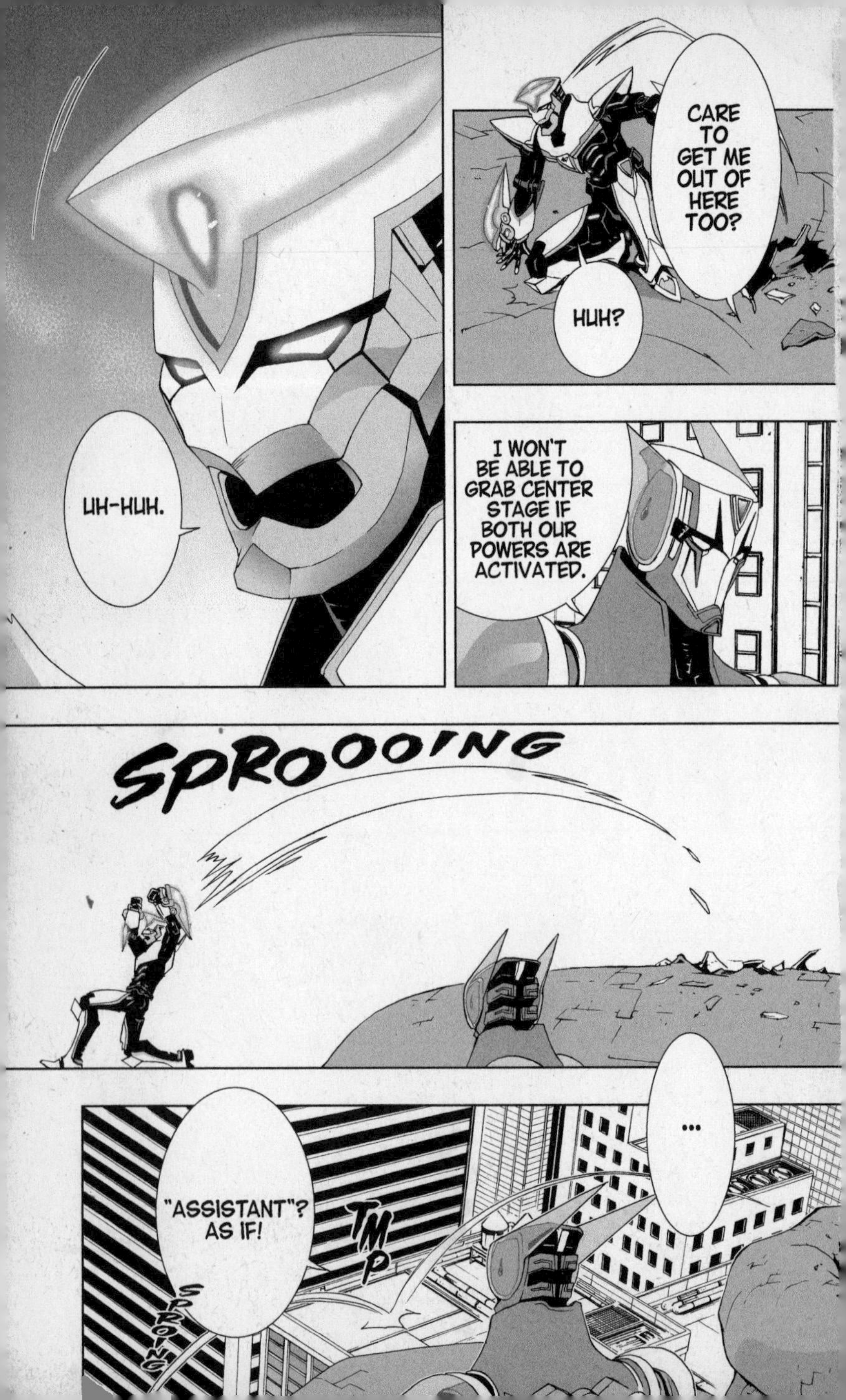
CARE TO GET ME OUT OF HERE TOO?
HUH?
I WON'T BE ABLE TO GRAB CENTER STAGE IF BOTH OUR POWERS ARE ACTIVATED.
UH-HUH.
SPROOOING
...
TMP
"ASSISTANT"? AS IF!
SPROING

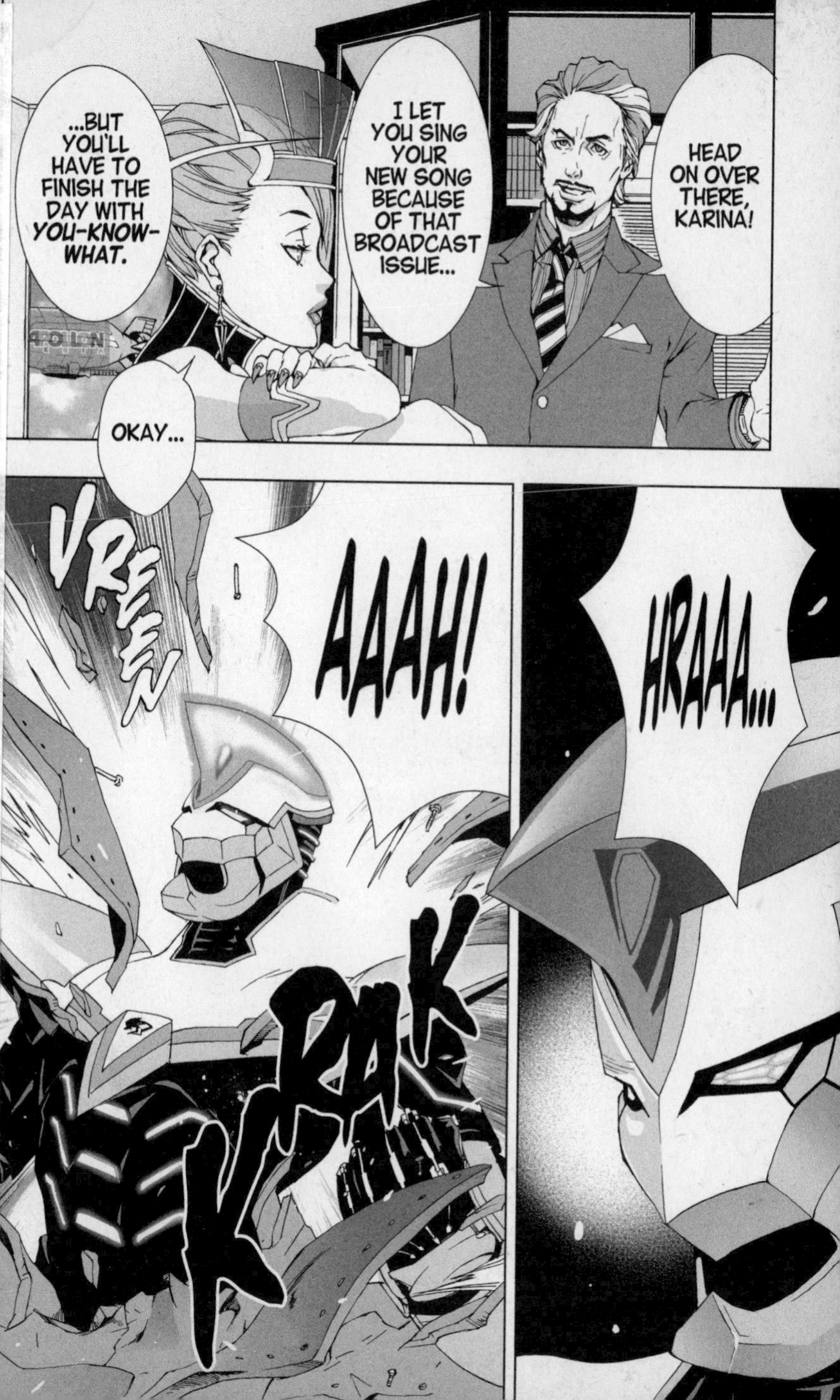
HEAD ON OVER THERE, KARINA!
I LET YOU SING YOUR NEW SONG BECAUSE OF THAT BROADCAST ISSUE...
...BUT YOU'LL HAVE TO FINISH THE DAY WITH *YOU-KNOW-WHAT.*
OKAY...
HRAAA...
AAAH!
VREEEN
KRAK

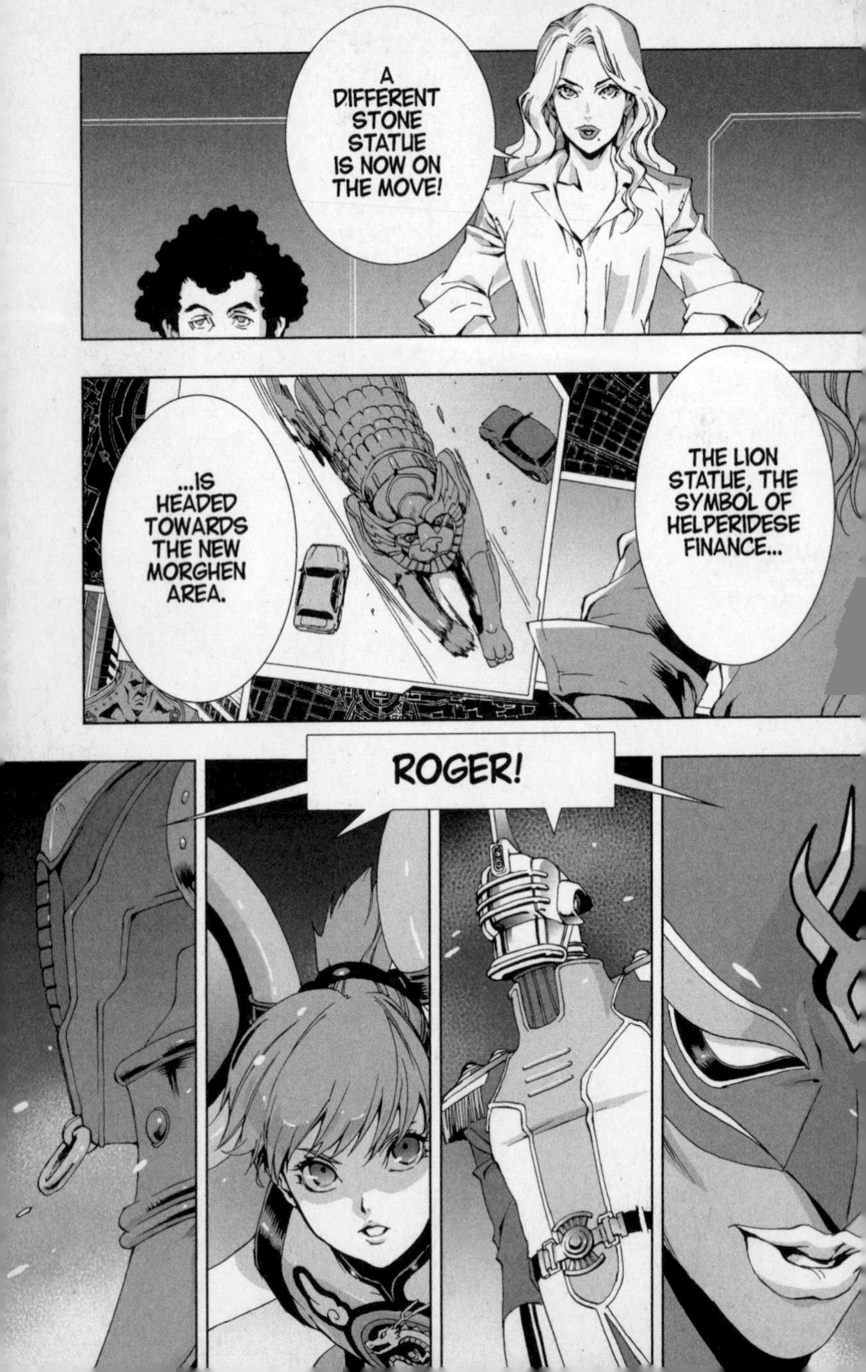
A DIFFERENT STONE STATUE IS NOW ON THE MOVE!
THE LION STATUE, THE SYMBOL OF HELPERIDESE FINANCE...
...IS HEADED TOWARDS THE NEW MORGHEN AREA.
ROGER!

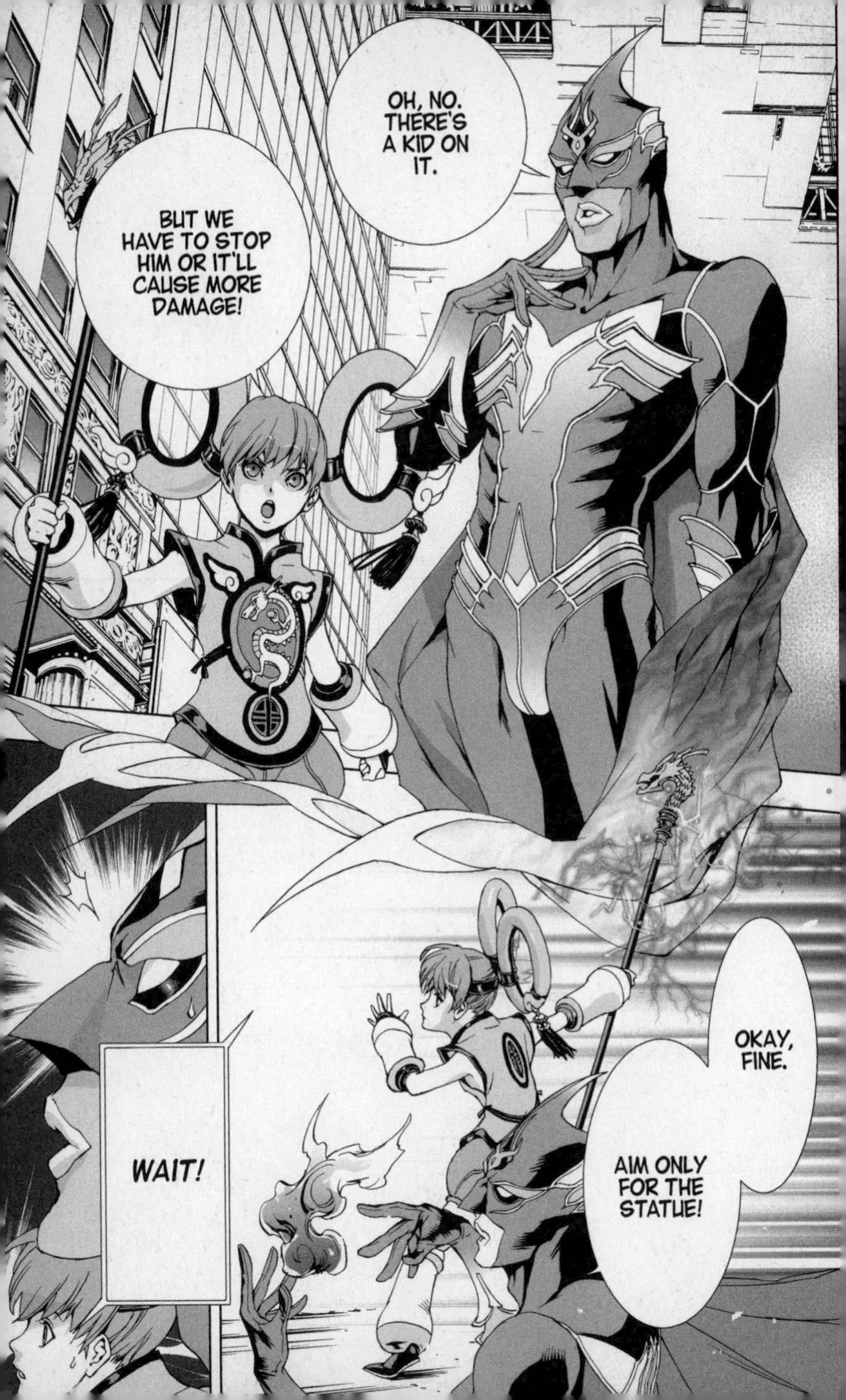
OH, NO. THERE'S A KID ON IT.
BUT WE HAVE TO STOP HIM OR IT'LL CAUSE MORE DAMAGE!
OKAY, FINE.
AIM ONLY FOR THE STATUE!
WAIT!

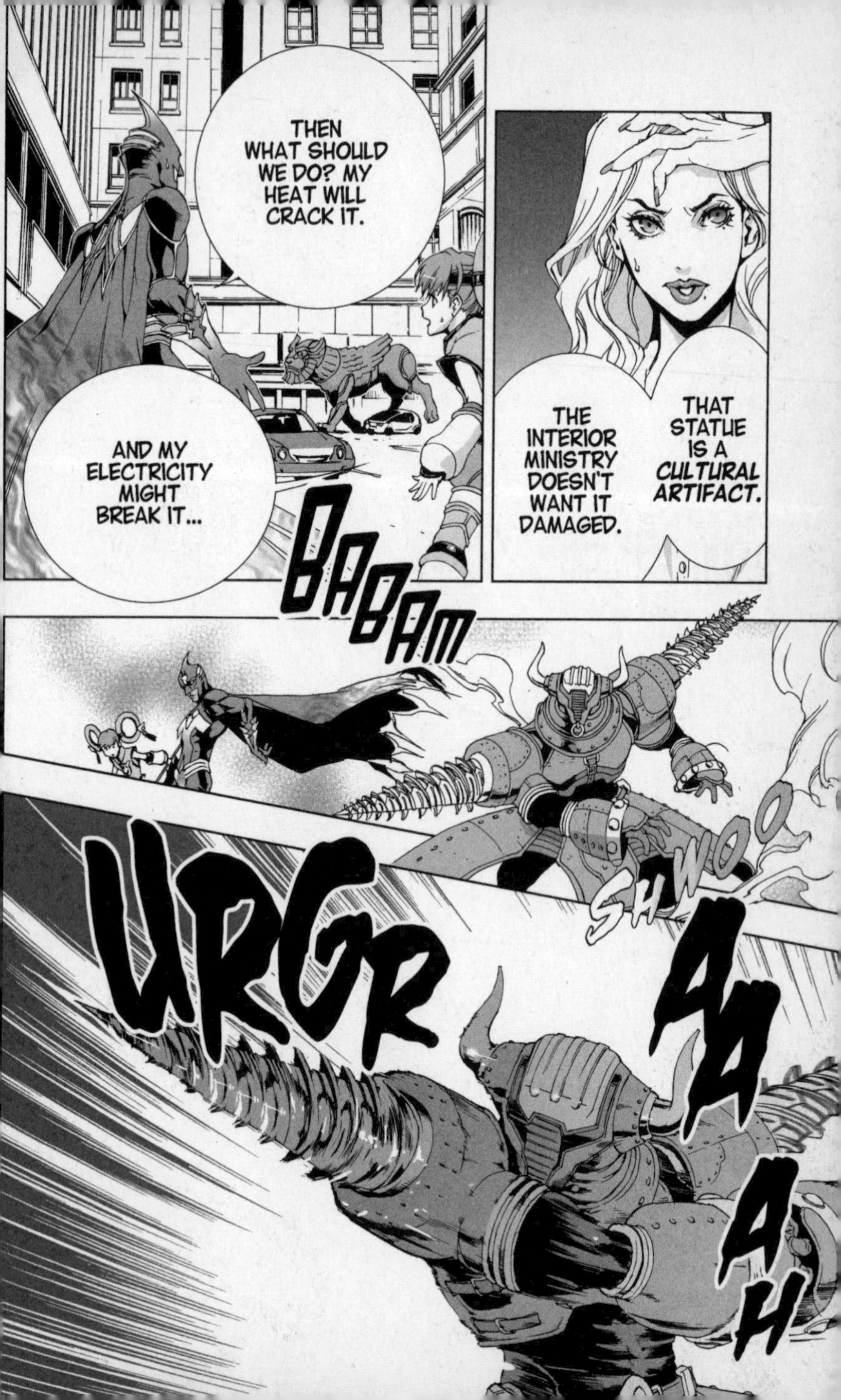
THAT STATUE IS A CULTURAL ARTIFACT.
THE INTERIOR MINISTRY DOESN'T WANT IT DAMAGED.
THEN WHAT SHOULD WE DO? MY HEAT WILL CRACK IT.
AND MY ELECTRICITY MIGHT BREAK IT...
BABAM
SHWOOO
URGRAAAH

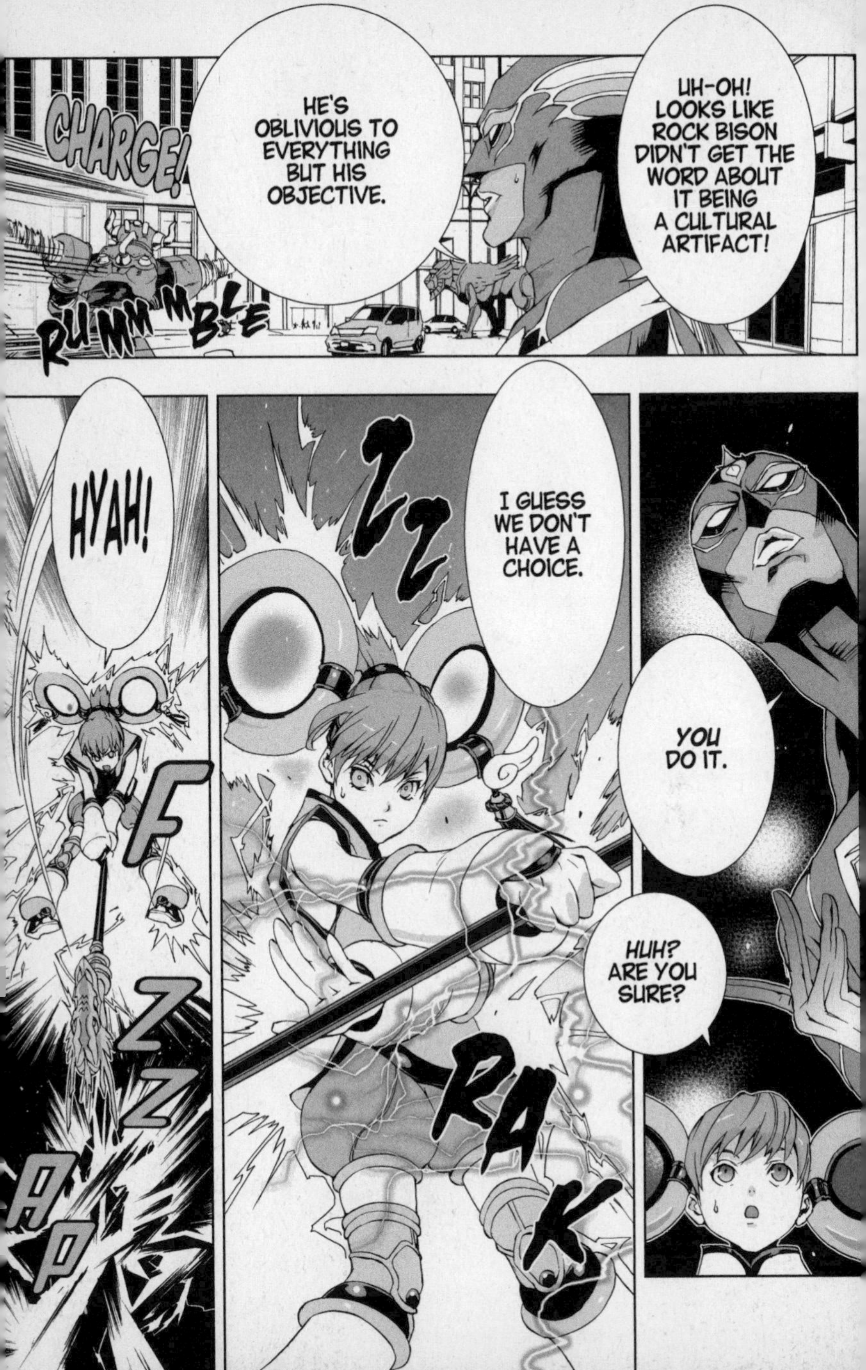
UH-OH! LOOKS LIKE ROCK BISON DIDN'T GET THE WORD ABOUT IT BEING A CULTURAL ARTIFACT!
HE'S OBLIVIOUS TO EVERYTHING BUT HIS OBJECTIVE.
CHARGE!
RUMMMBLE
YOU DO IT.
HUH? ARE YOU SURE?
I GUESS WE DON'T HAVE A CHOICE.
ZZ
RAK
HYAH!
FZZAP

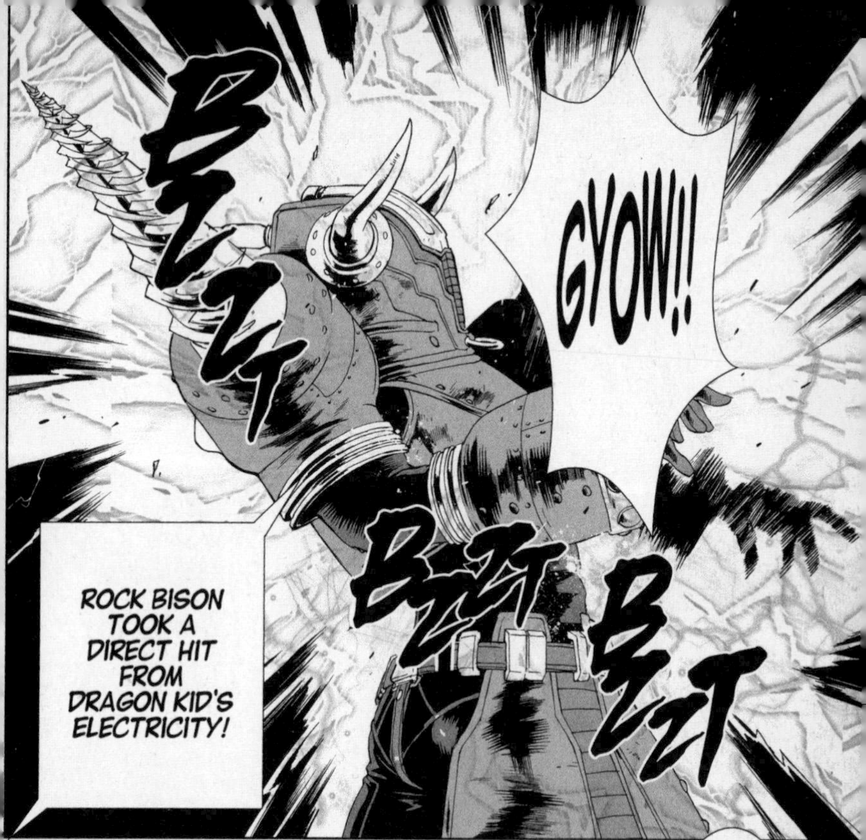
GYOW!!
BZZZT
BZZT
BZZT
ROCK BISON TOOK A DIRECT HIT FROM DRAGON KID'S ELECTRICITY!

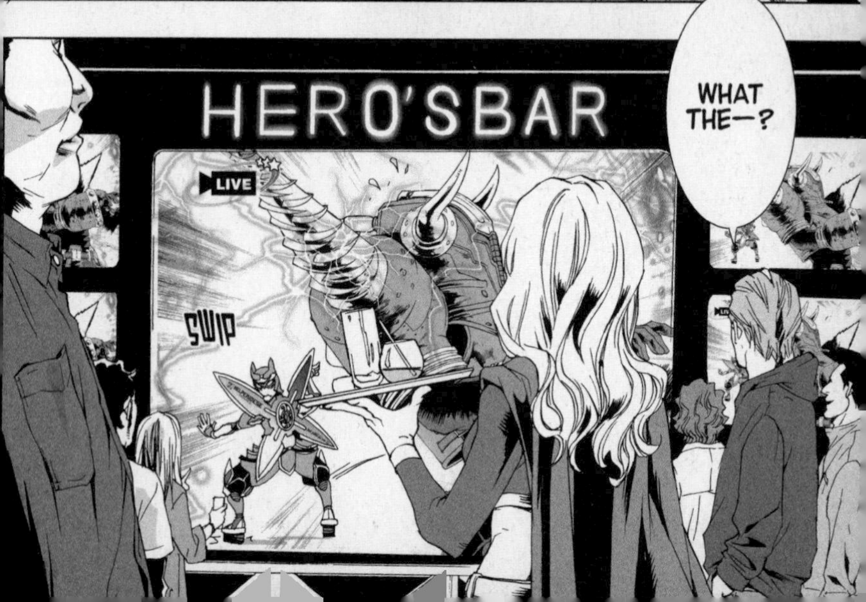
WHAT THE—?
HERO'SBAR
LIVE
SWIP

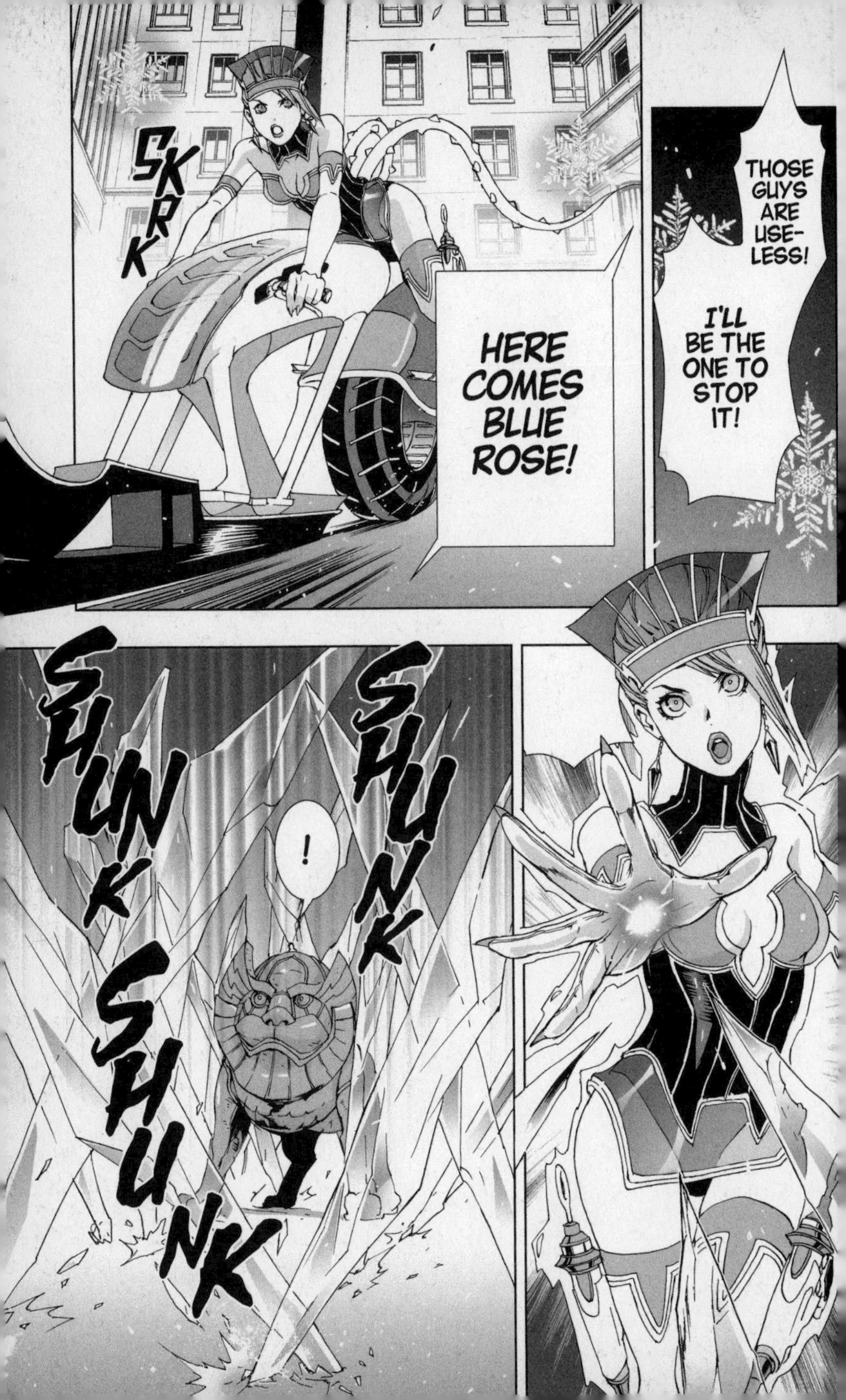
THOSE GUYS ARE USE-LESS!
I'LL BE THE ONE TO STOP IT!
SKRK
HERE COMES BLUE ROSE!
SHUNK
!
SHUNK
SHUNK

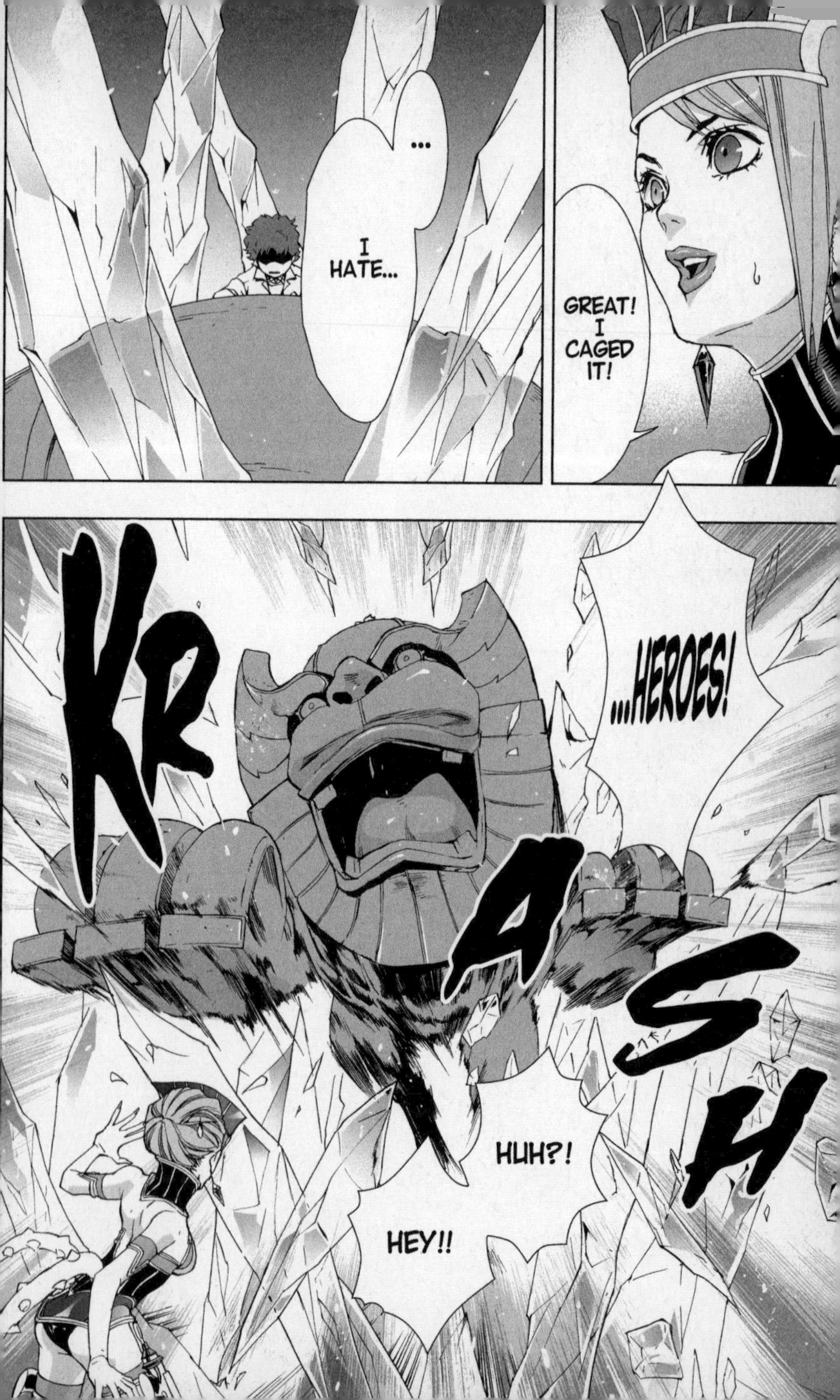
GREAT! I CAGED IT!
...
I HATE...
...HEROES!
KRASH
HUH?!
HEY!!

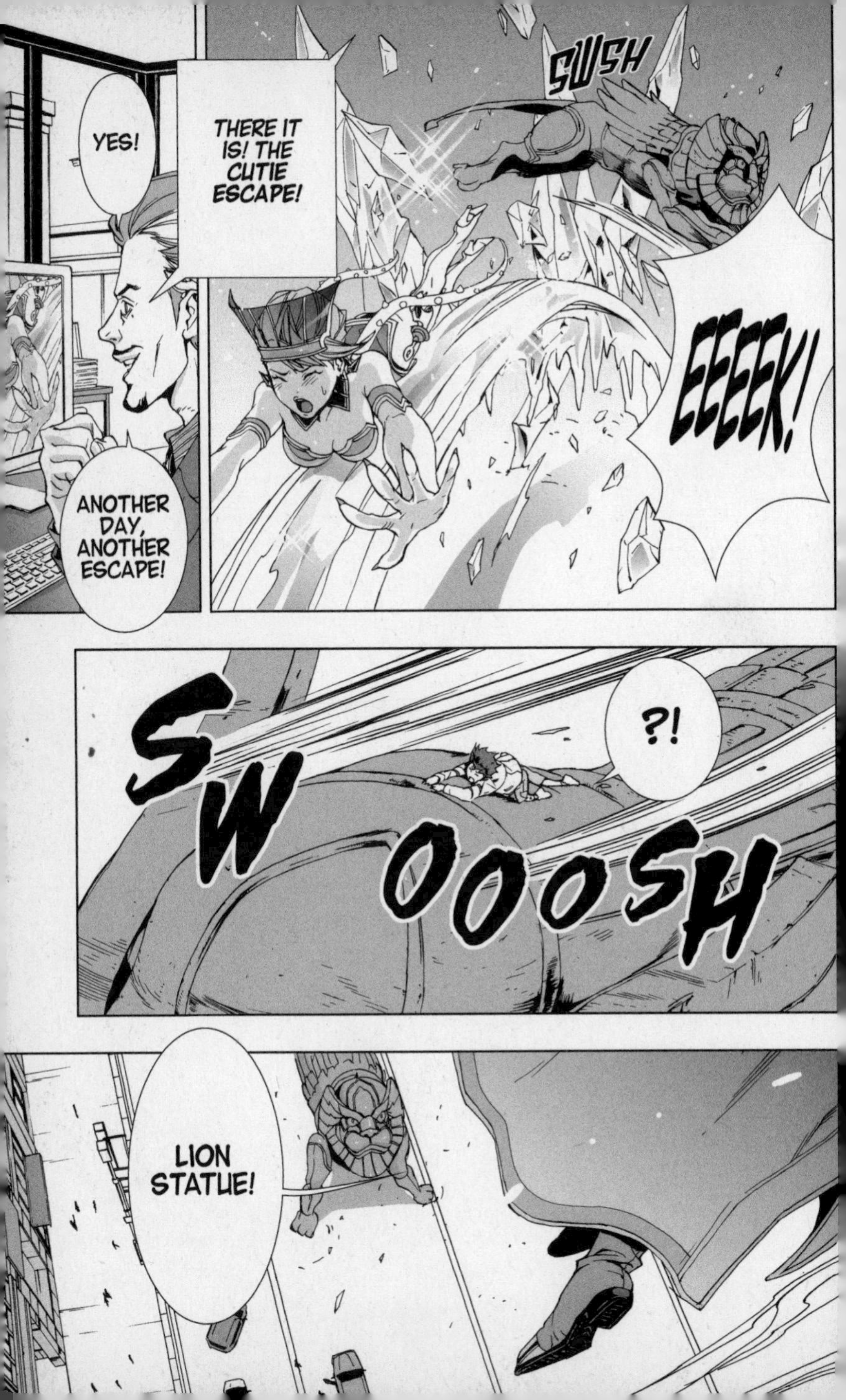
SWSH
EEEEK!
THERE IT IS! THE CUTIE ESCAPE!
YES!
ANOTHER DAY, ANOTHER ESCAPE!
?!
SWOOOSH
LION STATUE!

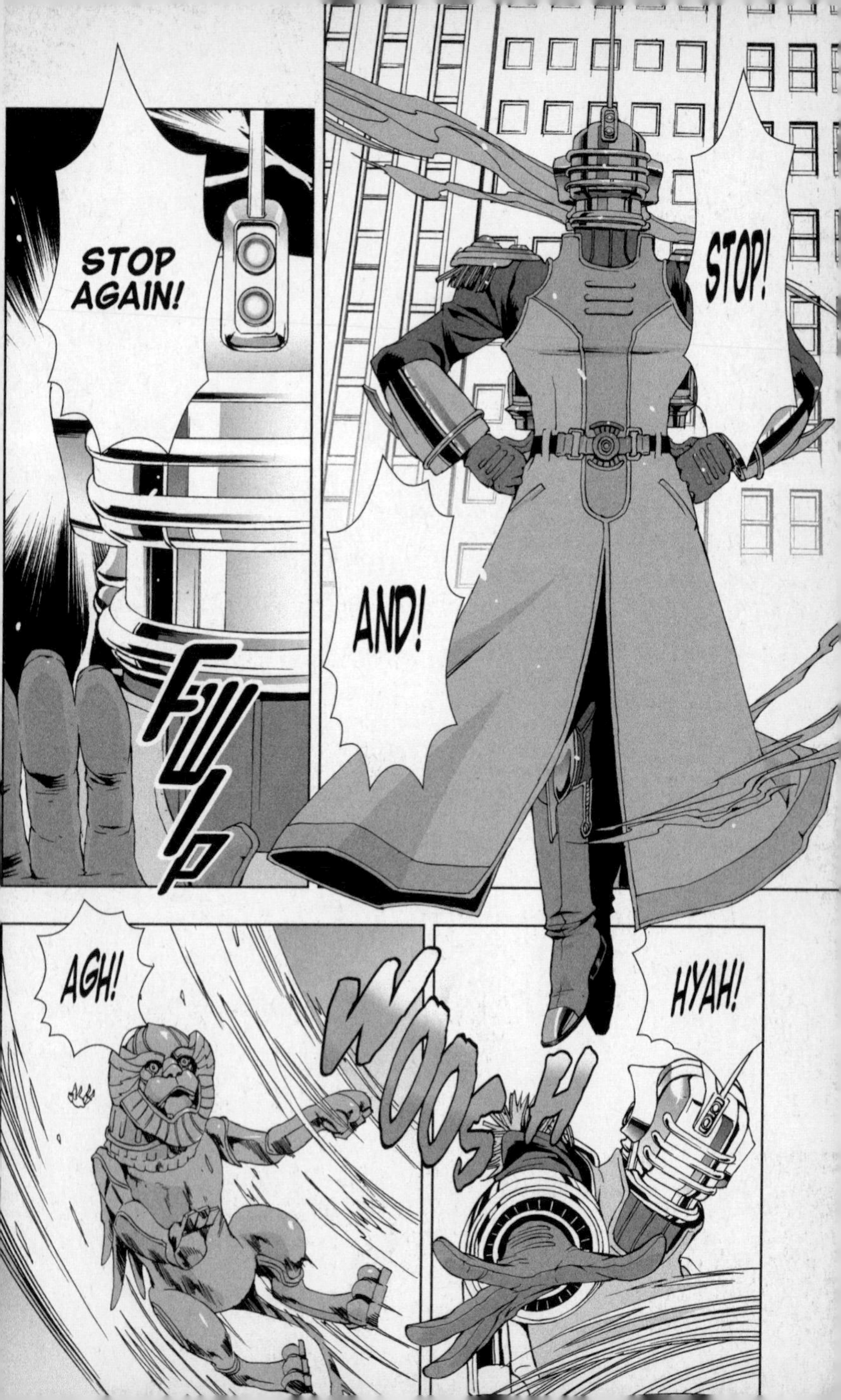
STOP!
AND!
STOP AGAIN!
FWIP
HYAH!
WOOSH
AGH!

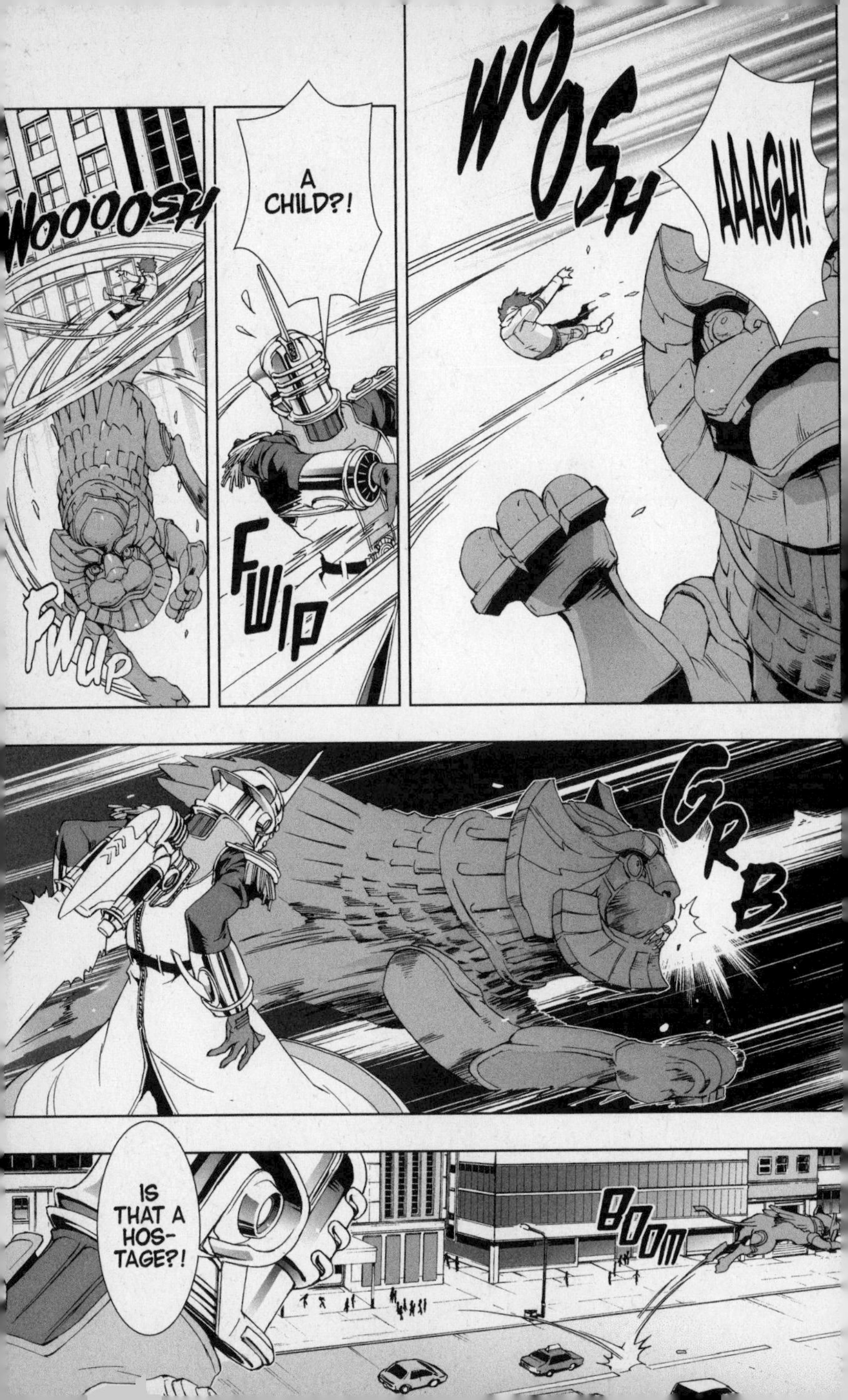
WOOSH
AAAGH!
A CHILD?!
FWIP
WOOOOSH
FWUP
GRB
IS THAT A HOS-TAGE?!
BOOM

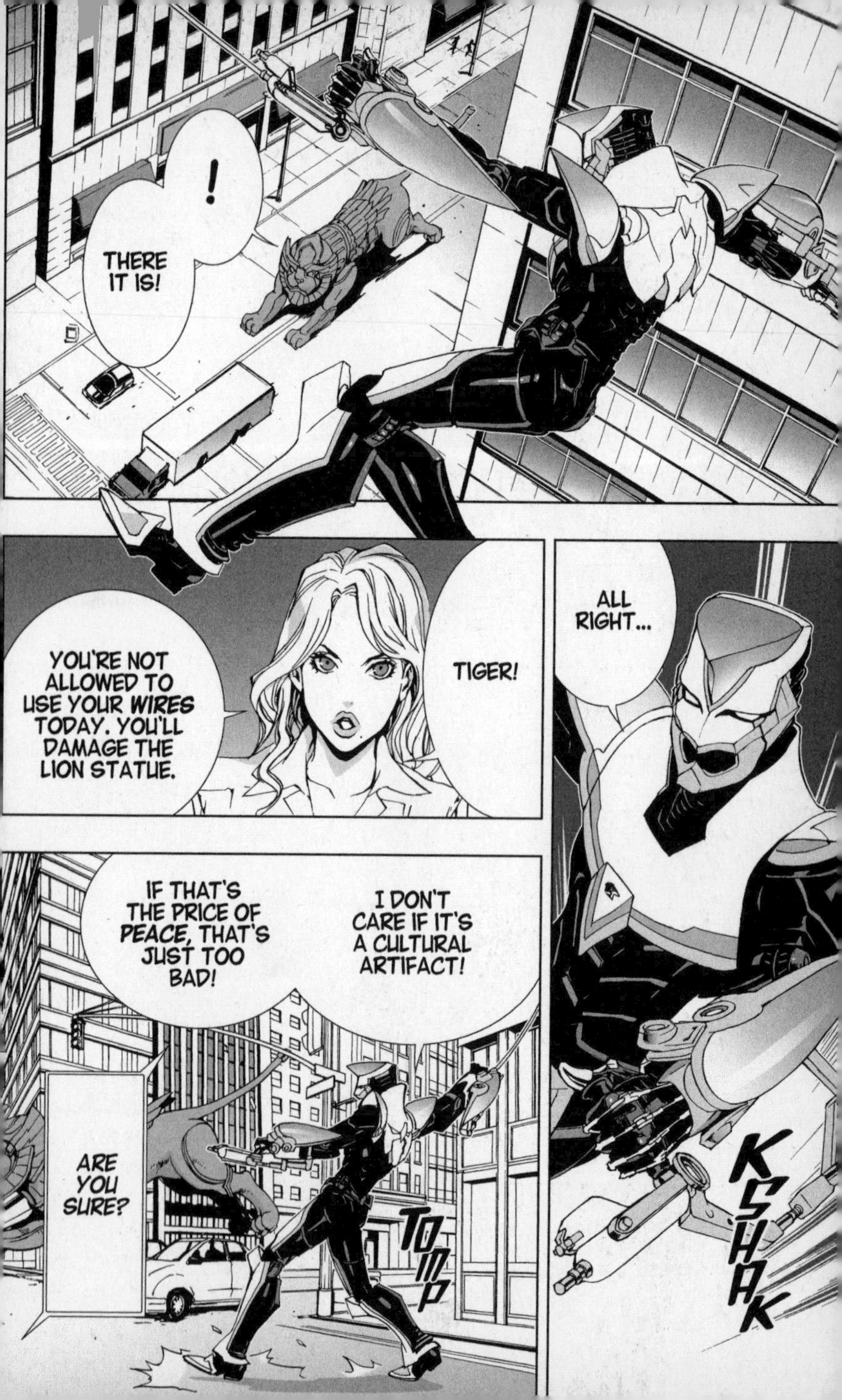
!
THERE IT IS!
ALL RIGHT...
KSHAK
TIGER!
YOU'RE NOT ALLOWED TO USE YOUR WIRES TODAY. YOU'LL DAMAGE THE LION STATUE.
I DON'T CARE IF IT'S A CULTURAL ARTIFACT!
IF THAT'S THE PRICE OF PEACE, THAT'S JUST TOO BAD!
TOMP
ARE YOU SURE?

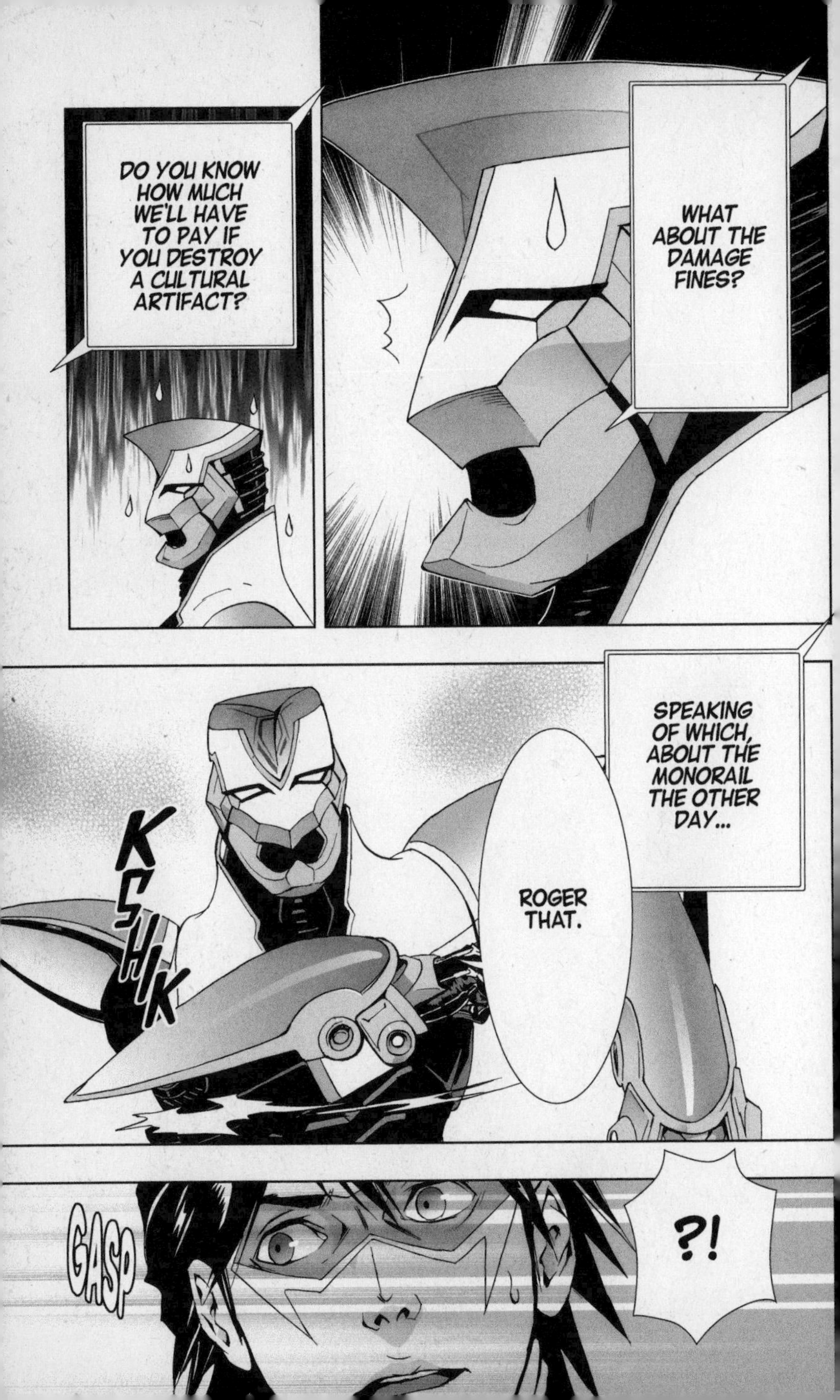
WHAT ABOUT THE DAMAGE FINES?
DO YOU KNOW HOW MUCH WE'LL HAVE TO PAY IF YOU DESTROY A CULTURAL ARTIFACT?
SPEAKING OF WHICH, ABOUT THE MONORAIL THE OTHER DAY...
ROGER THAT.
KSHIK
?!
GASP

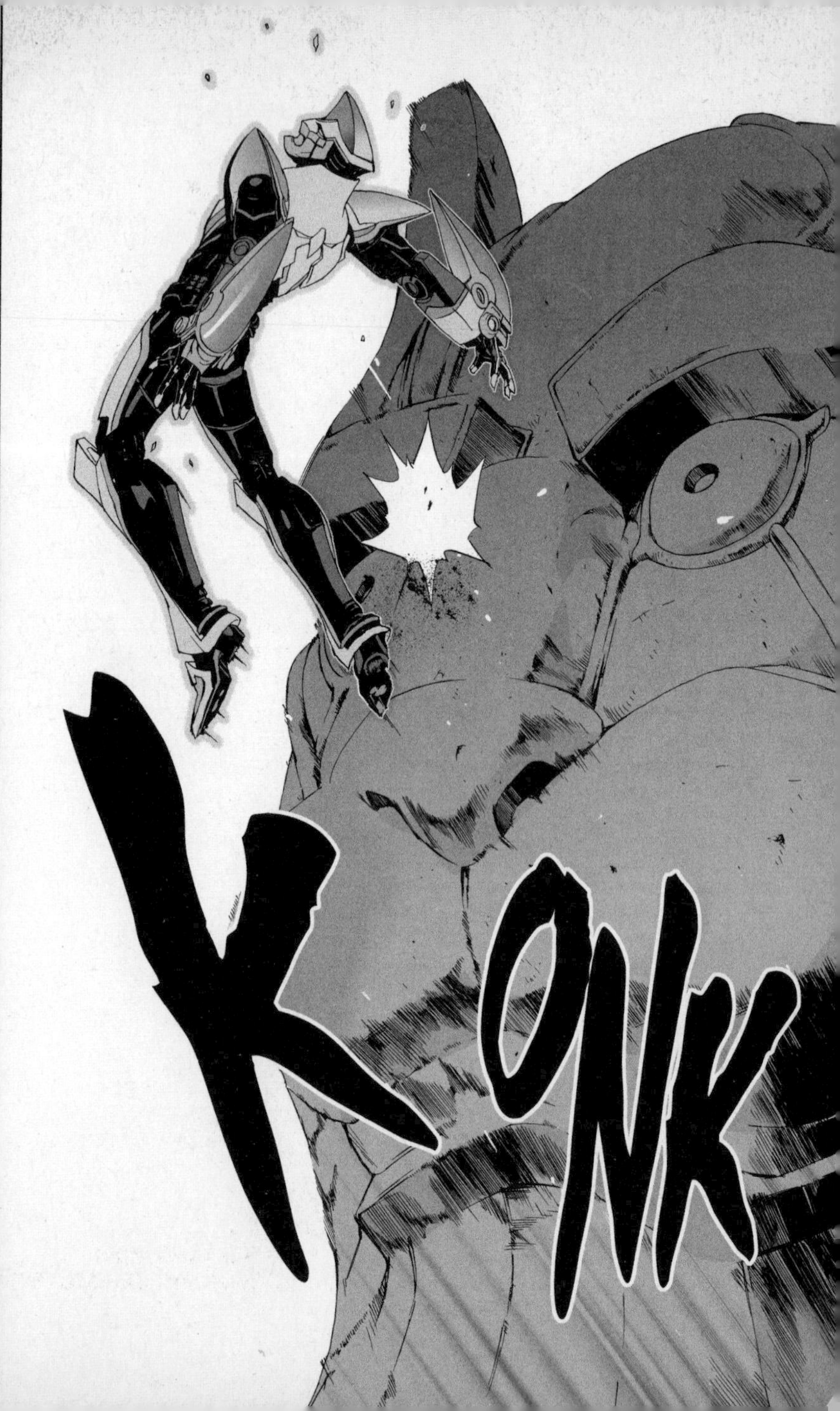
KONK

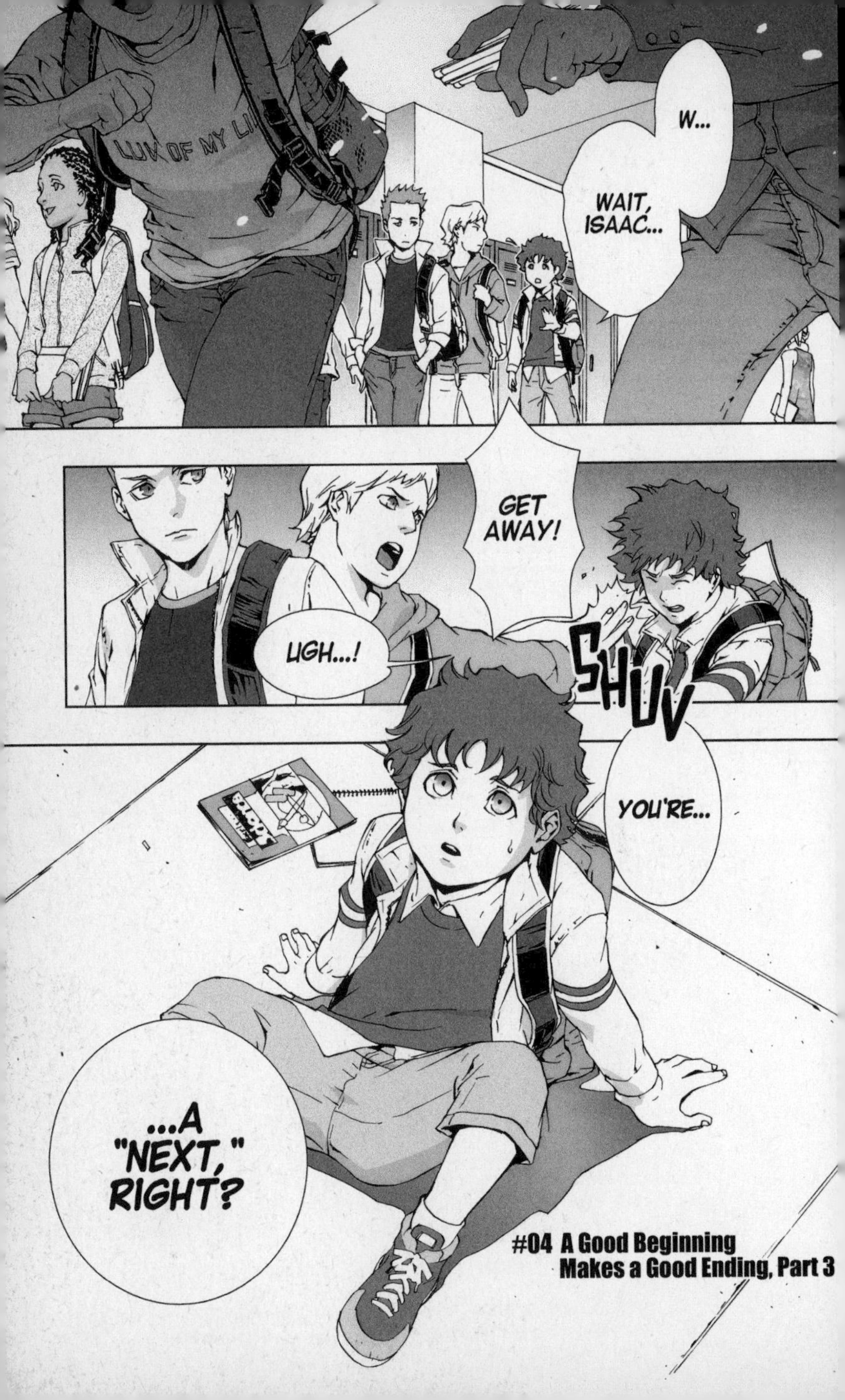
W...
WAIT, ISAAC...
LUV OF MY LI
GET AWAY!
UGH...!
SHUV
YOU'RE...
...A "NEXT," RIGHT?
#04 A Good Beginning Makes a Good Ending, Part 3

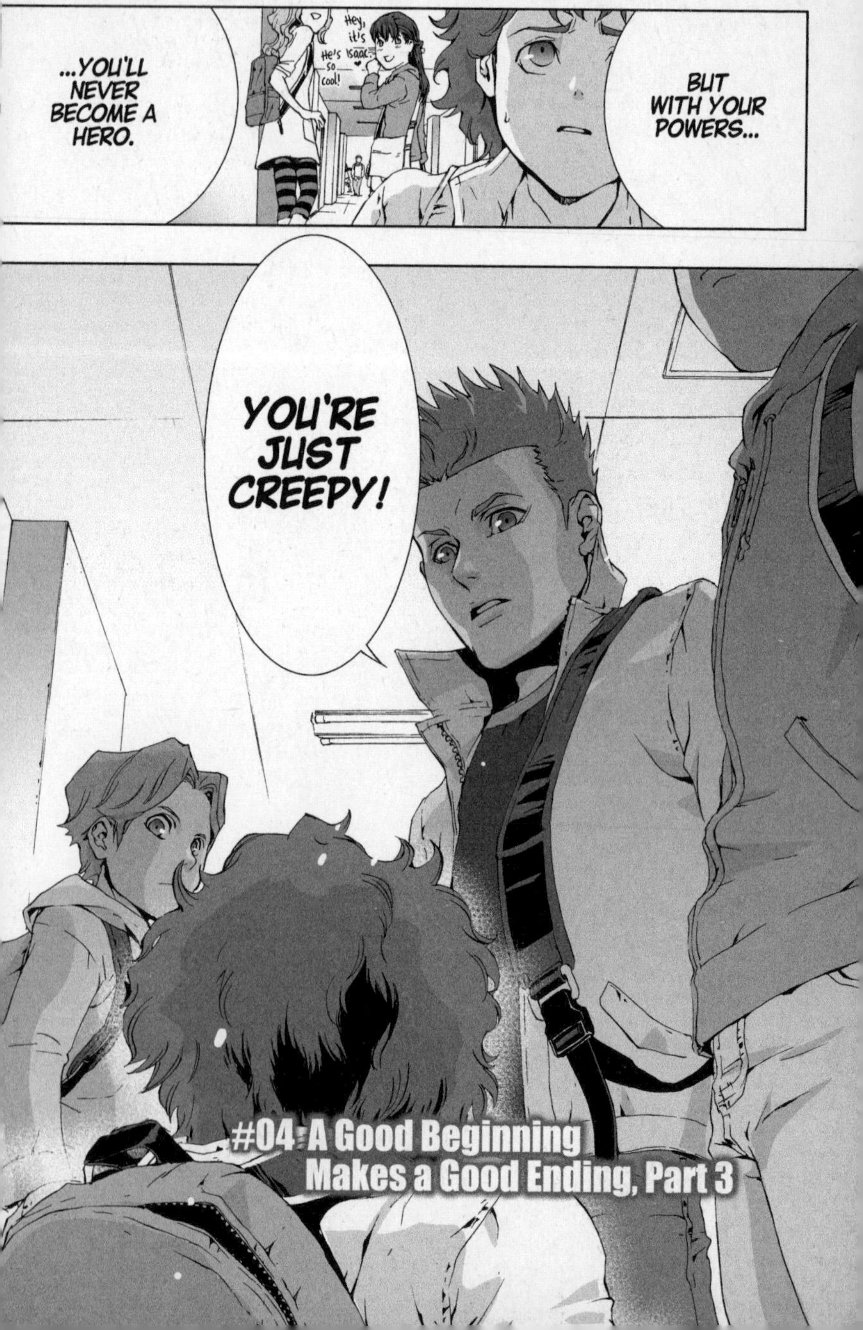
BUT WITH YOUR POWERS...
Hey, it's Isaac
He's so cool!
...YOU'LL NEVER BECOME A HERO.
YOU'RE JUST CREEPY!
#04 A Good Beginning Makes a Good Ending, Part 3

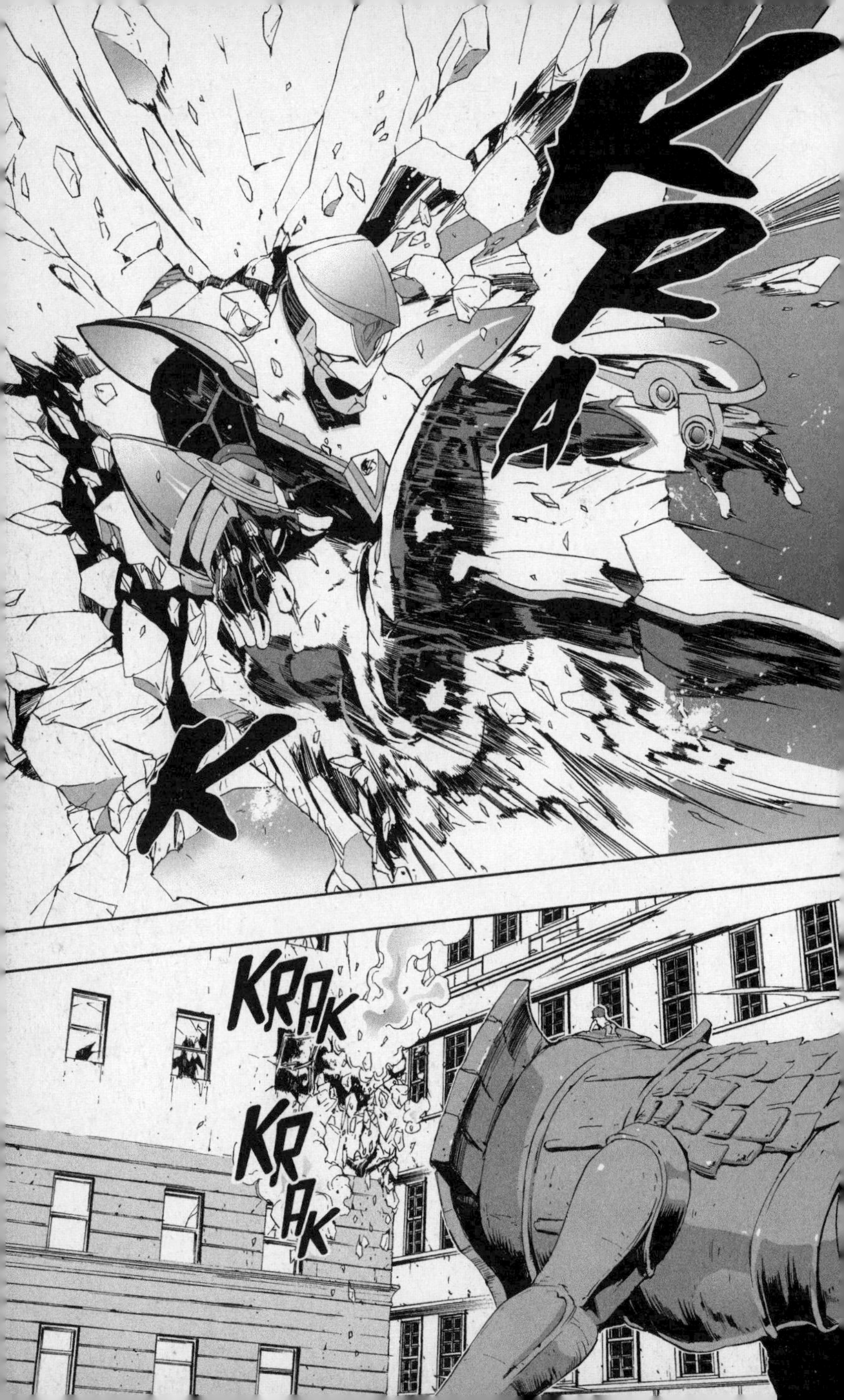
KRAK
KRAK
KRAK

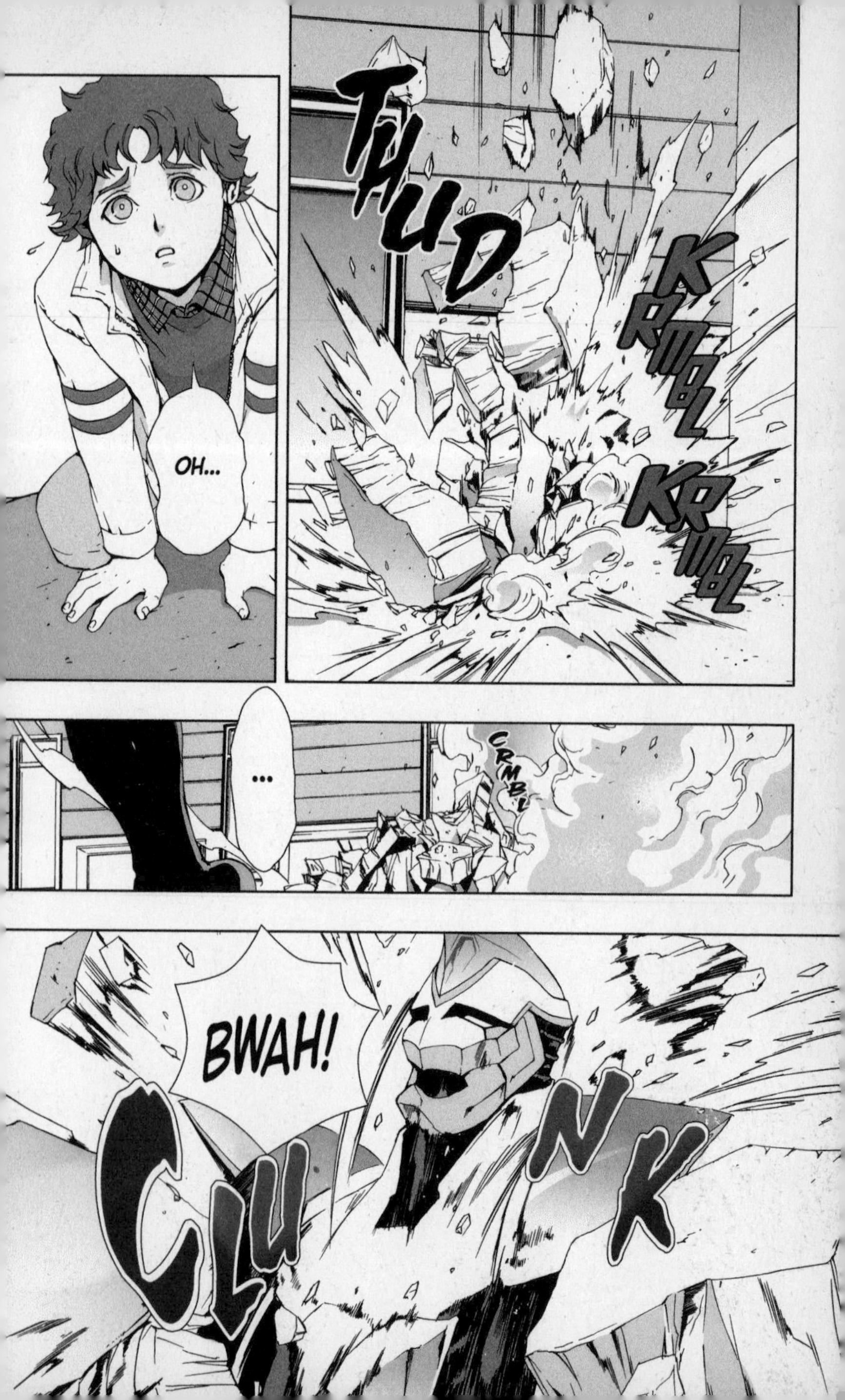
THUD
KRMBL
KRMBL
OH...
CRMBL
...
BWAH!
CLUNK

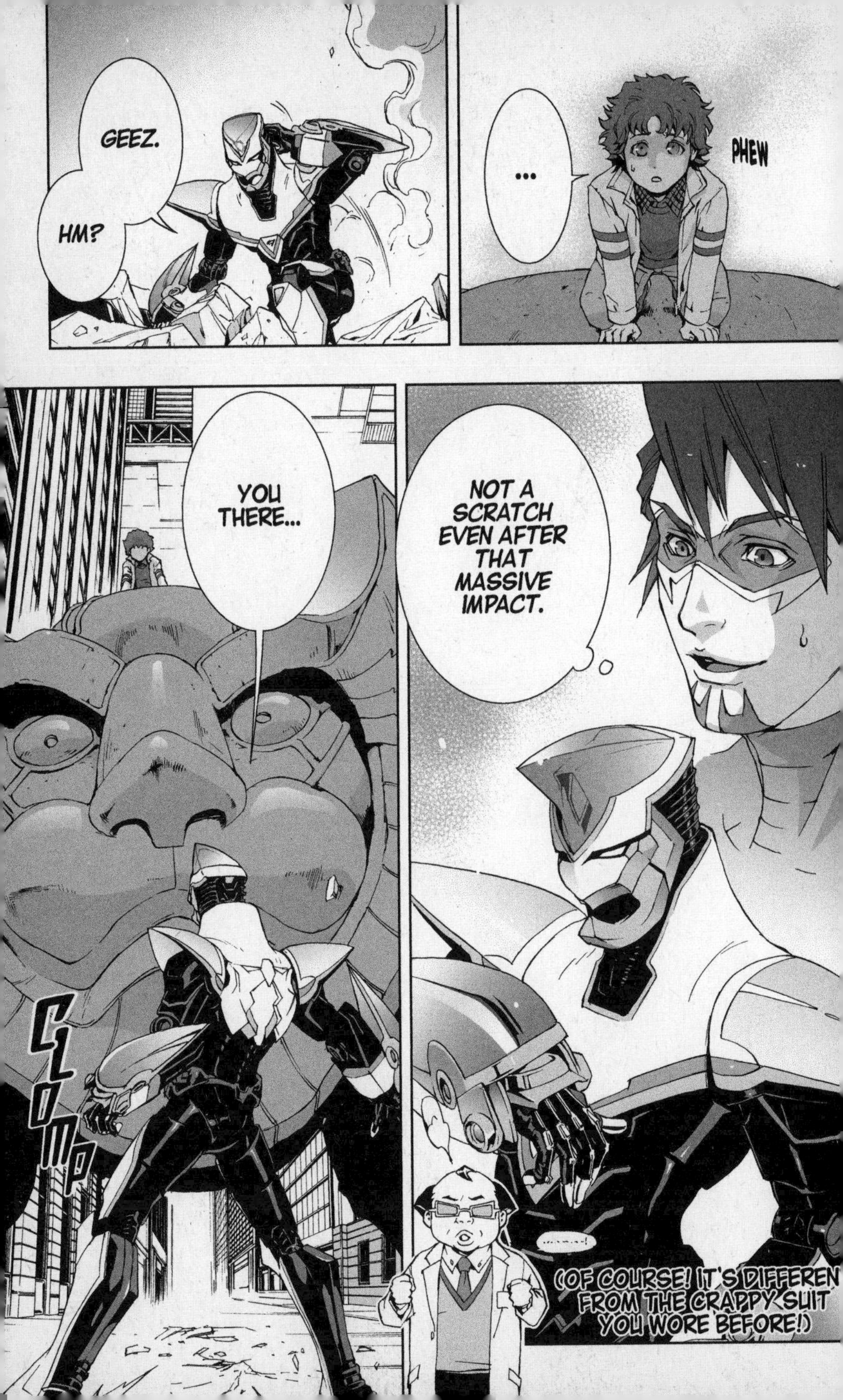
...
PHEW
GEEZ.
HM?
NOT A SCRATCH EVEN AFTER THAT MASSIVE IMPACT.
(OF COURSE! IT'S DIFFEREN
FROM THE CRAPPY SUIT
YOU WORE BEFORE!)
YOU THERE...
CLOMP

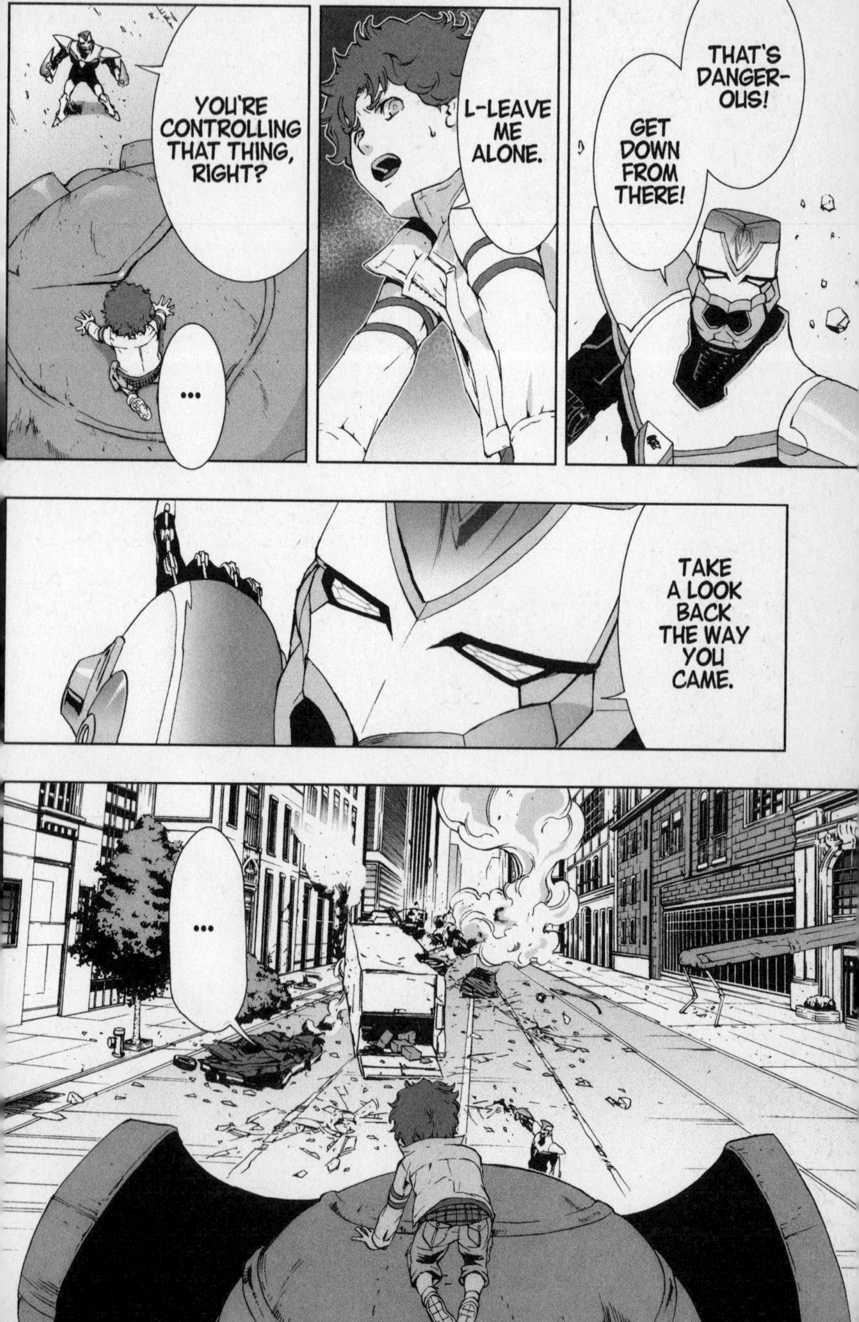
THAT'S DANGER-OUS!
GET DOWN FROM THERE!
L-LEAVE ME ALONE.
YOU'RE CONTROLLING THAT THING, RIGHT?
...
TAKE A LOOK BACK THE WAY YOU CAME.
...

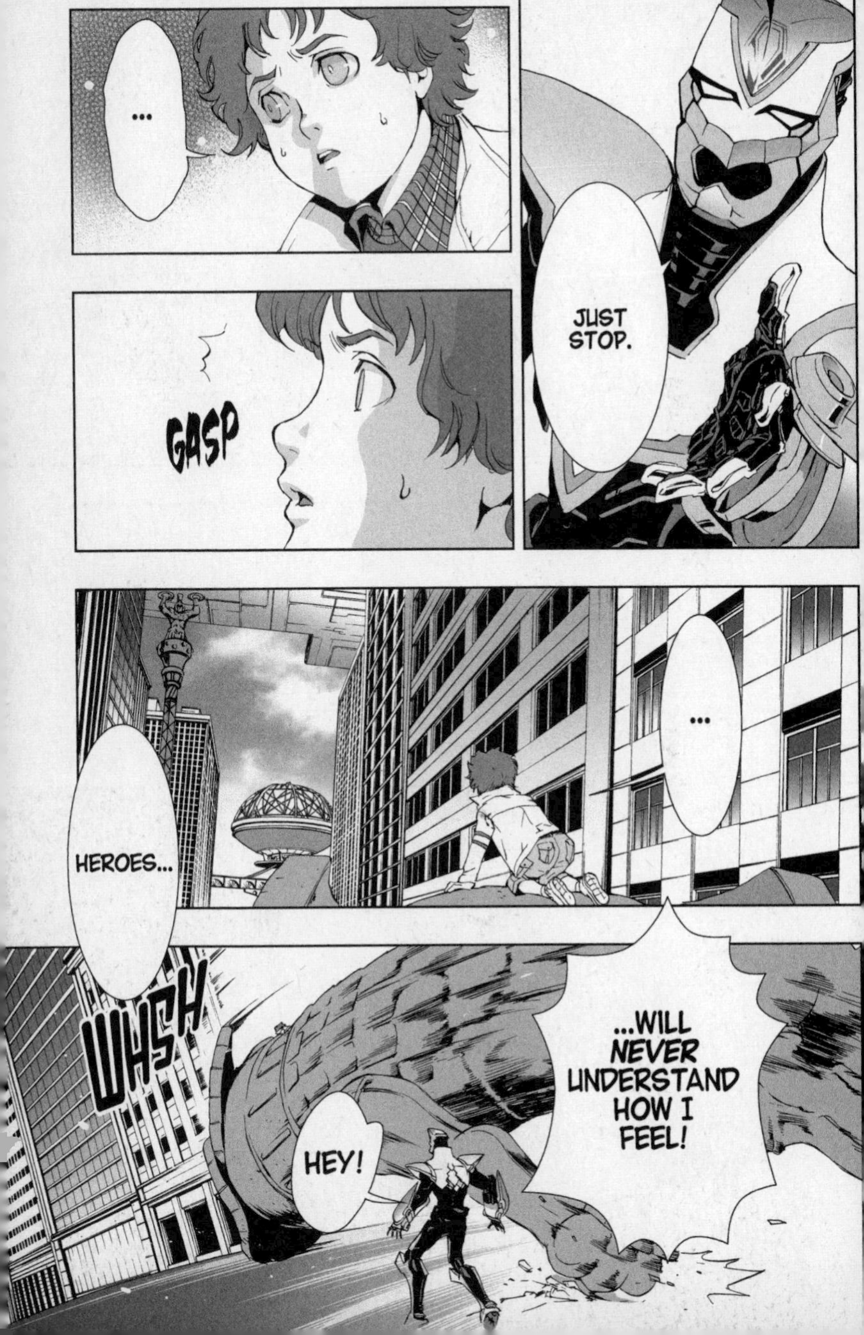
JUST STOP.
...
GASP
...
HEROES...
...WILL NEVER UNDERSTAND HOW I FEEL!
WHSH
HEY!

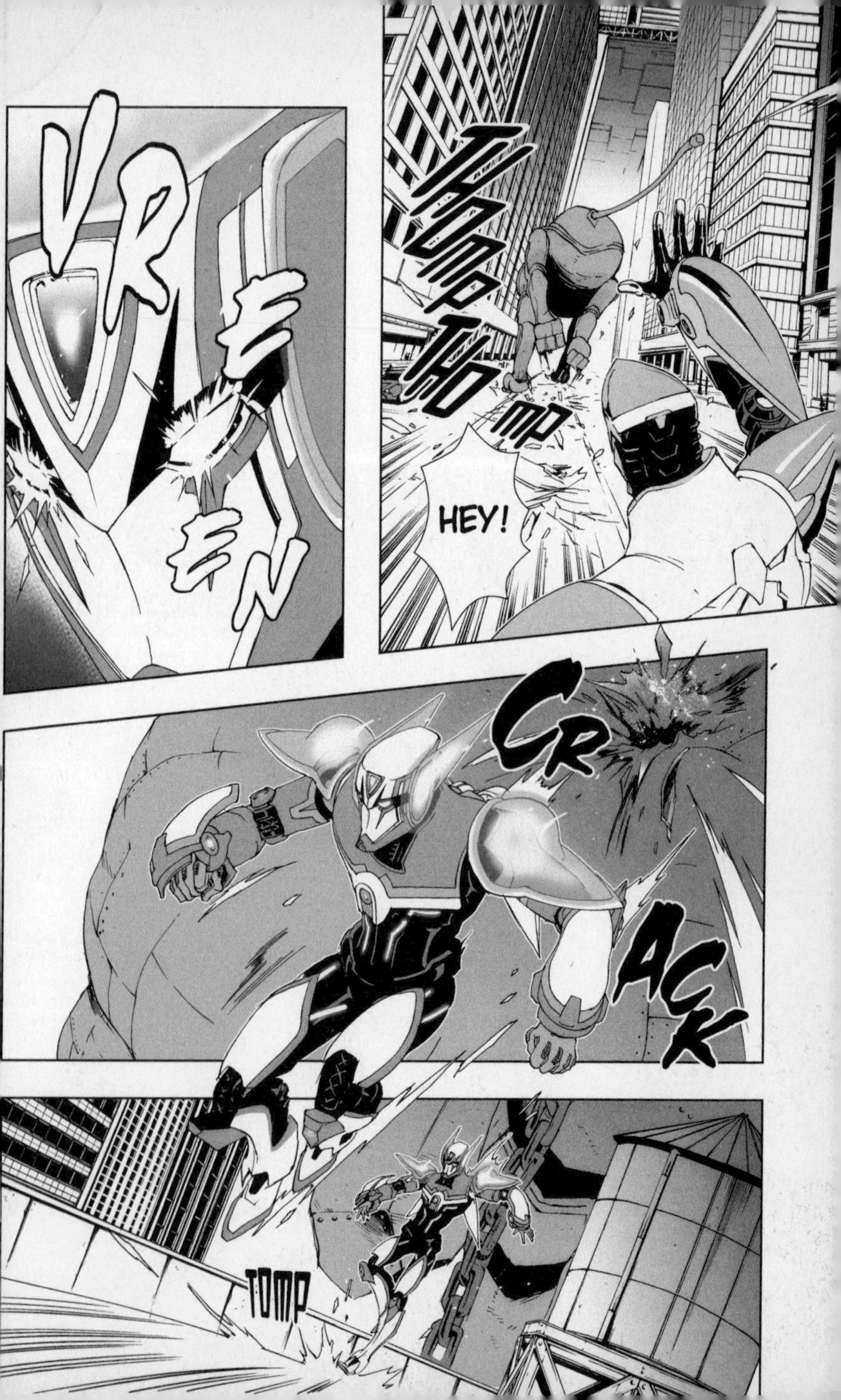
THOMP THOMP
HEY!
VREEN
CRACK
TOMP

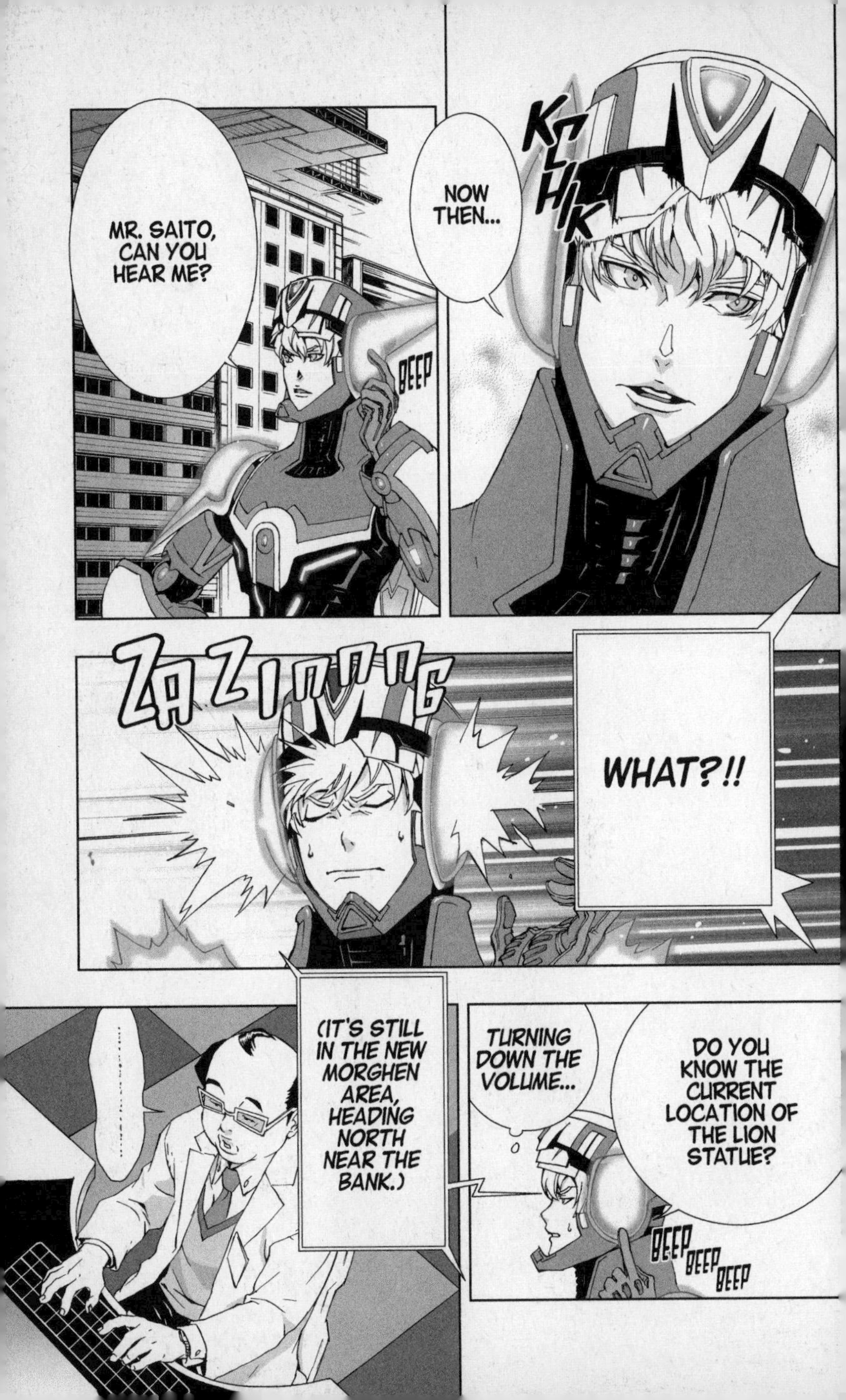
KCHIK
NOW THEN...
MR. SAITO, CAN YOU HEAR ME?
BEEP
WHAT?!!
ZAZINNNG
DO YOU KNOW THE CURRENT LOCATION OF THE LION STATUE?
TURNING DOWN THE VOLUME...
BEEP BEEP BEEP
(IT'S STILL IN THE NEW MORGHEN AREA, HEADING NORTH NEAR THE BANK.)
......

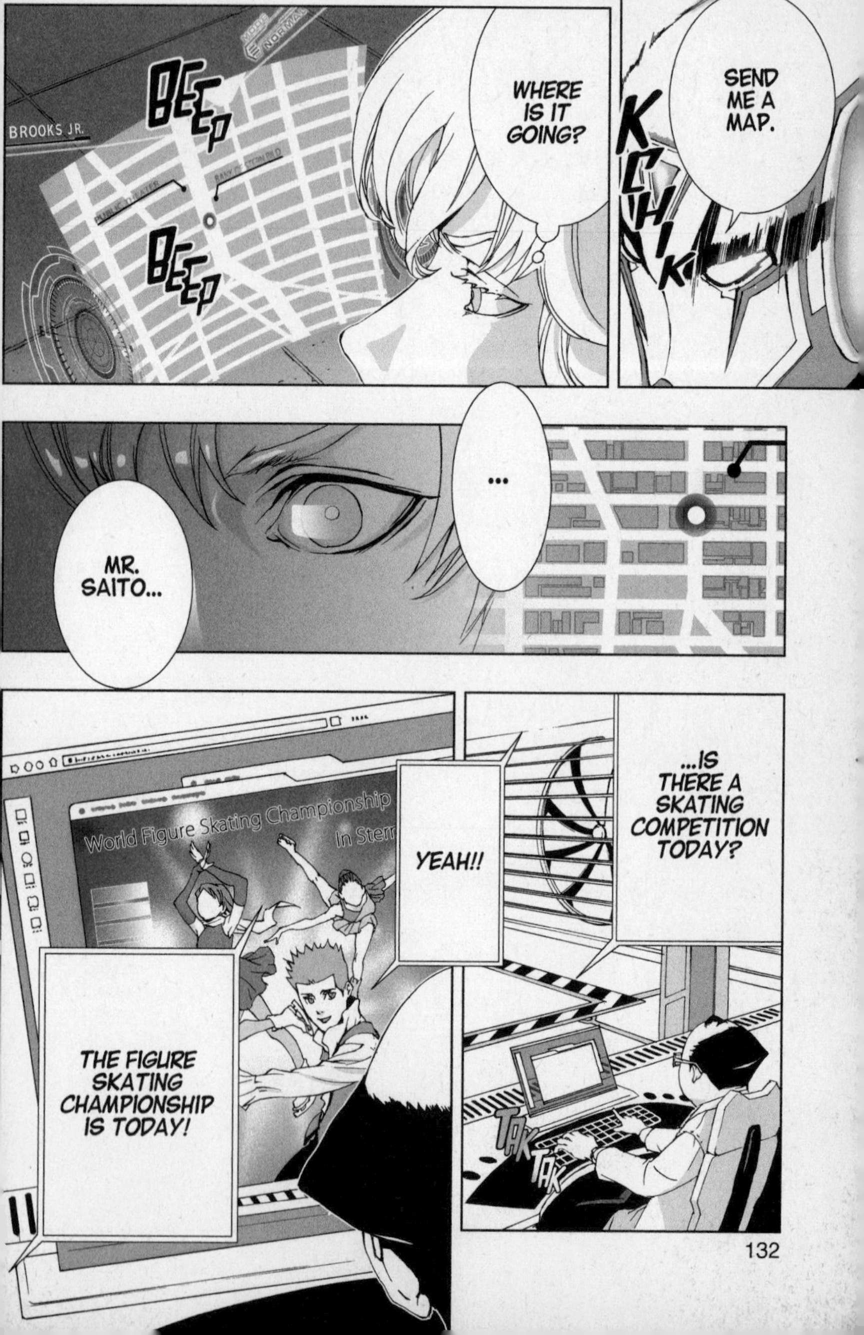
SEND ME A MAP.
KCHIK
WHERE IS IT GOING?
BROOKS JR.
NORMAL
BEEP
BEEP
...
MR. SAITO...
...IS THERE A SKATING COMPETITION TODAY?
YEAH!!
TAK TAK
World Figure Skating Championship
In Stern
THE FIGURE SKATING CHAMPIONSHIP IS TODAY!

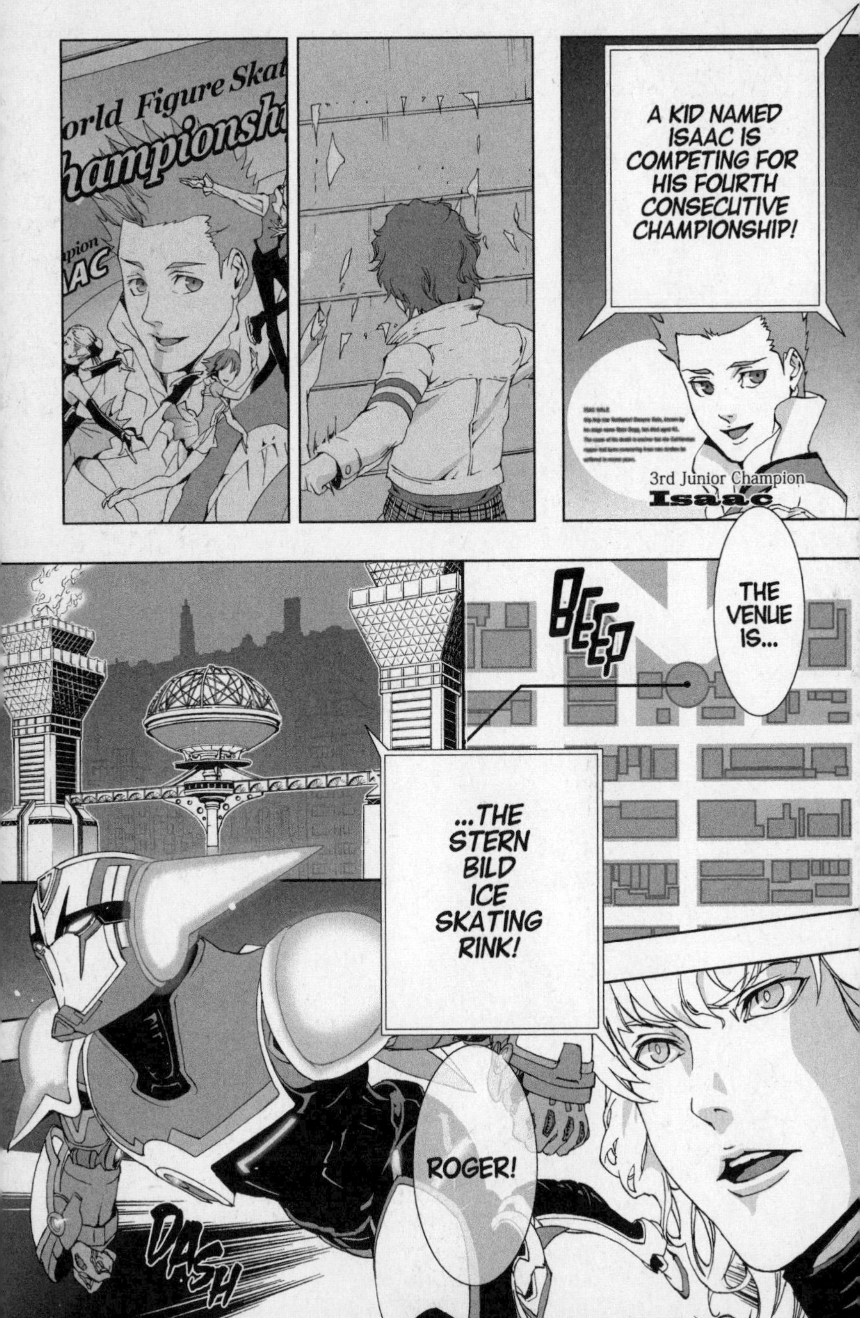

A KID NAMED ISAAC IS COMPETING FOR HIS FOURTH CONSECUTIVE CHAMPIONSHIP!
3rd Junior Champion
Isaac
BEEP
THE VENUE IS...
...THE STERN BILD ICE SKATING RINK!
ROGER!
DASH

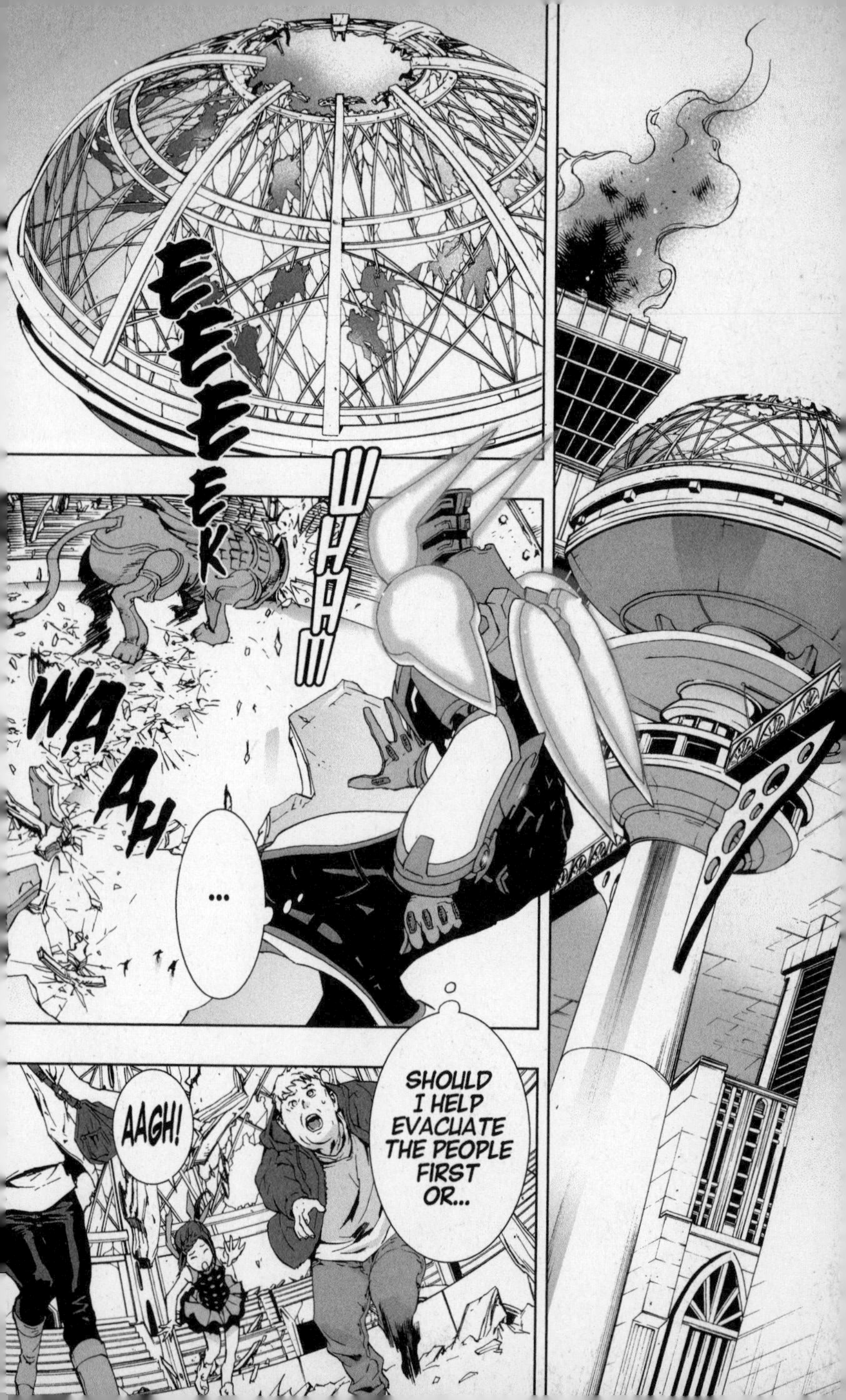
SHOULD I HELP EVACUATE THE PEOPLE FIRST OR...
EEEEEK
WHHAM
WAAAH
...
AAGH!

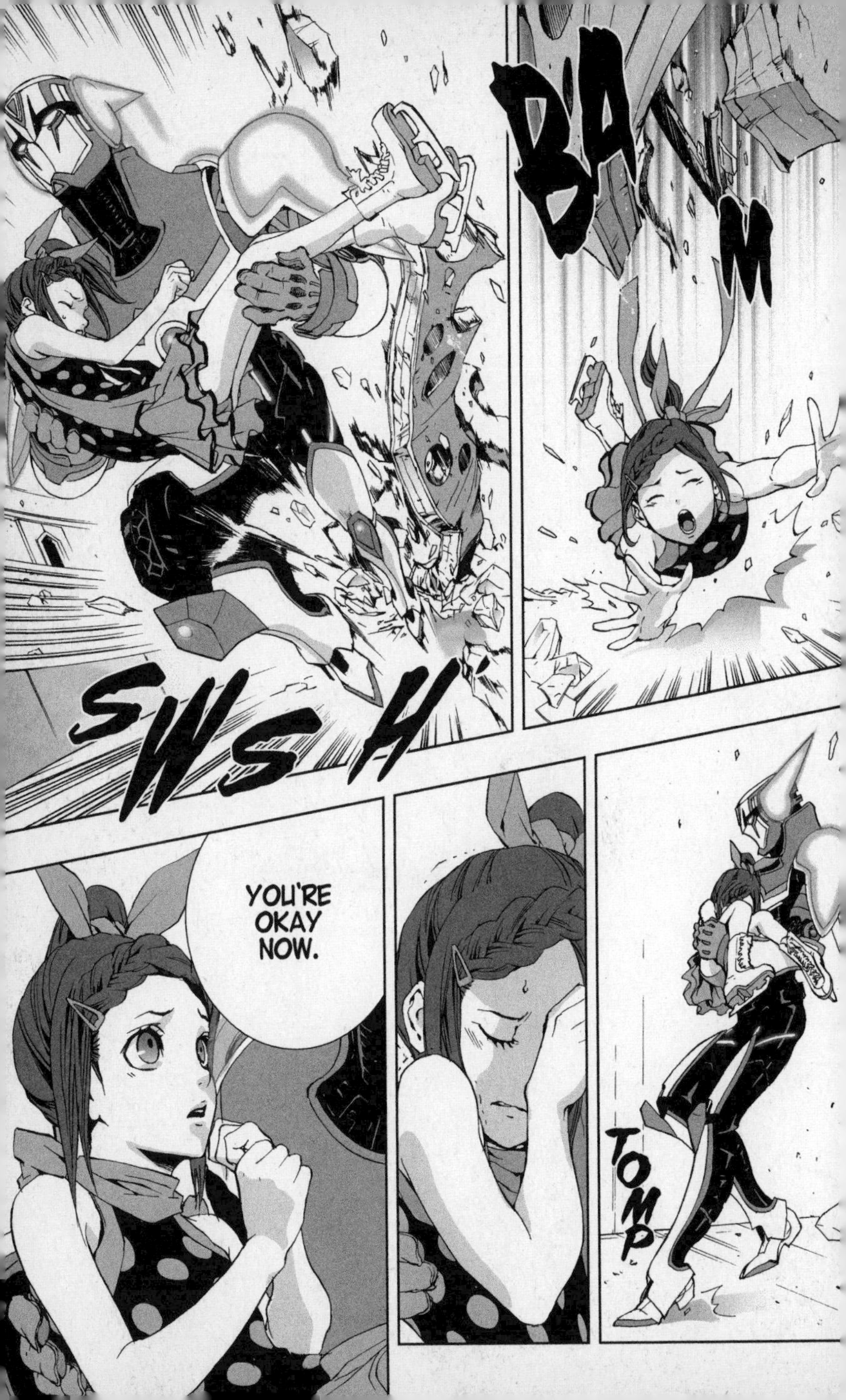
BAM
SWSH
TOMP
YOU'RE OKAY NOW.

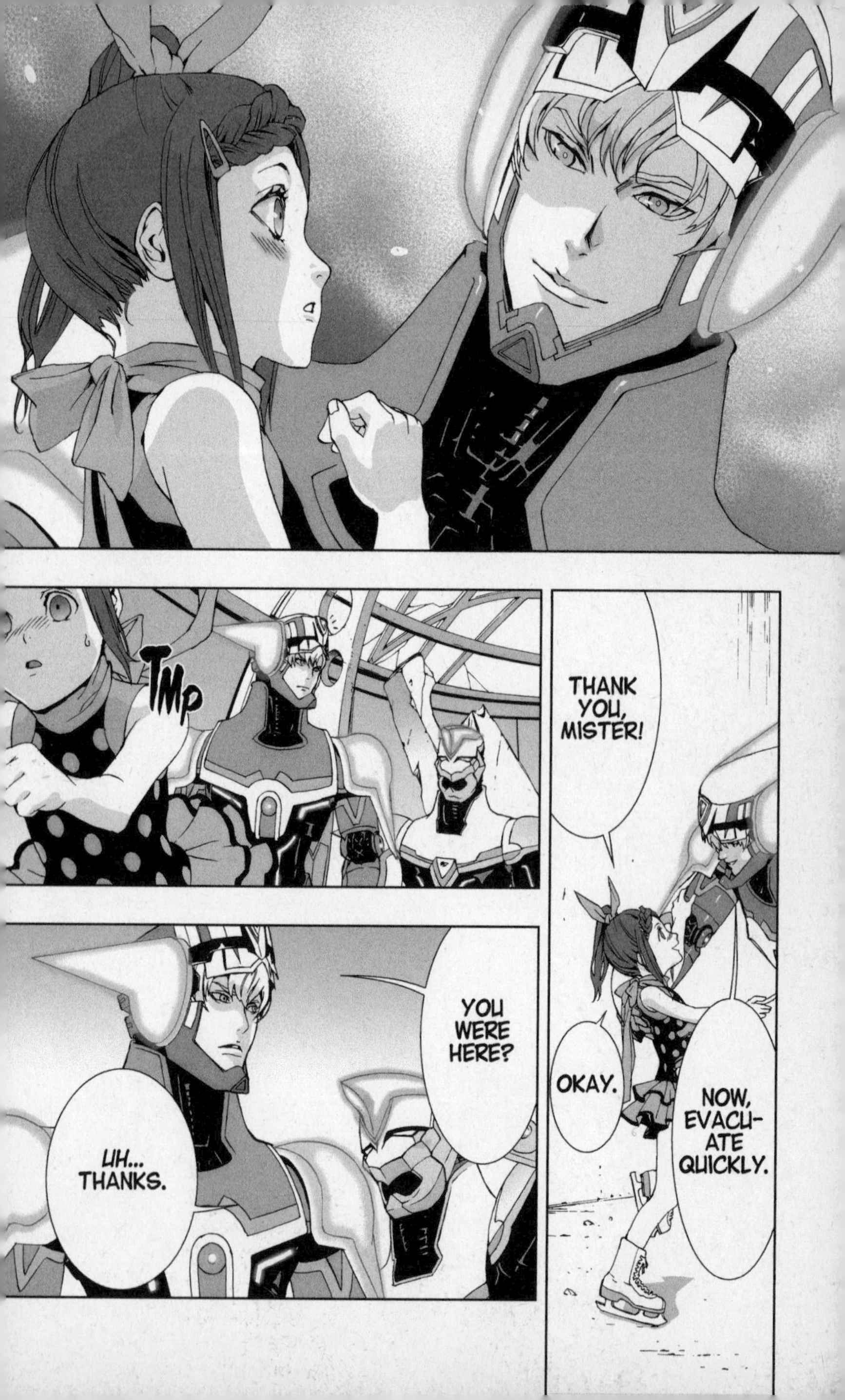
THANK YOU, MISTER!
NOW, EVACU-ATE QUICKLY.
OKAY.
TMP
YOU WERE HERE?
UH... THANKS.

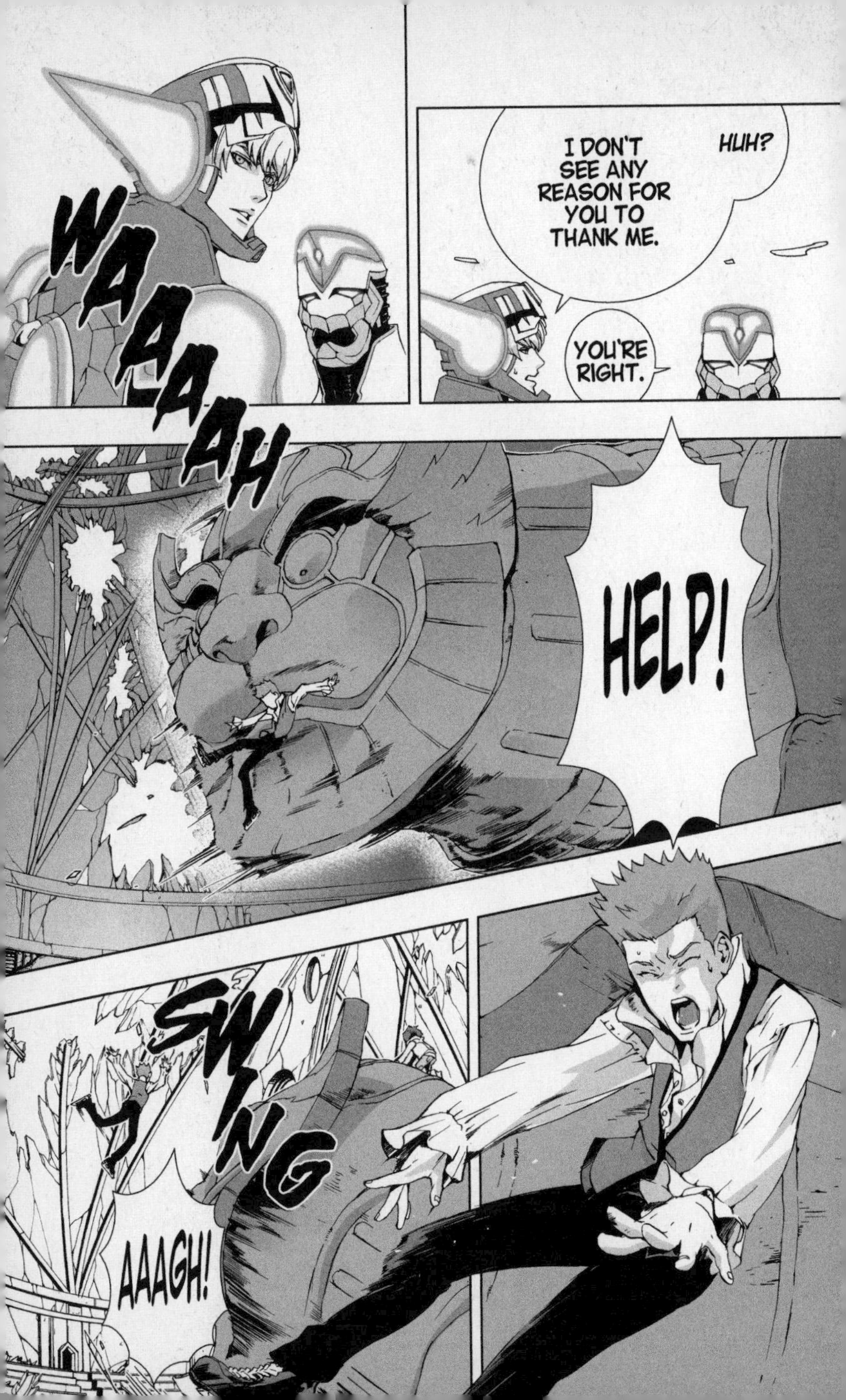
I DON'T SEE ANY REASON FOR YOU TO THANK ME.
HUH?
YOU'RE RIGHT.
WAAAAAH
HELP!
SWING
AAAGH!

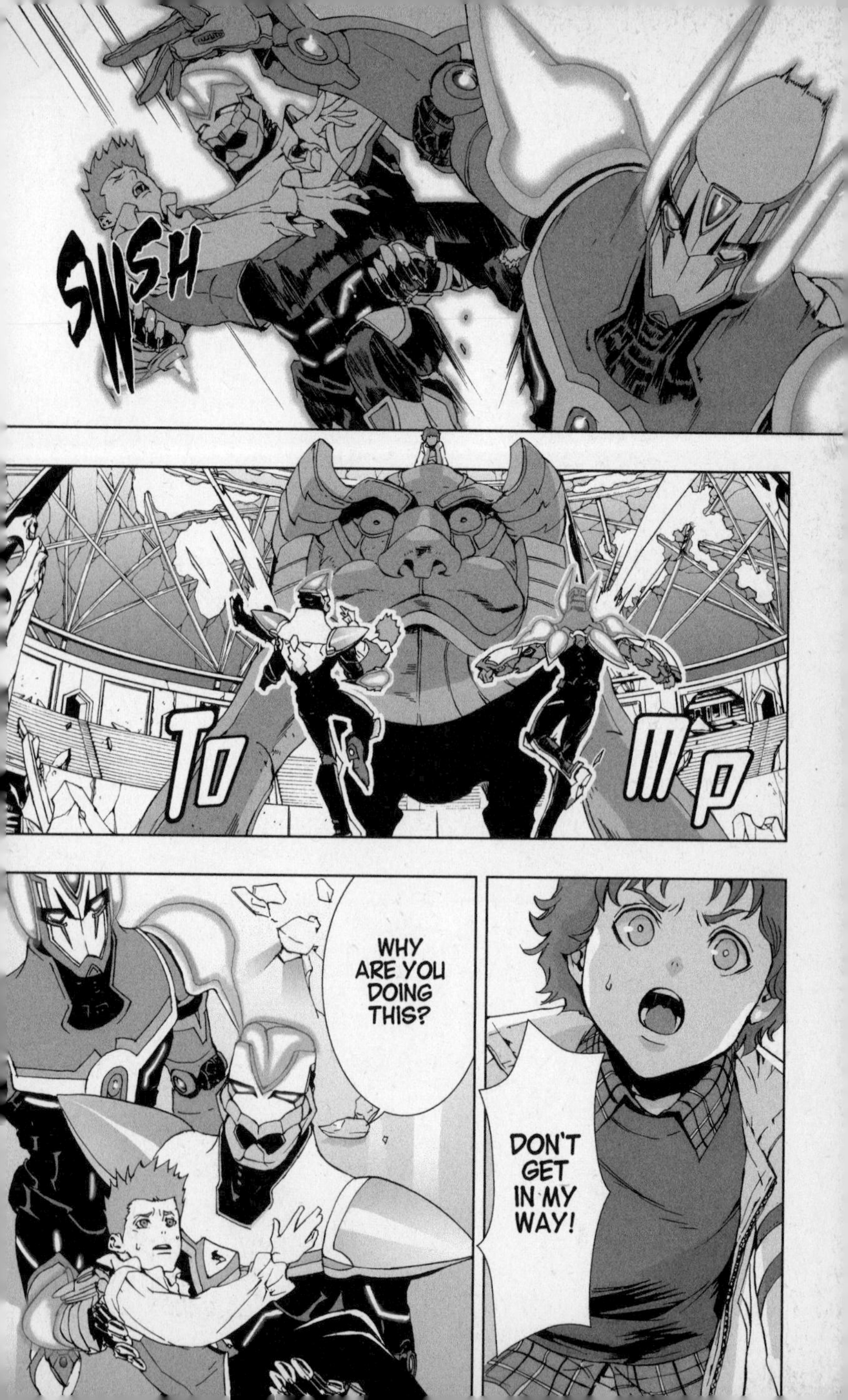
SWSH
To mp
DON'T GET IN MY WAY!
WHY ARE YOU DOING THIS?

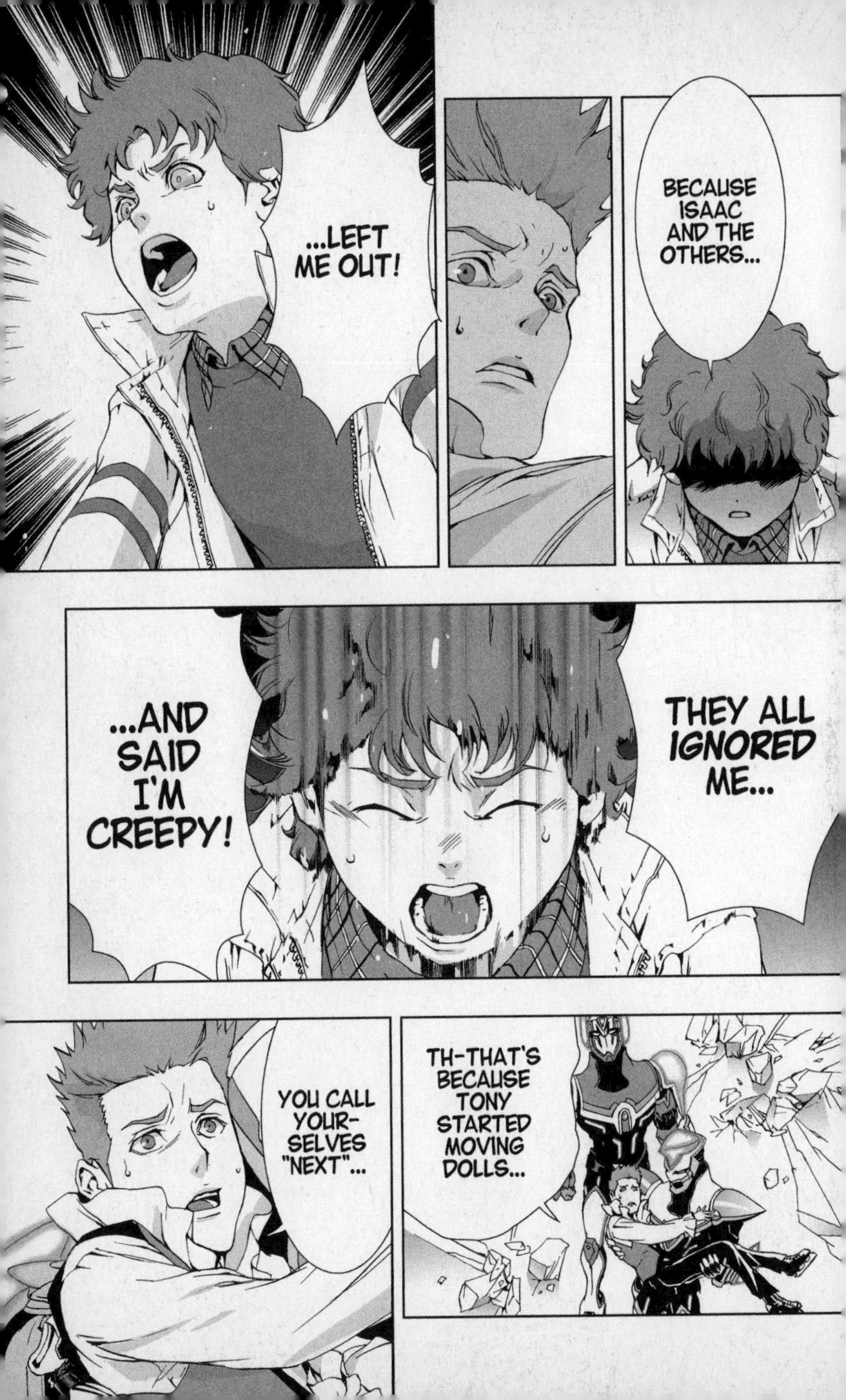
BECAUSE ISAAC AND THE OTHERS...
...LEFT ME OUT!
THEY ALL IGNORED ME...
...AND SAID I'M CREEPY!
TH-THAT'S BECAUSE TONY STARTED MOVING DOLLS...
YOU CALL YOUR-SELVES "NEXT"...

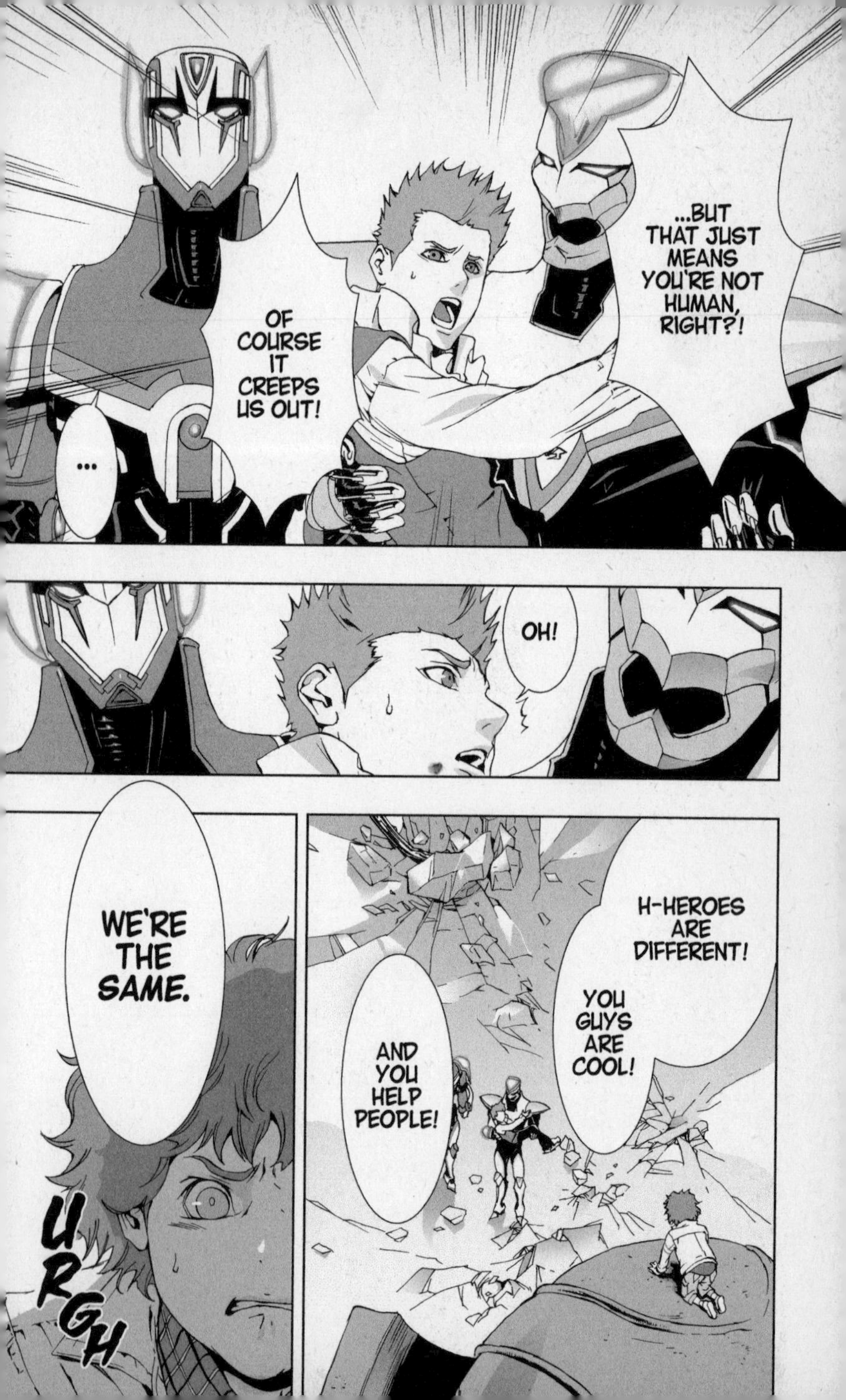
...BUT THAT JUST MEANS YOU'RE NOT HUMAN, RIGHT?!
OF COURSE IT CREEPS US OUT!
...
OH!
H-HEROES ARE DIFFERENT!
YOU GUYS ARE COOL!
AND YOU HELP PEOPLE!
WE'RE THE SAME.
URGH

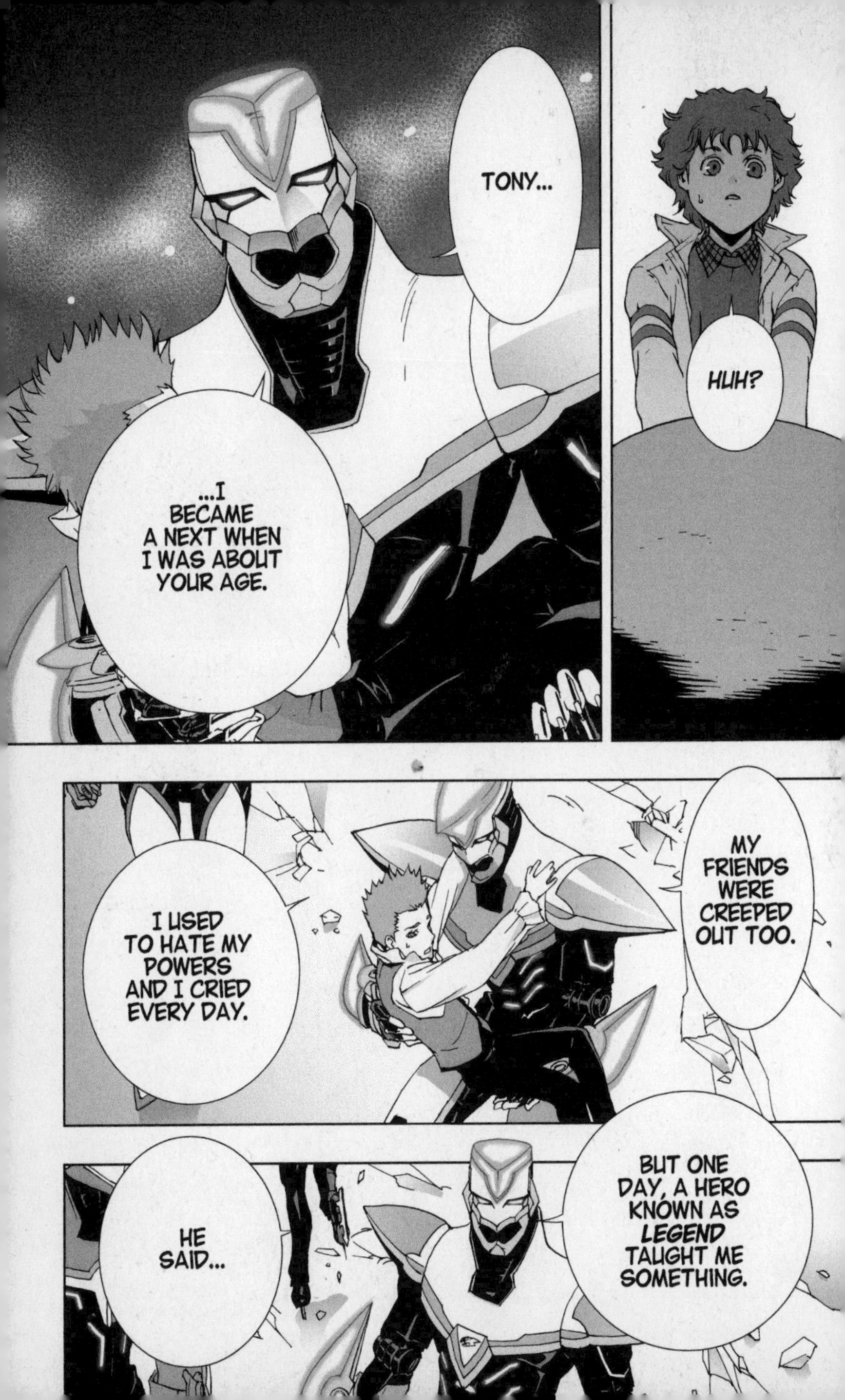
HUH?
TONY...
...I BECAME A NEXT WHEN I WAS ABOUT YOUR AGE.
MY FRIENDS WERE CREEPED OUT TOO.
I USED TO HATE MY POWERS AND I CRIED EVERY DAY.
BUT ONE DAY, A HERO KNOWN AS *LEGEND* TAUGHT ME SOMETHING.
HE SAID...

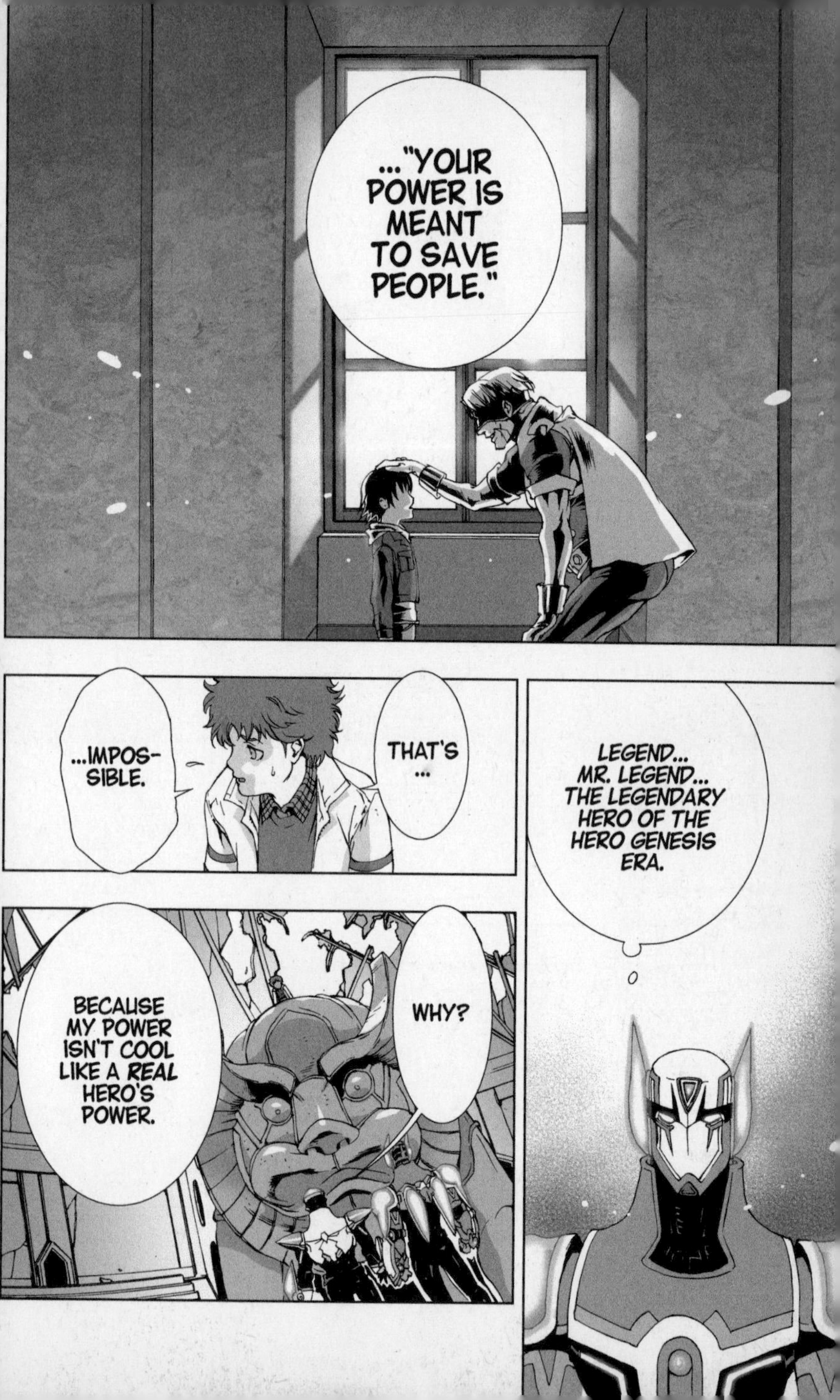
..."YOUR POWER IS MEANT TO SAVE PEOPLE."
LEGEND... MR. LEGEND... THE LEGENDARY HERO OF THE HERO GENESIS ERA.
THAT'S ...
...IMPOS-SIBLE.
WHY?
BECAUSE MY POWER ISN'T COOL LIKE A *REAL* HERO'S POWER.

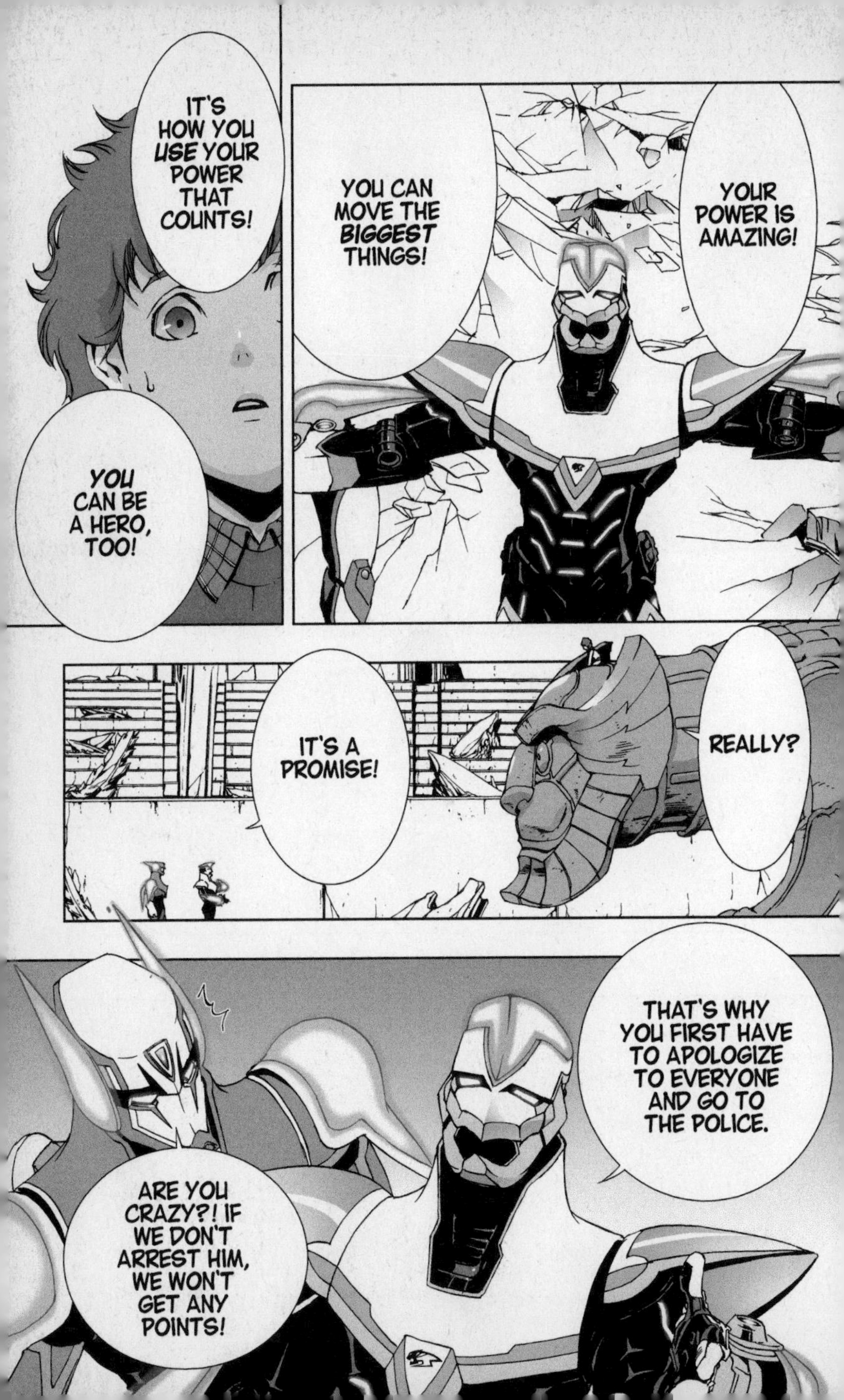
YOUR POWER IS AMAZING!
YOU CAN MOVE THE BIGGEST THINGS!
IT'S HOW YOU USE YOUR POWER THAT COUNTS!
YOU CAN BE A HERO, TOO!
REALLY?
IT'S A PROMISE!
THAT'S WHY YOU FIRST HAVE TO APOLOGIZE TO EVERYONE AND GO TO THE POLICE.
ARE YOU CRAZY?! IF WE DON'T ARREST HIM, WE WON'T GET ANY POINTS!

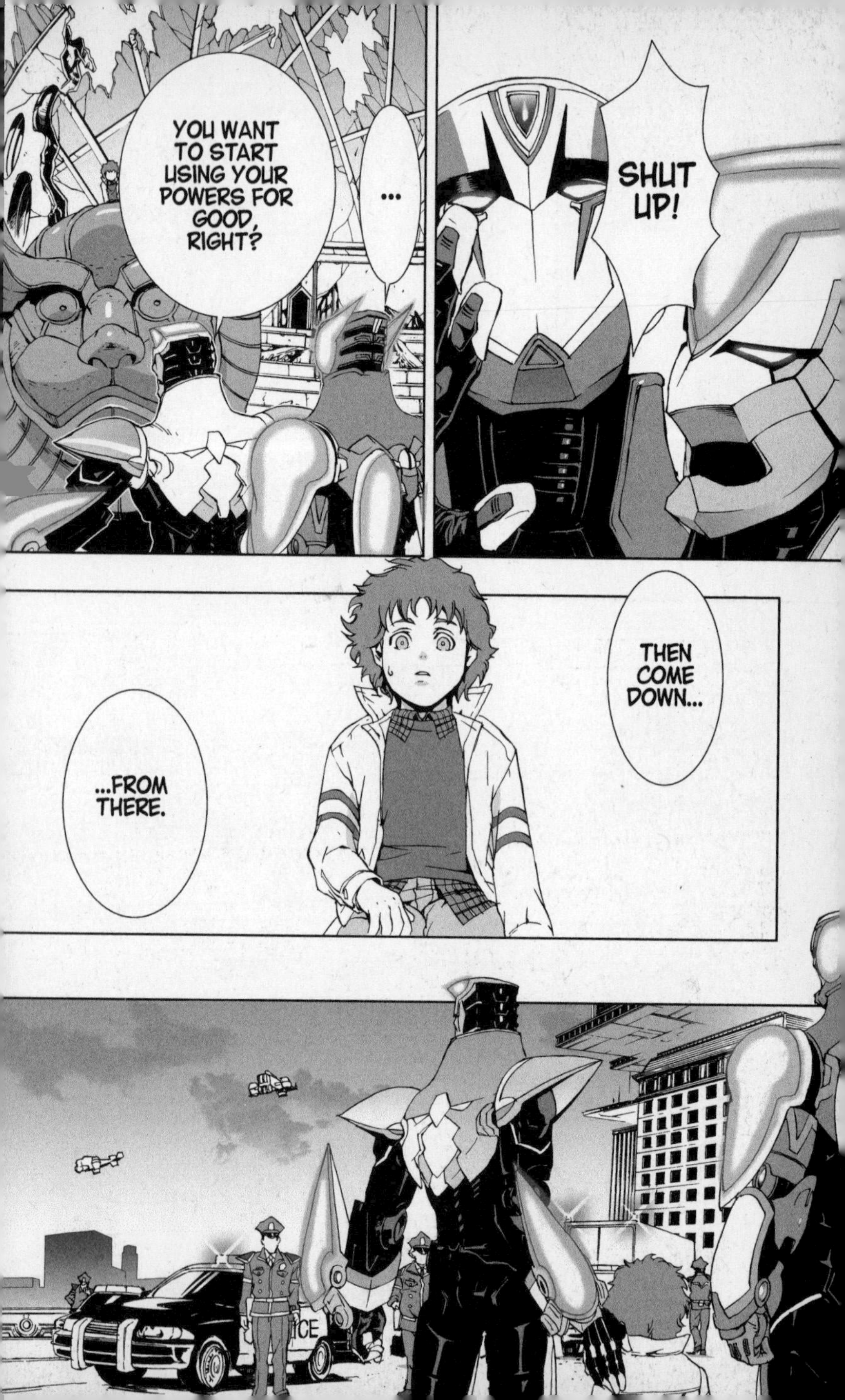
SHUT UP!
...
YOU WANT TO START USING YOUR POWERS FOR GOOD, RIGHT?
THEN COME DOWN...
...FROM THERE.

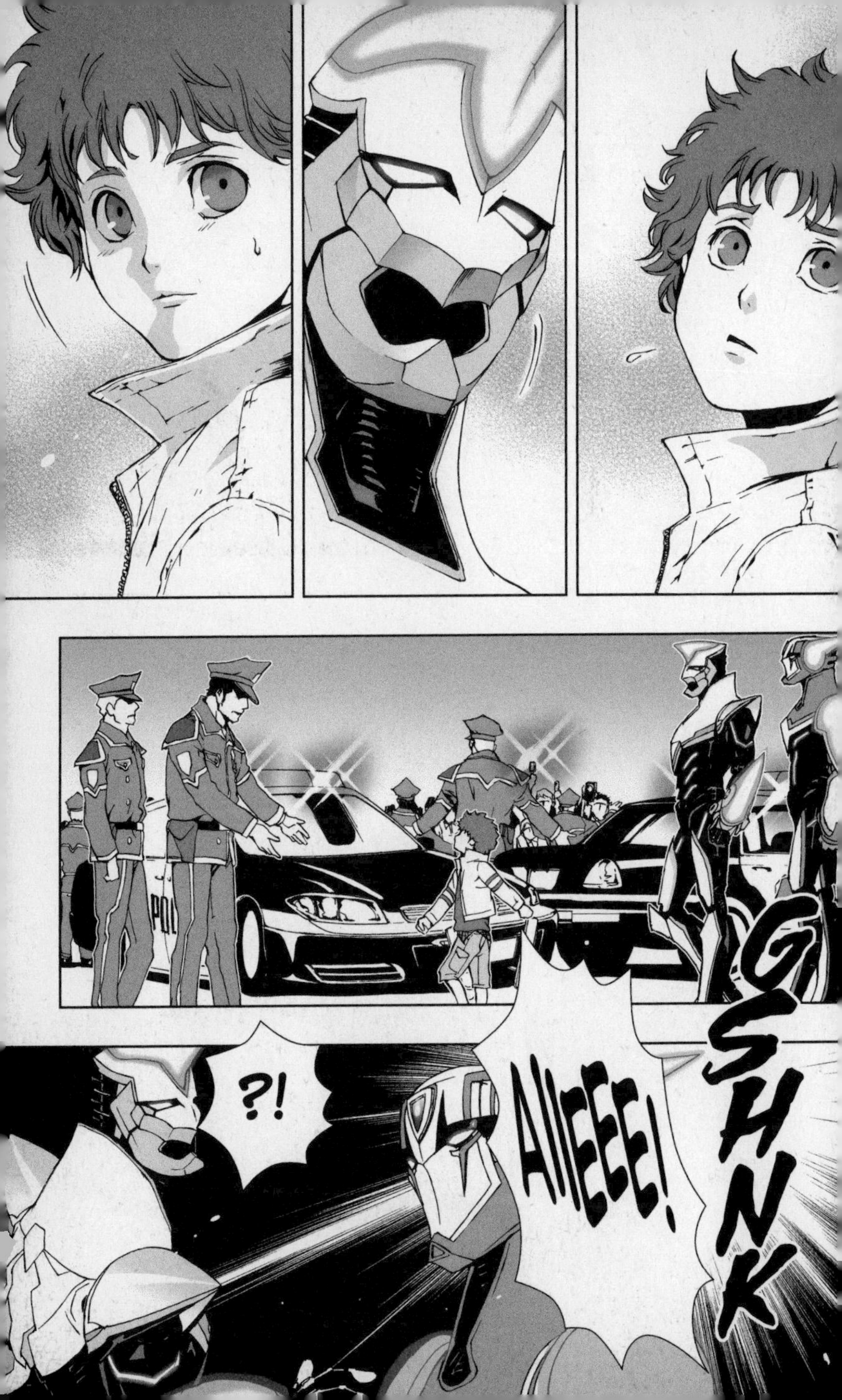
AIIEEE!
?!
SHNK

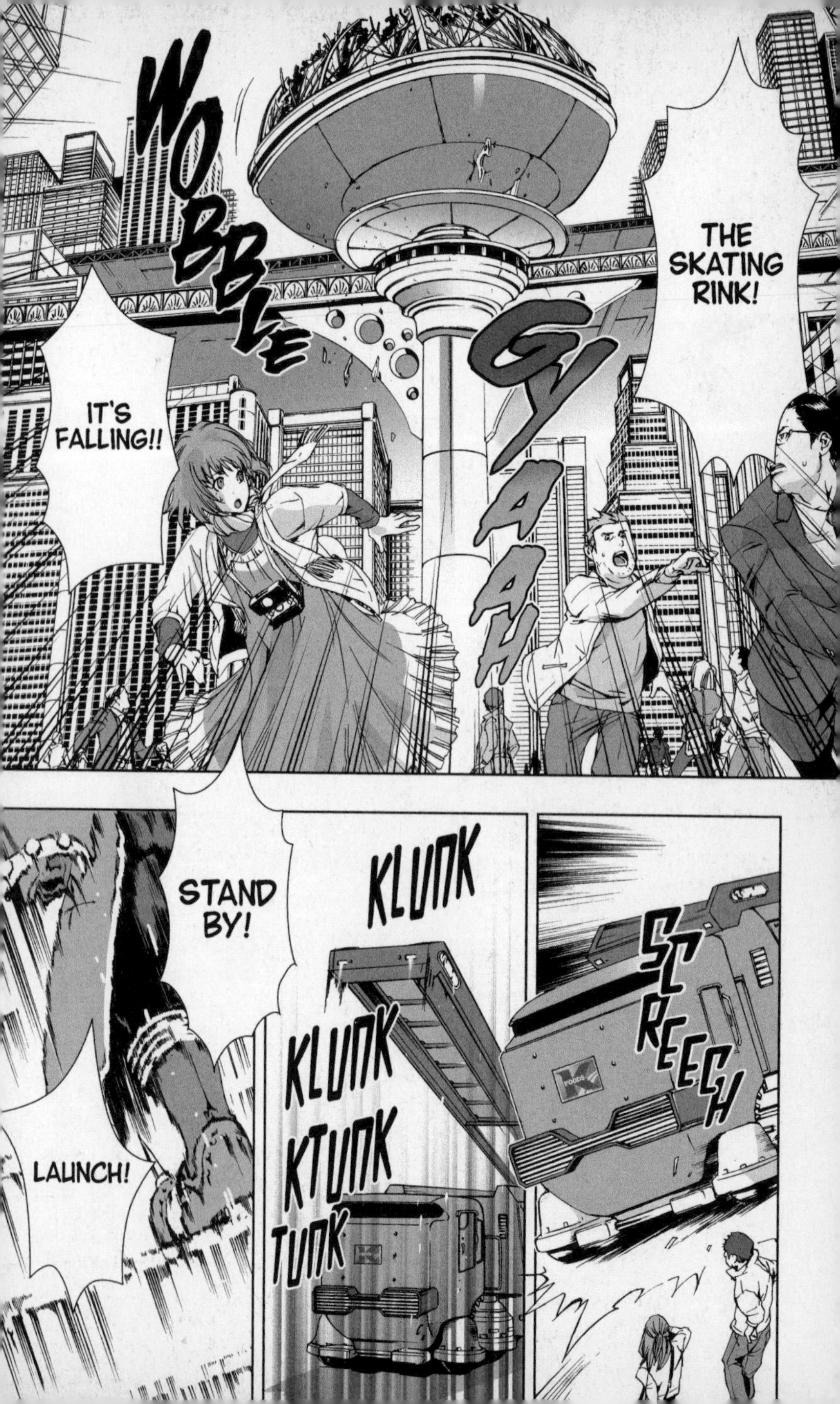
THE SKATING RINK!
WOBBLE
GYAAH
IT'S FALLING!!
SCREECH
KLUNK
KLUNK KTUNK TUNK
STAND BY!
LAUNCH!

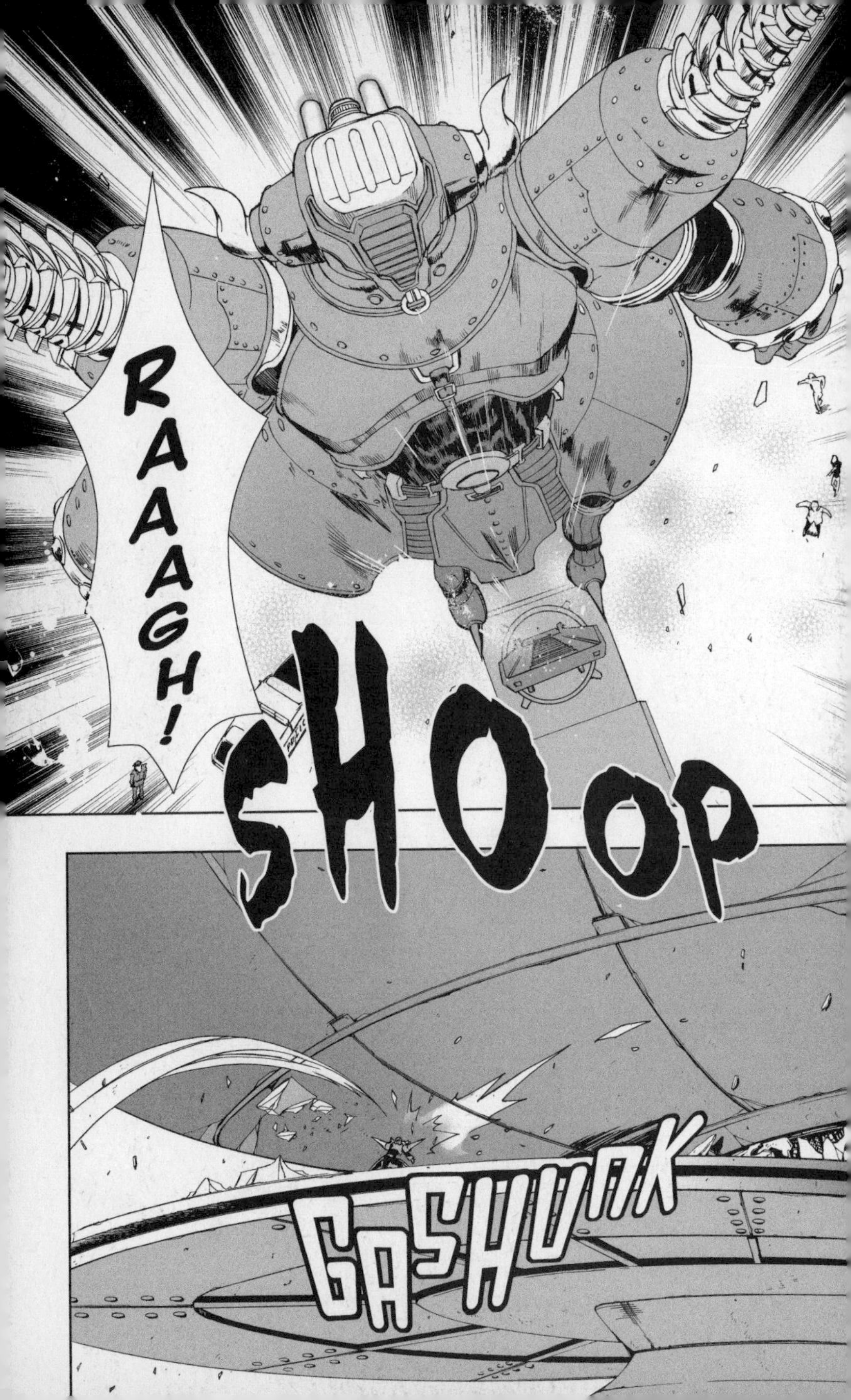
RAAAGH!
SHOOP
GASHUNK

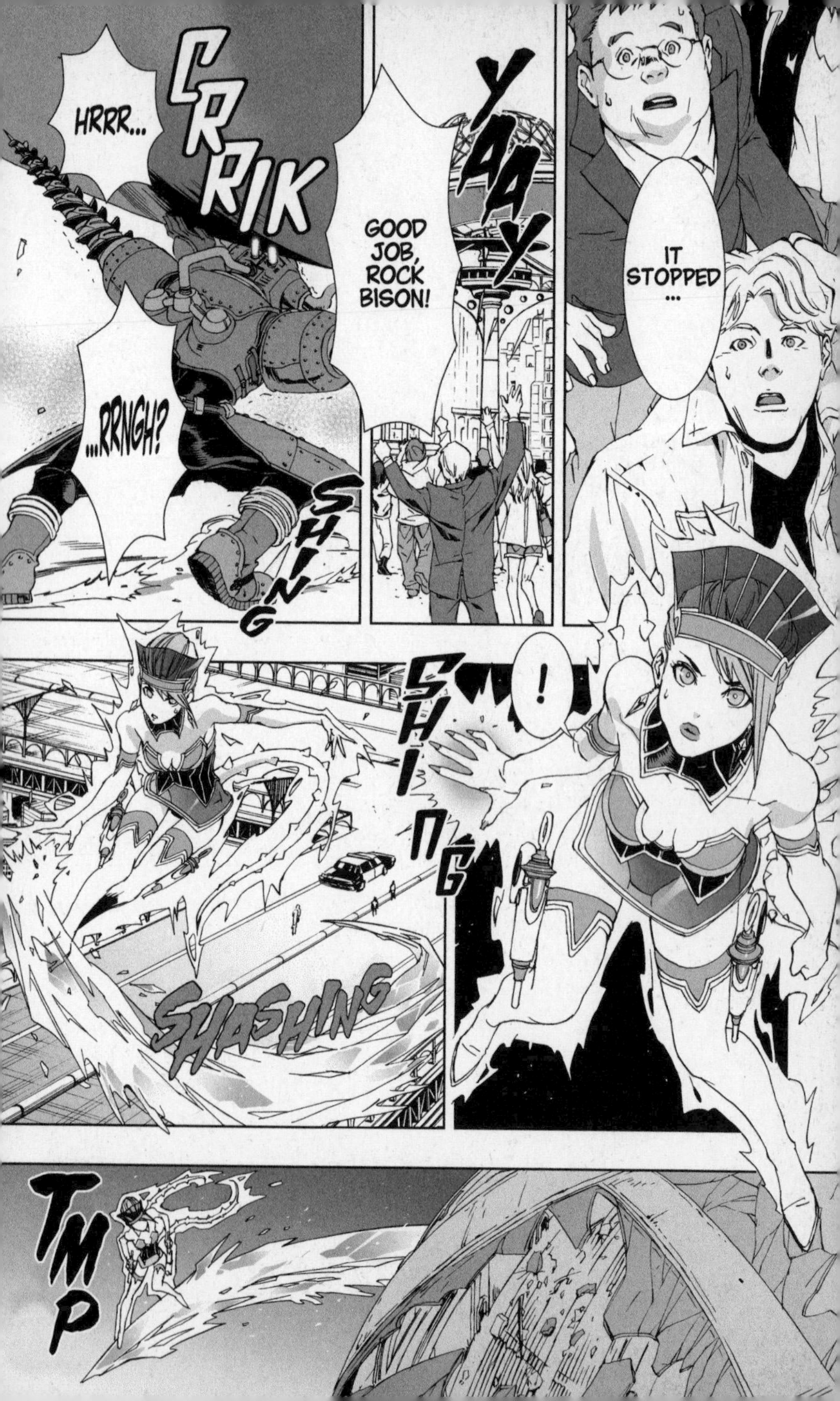
IT STOPPED ...
YAAAY
GOOD JOB, ROCK BISON!
HRRR...
CRRIK
...RRNGH?
SHING
!
SHING
SHASHING
TMP

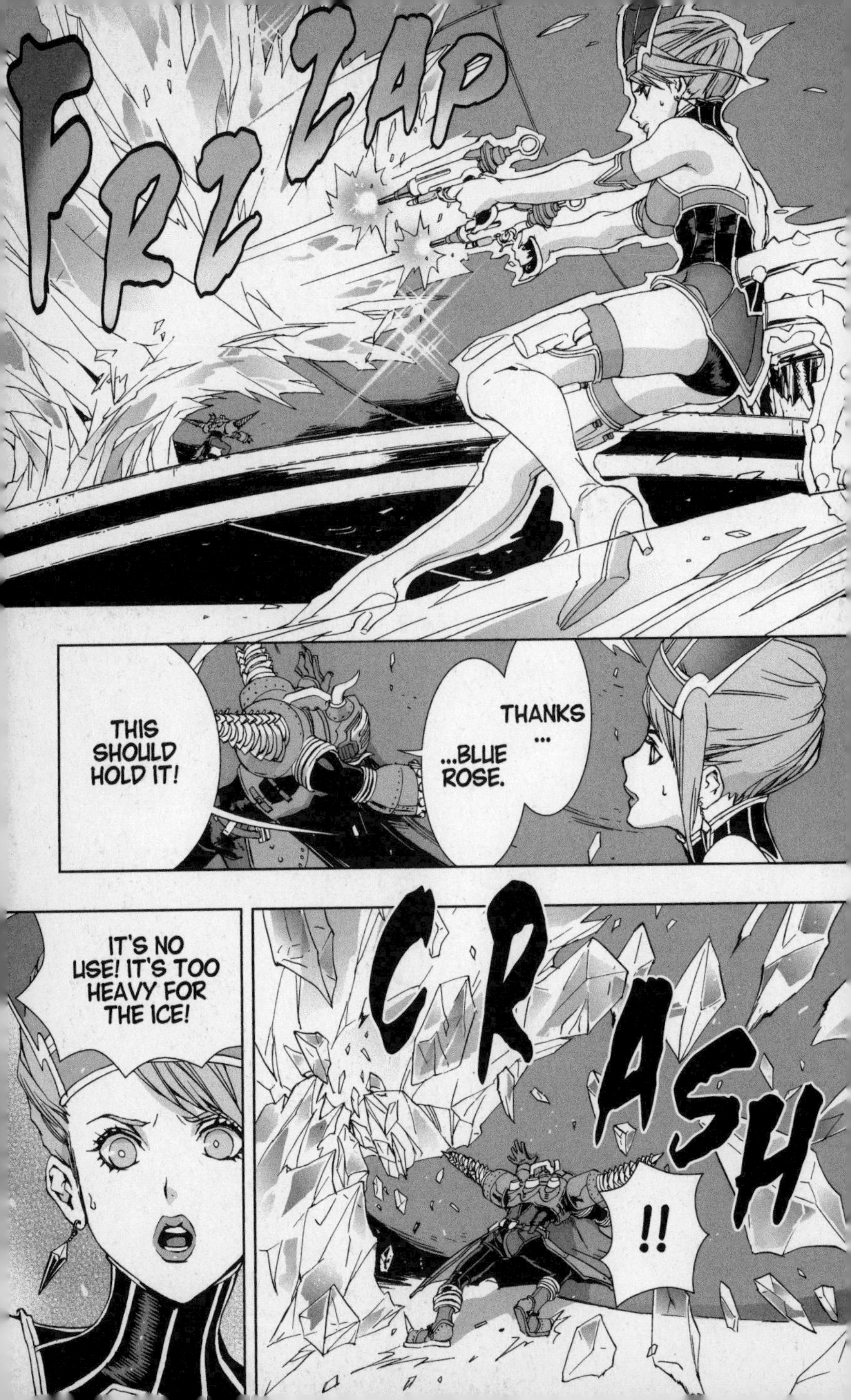
ZAP
FRZ
THANKS ... ...BLUE ROSE.
THIS SHOULD HOLD IT!
CRASH
!!
IT'S NO USE! IT'S TOO HEAVY FOR THE ICE!

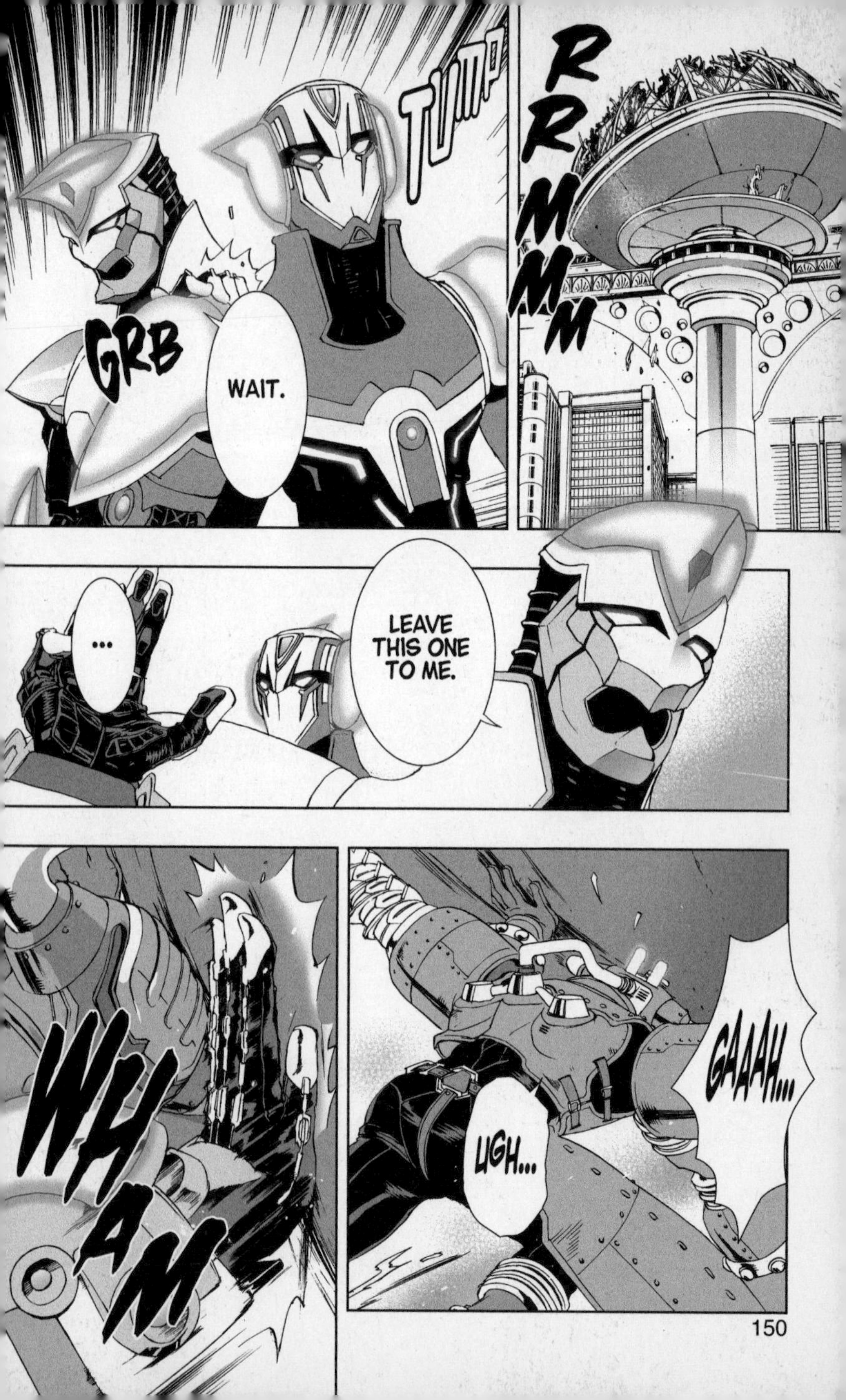
RRRMMMM
TUMP
WAIT.
GRB
LEAVE THIS ONE TO ME.
...
GAAAH...
UGH...
WHAM

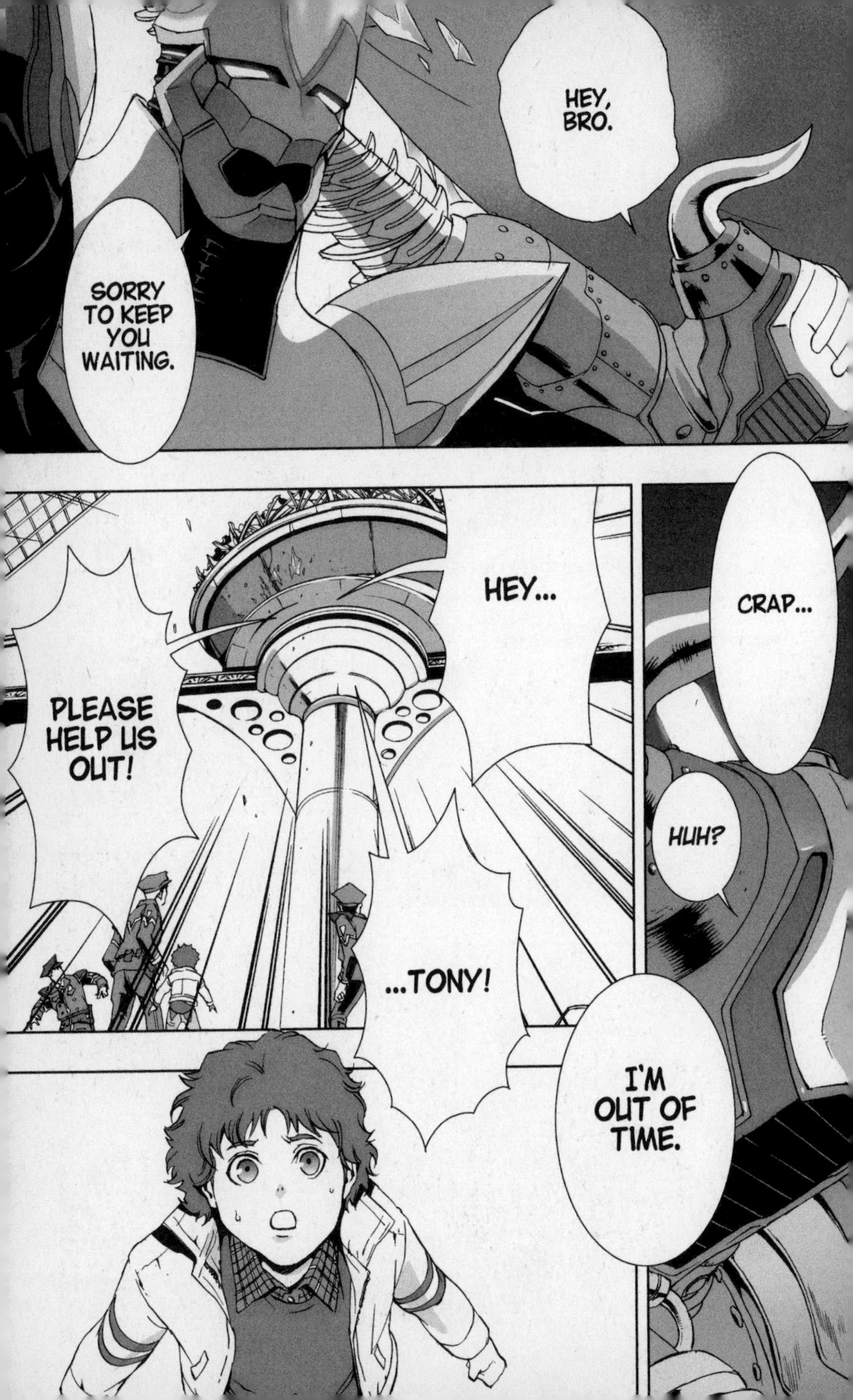
HEY, BRO.
SORRY TO KEEP YOU WAITING.
CRAP...
HUH?
I'M OUT OF TIME.
HEY...
PLEASE HELP US OUT!
...TONY!

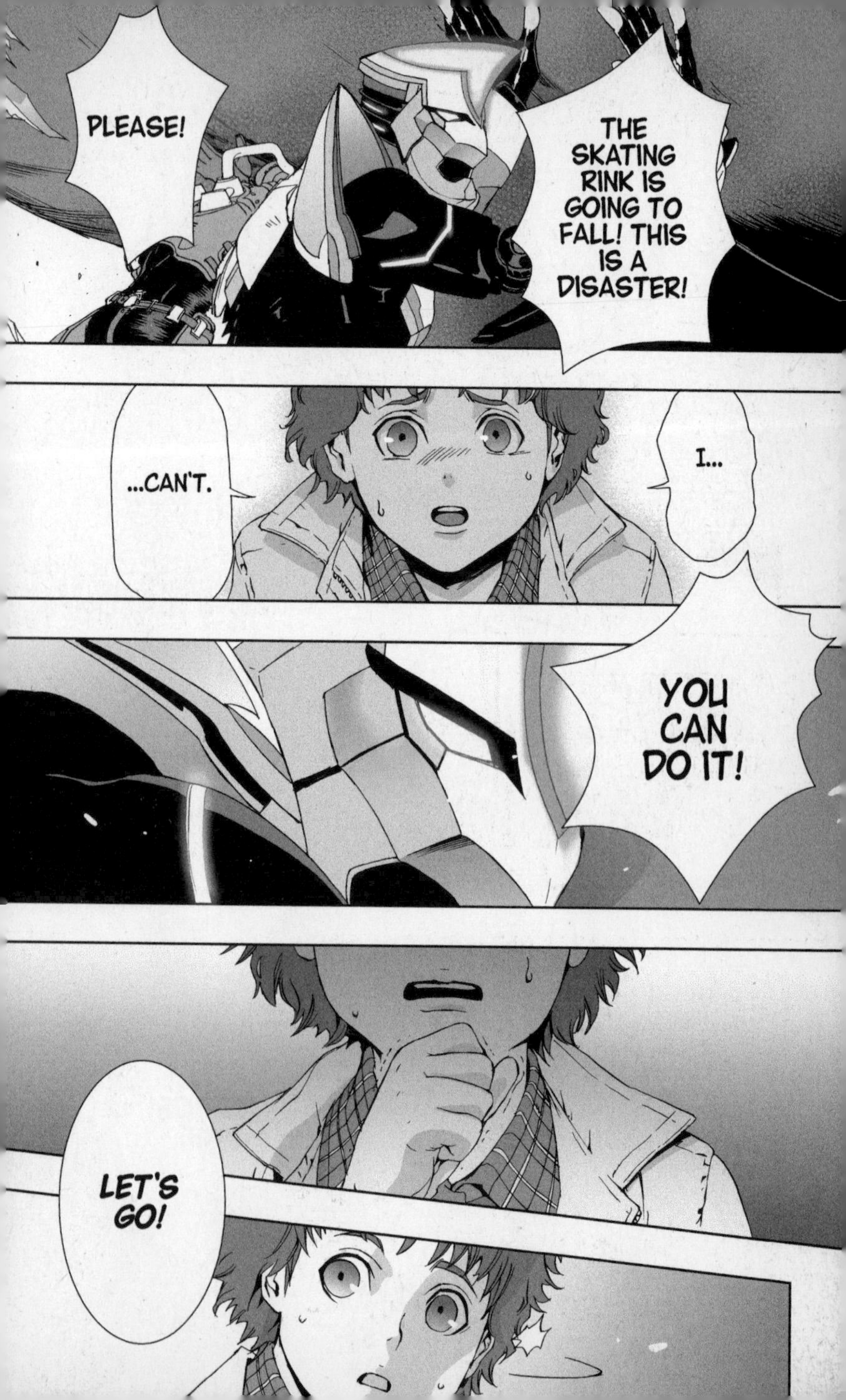
THE SKATING RINK IS GOING TO FALL! THIS IS A DISASTER!
PLEASE!
I...
...CAN'T.
YOU CAN DO IT!
LET'S GO!

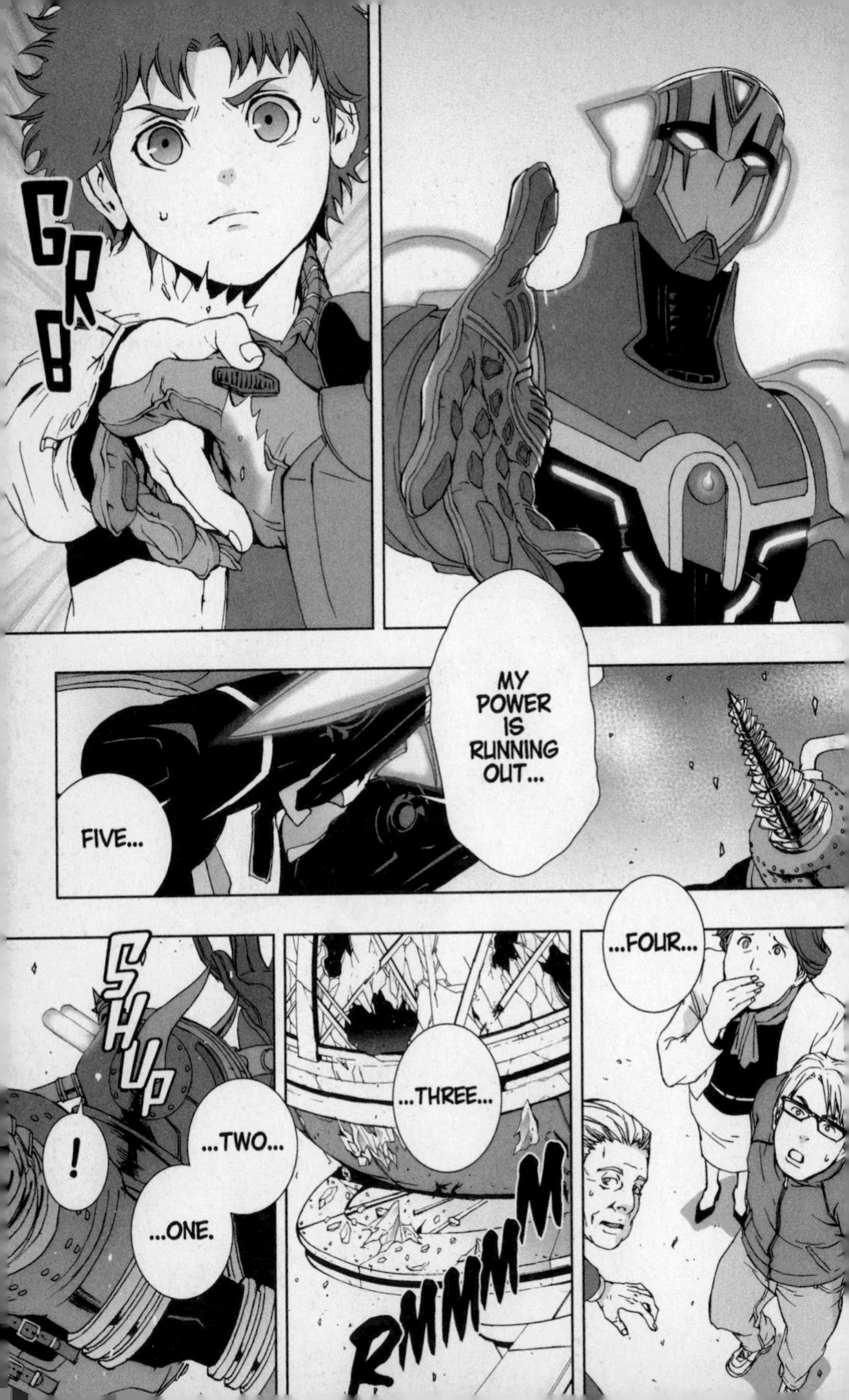
GRB
MY POWER IS RUNNING OUT...
FIVE...
...FOUR...
...THREE...
RMMMM
SHUP
!
...TWO...
...ONE.

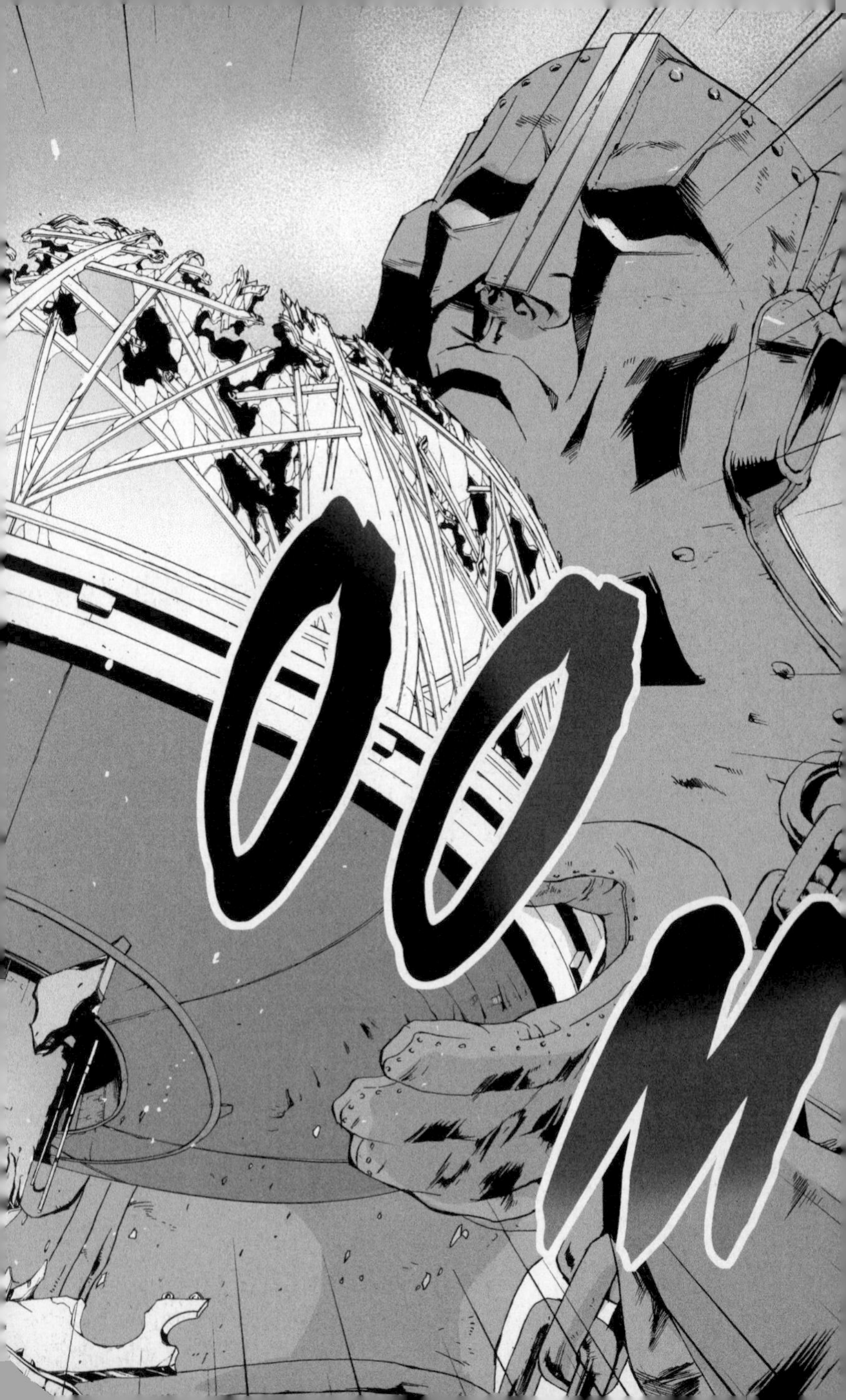
OOM

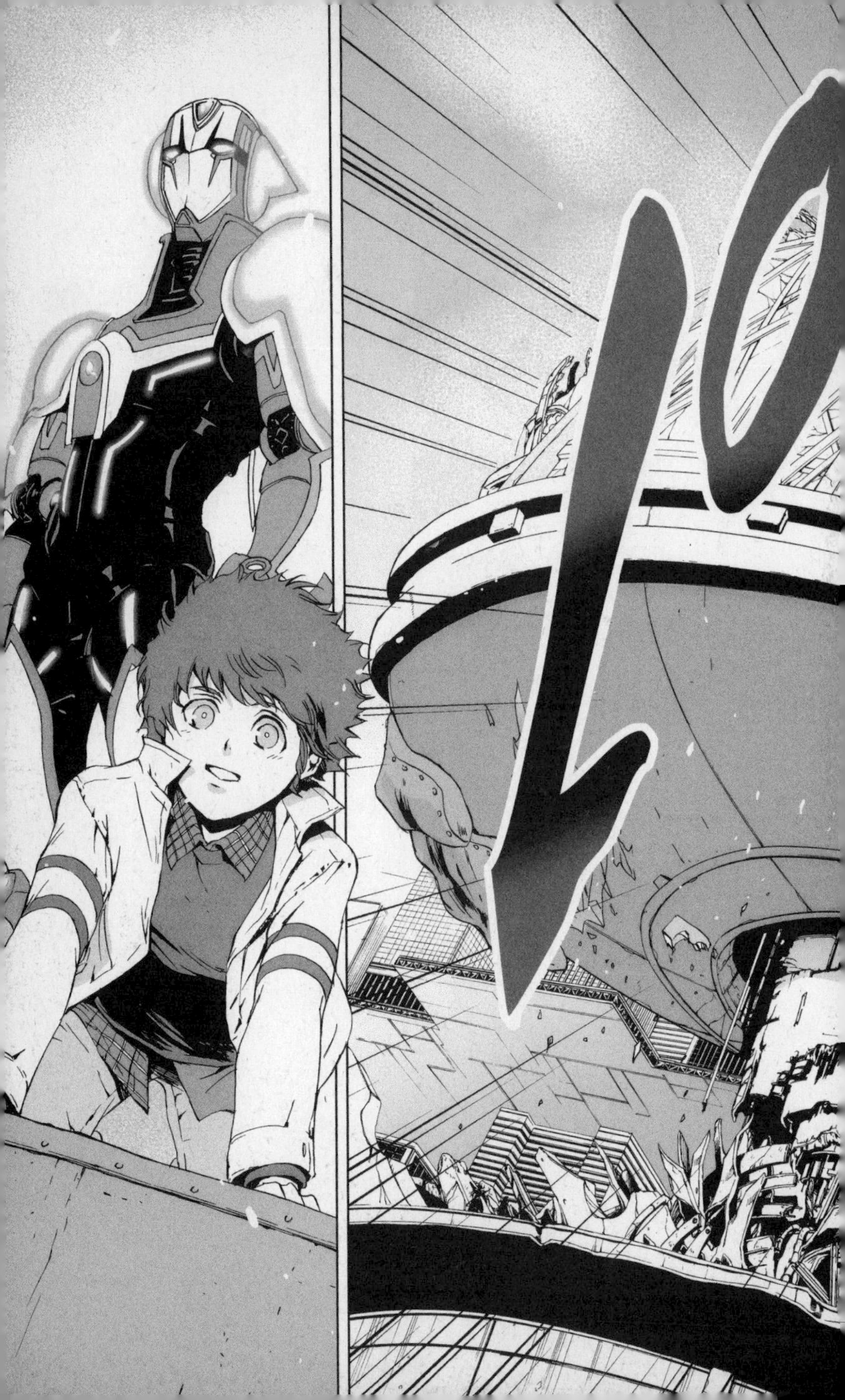

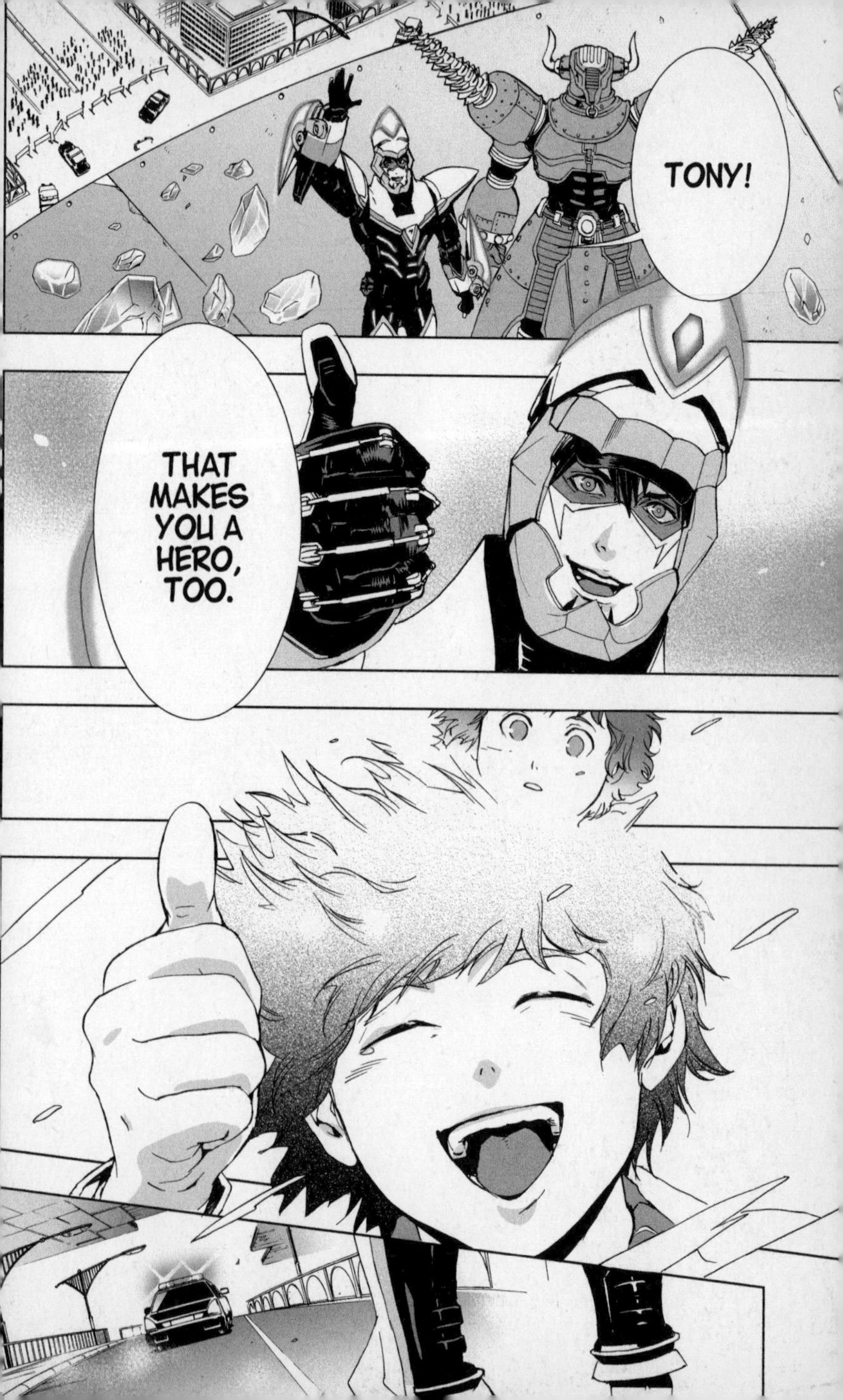
TONY!
THAT MAKES YOU A HERO, TOO.

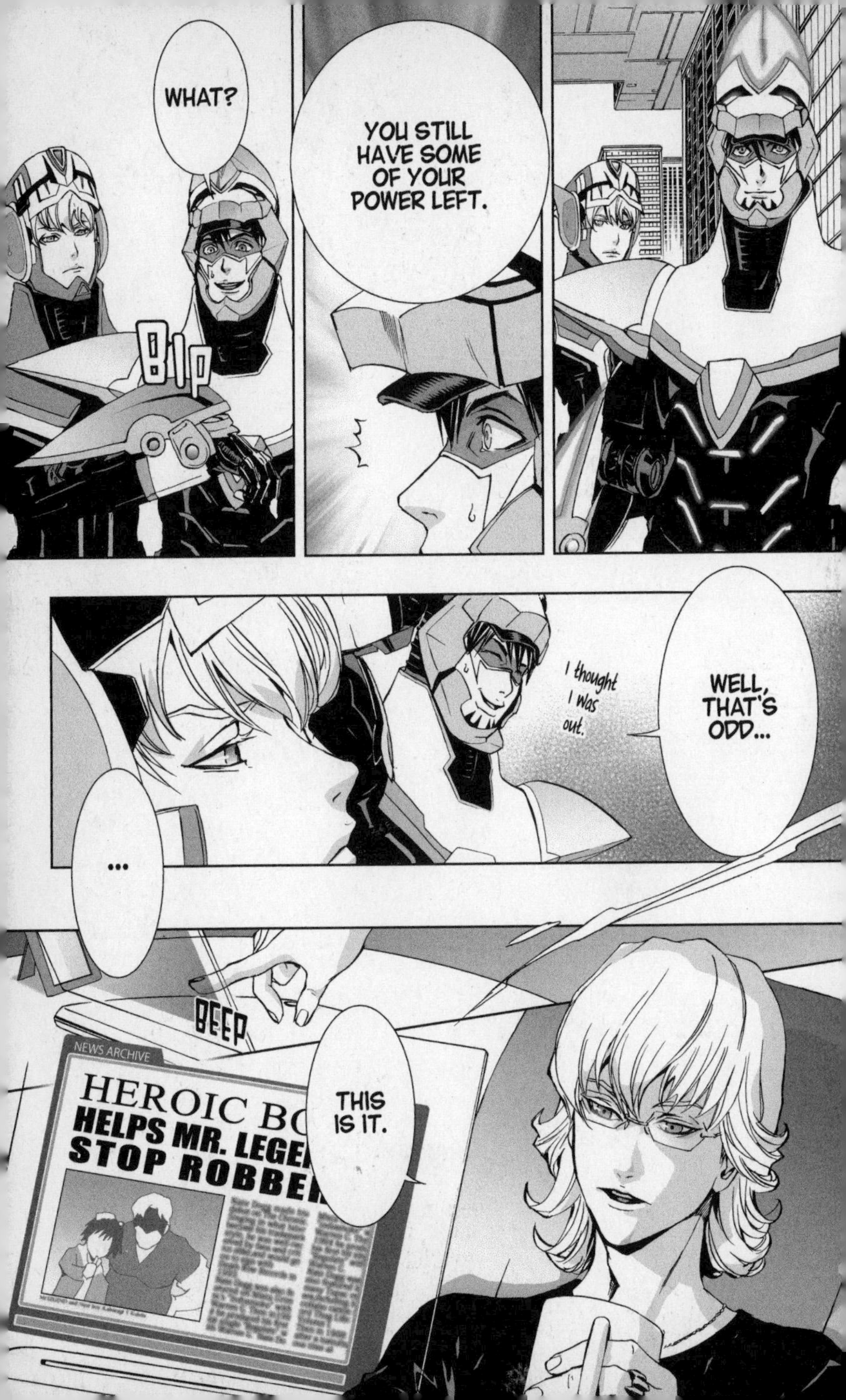
YOU STILL HAVE SOME OF YOUR POWER LEFT.
WHAT?
BIP
WELL, THAT'S ODD...
I thought I was out.
...
BEEP
THIS IS IT.
NEWS ARCHIVE
HEROIC BO
HELPS MR. LEGE
STOP ROBBE

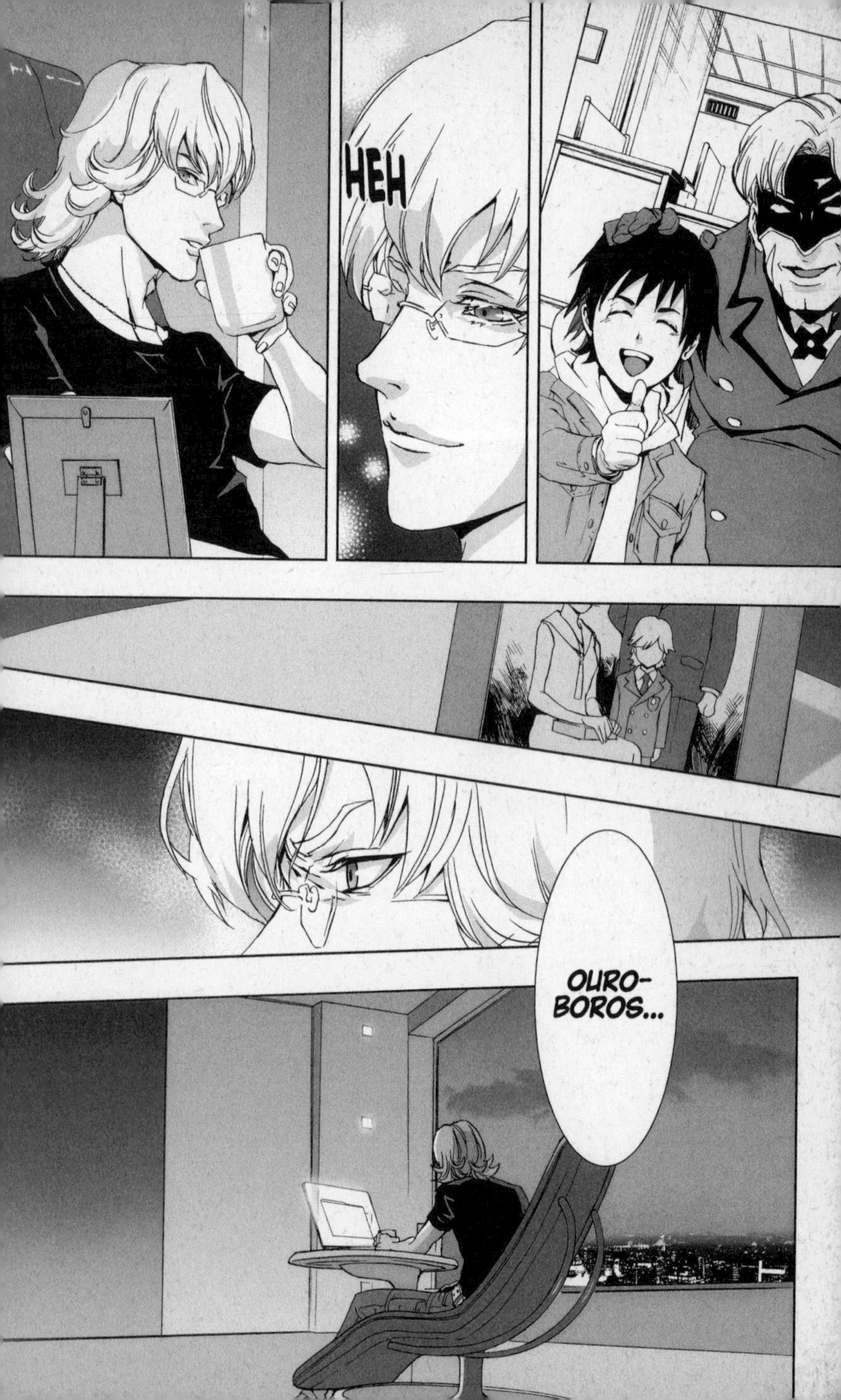
HEH
OURO-BOROS...

TIGER&BUNNY
To Be Continued

Mizuki Sakakibara

Assistants

Naoto Tsushima
Ayako Mayuzumi
Eri Saito
Sachiko Ito
Kiritachi
Beth

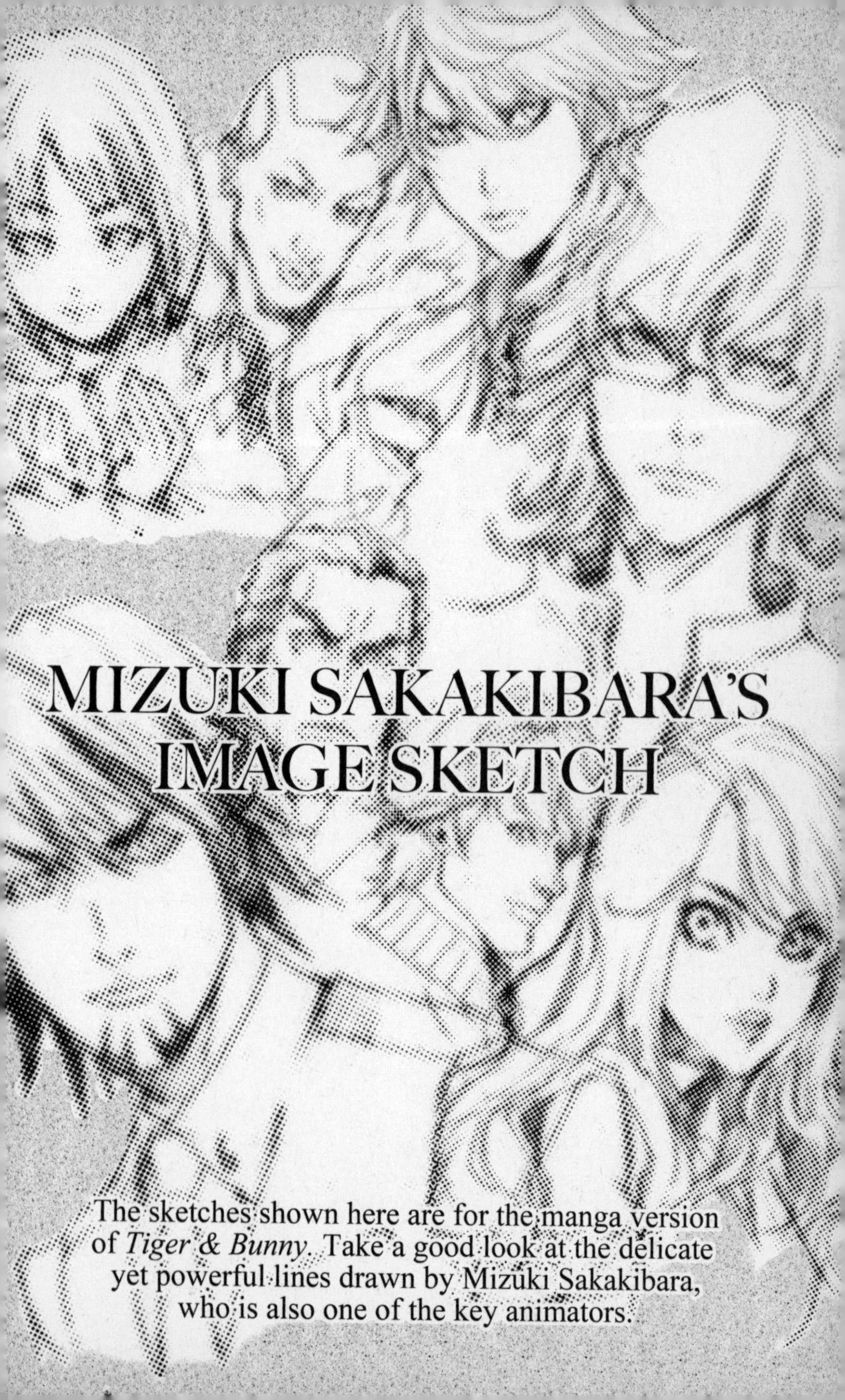

MIZUKI SAKAKIBARA'S IMAGE SKETCH

The sketches shown here are for the manga version of *Tiger & Bunny*. Take a good look at the delicate yet powerful lines drawn by Mizuki Sakakibara, who is also one of the key animators.

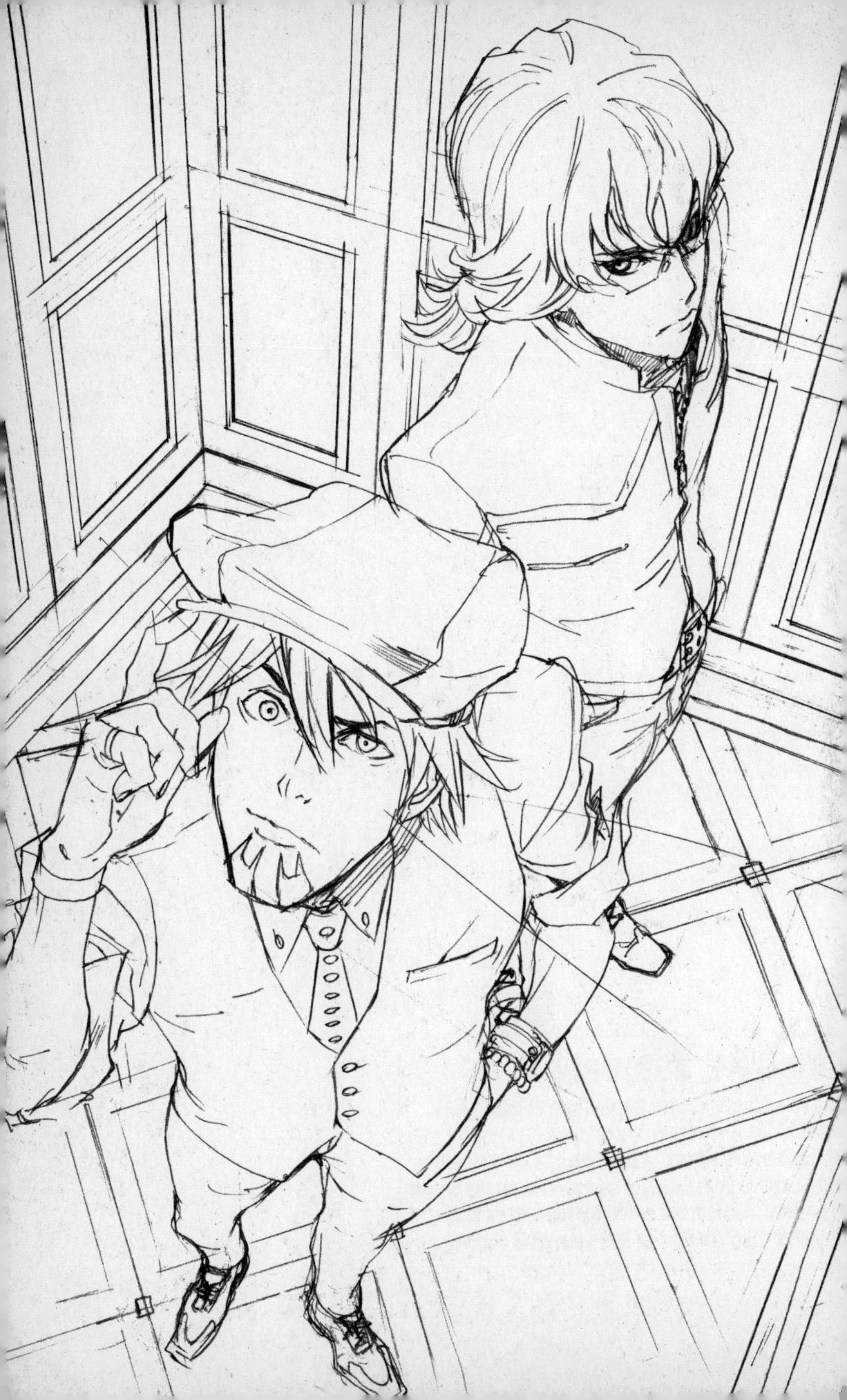

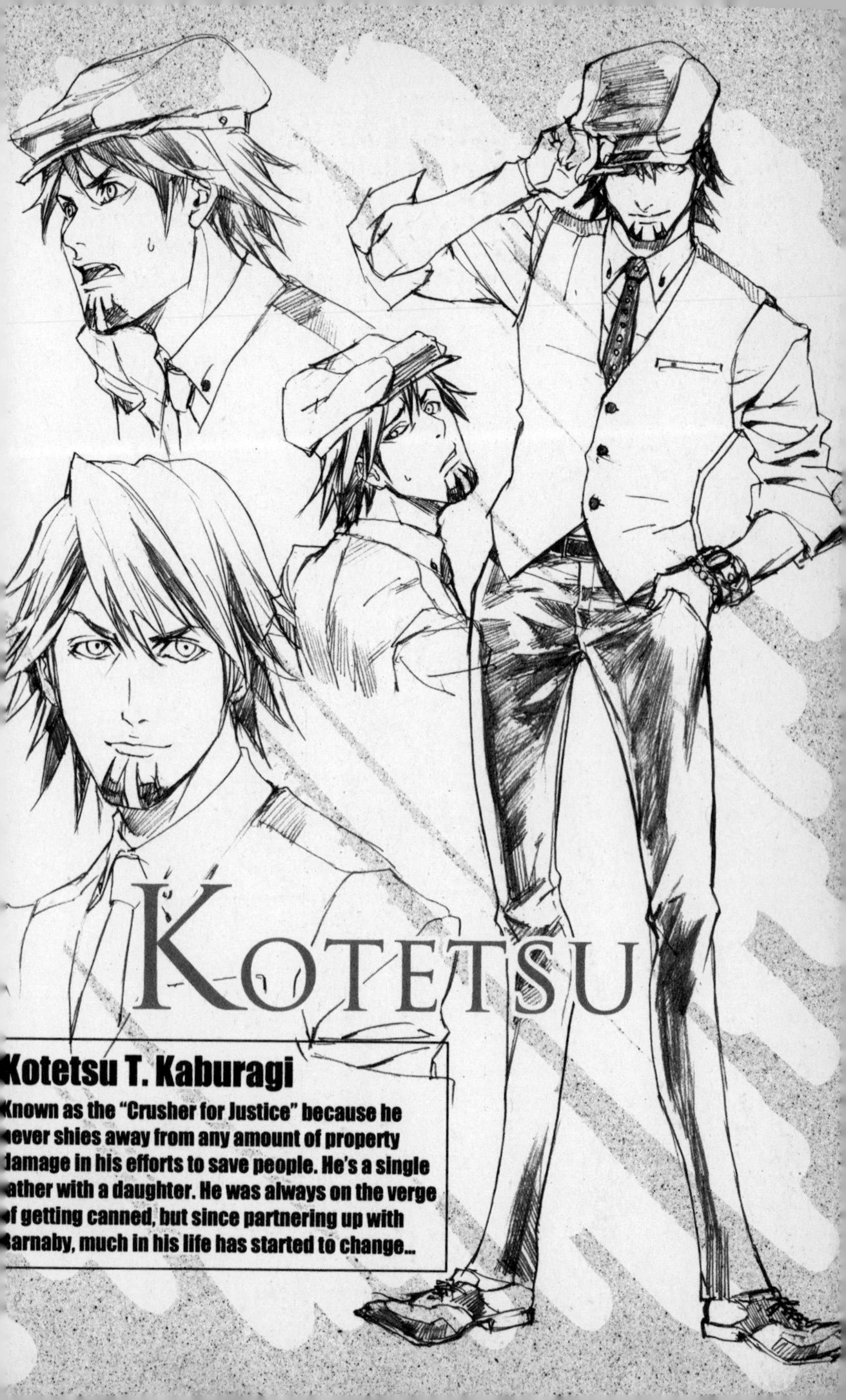
KOTETSU

Kotetsu T. Kaburagi

Known as the "Crusher for Justice" because he never shies away from any amount of property damage in his efforts to save people. He's a single father with a daughter. He was always on the verge of getting canned, but since partnering up with Barnaby, much in his life has started to change...

Barnaby Brooks Jr.

Even without a proper hero name, this super rookie attracts a lot of attention for his coolness and pragmatism, as well as for making his face public. Since forming a duo with Kotetsu, the two clash constantly, but they slowly build up trust as they tackle one incident after another.

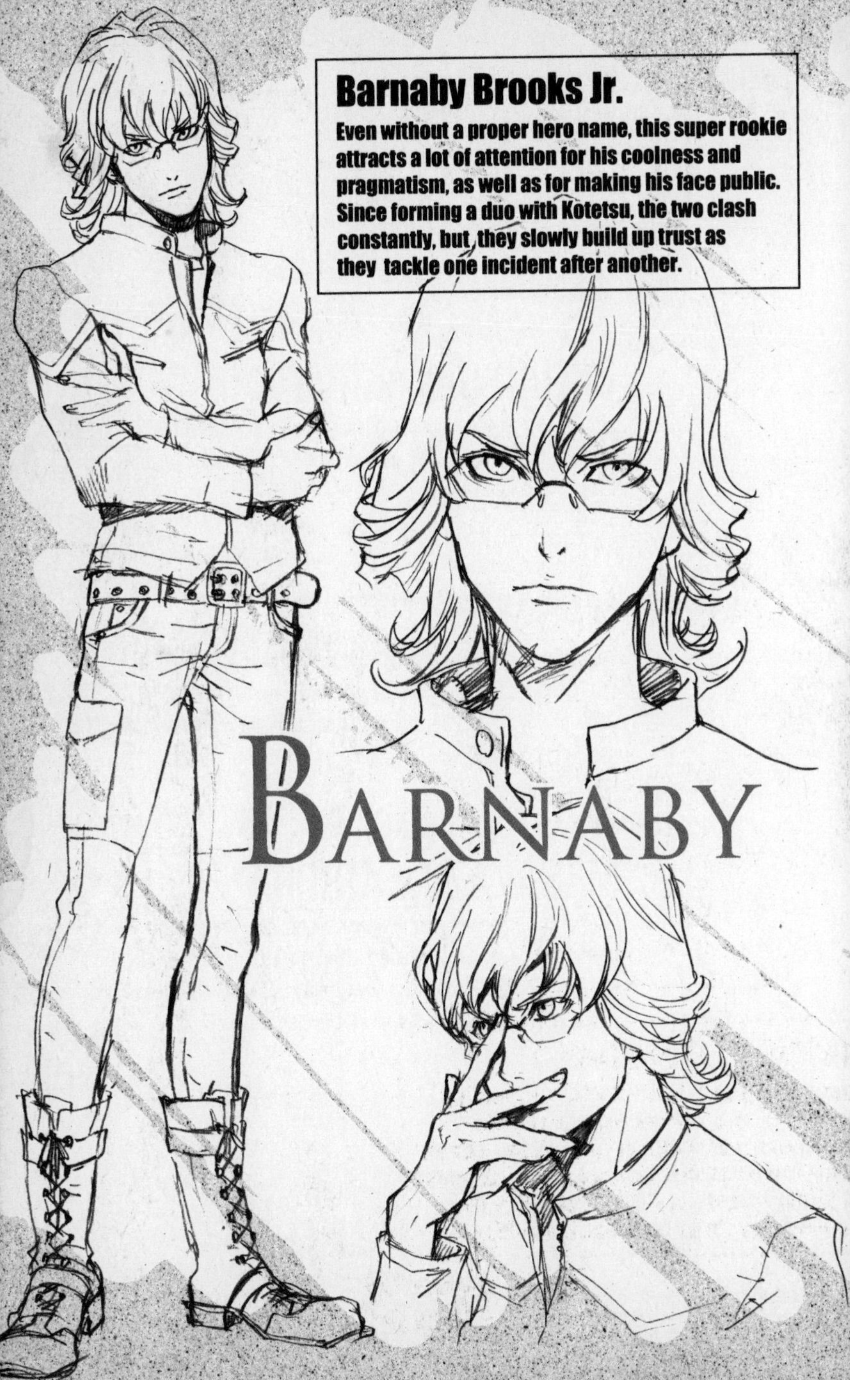
BARNABY

MIZUKI SAKAKIBARA

Mizuki Sakakibara's American comics debut was Marvel's *Exile* in 2002. Currently, *TIGER & BUNNY* is serialized in *Newtype Ace* magazine by Kadokawa Shoten.

MASAFUMI NISHIDA

Story director. *TIGER & BUNNY* was his first work as a TV animation scriptwriter. He is well known for the movie *Gachi☆Boy* and the Japanese TV dramas *Maoh*, *Kaibutsu-kun*, and *Youkai Ningen Bem*.

MASAKAZU KATSURA

Original character designer. Masakazu Katsura is well known for the manga series *WING MAN*, *Denei Shojo* (*Video Girl Ai*), *I"s*, and *ZETMAN*. Katsura's works have been translated into several languages, including Chinese and French, as well as English.

COMING **NEXT VOLUME**

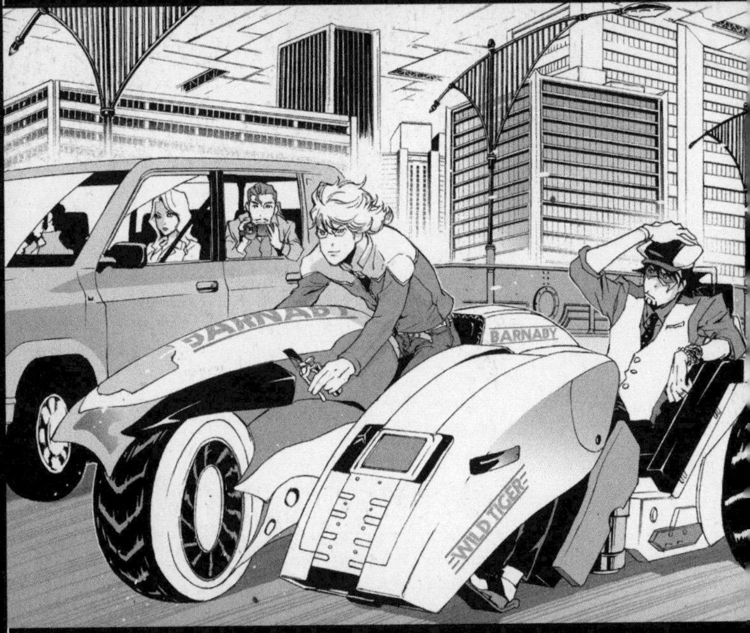
BARNABY
BARNABY
WILD TIGER

2

Kotetsu and Barnaby are the first NEXT superhero duo, but they've got a few differences to overcome if they're going to learn to work together. A reality TV show intruding into their daily lives doesn't help, but a bomb threat just might get them to cooperate. Then a misguided surprise party leads to a NEXT-involved diamond heist!

TIGER&BUNNY 1

VIZ Media Edition

Art **MIZUKI SAKAKIBARA**
Planning / Story **SUNRISE**
Original Script **MASAFUMI NISHIDA**
Original Character and Hero Design **MASAKAZU KATSURA**

First published in Japan in 2012 by KADOKAWA SHOTEN Co.,Ltd.,Tokyo.
English translation rights arranged with KADOKAWA SHOTEN Co.,Ltd.,Tokyo.

Translation & English Adaptation **LABAAMEN & JOHN WERRY, HC LANGUAGE SOLUTIONS**
Touch-up Art & Lettering **STEPHEN DUTRO**
Design **FAWN LAU**
Editor **MIKE MONTESA**

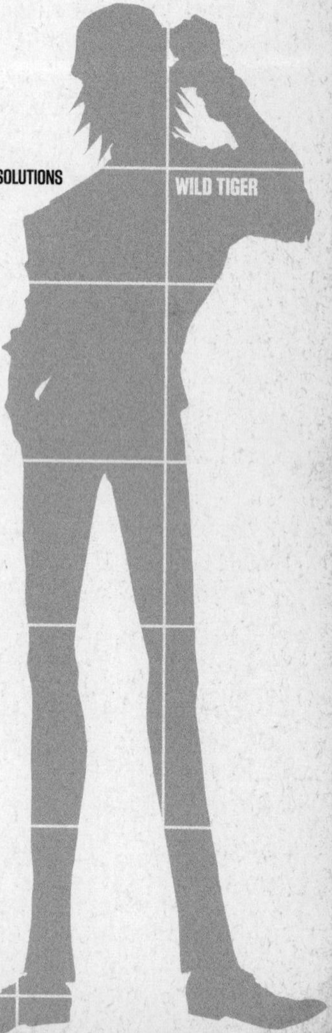

WILD TIGER

Printed in the U.S.A

Published by VIZ Media, LLC
P.O. Box 77010
San Francisco, CA 94107

10 9 8 7 6 5 4 3 2 1
First printing, April 2013

RATED T FOR TEEN

PARENTAL ADVISORY
TIGER & BUNNY is rated T for Teen and is recommended for ages 13 and up.

ratings.viz.com

viz media

www.viz.com

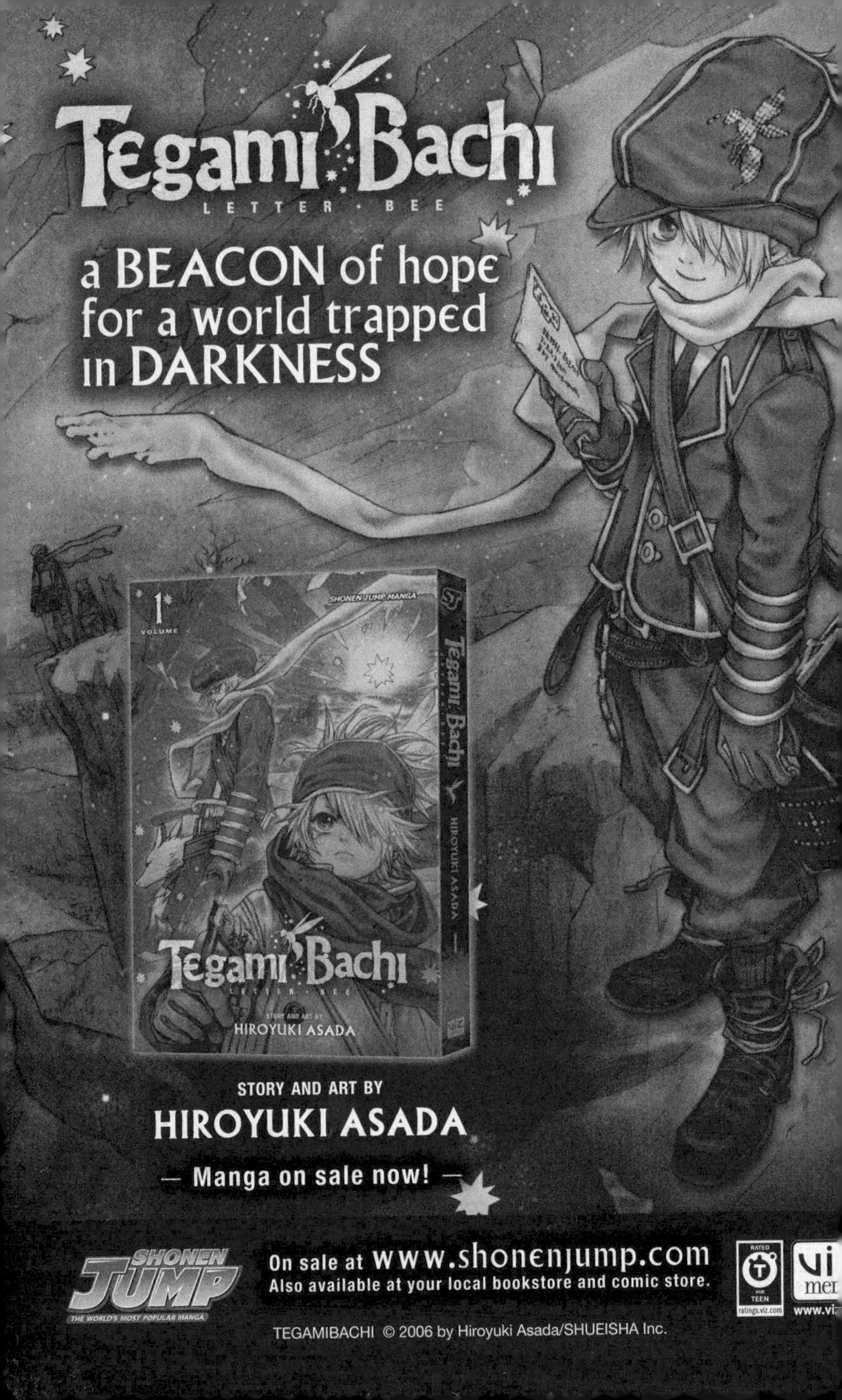
Tegami Bachi
LETTER · BEE
a BEACON of hope
for a world trapped
in DARKNESS
SHONEN JUMP MANGA
1
VOLUME
Tegami Bachi
LETTER · BEE
HIROYUKI ASADA
Tegami Bachi
HIROYUKI ASADA
STORY AND ART BY
HIROYUKI ASADA
— Manga on sale now! —
SHONEN JUMP
THE WORLD'S MOST POPULAR MANGA
On sale at www.shonenjump.com
Also available at your local bookstore and comic store.
RATED
T
FOR
TEEN
ratings.viz.com
TEGAMIBACHI © 2006 by Hiroyuki Asada/SHUEISHA Inc.

nter_the_world_of_

LOVELESS

story_+_art_by_YUN_KOUGA

2-in-1
EDITIONS

Each 2-in-1
edition includes
5 color pages and
50 pages of
ver-before-seen
BONUS comics,
rtist commentary
and interviews!

only $14.99!
($16.99 CAN / £9.99 UK)

Available at your local book store,
comic book shop or library, or online at:
store.viz.com

ⅤIZMⱯNGⱭ
Read manga anytime, anywhere!

From our newest hit series to the classics you know and love, the best manga in the world is now available digitally. Buy a volume* of digital manga for your:

- iOS device (**iPad®**, **iPhone®**, **iPod®** touch) through the **VIZ Manga** app

- Android-powered device (**phone or tablet**) with a browser by visiting VIZManga.com

- **Mac or PC computer** by visiting VIZManga.com

VIZ Digital has loads to offer:

- 500+ ready-to-read volumes
- New volumes each week
- FREE previews
- Access on multiple devices! Create a log-in through the app so you buy a book once, and read it on your device of choice!*

To learn more, visit www.viz.com/apps

* Some series may not be available for multiple devices.
Check the app on your device to find out what's available.

YOU'RE READING THE
WRONG WAY!

Tiger & Bunny reads from right to left, starting in the upper-right corner. Japanese is read from right to left, meaning that action, sound effects, and word-balloon order are completely reversed from English order.

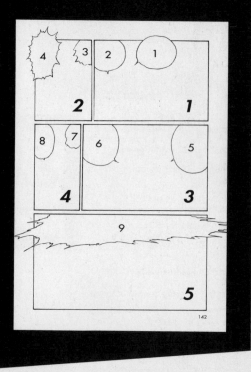